T0339955

MACROECONOMIC FLUCTUATIONS AND POLICIES

MACROECONOMIC FLUCTUATIONS AND POLICIES

EDOUARD CHALLE

TRANSLATED BY SUSAN EMANUEL

THE MIT PRESS

CAMBRIDGE, MASSACHUSETTS • LONDON, ENGLAND

This book was set in Melior and MetaPlus by Westchester Publishing Services.

Library of Congress Cataloging-in-Publication Data

Names: Challe, Edouard, author. | Emanuel, Susan, translator.
Title: Macroeconomic fluctuations and policies / Edouard Challe ; translated by Susan Emanuel.
Other titles: Fluctuations et politiques macroéconomiques. English
Description: Cambridge, MA : The MIT Press, [2019] | Includes bibliographical
   references and index.
Identifiers: LCCN 2018026937 | ISBN 9780262039550 (hardcover : alk. paper)
ISBN 9780262549295 (paperback)
Subjects: LCSH: Macroeconomics. | Business cycles.
Classification: LCC HB172.5 .C4413 2019 | DDC 339—dc23 LC record available
   at https://lccn.loc.gov/2018026937

Contents

Preface

This book is the result of fifteen years of teaching of macroeconomics at the advanced undergraduate level, at the Universities of Paris-Nanterre, Paris-Dauphine, Cambridge (UK), Columbia, and Ecole Polytechnique. Its goal is to address the basic tools of analysis of macroeconomic fluctuations and policies, while applying these tools to a number of concrete issues that are encountered today. How are recessions and crises propagated? Is unemployment the outcome of low aggregate demand or else of overly high labor costs? What instruments do central banks and governments possess to stimulate activity when private demand is too weak? And can monetary policy lose its effectiveness, as seems to have been the case in the aftermath of the Great Recession in many countries that have found themselves stuck into interminable "liquidity traps"? In this situation, are there "unconventional" macroeconomic policies that might be able to restore full employment? Is the flexibility of prices and wages always desirable or can it worsen the deflationary pressures experienced by countries facing major economic crises? Why do public authorities sometimes find it so difficult to keep up with their proclaimed objectives—for example, when it comes to controlling inflation or the public debt—and can one devise an institutional framework that would make macroeconomic policy both reliable and flexible? How do households' expectations influence the propagation of macroeconomic shocks and the effectiveness of economic policies? These are the types of questions that the concepts presented in this book hope to answer.

From a pedagogic standpoint, the book's specificity is to use a unified framework, of the "New Keynesian" type, that enables understanding the joint determination of output, employment, inflation, and interest rates. This framework is that which today dominates the macroeconomic analysis of business-cycle fluctuations in academic circles as well as at central banks and international institutions. Although the book introduces this framework at the undergraduate level, students who are pursuing the study of macroeconomics will later encounter the very same framework, extending in a variety of directions and dealing more systematicallywith intertemporal issues. In fact, one of the main motivations for writing this book was the desire to better connect undergraduate teaching with the more advanced tools taught at the graduate level and with the large body of policy-oriented research traditionally published in academic journals. The book's policy orientation may also make it useful for professional economists who want to strengthen or update their knowledge of macroeconomics either by returning to its foundations or by examining its most recent developments (for example, regarding the liquidity trap and the rationale for unconventional macroeconomic policies).

After a general introduction that presents some empirical and methodological elements, the bulk of the book is divided into four parts. Part I provides the foundations of the modern theory of business-cycle fluctuations through the notions of aggregate demand (chapter 2) and aggregate supply (chapter 3). Part II turns to the regular business cycle: it first examines how aggregate demand and supply interact and propagate the impact of macroeconomic shocks (chapter 4) and then pays special attention to the workings of the labor market over the business cycle (chapter 5). Part III is devoted to conventional macroeconomic policies: monetary policy (chapter 6) and fiscal policy (chapter 7). A few years ago, adding the term "conventional" would have been redundant, since these policies were the only ones being considered and applied in developed countries (except perhaps in Japan). After 2008, however, the central banks of many developed economies became constrained by the "zero lower bound" on short-term nominal interest rates. The principal consequence of this situation was that the conventional economic policies were either impossible to implement or else had effects very different than in normal times. Consequently, Part IV (explicitly revised for the English edition) is devoted to the liquidity trap and *unconventional* macroeconomic policies. Chapter 8 shows how a sufficiently powerful negative shock to aggregate demand (namely, the world financial crisis in 2008) might push an economy into a liquidity trap and then analyzes the particular nature of macroeconomic adjustments in this situation (as illustrated by the famous paradoxes of *flexibility*, *toil*, and *thrift*). Chapter 9 is devoted to unconventional monetary policies: forward guidance and large-scale asset purchases (including "quantitative easing" operations), as well as some more iconoclastic (and not yet tested) monetary policies such as the implementation of (very) negative interest rates or the change in the inflation target or even of monetary policy regime. Chapter 10 concludes the book with the study of the effects of fiscal policies and structural reforms in a liquidity trap.

This book has benefited from the benevolent criticism of several colleagues and friends to whom I express my gratitude: Stéphane Auray, Pierre Cahuc, Christophe Cahn, Hubert Kempf, Olivier Loisel, Eric Mengus, Jean-Baptiste Michau, Benoît Mojon, and Jean-Guillaume Sahuc. I would also like to thank Emily Taber, my editor at MIT Press, for her continuous help and support, the referees for they many useful comments, and Susan Emanuel for the translation of the book into English.

CHAPTER 1

INTRODUCTION: FROM BUSINESS-CYCLE MEASUREMENT TO MACROECONOMIC THEORY

Science is the great antidote to the poison of enthusiasm and superstition.

—Adam Smith ([1776] 1975)

The purpose of this introductory chapter is dual: first of all, it presents certain empirical elements on economic fluctuations that constitute the basic material on which the macroeconomic theory of the business cycle is built. It begins by recalling the notion of *gross domestic product* (GDP), notably from the point of view of the components of expenditure (consumption, investment, net exports, and government spending) and from the standpoint of production inputs (capital and labor). Then it shows how to break down a macroeconomic time series between its *trend* and its *cycle*, presents one of the most widely used breakdowns (the "Hodrick-Prescott filter"), and applies it to the measurement of the business cycle in the United States and the euro area since 1970. The second objective of the chapter is to clarify certain methodological choices that characterize the theoretical analysis of fluctuations proposed in the rest of the book. After having recalled the particular function of macroeconomic models (in contrast to the models utilized, say, in the natural sciences), it briefly presents the framework of analysis used throughout the book and, notably, the distinction it makes between macroeconomic "shocks" and their propagation. Finally, we discuss the way in which we are dealing with the expectations of economic agents for those parts of the book where it is necessary to specify them explicitly.

1.1 THE GROSS DOMESTIC PRODUCT AND ITS BREAKDOWN

The gross domestic product (GDP) of an economy is the sum of the value of its final goods and services produced in the course of a given period, –that is, after deducting the production of intermediate goods (the goods and services that disappear in the process of producing the final goods and services). This definition of GDP corresponds to the accounting notion of value added: the GDP of an economy is nothing else than the sum of the values added of all the firms that compose it.

1.1.1 COMPONENTS OF EXPENDITURE

GDP is identically equal to the expenditures of all the agents in the economy (households, firms, government, rest of the world) in the course of a given period. Therefore the following accounting identity is always verified:

$$Y = C + I + G + (X - M). \qquad (1.1)$$

$\uparrow$ GDP $\uparrow$ private consumption $\uparrow$ private GFCF + Δinventories $\uparrow$ gov't spending $\uparrow$ net exports

In the preceding equation, C is private consumption, I investment by firms, G government spending, X exports, and M imports. GFCF is the *gross fixed capital formation*, which corresponds to fixed investment (machines, computers, and so on), including investment that is required to simply maintain the existing fixed capital.[1] A change in inventories ("Δinventories") is considered a form of investment, since, from an accounting perspective centered on expenditures, it is interpreted as an acquisition of goods by the firm at the origin of their production. This is why GDP is equal to aggregate expenditure: by definition any service being produced is against an expenditure, and any good being produced necessarily finds itself in someone's hand (including, potentially, the firm that produced it). Finally, the term "net exports" $(X - M)$ represents the flow of goods and services bought by the rest of the world, net of the goods and services sold by the rest of the world to the domestic economy.

Equation (1.1) may be expressed either in nominal value, meaning in terms of monetary units of the current year, or in volume, meaning in terms of monetary units of a reference year. In the latter case, we speak of *real* GDP, of *real* consumption, and so on, since measures in volume eliminate by construction any variation in the value of goods and services that are due to the evolution of their nominal prices. Table 1.1 shows the decomposition of GDP (in nominal value) in the United States and the euro area in 2016. As in all developed countries, private consumption dominates

---

1. From this comes the "gross" in gross domestic product. Subtracting the depreciation of capital from the amount of fixed investment gives the *net* fixed investment; that is to say, the variation of the stock of fixed capital. Equation (1.1) with net investment instead of gross investment would give the net domestic product (NDP).

TABLE 1.1
GDP components in the United States and the euro area (2016).

	United States		Euro Area	
	bn $	% GDP	bn €	% GDP
GDP	18,624.5	100.0	10,742.7	100.0
Private consumption	12,820.7	68.8	5,883.2	54.8
Gross investment	3,057.2	16.4	2,172.0	20.2
Public spending	3,227.8	17.5	2,169.2	20.8
Net exports	−521.2	−2.8	469.9	4.3
Exports	2,214.6	11.9	4,929.2	45.9
Imports	2,735.8	14.7	4,459.3	41.6

Sources: US Bureau of Economic Analysis (BEA) and the Euro Area Business Cycle Network's (EABCN) Area-wide Model (AWM) database.

aggregate expenditure. Then come private investment, then government spending, and finally net exports.

1.1.2 NATIONAL INCOME

The *net* domestic product (NDP)–that is, GDP (Y) minus capital depreciation (δK)– is also identically equal to the total income drawn from production inputs over the course of an interval of time:

$$
\underset{\text{GDP}}{\underset{\uparrow}{Y}} - \underset{\text{capital depreciation}}{\underset{\uparrow}{\delta K}} = \underset{\text{labor income}}{\underset{\uparrow}{wL}} + \underset{\text{capital income}}{\underset{\uparrow}{\tilde{r}K}}.
$$

with $\tilde{r}$ standing for the return on capital (the income from capital divided by its stock).[2] We move from NDP to *net national income* (NNI), meaning the total income collected by a country's residents, by adding the *net transfers* coming from abroad, meaning the income associated with holding foreign capital (net of income from capital paid by the country's residents to the rest of the world) or the labor income that residents collect abroad (net of labor income paid by domestic firms to non resident workers). Thus, NNI is given by:

$$
NNI = \underset{\text{GDP}}{\underset{\uparrow}{Y}} + \underset{\text{net transfers}}{\underset{\uparrow}{T}} - \underset{\text{capital depreciation}}{\underset{\uparrow}{\delta K}} = \underset{\text{labor income}}{\underset{\uparrow}{wL}} + \underset{\text{capital income}}{\underset{\uparrow}{\tilde{r}K}} + \underset{\text{net transfers}}{\underset{\uparrow}{T}}.
$$

2. In practice, splitting NDP into labor and capital income is not straightforward in national accounting data due to the presence of independent workers whose total income mixes the two. Customarily, two-thirds of independent workers' income is attributed to labor income and one-third to capital income.

1.1.3 PRODUCTION INPUTS

Another way of considering GDP Y is from the standpoint of production inputs–notably the labor (L) and capital (K) inputs. Macroeconomists traditionally adopt a synthetic representation of the productive sector that links the quantity of output to the quantities of inputs by means of an aggregate production function. For example, we posit:

$$Y = ZK^\alpha L^{1-\alpha}, \ 0 < \alpha < 1, \tag{1.2}$$

where Z is total factor productivity (TFP for short) and α a constant.[3] From the perspective of explaining business-cycle phenomena, we will try to explain how the fluctuations of real GDP (in volume), or of real GDP per labor units of Y/L, manifest themselves as fluctuations in the inputs (K, L). When we take into account the variations in inventories as well as the depreciation of capital, the variation of the stock of fixed capital ΔK is given by:

$$\Delta K = \underbrace{\underbrace{I - \Delta\text{inventories}}_{\text{GFCF}} - \underbrace{\delta K}_{\substack{\uparrow \\ \text{capital depreciation}}}}_{\text{net fixed investment}}$$

In practice there are a number of difficulties associated with the measurement of the capital stock, the productive services that it provides, and its rate of depreciation. In particular, the heterogeneity of capital (think of the difference between an Apple computer and a milling machine) implies that both the lifetime of capital goods and the evolution of their market value may differ considerably across capital goods. We abstract from these difficulties here and just trust the national accountants when they compute the aggregate capital stock.

There are various ways of empirically measuring the labor units L. A useful and frequent shortcut is to consider the number of employees, but this approach measures the quantity of labor used in production only imperfectly because of potential variations in the hours worked per employed person. The closest thing to the true labor input is the number of hours worked, which may be broken down as follows:

$$L \quad = \quad \underset{\substack{\uparrow \\ \text{hours} \\ \text{worked}}}{Pop} \quad \times \quad \underset{\substack{\uparrow \\ \text{working-age} \\ \text{population}}}{\frac{N}{Pop}} \quad \times \quad \underset{\substack{\uparrow \\ \text{participation} \\ \text{rate}}}{\frac{E}{N}} \quad \times \quad \underset{\substack{\uparrow \\ \text{employment} \\ \text{rate}}}{\frac{L}{E}}$$

where the underbraces read: L = hours worked, Pop = working-age population, $\frac{N}{Pop}$ = participation rate, $\frac{E}{N}$ = employment rate, $\frac{L}{E}$ = hours worked per employee.

---

3. Empirically, TFP is not observed but rather treated as a residual once the other terms of the aggregate production function have been measured (and to be clear: Z is measured as $Y/K^\alpha L^{1-\alpha}$).

where N is the active population and E the number of employees. The population of working age is principally determined by long-term demographic trends and immigration; thus, its relation to the business cycle is weak. The participation rate is the fraction of the working age population who are active on the labor market–that is to say, either currently employed or else looking for employment. This variable is slightly procyclical because of workers situated on the margins of the labor market:[4] during a recession, more and more of the unemployed (especially the long-term unemployed) are discouraged by the state of the labor market and so stop actively looking for jobs, which tends to lower the participation rate; conversely, during economic expansions, growing numbers of people who were inactive on the labor market are attracted by the favorable prospects offered by the labor market and they start seeking jobs, which lifts the participation rate. The hours worked per employee (L/E) are mildly procyclical, due to the overtime hours (during expansion) and to partial unemployment (during recession). It is the employment rate (E/N)–or, in an equivalent way, its mirror image, the unemployment rate $(U = (N - E)/N)$–which contributes the most to fluctuations in total hours of work.

Combining equations (1.1) and (1.2) gives:

$$C + I + G + (X - M) = Y = Z K^\alpha L^{1-\alpha}.$$

The first equality shows how fluctuations in GDP may be broken down into the components of aggregate expenditures; the second equality shows that they are necessarily accompanied by fluctuations of production inputs. Before examining the cyclical properties of expenditures and inputs, a brief introduction to the measurement of business-cycle fluctuations is in order.

1.2 MEASURING BUSINESS-CYCLE FLUCTUATIONS

1.2.1 DECOMPOSITION BETWEEN TREND AND CYCLE

The first step in the measurement of the business cycle is the breaking down of each time series between a "trend" (or "secular") component and a "cyclical" component. This decomposition relies on the idea that the trend in a macroeconomic time series is determined by factors that influence the speed of long-run growth of the economy and that these factors do not play a predominant role in cyclical fluctuations.

Formally, we are trying to break down a time series x_t (for example, real private consumption between 1950 and 2015, which we will note as $\{C_t\}_{t=1950}^{2015}$) into the

---

4. We recall that a variable is *procyclical* (*countercyclical*) when its correlation with GDP is positive (negative). It is acyclical when this correlation is zero.

trend and cyclical components according to an equation of the form:

$$x_t = \tau_t^x + v_t^x,$$

where τ_t^x is the trend of x_t and v_t^x its cycle. In general we express the time series $\{x_t\}$ as a logarithm (which means we will use $c_t = \ln C_t$ [rather than C_t] in our example) since this will simplify the interpretation of the cyclical component and will allow for an easy comparison of the cyclical components of different series. In fact, if x_t is the series in logarithm, then its level is given by $X_t = e^{x_t}$ and the level of its trend by $T_t^x = e^{\tau_t^x}$. Now recall that, when y is close to 0, we have:

$$\ln(1 + y) \simeq y. \tag{1.3}$$

By using this approximation, we see that if x_t (the log series) is close to τ_t^x (its trend), we have:

$$v_t^x = x_t - \tau_t^x = \ln X_t - \ln T_t^x = \ln\left(1 + \frac{X_t - T_t^x}{T_t^x}\right) \tag{1.4}$$

$$\simeq \frac{X_t - T_t^x}{T_t^x}.$$

Equation (1.4) thus enables interpreting the cyclical component of the series (in logarithm, or log) as a *proportional deviation of the series from its own trend*. As such, the unit of measurement of the cycle is the percentage, and hence it is common to all series (we would say, for example, that "private consumption is 4 percent below trend in the third quarter of 2008, whereas investment is 10 percent below trend"). Thus we may compute the standard deviation of the cycle in private consumption (σ_c, in percent), and compare it with that in private investment (σ_i, also in percent) in order to conclude that private investment is a more volatile macroeconomic variable than private consumption–the average proportional deviation of private investment from its trend, as measured by the standard deviation of the cyclical component, is higher than the average proportional deviation of private consumption from its trend. This approach is systematically utilized in practice, except for series that are already expressed in the form of rates (in percent), such as the unemployment rate or the interest rate. In those cases, we calculate the level deviation (and not the proportional deviation) from the trend (for example, unemployment volatility is measured by the standard deviation of the unemployment rate and not of the log unemployment rate). Finally we note that the use of logarithms is obviously possible only for positive flows. Certain flows (for example, net exports) can be negative, in which case their cyclical component must be constructed from their level and not their log.

In practice, the breakdown of the series x_t into its trend and its cycle carries its share of arbitrariness, and numerous statistical breakdowns are possible. To summarize, a good decomposition should isolate the changes in the time series at cyclical frequencies (between two and six years), notably by dissociating them from movements of lower frequencies (with a duration longer than six years); and it should be easy to implement and be applicable to a large number of series. Hodrick and Prescott ([1981] 1997.) have proposed a decomposition that achieves a satisfactory compromise between these requirements; today the "HP filter" is one of the most-used tools in practice.

1.2.2 AN EXAMPLE: THE HODRICK-PRESCOTT FILTER

If we consider a time series constituted of $T + 1$ observations (from period 0 to period T inclusive), the Hodrick-Prescott filter–more commonly known as the "HP filter"– constructs the trend that minimizes the following quadratic loss function:

$$HP(\{x_t\}_{t=0}^T) = \underbrace{\sum_{t=0}^T (x_t - \tau_t^X)^2}_{\text{size of the cycle}} + \lambda \underbrace{\sum_{t=1}^{T-1} \left[(\tau_{t+1}^X - \tau_t^X) - (\tau_t^X - \tau_{t-1}^X) \right]^2}_{\text{smoothness of the trend}}, \lambda \geq 0. \tag{1.5}$$

The HP trend is the solution $\{\tau_t^X\}_{t=0}^T$ to this minimization problem, whose argument is the whole sequence $\{x_t\}_{t=0}^T$. The function to minimize contains two components. On the one hand, the trend should track the series; this is what ensures the first term of the objective function, which penalizes deviations of the trend at time t (τ_t^X) from the value of the series at time t (x_t). On the other hand, the trend should not change directions too abruptly; this is what is expressed by the second term of the objective function (1.5). Indeed, the term $\tau_t^X - \tau_{t-1}^X \simeq (T_t^X - T_{t-1}^X)/T_{t-1}^X$ (cf. equation (1.3)) is, in first approximation, the growth rate of the trend between period $t-1$ and period t, and similarly $\tau_{t+1}^X - \tau_t^X$ is the growth rate of the trend between period t and period $t+1$. The second term of the objective function thus penalizes the difference between these two growth rates; that is, it penalizes breaks in the trend and thereby guarantees that *the trend is smoother than the series*. Thus, the first term of the objective function tends to make the trend more spiky (by sticking to the original series), while the second term tends to smooth it (hence to deviate from the original series). The optimal trade-off between these two opposite forces is governed by the parameter λ, which indicates the relative weight of the smoothing motive in the construction of the trend. In the limit case where $\lambda = 0$, then the second term of (1.5) disappears, so that $x_t = \tau_t^X$ for any t; the trend then merely replicates the underlying series. Conversely, when $\lambda \to \infty$, then the first term disappears, and $\tau_{t+1}^X - \tau_t^X = \tau_t^X - \tau_{t-1}^X$ for any t. The growth rate of the trend is then constant; in other words, we have a linear trend. Conventional trend-cycle decompositions lie between these two extreme cases, with the implied size of the cyclical component depending on the choice of λ. This choice is arbitrary, but from the perspective of comparing the cyclicality of different macroeconomic series, it is essential to adopt a homogenous value of λ from one series to another. Ever since the work of Hodrick and Prescott (1997), λ is conventionally set at 100 in annual data; 1,600 in quarterly data; and 14,400 in monthly data.

1.2.3 EXPANSIONS AND RECESSIONS IN THE UNITED STATES AND IN EUROPE SINCE 1970

Figure 1.1 shows the HP cycles of GDP and the components of expenditure (against GDP, noted by the dotted line) in the United States. Figure 1.2 performs the same exercise for the euro area.[5] In both cases, the time series are quarterly (so we assume $\lambda = 1,600$ when implementing the HP filter) and expressed in logs (so that the cycles are expressed as proportional deviations from the trend). The shaded areas correspond to periods of recession, as reported by the National Bureau of Economic Research (NBER) for the United States and by the Center for Economic Policy Research (CEPR) for the euro area (which is that area of the world which uses the euro monetary unit). Each recession starts with a "peak" (the high point of a business cycle) and ends with a "trough" (its low point)

Observation of figures 1.1 and 1.2 suggests that business cycles are not symmetric: long phases of economic expansion are broken by phases of relatively shorter recessions. Finally, figure 1.3 shows the cyclicality of inputs in the United States over the same period (as the data frequency is annual in this case, we set the HP penalty λ to 100). In the short term, the variations in the labor input are predominant, with capital variations being of smaller magnitude and of greater inertia. We will periodically return to these empirical regularities later in the book.

1.2.4 MAIN SOURCES OF MACROECONOMIC DATA

Whenever possible, the notions discussed in the book are illustrated by suitable charts. For future reference and for the readers' interest, the list below records the main sources of data used by macroeconomists. All of them are accessible online and free of charge.

For the US economy, the website FRED (Federal Reserve Economic Data) collects macroeconomic and financial information disseminated in a multitude of databases. Such widely used databases include the national accounts from the US Bureau of Economic Analysis (BEA), the banking and financial data of the Federal Reserve Board, as well as data on employment, wages, and productivity from the US Bureau of Labor Statistics (BLS).

---

5. The common european currency was introduced for household payments only in 1999. The "euro area" between 1970 and 1999 is reconstructed by aggregating the national accounts of the countries that are nowadays part of the euro area.

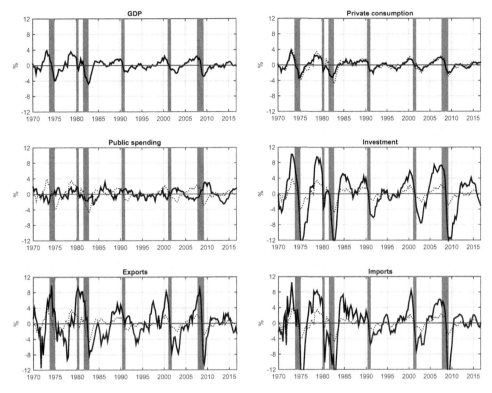

FIGURE 1.1
Cycles of GDP and its components in the United States. Shadowed areas correspond to periods of recession according to the National Bureau of Economic Research (NBER).
Sources: BEA (NIPA tables), NBER, and the author's calculations.

- **FRED**: https://fred.stlouisfed.org

- **BEA**: https://www.bea.gov/itable/index.cfm

- **Federal Reserve Board**: https://www.federalreserve.gov/data.htm

- **BLS**: https://www.bls.gov

For the euro area, the Area-wide Model (AWM) aggregates the national accounts of the countries that are currently part of the monetary union, as well as data on employment, productivity, prices, and wages. A great amount of euro area's financial and monetary data is accessible from the European Central Bank Statistical Data Warehouse, or via its monthly bulletins. Economic and social data of the area are gathered in the AMECO and Eurostat databases, which are both managed by the European Commission.

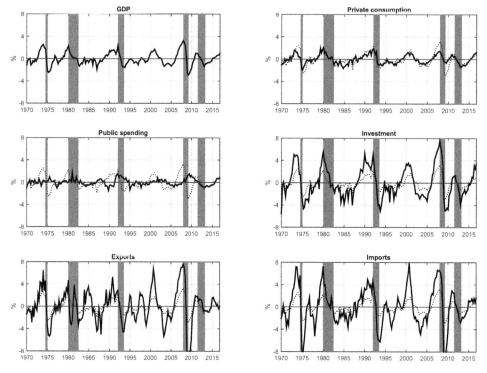

FIGURE 1.2
Cycles of GDP and its components in the euro area. Shadowed areas correspond to periods of recession according to the Center for Economic Policy Research (CEPR).
Sources: AWM database, CEPR, and the author's calculations.

- **Area Wide Model (AWM) database**: https://eabcn.org/page/area-wide-model

- **ECB Statistical Data Warehouse**: http://sdw.ecb.europa.eu

- **ECB Monthly Bulletins**: http://www.ecb.europa.eu/pub/economic-bulletin /html/index.en.html

- **AMECO**: http://ec.europa.eu/economy_finance/ameco/user/serie/SelectSerie .cfm

- **Eurostat**: http://ec.europa.eu/eurostat/home

For the United Kingdom, similar information can be found at the Office for National Statistics and the Bank of England:

- **Office for National Statistics**: https://www.ons.gov.uk

- **Bank of England**: https://www.bankofengland.co.uk/statistics

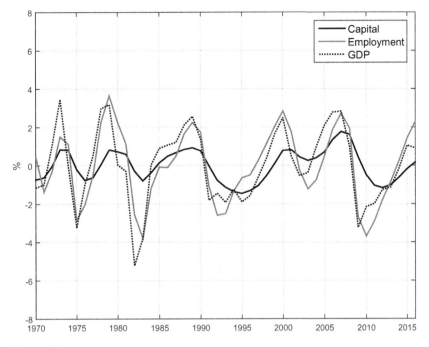

FIGURE 1.3
Cycles of capital and employment in the United States.
Sources: BEA (fixed asset tables), BLS (CES data), and the author's calculations.

Finally, the database of the Organization for Economic Co-operation and Development (OECD) is one of the most utilized for international comparisons. The website DB.nomics, maintained by CEPREMAP, also gathers international data from various sources:

- **OECD**: https://data.oecd.org

- **DB.nomics**: https://db.nomics.world

1.3   BUSINESS CYCLE THEORY

1.3.1   THE ROLE OF MODELS IN MACROECONOMIC THEORY
The empirical analysis of business cycles is designed to extract a certain number of regularities that characterize historical fluctuations and crises. The goal of macro-economic theory is to organize these observations in terms of *causal effects* and to exploit them for the purposes of *economic policy*. In order to do this, macro-economists use formal models, which are mathematical representations of the world

that surrounds them. The way in which economists conceive and use their models is distinctive and is sometimes a source of confusion. This confusion arises from the fact that economics is both a quantitative and social science: it bears on measurable notions (price, quantities, and so on) and does so by studying the choices of free individuals who are immersed in networks of complex interactions that are perpetually changing. The quantitative nature of its subject naturally pushes economics toward the mathematization of the world, but the complexity of social interactions prevents by nature the discipline from attaining the same degree of empirical accuracy as the so-called "exact" sciences. In this context, an economic model's prime utility does not lie so much in its empirical precision as in its capacity to represent, in a rigorous and parsimonious way, a specific economic mechanism that is seen as pertinent but whose workings would remain elusive in the absence of a *theoretically precise* formulation of the problem at hand. And therefore the simplicity of a macroeconomic model is commonly recognized as one of its prime qualities: without this simplicity, the model (whose purpose is to make intelligible and transparent a particular aspect of the socioeconomic world) quite simply would have no interest. And so the approach of the macroeconomist consists of starting from a simple model, whose mechanisms is perfectly understood, and then gradually enriching it so as to extend its domain of application and to test the robustness of its core mechanisms. This is precisely the way in which we will proceed here: by constructing the simplest possible macroeconomic model, then by gradually enriching it in subsequent chapters when necessary.

1.3.2 THE AGGREGATE SUPPLY-AGGREGATE DEMAND (AS-AD) MODEL AND ITS EXTENSIONS

The basic model that constitutes the guiding thread of this book is composed of three equations:

$$\textbf{IS} : y_t = \theta_t - \sigma(r_t - \bar{r});$$

$$\textbf{MP} : r_t = \bar{r} + \gamma(\pi_t - \bar{\pi});$$

$$\textbf{AS} : \pi_t = \pi_{t-1} + \kappa(y_t - y_t^n).$$

where σ, γ, and κ are nonnegative parameters. The first equation is the "IS curve," for "Investment-Saving," which is studied in detail in chapter 2. The IS curve states that in equilibrium output y_t (expressed in logarithm) is necessarily equal to aggregate demand, which can in turn be broken down into two parts: one component that depends negatively on the real interest rate r_t (as a deviation from its average value $\bar{r}$) that represents the systematic reaction of private expenditures (consumption, investment, and net exports) to this variable; and another term θ_t that summarizes the effects of all the factors that influence aggregate demand independently of variations in the real interest rate. Most of the time, we will simply consider θ_t as *exogenous* (i.e., determined outside the model) and we will study the effects of variations of θ_t (the "aggregate demand shocks") on the macroeconomic equilibrium. We will see, however, that in certain situations, considering θ_t as purely exogenous is a source of error. When this is the case (for example, when we study fiscal policy in chapters 7 and 10), we will make explicit the endogenous determination of θ_t and its dependence on the underlying macroeconomic shocks.

The second equation is the "MP curve," for "Monetary Policy," which is also presented in chapter 2. In the type of economy that we are considering, the macroeconomic equilibrium is not complete as long as the behavior of the real interest rate (the r_t in the IS curve) is not specified. The MP curve describes the evolution of this rate as it results from the monetary policy implemented by the central bank. The most widespread monetary policy regime in developed countries is some form of (more or less explicit) "inflation targeting." Under this regime, the central bank attempts to to stabilize inflation π_t around a target $\bar{\pi}$ (typically 2 percent) and adopts (when possible) a monetary policy aimed at gradually correcting any deviation of inflation from this target (by raising r_t when π_t exceeds $\bar{\pi}$, and vice versa).[6]

The third equation is the "AS curve," for "Aggregate Supply," which is covered in chapter 3. The AS curve results from the behavior of firms; more precisely, the way in which firms respond to the demand for their goods (by the consumers, the other firms, the rest of the world, and the government) by adjusting either their selling prices or their production or both.[7]

From chapter 5 onward this basic analytical framework is enriched in various directions *but only in the dimension where it is necessary, given the question at hand.* For example, the AS curve is modified in chapter 5 to explicitly study worker flows and fluctuations in unemployment, without any modification to the IS and MP curves. One part of chapter 6 is devoted to optimal monetary policy and therefore replaces the MP curve by the value of the real interest rate that maximizes social welfare (under certain assumptions about society's preferences toward inflation and output stabilization); but in that case the IS and AS curves are kept identical to those above. Similarly, when we study fiscal policy in chapter 7, the IS and AS curves are explicitly derived from a general-equilibrium analysis (the only analytical framework that allows the studying of fiscal policy in a coherent way) but under a set of assumptions that is more restrictive than in chapter 2. Finally, the third part of the book, devoted to the liquidity trap, shows that when short-term nominal interests reach their "zero lower bound," then the central bank is no longer able to manipulate the real interest rate as it wishes. Thus the real interest rate is no longer described by

6. This form of inflation targeting is sometimes called "flexible" because the correction of the deviations of inflation from its target is gradual and not immediate. We examine whether this gradualism is warranted or not in chapter 6.

7. The "New Keynesian" aggregate supply mechanism used throughout this book was originally introduced into macroeconomic analysis by Mankiw (1985) and Blanchard and Kiyotaki (1987).

the MP curve (it instead depends on future inflation, as we will see), but this does not require any change in the IS or the AS curves. Thus this book adopts a modular approach that facilitates the understanding of the key business-cycle mechanisms while opening up vast domains of applications.

1.3.3 SHOCKS, PROPAGATION, AND EXPECTATIONS

From a methodological point of view, the framework of analysis adopted here rests upon the general idea that the economy is hit by macroeconomic shocks that are considered to be exogenous; these shocks are then propagated to macroeconomic variables (output, employment, inflation, interest rate) due to the behavioral responses of economic agents (both private agents and policy makers). Formally, in the three equations (IS, MP, and AS) above, the aggregate shocks show up as variations in θ_t (the "aggregate demand shocks") as well as in y_t^n (the "aggregate supply shocks"), and the reactions of agents to these aggregate shocks trigger endogenous adjustments of r_t, y_t, and π_t. The representation of the macroeconomic equilibrium as resulting from the endogenous propagation of exogenous shocks goes back to the work of Ragnar Frish (1933) and Eugene Slutzky (1937), and this is the one that today dominates the macroeconomic analysis of business-cycle fluctuations.

Note that the elementary model above is almost static: it describes the macroeconomic equilibrium in period t as a function of macroeconomic shocks in period t and of the equilibrium in period $t-1$ (since the AS curve features past inflation π_{t-1}). Therefore this model, which we will construct and utilize as is in Parts I and II of this book, does not require any particular assumption about the way in which agents form their expectations about the future values of economic variables. In Part III and IV, however, certain variants of the basic model will incorporate a forward-looking dimension, in the sense that some variables that are determined in the future (in period $t+1$, $t+2$, etc.) will influence the equilibrium in the current period (for example, in a liquidity trap the real interest rate r_t is no longer determined by the MP curve above but instead by expectations of future inflation). When this is the case, we will compute the current equilibrium (in period t) under two assumptions. First, we will assume that economic agents form their expectations by using the "true" economic model; for example, they use the AS curve of period $t+1$ ($\pi_{t+1} = \pi_t + \kappa(y_{t+1} - y_{t+1}^n)$) to predict inflation in period $t+1$ rather than using an arbitrary forecasting rule. More generally, agents' expectations will be assumed to be consistent with all the equations of the economic model within which they are operating. Such expectations are called "rational" because they imply that economic agents are making an optimal use of whatever information they have, including the current equilibrium as well as the model that describes its evolution over time.[8] The second assumption we will make, in addition to rational expectations, is that

---

8. We will study in detail the nature and implications of the assumption of rational expectations in chapter 6.

there are no aggregate shocks after period t. That is, we will study the effect of current aggregate shocks by taking into account their potential effects on future equilibrium variables (for example, when a current shock affects future inflation due to the form of the AS curve) but deliberately ignoring the fact that these future variables might also be moved by some future aggregate shocks that are not yet known. This implies that, conditional upon the aggregate shocks occurring in the current period t, there is no difference between the *expected* value of a variable *ex ante* (for example, the expectation of future inflation π_{t+1}^e) and its *realized* value *ex post* (π_{t+1}). Agents forming rational expectations in this (fictitious) world without future shocks are said to have *perfect foresight*.

FOUNDATIONS: AGGREGATE DEMAND AND SUPPLY

Aggregate Demand

The outstanding faults of the economic society in which we live are its failure to provide for full employment and its arbitrary and inequitable distribution of wealth and incomes … . For if effective demand is deficient, not only is the public scandal of wasted resources intolerable, but the individual enterpriser who seeks to bring these resources into action is operating with the odds loaded against him. The game of hazard which he plays is furnished with many zeros, so that the players as a whole will lose if they have the energy and hope to deal all the cards … . But if effective demand is adequate, average skill and average good fortune will be enough.

—John Maynard Keynes ([1936] 2017)

The idea that aggregate demand (AD) contributes to determining the economic equilibrium coincides with the birth of macroeconomics: it was introduced by J. M. Keynes, who saw the Great Depression as the manifestation of an inefficient shortage in the demand for goods and services rather than a disruption in the productive capacity of the economy or the outcome of an overaccumulation of capital. This chapter is devoted to the determinants of aggregate demand and its fluctuations. As we shall see, the level of aggregate demand that prevails in an economy depends not only on the spending behavior of the private sector (households, firms, rest of the world) but also on economic policy, as implemented by the government (for fiscal policy) and the central bank (for monetary policy). In particular, we will see that private expenditure depends on the real interest rate in the economy, which results from the more or less expansionary nature of the monetary policy followed by the central bank. In order to understand this interconnection between private and public decisions, we will proceed in two stages. First of all, we will study the determinants of aggregate demand, *taking monetary policy as given*. The aggregation of the expenditure decisions of all agents will enable us to construct the *IS curve* (for "Investment-Saving"), namely a relation linking aggregate demand and the real interest rate, and potentially perturbed by other factors that we will consider to be exogenous and will interpret as "aggregate demand shocks." Formally, the IS curve will have the following form:

IS : $y_t = \theta_t - \sigma \, (r_t - \bar{r})$,

where y_t is output (in logarithm), r_t the real rate of interest, $\bar{r}$ its average value, $\sigma \geq 0$ a constant, and θ_t an exogenous variable summarizing demand conditions independently of the effects of the real interest rate.

In the second stage, we will show how the real interest rate r_t that occurs in the IS curve follows from the monetary policy stance of the central bank; at this stage, we will be content with summarizing this stance by an increasing relation between the real interest rate and the deviation of inflation from a target value, which we will label as *MP curve* (for "Monetary Policy"). The MP curve that we will consider will have the following simple form:

MP : $r_t = \bar{r} + \gamma \, (\pi_t - \bar{\pi})$,

where $\bar{\pi}$ is the inflation target and $\gamma \geq 0$ a constant. Taken together, the IS and MP curves generate a (decreasing) relation between inflation and output, namely the *AD curve* (for "Aggregate Demand"):

AD : $y_t = \theta_t - \gamma \sigma \, (\pi_t - \bar{\pi})$.

The AD curve will form one of the two basic blocks of the macroeconomic model that we will use throughout this book.[1] Since the construction of the AD curve from the IS and MP curves is almost direct, the major part of this chapter is devoted to the derivation of the IS curve and to the description of the underlying behaviors of private agents.

2.1 THE REAL INTEREST RATES AND THE MACROECONOMIC EQUILIBRIUM

Equation (1.1) in the preceding chapter outlines the various components of the total demand addressed to firms, which in equilibrium necessarily is equal to total output. Thus at any period t we have:

---

1. The second block of the model will be the AS curve (for "Aggregate Supply"), which defines another relation, increasing this time, between y_t and π_t. We will study the AS curve in chapter 3.

$$Y_t = C_t + I_t + XM_t + G_t,$$

where C_t is consumption, I_t investment, XM_t net exports, and G_t government spending. In what follows, I will show that the components of private spending (that is to say, C_t, I_t, and XM_t) are all *decreasing* in the real interest rate, denoted by r_t (by contrast, G_t is determined by the government and supposed to be independent of r_t for simplicity). The *real* interest rate represents the anticipated cost of borrowing or the anticipated return on a financial investment, as expressed in terms of consumption goods. By contrast, the *nominal* rate of interest, which will be denoted as i_t, represents the cost of borrowing or the return on investment in terms of *monetary units* (e.g., in US dollars). Although in practice loans and borrowing are systematically expressed in nominal terms, it is actually the real interest rate (and not the nominal interest rate) that influences the spending behavior of private agents. The two differ from each other due to the anticipated rate of inflation, which introduces a gap between the nominal return of an investment (or the nominal cost of a loan) and its real return—meaning the quantity of goods that the nominal interest on the investment enables to purchase. Formally, the relation between the two interest rates is given by:

$$1 + r_t = \frac{1 + i_t}{1 + \pi_{t+1}}, \tag{2.1}$$

with r_t the real interest rate between period t and period $t + 1$, i_t the nominal interest rate between period t and period $t + 1$, and π_{t+1} the anticipated rate of inflation between period t and period $t + 1$. An important difference between the nominal interest rate and the real interest rate is that the former is known at time t, at the moment when the financial transaction takes place, whereas the latter must be anticipated, since it depends on the inflation realized in period $t + 1$, which in general is not yet known in period t. Thus, the macroeconomic shocks that occur in period $t + 1$ (but that were not known in period t) induce a gap between realized inflation and anticipated inflation and hence a gap between the real interest rate r_t *ex ante* and the return on investment *ex post*. However, as discussed in the preceding chapter, the approach throughout this book is to study the propagation of a macroeconomic shock occurring in the current period (i.e., at time t) by leaving out future shocks (in periods $t + 1, t + 2, \ldots$), which enables us to reason under the hypothesis of *perfect foresight*. This is a useful simplification, which by construction equalizes expected inflation for time $t + 1$ and realized inflation at time $t + 1$ and thus equalizes the real interest rate between time t and time $t + 1$ with the *ex post* return on investment at time $t + 1$. By converting equation (2.1) into log and by using the approximation (1.3), we see that:

$$\textbf{FE}: r_t \simeq i_t - \pi_{t+1}, \tag{2.2}$$

and it is this expression, called the Fisher equation, that we will use in the rest of this book.

Interest rates have variable maturities, ranging from a day to several decades, and we will study in chapter 6 the relation between the interest rates of different maturities (the "term structure of interest rates"). For the moment, let us note that the interest rates that influence decisions about expenditures on the part of households and (nonfinancial) firms are *real* interest rates of relatively long maturity, running from one to several years, which corresponds to the time horizon over which private agents make their borrowing and investment decisions. Consequently, it is these interest rates that the central bank tries to influence in its conduct of monetary policy.

2.2   Private Consumption

We saw in chapter 1 that consumption is the largest component of aggregate expenditures. Consequently, we start our exposition of aggregate demand by describing the consumption behavior of the households. According to the modern theory of consumption, private consumption results from the optimal choices of the households, taking into account their preferences and the constraints they are facing. Assuming that the marginal utility of consumption is decreasing, then households wish to *smooth their consumption over time*—that is to say, to insulate their current consumption from fluctuations in their current disposable income. Households seek to smooth their consumption by saving (or by reducing their indebtedness) when current income is particularly high, so that future consumption also rises (in addition to current consumption); or conversely, by going into debt (or liquidating assets) when income is particularly low, so as to immediately benefit from the greater future income. This smoothing of consumption relies on free variations in savings, which can be thwarted by financial constraints such as debt constraints. Ultimately it is the relative power of the consumption-smoothing motive and the financial constraints besetting households that determines the cyclical behavior of aggregate consumption.

2.2.1   Household Preferences and Constraints

We will assume that the economy is populated by a large number of households. The intertemporal utility of household j as of period t takes the following form:[2]

$$U_t^j = \sum_{k=0}^{n} \left(\frac{1}{1+\rho} \right)^k \ln C_{t+k}^j \tag{2.3}$$

$$= \ln C_t^j + \left(\frac{1}{1+\rho} \right) \ln C_{t+1}^j + \left(\frac{1}{1+\rho} \right)^2 \ln C_{t+2}^j + \dots + \left(\frac{1}{1+\rho} \right)^n \ln C_{t+n}^j,$$

---

2. In the appendix to chapter 3 we will generalize these preferences to incorporate a trade-off between labor and leisure, and in chapter 7 we will consider a general equilibrium model with a dynastic infinitely lived representative household (such that $n \to \infty$ for all j).

where C_t^j is the household's consumption in period t, $n \geq 0$ its horizon (which depends, among other things, on the age of the household) and $\rho > 0$ its rate of time preference, meaning its degree of "impatience"—the higher ρ, the less is future consumption valued relative to present consumption. As we will see, for this reason a high value of ρ tends to generate—all else equal—a low level of savings.

The household faces, in each period t, the following budget constraint:

$$ C_t^j \;+\; \underbrace{A_t^j - A_{t-1}^j}_{\text{net financial savings}} \;=\; \underbrace{r_{t-1} A_{t-1}^j}_{\text{asset income}} \;+\; \underbrace{\frac{W_t}{P_t} L_t^j}_{\text{labor income}} \;-\; T_t^j. \tag{2.4} $$

$\underset{\text{consumption}}{\uparrow}$ $\qquad\qquad\qquad\qquad\qquad\qquad\qquad\qquad\quad \underset{\text{taxes (minus transfers)}}{\uparrow}$

$$\underbrace{\qquad\qquad\qquad\qquad\qquad\qquad}_{\text{disposable income}}$$

In this expression L_t^j is the quantity of labor supplied by the household; W_t the nominal wage (e.g., in US dollars), which for simplicity we assume to be common to all employees; and P_t is the nominal price level (also in US dollars). Thus, W_t/P_t is the real wage received by households—meaning the number of units of consumption goods that one unit of labor enables to purchase. Labor income $(W_t/P_t) L_t^j$ in equation (2.4) refers therefore to the total quantity of consumption goods that the household might acquire thanks to its labor supply, if the household devoted all its current income to that.[3] A_t^j denotes the household's *asset wealth* (measured at the end of period t), while $S_t^j = A_t^j - A_{t-1}^j$ stands for *net financial savings*, meaning the *variation* in asset wealth. We see that asset wealth is a stock, whereas savings is a flow; it is by accumulating saving flows that asset wealth is accumulated over time. Of course, asset wealth contributes (along with labor income) to the disposable income of the household (see the term $r_{t-1} A_{t-1}^j$), which might in turn accrue to future savings and hence to further asset accumulation, and so on. Asset wealth A_t^j is positive when the household is a net lender and negative when it is a net debtor (which is possible inasmuch as future labor income can be used to pay off the debt). Finally, the household pays taxes and receives transfers from the government, and we denote as T_t^j the total value of taxes net of transfers (noticing that T_t^j is negative for a household that receives more than it contributes). Again, for the sake of simplicity, we assume here that this net contribution is lump sum rather than proportional to income.[4]

The solvency of the household requires that it satisfy its *intertemporal budget constraint* (IBC): in one way or another current and future labor income flows $((W_{t+k}/P_{t+k})L_{t+k}^j, \quad k = 0, 1, \ldots, n)$, as well as accumulated asset wealth

---

3. In other words, the budget constraint in equation (2.4) is expressed in *real* terms, meaning that both resources (on the right) and their uses (on the left) are measured in terms of consumption goods. We might convert the same constraint into nominal form by multiplying all terms by the price level P_t.

4. This simplifying assumption is relaxed in chapter 7, which is devoted to fiscal policy.

$(A_{t-1}^j(1+r_{t-1}))$, must be sufficient to cover the consumption flows taking place from the current period onward $(C_{t+k}^j, \; k=0,1,\ldots,n)$. We construct the household's IBC by using the budget constraint of each period $t+k, \; k=0,1,\ldots,n$ in such a way as to eliminate all the A_{t+k}^js. The budget constraint of each period is written as

$$k=0: C_t^j + A_t^j = A_{t-1}^j(1+r_{t-1}) + (W_t/P_t)L_t^j - T_t^j;$$

$$k=1: C_{t+1}^j + A_{t+1}^j = A_t^j(1+r_t) + (W_{t+1}/P_{t+1})L_{t+1}^j - T_{t+1}^j;$$

$$\vdots$$

$$k=n: C_{t+n}^j = A_{t+n-1}^j(1+r_{t+n-1}) + (W_{t+n}/P_{t+n})L_{t+n}^j - T_{t+n}^j.$$

Notice that we have set $A_{t+n}^j=0$ in the budget constraint of period $t+n$; since consumption beyond period $t+n$ is not valued, it would make no sense to choose $A_{t+n}^j>0$; and since the household has no labor income beyond period $t+n$, nobody would agree to be its creditor at that time and so it is impossible to have $A_{t+n}^j<0$. Thus we necessarily have $A_{t+n}^j=0$.

By using the second line to eliminate A_t from the first, we obtain

$$C_t^j + \frac{C_{t+1}^j}{1+r_t} + \frac{A_{t+1}^j}{1+r_t} = A_{t-1}^j(1+r_{t-1}) + \frac{W_t}{P_t}L_t^j - T_t^j + \frac{\frac{W_{t+1}}{P_{t+1}}L_{t+1}^j - T_{t+1}^j}{1+r_t}.$$

And by repeating this operation, that is by using equation (2.4) with $k=2$ in order to eliminate A_{t+1}^j from the preceding equation, then using equation (2.4) with $k=3$ to eliminate A_{t+2}^j, and so on until $k=n$, we obtain the IBC:

$$\underbrace{\sum_{k=0}^{n} \frac{C_{t+k}^j}{\Pi_{m=0}^{k-1}(1+r_{t+m})}}_{\text{present value of consumption flows}} = \underbrace{A_{t-1}^j(1+r_{t-1})}_{\text{assets and interest}} + \underbrace{\sum_{k=0}^{n} \frac{\frac{W_{t+k}}{P_{t+k}}L_{t+k}^j - T_{t+k}^j}{\Pi_{m=0}^{k-1}(1+r_{t+m})}}_{\text{present value of disposable labor income}}.$$

$$\underbrace{\phantom{A_{t-1}^j(1+r_{t-1}) + \sum_{k=0}^{n} \frac{\frac{W_{t+k}}{P_{t+k}}L_{t+k}^j - T_{t+k}^j}{\Pi_{m=0}^{k-1}(1+r_{t+m})}}}_{\text{total wealth}}$$

$$(2.5)$$

In other words, the IBC requires that the *present value of consumption flows* be covered by *total wealth*, meaning accumulated asset wealth (including interest) *plus* the present value of labor income (net of taxes).

The intertemporal budget constraint always holds (it is not possible to escape it, and it is optimal to exhaust it), but in general this is not the only constraint weighing on households. Many households also face a *debt constraint*, which imposes a ceiling on the amount of debt they can contract in every period. In other words, in many situations a household cannot take on a debt as high as the present value of its labor income net of taxes (which is what the IBC in principle permits). Let us illustrate why with the help of a (deliberately) extreme example. Let us assume that the household is so impatient that it values only its present consumption. We then have $\rho = \infty$, such that the intertemporal utility becomes $\mathcal{U}_t = \ln C_t$, and thus the household chooses $C_{t+1}^j = C_{t+2}^j = \ldots = C_{t+n}^j = 0$. In addition, let us assume (again for simplicity) that the household starts its working life in period t without any asset or debt, so that $A_{t-1}^j = 0$. Nevertheless, this household will work until period $t+n$, and so it will receive the corresponding labor income. According to the IBC (equation (2.5)), and given the fact that $C_{t+1}^j = C_{t+2}^j = \ldots = 0$, the household's consumption in period t is given by

$$C_t^j = \sum_{k=0}^{n} \frac{\frac{W_{t+k}}{P_{t+k}} L_{t+k}^j - T_{t+k}^j}{\Pi_{m=0}^{k-1} (1 + r_{t+m})}.$$

Moreover, since the current labor income (net of taxes) of the household is $(W_t/P_t) L_t^j - T_t^j$, equation (2.4) implies that in order to reach C_t^j the household must take on a debt in the following amount:

$$-A_t^j = C_t^j - \frac{W_t}{P_t} L_t^j + T_t^j = \sum_{k=1}^{n} \frac{\frac{W_{t+k}}{P_{t+k}} L_{t+k}^j - T_{t+k}^j}{\Pi_{m=0}^{k-1} (1 + r_{t+m})}.$$

This level of debt implies that the household *should devote its entire future labor income to reimbursing it*. No lender would accept extending credit to the household at this point, since it would then be too tempting for the household to default on the debt. In the case we are considering, the household would have absolutely nothing to lose by defaulting, since the reimbursement of the debt implies zero consumption throughout all periods. The example just described is extreme, but it does illustrate a much more general phenomenon: many households cannot go into debt as much as they would like and would be consistent with their IBC, because the corresponding debt level would overly increase the risk of nonrepayment to the lender. In practice, many households face debt constraints, which are imposed by lenders in order to limit the risk of default.

A simple and realistic representation of this debt constraint consists of assuming that the debt at the end of period t cannot be such that its total cost in period $t+1$ (that is, the payment of interest plus the repayment of the capital) would exceed an exogenous limit $\bar{D}_t$, which might vary over time. This debt constraint takes the following form:

$$(1 + r_t) A_t^j \geq \bar{D}_t, \quad \text{with } \bar{D}_t \leq 0. \tag{2.6}$$

$\bar{D}_t$ is negative or zero since it is a debt constraint—when $\bar{D}_t = 0$, households cannot go into debt, implying that their asset wealth A_t^j cannot be negative; when $\bar{D}_t < 0$, the debt constraint is less tight—the asset wealth of the household can be negative but never lower than $\bar{D}_t / (1 + r_t)$.

The inequality constraint in equation (2.6) might be binding or not, depending on whether the optimal choice of consumption implied by the maximization of intertemporal utility in equation (2.3) under the IBC alone (equation (2.5)) gives a value of A_t^j that does or does not violate the inequality in equation (2.6). When this consumption choice implies that the inequality in equation (2.6) is satisfied, then the debt constraint imposes no additional constraint on the household's choices relative to the IBC. A household whose consumption choices are not affected by the debt constraint is called a *Ricardian* household. On the other hand, when the choice of A_t^j under the IBC implies that the inequality in equation (2.6) is violated, then it means that the inequality constraint in equation (2.6) binds. In this situation, the household's optimal behavior consists of taking on as much debt as the debt constraint allows, to the point that its asset wealth reaches the level $A_t^j = \bar{D}_t / (1 + r_t)$ (≤ 0). A household whose consumption choice is determined by the debt constraint is called *Keynesian*.[5]

2.2.2 RICARDIAN HOUSEHOLDS

By definition, a Ricardian household is a household whose intertemporal consumption choice implies that the inequality constraint in equation (2.6) is not (and will never be) binding, so that we can simply ignore it when solving for the optimal consumption plan. Thus a Ricardian household chooses, in each period, the level of consumption C_t^j that maximizes intertemporal utility in equation (2.3) under the IBC given by equation (2.5). The Lagrangian function corresponding to this problem is written:

$$\mathcal{L}_t = \underset{\substack{\uparrow \\ \text{intertemporal utility}}}{\mathcal{U}_t^j}$$

$$+ \Lambda_t^j \underbrace{\left\{ A_{t-1}^j (1 + r_{t-1}) + \sum_{k=0}^{n} \frac{\frac{W_{t+k}}{P_{t+k}} L_{t+k}^j - T_{t+k}^j}{\Pi_{m=0}^{k-1} (1 + r_{t+m})} - \sum_{k=0}^{n} \frac{C_{t+k}^j}{\Pi_{m=0}^{k-1} (1 + r_{t+m})} \right\}}_{\text{IBC}},$$

---

5. The terminology may seem badly chosen since there are no "Ricardian" households in the sense as described in the work of David Ricardo, nor are there financially constrained "Keynesian" households in the work of John Maynard Keynes. However, these terms have become so customary that it could be confusing not to use them.

where Λ^j is the Lagrange multiplier associated with the IBC. The first-order conditions associated with the choices of C_t^j and C_{t+1}^j are given by:

$$\frac{\partial \mathcal{L}_t}{\partial C_t^j} = \frac{1}{C_t^j} - \Lambda_t^j = 0 \ \text{ and } \ \frac{\partial \mathcal{L}_t}{\partial C_{t+1}^j} = \left(\frac{1}{1+\rho}\right) \frac{1}{C_{t+1}^j} - \frac{\Lambda_t^j}{1+r_t} = 0. \tag{2.7}$$

By using these two equations to eliminate Λ^j, we find

$$\frac{C_{t+1}^j}{C_t^j} = \frac{1+r_t}{1+\rho}. \tag{2.8}$$

We note that, in a first approximation, when r_t and ρ are sufficiently small (so that C_{t+1}^j / C_{t+1}^j is close to 1) we have[6]

Keynes-Ramsey : $\dfrac{C_{t+1}^j - C_t^j}{C_t^j} \simeq r_t - \rho.$ $\tag{2.9}$

The preceding relation (either in its exact form in (2.8) or in its approximate form in (2.9)) is called the *Keynes-Ramsey rule*. This rule summarizes the phenomenon of *intertemporal substitution in consumption* following from a change in the real interest rate r_t. More precisely, a rise in r_t increases the slope of the consumption path, since it pushes households to consume less in the current period so as to save more money (or reduce their debt) and thus consume more in the future. Conversely, a drop in the real interest rate discourages savings and, hence, lowers future consumption relative to present consumption: the slope of the consumption path is reduced.

The Keynes-Ramsey rule determines the *slope* of the consumption path, meaning the rates of consumption growth between any two successive periods, but the rule does not determine the *level* of this path. It is the IBC that determines what the highest possible consumption levels can be, given the optimal slope of the consumption path. Hence, the use of the Keynes-Ramsey rule (in any period $t+k \geq t$) jointly with the IBC allows a determination of all the optimal consumption levels as of period t. This calculation may be complex in the general case, but under

---

6. This follows from the approximation in equation (1.3) in chapter 1. Indeed, turning equation (2.8) into log gives:

$$\ln\left(1 + \frac{C_{t+1}^j - C_t^j}{C_t^j}\right) = \ln(1+r_t) - \ln(1+\rho),$$

and, hence, equation (2.9) when r_t, ρ, and $(C_{t+1}^j - C_t^j)/C_t^j$ are close to zero.

the preferences that we have assumed we can calculate these consumption levels explicitly. Indeed, by using equation (2.8), for $k = 0, 1, 2, \ldots$, we may eliminate C^j_{t+1}, C^j_{t+2}, C^j_{t+3}, ... from the expression of the present value of consumption flows in equation (2.5) and obtain[7]

$$\sum_{k=0}^{n} \frac{C^j_{t+k}}{\Pi_{m=0}^{k-1} (1+r_{t+m})} = C^j_t + \frac{C^j_{t+1}}{1+r_t} + \frac{C^j_{t+2}}{(1+r_t)(1+r_{t+1})} + \cdots$$

$$+ \frac{C^j_{t+n}}{(1+r_t)(1+r_{t+1})\cdots(1+r_{t+n-1})}$$

$$= C^j_t + \frac{1}{1+r_t}\left[\frac{1+r_t}{1+\rho}C^j_t\right]$$

$$+ \frac{1}{(1+r_t)(1+r_{t+1})}\left[\frac{(1+r_t)(1+r_{t+1})}{(1+\rho)^2}C^j_t\right] + \cdots$$

$$+ \frac{1}{(1+r_t)(1+r_{t+1})\cdots(1+r_{t+n-1})}$$

$$\times \left[\frac{(1+r_t)(1+r_{t+1})\cdots(1+r_{t+n-1})}{(1+\rho)^n}C^j_t\right]$$

$$= \left[1 + \frac{1}{1+\rho} + \left(\frac{1}{1+\rho}\right)^2 + \cdots + \left(\frac{1}{1+\rho}\right)^n\right]C^j_t$$

$$= \left(\frac{1+\rho}{\rho}\right)\left[1 - \left(\frac{1}{1+\rho}\right)^{n+1}\right]C^j_t.$$

By using the latter expression together with the IBC (equation (2.5)), we obtain the consumption in period t of a Ricardian household j (which is therefore noted as $C^{R,j}_t$) with a planning horizon $t + n$:

$$C^{R,j}_t = \underbrace{\frac{\rho}{1+\rho}\left[1 - \left(\frac{1}{1+\rho}\right)^{n+1}\right]^{-1}}_{=\Upsilon, \text{ with } 0 < \Upsilon < 0} \times \underbrace{\left[A^j_{t-1}(1+r_{t-1}) + \sum_{k=0}^{n}\frac{(W_{t+k}/P_{t+k})L^j_{t+k} - T^j_{t+k}}{\Pi_{m=0}^{k-1}(1+r_{t+m})}\right]}_{\text{total wealth}}.$$

(2.10)

7. To go from the third to the fourth line we use the fact that, for any x, $1 + x + x^2 + \ldots + x^n = (1 - x^{n+1})/(1-x)$.

Thus, a Ricardian household *consumes a fraction Υ of its total wealth*; that is to say, the sum of its asset wealth and the present value of labor income, net of taxes. This fraction is all the higher when the household is impatient (which means that ρ is high), since impatience favors present consumption over future consumption. It is also all the higher as n is low: as the horizon becomes shorter, it becomes less and less profitable to save for the future; in the limit, when $n = 0$, we have $\Upsilon = 1$, meaning that the household consumes its entire asset wealth (we then have $C_t^{R,j} = A_{t-1}^j (1 + r_{t-1}) + (W_t/P_t) L_t^j - T_t^j$, and therefore $A_t^j = 0$). In period t, $A_{t-1}^j (1 + r_{t-1})$ is given (since A_{t-1}^j and r_{t-1} have been determined in period $t-1$), but consumption at time t responds to any variation in the path of labor income (net of taxes). It also responds to variations in the real interest rate: high interest rates reduce the present value of future income, which tends to lower current consumption.

Equation (2.10) is the modern version of the so-called *permanent income hypothesis,* originally formulated by Milton Friedman (1957). According to Friedman, and contrary to what Keynes ([1936] 2017) himself wrote, households do not consume a fraction of their *current* income, but instead a fraction of their *permanent* income—that is, the part of income that is not affected by its transitory fluctuations. Thus, an increase in income perceived as permanent will have a large effect on consumption, whereas an increase that is perceived as transitory will not affect current consumption very much (with most of the gain in income being saved, in order to smooth consumption over time).

Equation (2.10) illustrates this point. Let us suppose that the horizon n is sufficiently long, such that the term Υ becomes close to $\rho/(1 + \rho)$. Since we think of ρ as being of the same order of magnitude as the real rate of interest (a few percentage points), the term $\rho/(1 + \rho)$ is low. Thus, a one-shot increase of $(W_t/P_t) L_t^j - T_t^j$, which would take place only in period t, would only have a very small impact on $C_t^{R,j}$. However, a permanent increase in $(W_t/P_t) L_t^j - T_t^j$ has a potentially important effect since it affects the full present value of labor income flows. In the special case where $n \to \infty$ and $r_t = \rho$ for all t, we have $\sum_{i=0}^{n} 1/\Pi_{j=0}^{i-1} (1 + r_{t+i}) = 1/\Upsilon$, so that a permanent increase in $(W_t/P_t) L_t^j - T_t^j$ lifts $C_t^{R,j}$ one for one. Thus, under these assumptions the marginal propensity to consume (MPC for short) out of a *permanent* increase in income is equal to 1, while the MPC out of a purely *transitory* increase in income is equal to $\rho/(1 + \rho) \simeq r_t \ll 1$.

Empirical estimates of the aggregate consumption response to transitory income changes find a much larger response than that implied by the strict permanent income hypothesis (see, e.g., Campbell and Mankiw 1989). The prevailing interpretation of this result is that many households are *not* Ricardian, so that the economy-wide MPC out of transitory income changes averages the MPCs of Ricardian households (small) and the MPCs of non-Ricardian households (possibly large). We now turn to the consumption behavior of those households and the way they affect the aggregate consumption function.

2.2.3 KEYNESIAN HOUSEHOLDS

By definition, a Keynesian household is a household that faces a binding debt limit. The debt limit is binding if the consumption level $C_t^{R,j}$ (that is, the level implied by household preferences and the IBC only) implies an asset wealth A_t that violates the debt constraint (2.6). If the constraint (2.6) is binding in period t then the asset wealth of the household is simply $A_t = \bar{D}_t/(1+r_t)$ (≤ 0), because it cannot fall at a lower level. Replacing A_t by $\bar{D}_t/(1+r_t)$ in the period t budget constraint (2.4), we see that the consumption of a Keynesian household (henceforth $C_t^{K,j}$) is given by:

$$C_t^{K,j} = -\frac{\bar{D}_t}{1+r_t} + (1+r_{t-1}) A_{t-1}^j + \frac{W_t}{P_t} L_t^j - T_t^j. \tag{2.11}$$

This expression for the individual consumption of a debt-constrained household teaches us a number of things. First of all, we see that this consumption level does not depend on the present value of all future disposable labor income flows but only on *current* disposable income; this is the precise sense in which this behavior could be called "Keynesian." This Keynesian behavior on the part of a subset of the households has important implications for the way the economy responds to aggregate conditions. Let us mention a few here:

- Changes in the real interest rate r_t affect consumption through the *borrowing capacity* of Keynesian households: a rise in r_t raises the total burden of the debt *ex post*; hence it reduces the amount that these households can borrow *ex ante* (the term $-\bar{D}/(1+r_t) \geq 0$ is lower) and force them to cut their consumption demand $C_t^{K,j}$. This mechanism thus complements the intertemporal substitution in consumption on the part of Ricardian households, which implied a fall in their consumption ($C_t^{R,j}$) following a rise in the real interest rate (due to intertemporal substitution in consumption).

- Temporary changes in taxes have a large effect on Keynesian households' consumption demand, while they have a marginal effect on Ricardian households' consumption demand (since the latter does not respond to current disposable income but to the full present value of all disposable income flows). Hence the impact of fiscal policy shocks may substantially differ depending on the number of Keynesian households in the economy. This is examined in detail in chapter 7.

- Similarly, changes (even temporary) in the real wage have a large impact on the consumption demand of Keynesian households. We will see in chapter 7 that this greater consumption demand in turn contributes to push up the real wage, potentially setting in motion a powerful feedback loop between the real wage and aggregate demand.

- Finally, time variations in the debt constraint mechanically induce variations in Keynesian households' consumption demand (formally, a tightening of the debt constraint, meaning a rise in $\bar{D}_t$, reduces $C_t^{K,j}$). This channel explains why aggregate consumption responds positively to financial innovations, which tend to relax the debt constraint, but responds negatively to financial crises that generate a tightening of the debt constraint. We will study in more detail the channel of forced deleveraging induced by the tightening of the debt constraint in chapter 8.

An important–and by nature empirical–question is how many households actually behave like Keynesian households in practice. In principle, these households are those who are "poor" in the sense of being at (or close to) the debt limit, and they could be measured in this way in wealth surveys. However, one must be careful as to use the proper wealth concept here: many households are "wealthy" in the sense of owning a house or a car but in fact have very little cash ahead of them to provide for current consumption. Such households are likely to behave like Keynesian households while having a high recorded net worth, so just looking at the distribution of net worth in wealth surveys may significantly underestimate the true share of Keynesian households. Kaplan, Violante, and Weidner (2014) attempt to measure the share of Keynesian consumers in a number of OECD countries by including not only poor households, but also those households that are wealthy due to home ownership yet nevertheless hold little liquid wealth and are thus likely constrained in their daily nondurables consumption (these latter households are labeled by the authors as the "wealthy hand-to-mouth"). They estimate the total share of Keynesian consumers to lie between 20 percent and 35 percent, depending on the country.

2.2.4 Aggregate Consumption

Aggregate consumption C_t results from the aggregation of the consumption decisions of Ricardian and Keynesian households. What form does the aggregate "consumption function" take, and what are its principal arguments? First, we notice that the consumption levels of both Keynesian and Ricardian households respond negatively to a rise in the real interest rate r_t: Keynesian households because this hike reduces their debt capacity, and Ricardian households because it induces them to delay consumption spending. Therefore aggregate consumption is unambiguously decreasing in r_t. In the same way, current labor income $(W_t/P_t)\, L_t^j$ influences positively the consumption of both household types. This income is in turn closely tied to current output Y_t, which determines the income of all households in the economy.[8]

---

8. As indicated in the previous chapter, aggregate household income is not identically equal to output due to the depreciation of capital and the net transfers coming from abroad. Having said that, output remains the main determinant of current income, so the two are highly correlated.

Thus aggregate consumption is unambiguously increasing in current output Y_t. Conversely, aggregate consumption is negatively affected by net tax contributions (whose total value is T_t), due to the impact of taxes on the disposable income of all households. Finally, to the extent that the consumption of Ricardian households responds to anticipated variations in disposable labor income flows, it responds positively to the future values of output (Y_{t+1}, Y_{t+2}, ...) and negatively to the future values of taxes (T_{t+1}, T_{t+2}, ...).

For the sake of simplicity, we will overlook here the effects of future income and taxes (Y_{t+1}, T_{t+1}, ...) on current consumption. Strictly speaking, this is equivalent to assuming that all consumers are Keynesian in the sense defined above; that is, they are financially constrained. A looser interpretation of this assumption is that the future values of income and taxes do influence current aggregate consumption, but that these effects may be usefully overlooked, at least in a first approximation, in order to study a certain number of macroeconomic issues. Having said that, temporarily abstracting from these effects does not mean ignoring them altogether, and they must be reintroduced into the analysis whenever this is necessary. This will notably be the case when we will study the effects of fiscal policy, since fiscal policy generally causes a variation in public debt that influences future taxes in a manner that may affect current consumption-saving choices retroactively. Thus, when we study fiscal policy in chapters 7 and 10, these Ricardian effects of future income and taxes on present consumption will occupy the space that they deserve. For the present, we will merely assume that the *aggregate consumption function* has the following form:

$$C_t = C(\underset{-}{r_t}, \underset{-}{\bar{D}_t}, \underset{+}{\rho}, \underset{+}{Y_t}, \underset{-}{T_t}). \tag{2.12}$$

2.3   INVESTMENT

We saw in chapter 1 that, within national accounting, investment gathers together gross fixed capital formation (GFCF) as well as the variation in firm inventories. Given the small size of inventories in GDP (of the order of 0.5 percent of GDP), we will overlook their variations here and simply identify investment with variations in the stock of fixed capital. This stock of capital consists of any good that is not destined for current consumption (machines, computers, software, public transportation, industrial buildings, and so on).

For the sake of simplicity we will assume that the economy is composed of a large number of identical firms and we will therefore study the behavior of the representative firm. This firm chooses the quantities of inputs it uses (capital and labor) in such a way as to maximize profits. Suppose there is a construction delay, such that the amount of capital accumulated in the current period (K_t) only serves to produce in the next period:

$$Y_{t+1} = Z_{t+1} K_t^\alpha (L_{t+1}^d)^{1-\alpha}, \, 0 < \alpha < 1,$$

where L_t^d is the quantity of labor utilized (d stands here for labor *demand* by the firm) and $Z_t > 0$ is total factor productivity. A fraction δ of capital depreciates in every period. Hence, the equation describing the accumulation of capital is given by:

$$K_t = I_t + (1 - \delta) K_{t-1}. \tag{2.13}$$

It is simplest to think of firms as borrowing, in every period, the goods that will form the capital stock. In period t the firm chooses the amount of capital that maximizes (appropriately discounted) next period's profits—that is, it maximizes[9]

$$\Pi_{t+1} = \underbrace{\frac{1}{1+r_t}}_{\text{disc. factor}} \Big[\underbrace{Z_{t+1} K_t^\alpha \left(L_{t+1}^d\right)^{1-\alpha}}_{\text{output}} + \underbrace{(1-\delta) K_t}_{\text{undepreciated capital}} - \underbrace{(1+r_t) K_t}_{\text{financing cost}}$$

$$- \underbrace{(W_{t+1}/P_{t+1}) L_{t+1}^d}_{\text{labor cost}} \Big]. \tag{2.14}$$

The choice of capital solves the first-order condition $\partial \Pi_{t+1}/\partial K_t = 0$. Hence, the optimal stock of capital satisfies

$$\underbrace{\alpha Z_{t+1} K_t^{\alpha-1} \left(L_{t+1}^d\right)^{1-\alpha}}_{\text{marginal product of capital}} = \underbrace{r_t + \delta}_{\text{user cost of capital}}. \tag{2.15}$$

Note that the *user cost of capital* incorporates, in addition to the real cost of the loan—the real interest rate, r_t—the fraction δ of the capital stock that is destroyed in the course of the production process and that must be reinvested in order to maintain the stock of capital at its existing level. More generally, the user cost of capital encompasses the interest burden as well as all the costs linked to the use of fixed capital other than the interests.[10]

9. This formulation takes the price of output as the numeraire and implicitly assumes, for simplicity, that the relative price of capital is equal to 1; that is, output and investment goods are effectively the same good.

10. Equation (2.15) implicitly assumes that the representative firm can choose $I_t < 0$. When that is the case, its capital is sold on the secondary market (so that the total supply of goods increases). In practice, installed capital is often difficult, if not impossible, to resell. If we add the constraint $I_t \geq 0$ to the firm's program, then the corner solution $I_t = 0$ may prevail—for example, when the stock of capital K_t is already high or expected future productivity Z_{t+1} particularly low.

Taking L_{t+1}^d as given, the solution to equation (2.15) is unique since the marginal product of capital is decreasing in K_{t+1} (due to the concavity of the production function). By using equation (2.13) to replace K_t by its value in equation (2.15), we find that the demand for investment by the representative firm in period t is given by

$$I_t = K_t - (1 - \delta) K_{t-1}$$

$$= \left(\frac{\alpha Z_{t+1}}{r_t + \delta} \right)^{\frac{1}{1-\alpha}} L_{t+1}^d - (1 - \delta) K_{t-1},$$

which we may summarize in the following *aggregate investment function*:

$$I_t = I(r_t, Z_{t+1}). \tag{2.16}$$
$$\underset{-}{} \quad \underset{+}{}$$

To summarize, a high real interest rate discourages investment, while a rise in expected future productivity stimulates it.

2.4 NET EXPORTS

The last component of private demand that we are studying is the balance of trade—that is, net exports (exports minus imports). This corresponds to the net demand for goods and services that is addressed to the domestic economy by the rest of the world. Figure 2.1 shows the behavior of exports and imports in the United States and the euro area since 1970. Although the two components of net exports are highly correlated (such that $X - M$ is much smaller than X or M alone), X and M are both large and thus may contribute significantly to the business cycle.

We are going to see that, like the other components of aggregate demand, net exports tend to decrease after a rise in a country's real interest rate. Now let us be more specific about the assumptions underlying our analysis:

- The economy under consideration is a *small open economy*, which means that global variables (such as world GDP Y_t^W, the world real interest rate r_t^W, and so on) have an impact on the domestic economy but not the other way around. The alternative assumption is that of a closed world economy composed of different zones interacting in general equilibrium, such that all macroeconomic variables (such as domestic and world GDP, domestic and world inflation, and so on) are all determined jointly and simultaneously. Such an analysis would be a lot more complicated than under the assumption of a small open economy,

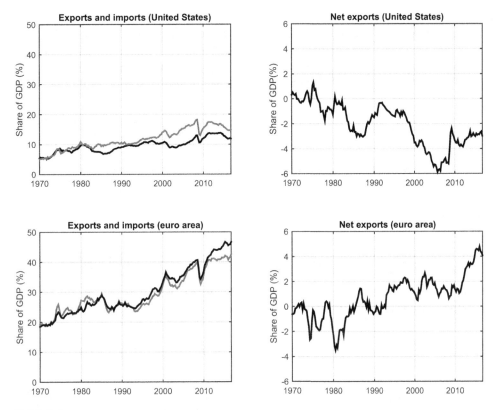

FIGURE 2.1
Exports and imports in the United States and the euro area.
Sources: AWM database, BEA (NIPA tables), and the author's calculations.

while the latter remains satisfactory at least as a first approximation for most issues in international economics.

- The exchange rate regime is one of *floating exchange rates*, so that the flows of goods, services, and capital trigger variations in the value of the domestic currency that are not systematically offset by central bank interventions. This is the exchange-rate regime that has been most widespread in developed economies since the collapse of the Bretton Woods system in 1973. The predominance of floating exchange rates in the developed world has tended to extend over time to developing and transition economies after it became apparent that fixed exchange rate regimes exposed countries to harmful currency crises (for example, several Southeast Asian countries experienced major currency and economic crises in 1997).

- *Capital mobility is perfect*, which means that investors promptly attempt to arbitrage away any returns differential between assets that are labeled in the different currencies that they are spotting. These speculative operations imply that interest rates and exchange rates are linked to each other through several no-arbitrage conditions, and it is those conditions that determine the equilibrium value of the domestic currency relative to other currencies (i.e., the nominal exchange rate). The assumption of prefect capital mobility is satisfactory when it comes to describing the currency markets of most developed countries. However, it is not an adequate description of countries practicing capital controls, as is the case of a number of developing and transition countries (including some large countries like China).

2.4.1 EXCHANGE RATES AND PRICE COMPETITIVENESS

2.4.1.1 THE NOMINAL EXCHANGE RATE

Let us start by recalling a few concepts necessary for the study of the effect of interest rates on a country's price competitiveness. The *nominal* exchange rate is the price of one unit of foreign currency in units of the domestic currency. For example, the US dollar-euro exchange rate is given by:

$$E_{\$/\euro} = 0.8\ \$/\euro.$$

This way of writing the nominal exchange rate, called direct, is the one most frequently utilized. Nevertheless the same exchange rate may be expressed in indirect form; that is, in terms of the number of units of foreign currency that can be purchased with one unit of the domestic currency:

$$E_{\$/\euro}^{\text{indirect}} = \left(E_{\euro/\$}\right)^{-1}\ \$/\euro.$$

Expressed in direct form, a hike in the nominal exchange rate E corresponds to a *depreciation* of the domestic currency, since it takes more units of the domestic currency to purchase one unit of foreign currency (for example if $E_{\$/\euro}$ shifts from 1.0 to 1.2, then the euro becomes more expensive for US residents).

2.4.1.2 THE REAL EXCHANGE RATE

The *real* exchange rate is the *real price of foreign goods*; that is, the price of goods purchased abroad, converted in the domestic currency, over the price of goods purchased in the domestic economy. Formally, the real exchange rate is given by:

$$Q_{\$/\euro} = \frac{E_{\$/\euro}P_{\euro}}{P_{\$}}. \tag{2.17}$$

where $E_{\$/€}$ is the (direct) nominal exchange rate (in our example, expressed in $\$/€$), $P_€$ the price of foreign goods (hence, expressed in $€$), and $P_\$$ the price of goods in the domestic economy (in $\$$).

2.4.1.3 Impact of Price Competitiveness on Net Exports

To understand intuitively the impact of the real exchange rate on a country's price competitiveness, and thereby on its net exports, let us review the following simple example. Suppose that the United States and the euro area produce different goods (one per country) while households in both regions enjoy utility from consuming both goods. Assuming logarithmic preferences, a US household will solve

$$\max_{C_{US},C_{EA}} \; (1-\nu)\ln C_{US} + \nu \ln C_{EA}, \;\; 0 < \nu < 1,$$

subject to

$$P_\$ C_{US} + E_{\$/€} P_€ C_{EA} = I_\$.$$

Here C_{US} and C_{EA} denote the consumption by a US household of the goods produced in the US and the euro area, respectively; the constant ν measures the relative importance of euro area–produced goods in the utility of this household; and $I_\$$ is the household's nominal income. The budget constraint is expressed in nominal terms and reflects the impact of the $\$/€$ nominal exchange rate on the cost of foreign goods to the domestic household. Dividing both sides of the nominal budget constraint by $P_\$$ to reformulate it in real terms and using equation (2.17), we obtain

$$C_{US} + Q_{\$/€} C_{EA} = I_\$/P_\$,$$

which makes it clear that the real exchange rate is the real price of foreign goods (euro area–produced goods, in our example). Substituting this latter constraint into the objective, computing the first-order condition, and rearranging, we find the demand for euro area–produced goods by US households to be

$$C_{EA}\left(Q_{\$/€}\right) = \left(\nu \frac{I_\$}{P_\$}\right) Q_{\$/€}^{-1},$$

so the consumption of the foreign good declines with its real price.[11]

---

11. Logarithmic preferences imply that a constant share ν of real income $I_\$/P_\$$ is devoted to the consumption of foreign goods ($Q_{\$/€} C_{EA}$). This property is specific to log preferences and does not hold away from this specification.

This simple example illustrates that, under standard preferences over domestic and foreign goods, we should expect *the quantity of imports to decline with the real exchange rate*. But note that in our example a symmetric reasoning applies to euro area consumers, for whom the (direct) real exchange rate is

$$Q_{\text{€}/\$} = \frac{E_{\text{€}/\$}P_\$}{P_\text{€}} = \frac{1}{E_{\$/\text{€}}}\frac{1}{P_\text{€}/P_\$} = \frac{1}{Q_{\$/\text{€}}}.$$

Therefore, a rise in $Q_{\$/\text{€}}$ is a fall in $Q_{\text{€}/\$}$, which will, under the same preferences, trigger a rise in the consumption of US-produced goods by euro area consumers. Thus, if $Q_{\$/\text{€}}$ rises, then not only do imports decline but *exports also rise*.

Does the fall in imports and the rise in exports necessarily improve the real value of net exports? Not necessarily, because the depreciation of the domestic currency *raises the relative price of imported goods, which goes toward deteriorating net exports*. For net exports to rise, it must be that the impact of the rise in the real exchange rate on quantities (i.e., the rise in exports and the fall in imports) dominates this terms-of-trade effect (i.e., the rise in the real price of imports). To see this formally, proceed with the same simple example as above, assuming that the consumption of euro area–produced goods by US residents are the only US imports (and the other way around), and that households in the two countries share the same preferences. To buy a quantity C_{EA} of goods produced in the euro area, US households must pay € $P_\text{€}C_{EA}$, so the value of their imports in terms of domestic currency units is \$ $E_{\$/\text{€}}P_\text{€}C_{EA}$. It follows that the real value of these imports (i.e., the dollar value divided by $P_\$$) is $Q_{\$/\text{€}}C_{EA}$. On the other hand, the US dollar value of exports (i.e., the consumption of US-produced goods by euro area residents) is \$ $P_\$C_{US}^*$, or C_{US}^* in real terms. By symmetry with C_{EA} above, C_{US}^* is given by

$$C_{US}^* = \left(v\frac{I_\text{€}}{P_\text{€}}\right)Q_{\text{€}/\$}^{-1} = \left(v\frac{I_\text{€}}{P_\text{€}}\right)Q_{\$/\text{€}}.$$

It follows that the real value of US net exports is

$$XM_\$ = C_{US}^* - Q_{\$/\text{€}}C_{EA} = \left(v\frac{I_\text{€}}{P_\text{€}}\right)Q_{\$/\text{€}} - \left(v\frac{I_\$}{P_\$}\right),$$

which (holding prices constant) is increasing in the real exchange rate $Q_{\$/\text{€}}$. Therefore, in our simple example *net exports XM_t increase with the real exchange rate Q_t*. Note that this property follows from the fact that the effects of changes in the real exchange rate on the price and quantity of imports exactly offset each other, leaving the real value of imports unchanged (at $vI_\$/P_\$$). It follows that the changes in net exports follow from changes in exports only, and the latter rise with the real exchange rate. While this property would not necessarily hold under alternative preferences over domestic and foreign goods, the logarithmic specification remains a natural benchmark with which to start.

Finally, the real exchange rate is not the only determinant of net exports; the cyclical position of the economy relative to the rest of the world also affects both its exports and imports. This is because, when the domestic economy is in expansion, domestic aggregate demand Y_t increases and a portion of this demand is addressed to firms located elsewhere in the world. This tends to stimulate imports and thus hurts net exports. Conversely, when demand from the rest of the world Y^w is high, part of it is directed at domestic firms, which stimulates exports. We summarize the effects of both price competitiveness and the business cycle on net exports by the following *net export function*:

$$XM_t = XM(\underset{+}{Q_t}, \underset{-}{Y_t}, \underset{+}{Y_t^w}).$$

2.4.2 CAPITAL FLOWS AND INTEREST RATE PARITIES

The preceding equation does not feature the real interest rate r_t. In order to comprehend how the latter influences net exports, we need to understand how it affects *capital flows* and therefore the nominal and real exchange rates.

The transactions of a country with the rest of the world are not limited to trades of goods and services but also involve financial transactions. For example, this is the case when a European bank buys US Treasury bonds from a US-based bank. From the viewpoint of the euro area, this is a capital outflow, since it is a debt issued by the US federal government and now owed to European residents. A financial transaction of this type involves a prior currency trade—here a purchase of US dollars (the currency in which the traded asset is denominated) against euros. The currency market aggregates all the currency transactions that result from the flows of goods and capital, and the nominal exchange rate is the equilibrium price of all these transactions. Thus, if euro area residents start to, for example, massively purchase dollar-denominated bonds, this triggers an appreciation of the US dollar relative to the euro—or equivalently, a depreciation of the euro. The nominal exchange rate $E_{\$/€}$ falls, since it now takes fewer US dollars to buy a euro.

2.4.2.1 UNCOVERED INTEREST RATE PARITY

The capital flows between countries result from investors' trades in financial assets. As soon as a difference in expected returns is spotted, investors may borrow in one currency, lend in another currency, and cash in the difference between the cost of the debt and the return on the loan. These operations on the currency market are called *carry trade*. When carry trading, investors contribute at any point in time to restoring the equality of expected returns. The condition of equality of expected returns in currency markets is called the *uncovered interest rate parity*, or UIP for short.

To derive the UIP, let us put ourselves in the position of a US-based investor who has $1 to invest at a certain time horizon (say a year), either inside the United States or in the euro area. Two investment strategies are offered to that investor:

1. to lend $1 at the nominal interest rate $i_{\$,t}$ in his country of residence and thus receive $\$(1 + i_{\$,t})$ at the maturity of the loan;

2. to carry out an international financial transaction, that is:

- to purchase € $1/E_{\$/€,t}$;

- to lend these € $1/E_{\$/€,t}$ euros at the (euro-denominated) nominal interest rate $i_{€,t}$ and hence receive € $(1 + i_{€,t})/E_{\$/€,t}$ at maturity;

- to resell these € $(1 + i_{€,t})/E_{\$/€,t}$ at the exchange rate $E_{\$/€,t+1}$ at maturity and thus recuperate $\$(1 + i_{€,t})E_{\$/€,t+1}/E_{\$/€,t}$.

Assuming that investors are risk neutral (or that there is no currency risk), the nominal returns associated with the two investment strategies should be identical. We should thus have

$$1 + i_{\$,t} = (1 + i_{€,t}) \frac{E_{\$/€,t+1}}{E_{\$/€,t}}, \tag{2.18}$$

which is precisely the UIP.

When the UIP holds, investors expect to earn nothing from carry trading. In principle, violation of the UIP in one direction or the other should push investors to undertake some financial transactions in order to seize the nascent profit opportunities—and in so doing eliminate those opportunities. For example, if $1 + i_{\$,t} < (1 + i_{€,t})E_{\$/€,t+1}/E_{\$/€,t}$, then investors would find it worthwhile to borrow in US dollars (at the nominal interest rate $i_{\$,t}$), use the borrowed amount to purchase euros and invest them at the nominal interest rate $i_{€,t}$, and then resell them at maturity to reimburse the (dollar-denominated) original loan. These operations translate into a rise in the demand for euros against the US dollar and hence a depreciation of the US dollar in period t. The implied rise in $E_{\$/€,t}$ then goes toward restoring equation (2.18). The converse is true if $1 + i_{\$,t} > (1 + i_{€,t})E_{\$/€,t+1}/E_{\$/€,t}$.

In practice, engaging aggressively into such carry trading can be quite risky for investors, given the uncertainty surrounding the future values of the nominal exchange rate. The presence of this currency risk and the difficulty to hedge it tend to limit the buying and selling pressures that risk-averse investors are willing to exert on a misaligned exchange rate. As a result, UIP rarely holds up in practice. However, it remains a useful benchmark in that it summarizes one of the main forces that affects the nominal exchange rate at any point in time—namely the nominal interest rate differential between countries.

In the context of a short-run equilibrium analysis, we may take $E_{\$/\euro,t+1}$ (the nominal exchange rate that will prevail, say, in a year's time) as given. So the UIP shows how the *current* nominal exchange rate (here, $E_{\$/\euro,t}$) adjusts as a function of the nominal interest rate differential. That is, holding constant the foreign nominal interest rate ($i_{\euro,t}$) and the future nominal exchange rate ($E_{\$/\euro,t+1}$), the UIP shows how the current nominal exchange rate $E_{\$/\euro,t}$ adjusts after changes in the domestic nominal interest rate $i_{\$,t}$. In this spirit, let us rewrite the UIP as follows:

$$E_{\$/\euro,t} = \frac{1+i_{\euro,t}}{1+i_{\$,t}}E_{\$/\euro,t+1}.$$

For example, all else being equal, a fall in the domestic interest rate generates a capital *outflow* that depreciates the domestic currency (i.e., $E_{\$/\euro,t}$ rises).

2.4.2.2 REAL INTEREST RATE PARITY

In the same way that the UIP ties the nominal exchange rate to a nominal interest rate differential, the *real interest rate parity* (RIP) ties the *real* exchange rate to a real interest rate differential. In our US euro area example, we go from the UIP to the RIP by rewriting the UIP as follows:

$$\frac{1+i_{\$,t}}{\frac{P_{\$,t+1}}{P_{\$,t}}} \times E_{\$/\euro,t} \times \frac{P_{\euro,t}}{P_{\$,t}} = \frac{(1+i_{\euro,t})}{\frac{P_{\euro,t+1}}{P_{\euro,t}}} \times E_{\$/\euro,t+1} \times \frac{P_{\euro,t+1}}{P_{\$,t+1}}.$$

By the definitions of the real interest rate (equation (2.1)) and of the real exchange rate (equation (2.17)), the preceding equation may be rewritten as follows:

$$(1+r_{\$,t})\,Q_{\$/\euro,t} = (1+r_{\euro,t})\,Q_{\$/\euro,t+1}.$$

Thus, if we consider the future real exchange rate Q_{t+1} as given, the current real exchange rate Q_t between an open economy (with real interest rate r_t) and the rest of the world (with real interest rate r_t^w) can be written like this:

$$Q_t = \frac{1+r_t^w}{1+r_t}Q_{t+1}.$$

This expression states that, for example, an increase in the domestic real interest rate r_t is associated with a *real* currency appreciation (a drop of Q_t), which makes the domestic economy less price-competitive—and the other way around. And since we have $XM_t = XM(\underset{+}{Q_t},\ \underset{-}{Y_t},\ \underset{+}{Y_t^w})$, we may rewrite the *net export function* as follows:

$$XM_t = XM(\underset{-}{r_t}, \underset{-}{Y_t}, \underset{+}{Y_t^w}, \underset{+}{r_t^w}, \underset{+}{Q_{t+1}}). \tag{2.19}$$

2.5 AGGREGATION OF EXPENDITURES

2.5.1 THE IS CURVE

We can now aggregate the spending behaviors described so far (equations (2.12), (2.16), and (2.19)) to obtain the following expression for aggregate demand:[12]

$$Y_t = \underbrace{C(r_t, \bar{D}_t, \rho, Y_t, T_t)}_{\text{consumption}} + \underbrace{I(r_t, Z_{t+1})}_{\text{investment}} + \underbrace{XM(r_t, Y_t, Y_t^W, r_t^W, Q_{t+1})}_{\text{net exports}} + \underbrace{G_t}_{\text{gov't spending}}. \qquad (2.20)$$

Notice that Y_t appears on both sides of this expression, because total expenditures Y_t include consumption expenditures as well as net exports, both of which depend on income and hence on expenditures. So we have, potentially, a multiplier effect passing through consumption—an increase in income stimulates consumption, which itself stimulates spending, output, and income, which in turn stimulates consumption, etc. On the other hand, we have an offsetting effect passing via the net exports, since an increase in income stimulates imports, which *reduces* net exports and thus spending and income. Regarding the first effect, recall that total household consumption aggregates the consumption behavior of *Ricardian* and *Keynesian* consumers. While Keynesian households respond about one for one to changes in their disposable income, Ricardian households only respond to changes in *permanent* income, and the latter is much smoother than current income (as many income changes are only temporary). Consequently, we should expect aggregate consumption demand to respond less than one for one to changes in current income–that is, $\partial C_t / \partial Y_t < 1$. The second effect, on the other hand, implies that net exports tend to fall with income—$\partial XM_t / \partial Y_t < 0$. Taken together, these two effects imply that the right-hand side of equation (2.20) increases less than one for one with income:

$$\underbrace{\frac{\partial C_t}{\partial Y_t}}_{\in (0,1)} + \underbrace{\frac{\partial XM_t}{\partial Y_t}}_{\leq 0} < 1. \qquad (2.21)$$

This latter property implies that the *equilibrium* response of output Y_t to the real interest rate r_t (that is, the response that takes into account the feedback from Y_t to C_t and XM_t) has the same (negative) sign as the direct responses of C_t, I_t, and XM_t to r_t. To verify this formally, assume that the functions $C(\cdot)$, $I(\cdot)$, and $XM(\cdot)$ are

---

12. The last component of aggregate demand is government spending G_t. It is chosen by the government, and as such we will consider it to be exogenous. We will study in detail in chapters 7 and 10 the effects of fiscal shocks, once we have properly constructed the intertemporal budget constraint of the government.

all differentiable, and use this property to compute the total differential of equation (2.20). One gets:

$$\underbrace{\left(1 - \frac{\partial C_t}{\partial Y_t} - \frac{\partial XM_t}{\partial Y_t}\right)}_{>0 \text{ (by eq. (2.21))}} dY_t = \underbrace{\left(\frac{\partial C_t}{\partial r_t} + \frac{\partial I_t}{\partial r_t} + \frac{\partial XM_t}{\partial r_t}\right)}_{<0} dr_t + \text{ other terms.}$$

Thus, provided that inequality in (2.21) holds and that all functions are differentiable, equation (2.20) implicitly defines an *aggregate demand function* of the form

$$Y_t = Y(\underset{-}{r_t}, \underset{+}{\Theta_t}), \tag{2.22}$$

where

$$\Theta_t = \Theta(\underset{-}{\bar{D}_t}, \underset{+}{\rho}, \underset{-}{T_t}, \underset{+}{Z_{t+1}}, \underset{+}{Y_t^W}, \underset{+}{r_t^W}, \underset{+}{Q_{t+1}}). \tag{2.23}$$

Equations (2.22) and (2.23) are just a rewriting of the aggregate demand equation (2.20) that makes it depend (tautologically) on two arguments: the real interest rate r_t (negatively) and a composite variable Θ_t (positively) that summarizes all the factors boosting aggregate demand independently of shifts in the real interest rate. For example, an increase in world GDP stimulates exports and hence increases aggregate demand in the domestic economy at any given real interest rate r_t. In the same manner, expectations of high future productivity (Z_{t+1}) increase investment demand and hence aggregate demand, and so on. The formulation of aggregate demand according to equations (2.22) and (2.23) recognizes that all these demand factors affect Y_t via their effect on Θ_t. Put differently, Θ_t is a "sufficient statistic" for all the aggregate demand shocks that hit the economy.

Expression (2.22) features the *level* of output and is *nonlinear*. In the rest of this book, we will work with a *log-linear* approximation to equation (2.22), which will thus feature log output $y_t = \ln Y_t$ in place of the output level Y_t. In the appendix to this chapter, it is shown that in the vicinity of the average level of output $\bar{Y} = Y(\bar{r}, \bar{\Theta})$, where $\bar{r}$ and $\bar{\Theta}$ are the average values of r_t and Θ_t, equation (2.22) is, in a first approximation, equivalent to:

$$\textbf{IS}: y_t = \theta_t - \sigma\,(r_t - \bar{r})\,, \ \sigma > 0. \tag{2.24}$$

Equation (2.24) is the *IS curve* (for "Investment-Savings"), which summarizes the systematic negative relation between log output (y_t) and the real interest rate (as a deviation from its average value, $r_t - \bar{r}$). This relation is parameterized by θ_t, which is (in the vicinity of $(r_t, \Theta_t) = (\bar{r}, \bar{\Theta})$) an increasing function of the underlying demand parameter Θ_t. In what follows, we will simply refer to θ_t as the aggregate demand parameter, or even more simply as the aggregate demand shock. The fact that equation (2.24) is linear will greatly facilitate the analysis in the chapters that follow, especially when we use the IS curve in conjunction with other behavioral equations or equilibrium conditions. In addition, the fact that equation (2.24) expresses output in logarithm (and not as a level) enables expressing variations in output in terms of proportional deviations from the mean. Indeed, the approximation in equation (1.3) implies that when Y_t is close to $\bar{Y}$ we have

$$y_t \simeq \bar{y} + \frac{Y_t - \bar{Y}}{\bar{Y}},$$

so that $\mathrm{d}y_t = \mathrm{d}Y_t / \bar{Y}$ (in percent). From this perspective, $-\sigma$ in equation (2.24) is the *semi-elasticity of output with respect to the real interest rate*, meaning the proportional drop of output $(\mathrm{d}Y_t / \bar{Y})$ induced by a variation in the level of the real interest rate $(\mathrm{d}r_t)$.[13] For example, when the level of the real interest rate goes from 3 percent (its average level, say) to 4 percent, then aggregate demand drops σ percent below the mean.

2.5.2 RELATION WITH THE IS-LM MODEL

Equation (2.24) above generalizes the IS curve of the basic IS-LM model in two directions. First, equation (2.24) incorporates the fact that all the components of private demand (and not only firms' investment) depend negatively on the real interest rate. Second, and more fundamentally, equation (2.24) makes perfectly clear the fact that it is the *real* interest rate (and not the *nominal* interest rate) that governs spending decisions. In the IS-LM model, the price level is assumed to be constant $(=\bar{P})$ and hence the real and nominal interest rates coincide. In that special case we may replace r_t by i_t and therefore write the IS curve as follows (ignoring time indices, since the IS-LM model is purely static):

$$\textbf{IS}: y = \theta - \sigma\,(i - \bar{\imath}). \tag{2.25}$$

In the IS-LM model, the nominal interest rate i is itself determined by the equilibrium on the money market—the money supply M^s being considered as exogenous and controlled by the central bank (the underlying assumption being that the monetary base, which is effectively controlled by the central bank, maintains a stable

---

13. Recall that an elasticity is a ratio of proportional variations (both expressed in percent), whereas a semi-elasticity is the ratio of a proportional variation to a variation in level. Here the variation in level is that of r_t, which induces a variation in the level of y_t (output in log) and hence, in first approximation, a *proportional* variation of Y_t (output in level).

relation with M^s). Equilibrium on the money market, coupled with a money demand function that is increasing in output (due to the transaction motive) but decreasing in the nominal interest rate (due to the opportunity cost of holding money), gives the usual LM curve (here in log-linear form):

$$\textbf{LM}: m^s - \bar{p} = ay - bi, \ a, b > 0. \tag{2.26}$$

Finally, the underlying assumption of the IS-LM model is that aggregate supply responds one for one to variations in aggregate demand, such that equations (2.25) and (2.26) are suffice to characterize the equilibrium (y, i) as a function of the exogenous parameters (θ and $m^s - \bar{p}$). Graphically, the equilibrium is located at the intersection of the IS and LM curves on the (y, i) plane (see figure 2.2).

The macroeconomic model we use throughout the book departs from the basic IS-LM model in the direction of more generality and greater realism. First, it allows macroeconomic shocks to influence not only output but also prices and inflation. Thus equation (2.24) is correct but (2.25) is not, since in general $r_t = i_t - \pi_{t+1} \neq i_t$. Second, the model we will be using replaces the assumption that the central bank targets the money supply M^s with the alternative assumption that the central bank *adjusts the path of nominal short-term interest rates in a manner to influence the real interest rate r_t*. Finally, the analysis of the following chapters will depart from the basic IS-LM model by not assuming that firms passively adjust their production to respond one for one to changes in demand. Some firms will adjust their selling price in response to changes in macroeconomic conditions, so aggregate shocks will be buffered by price adjustments.

2.6 MONETARY POLICY AND AGGREGATE DEMAND

2.6.1 THE MONETARY POLICY CURVE

Nowadays central banks set the path of nominal short-term interest rates in such a way as to influence the real interest rate—meaning the rate of interest that matters for private agents. We will describe in detail the procedures and channels of transmission of monetary policy in chapter 6. For the time being, we need not go into so much detail. It suffices to observe that the ultimate goal of the central bank is to influence aggregate demand in such a way as to best stabilize inflation and output. Thus it is indeed the *real* interest rate r_t (the one that occurs in the IS curve) that the central bank seeks to influence by its monetary policy. Following Romer (2000), we will simply assume that the real interest rate that the central bank implements follows a reaction function of the type:

$$\textbf{MP}: r_t = \bar{r} + \gamma \left(\pi_t - \bar{\pi} \right), \ \gamma \geq 0, \tag{2.27}$$

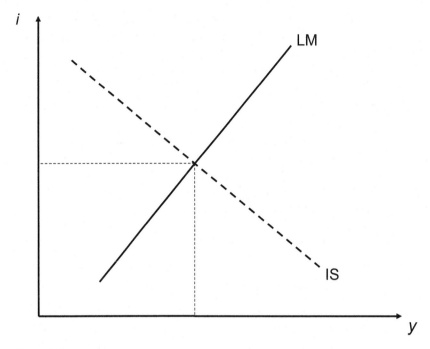

Figure 2.2
The IS-LM model.

which we will call the *MP curve*, for monetary policy. The term $\bar{\pi}$ in the MP curve is the inflation target. When inflation is on target, the central bank maintains the real interest rate at its average level $\bar{r}$. The term $\gamma \, (\pi_t - \bar{\pi})$ corresponds to the systematic response by the central bank to the deviations of inflation from its target. When realized inflation π_t is excessive, the central bank aims to reduce aggregate demand in order to limit inflationary pressures, and it does so by increasing r_t above its average value $\bar{r}$. Conversely, a level of inflation below target means that the central bank can stimulate aggregate demand (by lowering r_t) without risking excess inflation. The MP curve epitomizes the monetary regime of *inflation targeting*, which has been more or less explicitly adopted by all central banks in developed countries in the past twenty-five years. Note that according to equation (2.27), the real interest rate only responds to deviations of inflation from target but not to deviations of *output* from an output target. However, the second exercise at the end of the chapter shows that adding such output deviations is inconsequential, provided that the central bank does not respond too strongly to them.

2.6.2 The Aggregate Demand Curve
By using the MP curve (equation (2.27)) to replace r_t by its value in the IS curve (equation (2.24)), we obtain the *AD curve*, for aggregate demand:

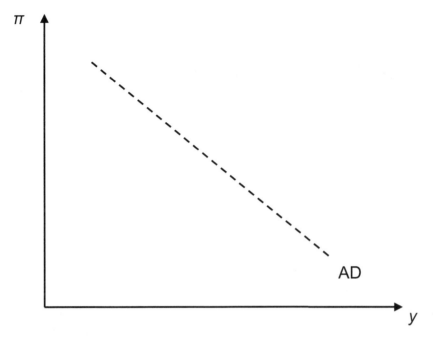

FIGURE 2.3
The AD curve. When inflation is high, the central bank adopts a restrictive monetary policy, which tends to contract aggregate demand and output.

$$\mathbf{AD} : y_t = \theta_t - \gamma \sigma \left(\pi_t - \bar{\pi} \right). \tag{2.28}$$

In the (y, π) plane, the AD curve is decreasing with slope $-1/\gamma \sigma$, and its exact position in the plane is parameterized by θ_t (see figure 2.3). The AD curve is decreasing due to the automatic component of monetary policy; an elevated value of π_t leads the central bank to adopt a more contractionary monetary policy—that is, to raise the real interest rate r_t (see the MP curve), which reduces aggregate demand y_t (by the IS curve). This effect of systematic stabilization of inflation is even more pronounced when the central bank's response to inflation deviations from target (γ) and/or the response of aggregate demand to the real interest rate (σ) are elevated. The case where $\gamma = \infty$ corresponds to extreme inflation targeting, to the point that the AD curve is horizontal (the central bank never lets inflation deviate from $\bar{\pi}$). Conversely, the case where $\gamma = 0$ corresponds to a lax central bank that never tries to stabilize inflation at its target; in this case the AD curve is vertical at $y_t = \theta_t$.

The AD curve constitutes the first block of short-term macroeconomic equilibrium. The second block, the AS curve, is the subject of the next chapter.

2.7 EXERCISES

2.7.1 THE IS-LM MODEL

Relying on section 2.5.2 above, analyze graphically and analytically and then explain intuitively the impact on the macroeconomic equilibrium of a money-supply shock dm^s, and then of an exogenous aggregate demand shock $d\theta$.

2.7.2 THE AD CURVE WITH A HYBRID MP CURVE

Suppose that the MP curve takes the form

$$r_t = \bar{r} + \gamma_\pi \left(\pi_t - \bar{\pi} \right) + \gamma_y \left(y_t - \bar{y} \right),$$

where $\gamma_\pi, \gamma_y > 0$. Show that the AD curve has exactly the same form as equation (2.28) above, up to a redefinition of θ_t and γ. Explain intuitively how and why γ_y affects the slope of this AD curve.

2.7.3 OPTIMAL ACCUMULATION AND DECUMULATION OF WEALTH

Call $R_t = (W_t/P_t) L_t^j - T_t^j$ the after-tax labor income of a Ricardian household at time t, and assume that this household lives indefinitely (i.e., the planning horizon n goes to infinity), and that the real interest rate r_t is equal to ρ at all times. Then the consumption function (2.10) becomes

$$C_t^R = \frac{\rho}{1+\rho} \left(A_{t-1}^R (1+\rho) + \sum_{k=0}^{\infty} \frac{R_{t+k}}{(1+\rho)^k} \right).$$

Assume that the household has no wealth at the beginning of time $t = 0$ (i.e., $A_{-1}^R (1+\rho) = 0$). Compute and discuss the optimal paths of consumption and asset wealth for the following paths of R_t:

1. $R_t = R \geq 0$ from $t = 0$ to $t = T-1$ ($T \geq 1$), then $R_t = R + \Delta R$ ($\Delta R > 0$), from $t = T$ onward (anticipated, permanent income shock);

2. $R_t = R + \Delta R$ from $t = 0$ to $t = T-1$, then $R_t = R$ from $t = T$ onward (unanticipated, transitory income shock);

3. $R_t = R$ from $t = 0$ to $t = T-1$, then again from $t = T + m + 1$ ($m \geq 0$), but $R_t = R + \Delta R \geq 0$ from $t = T$ to $t = T + m$ (anticipated, transitory income shock).

2.7.4 EXCHANGE RATE OVERSHOOTING

We are considering a small open economy whose output is determined by the following equations ($t = 0, 1, \ldots$):

IS : $y_t = \dfrac{1}{2} \left(e_t + \bar{p}^w - p_t \right)$,

LM : $m_t^s - p_t = y_t - i_t$,

UIP : $i_t = \bar{\imath}^w + e_{t+1} - e_t$,

where y_t is log output, p_t the log nominal price level, e_t the nominal exchange rate, m_t^s the money supply (assumed to be exogenous and perfectly controlled by the central bank), and i_t the nominal interest rate. The world log price level and nominal interest rate are $\bar{p}^w$ and $\bar{\imath}^w$, respectively, assumed here to be constant and normalized to zero henceforth. p_t is fixed in the short run but flexible in the long run. More precisely, assuming that the economy was in long-run equilibrium in period $t-1$, then p_t does not adjust after an unanticipated shock to m_t^s in period t, so that $p_t = p_{t-1}$. However, p_t fully adjusts to the shock in period $t+1$. Hence, at time $t+1$ output returns to its natural level, which is normalized to zero.

1. Explain intuitively the equations of the model.

2. Suppose that the central bank has set $m_0^s = 0$ and that this quantity of money is anticipated to be permanent. Compute the long-run equilibrium starting from period $t = 1$ onward.

3. Suppose that in some period $T \geq 2$ the quantity of money suddenly contracts to $m_T^s = -1$, and that this shock is expected to be permanent. Compute the equilibrium value of the exchange rate in the short run (e_T) and in the long run (e_{T+1}) and explain your results intuitively.

2.8 APPENDIX: THE LOG-LINEAR IS CURVE

The transformation of the nonlinear IS curve in terms of levels (equation (2.22)) to the log-linear IS curve (equation (2.24)) requires a first-order Taylor expansion around the mean point $(\bar{r}, \bar{\Theta})$. That is, in the vicinity of $(\bar{r}, \bar{\Theta})$ we can approximate $Y(r_t, \Theta_t)$ as follows:

$$Y(r_t, \Theta_t) \simeq \bar{Y} + Y_r(\bar{r}, \bar{\Theta})(r_t - \bar{r}) + Y_\Theta(\bar{r}, \bar{\Theta})(\Theta_t - \bar{\Theta}), \qquad (2.29)$$

where $Y_r(\bar{r}, \bar{\Theta})$ and $Y_\Theta(\bar{r}, \bar{\Theta})$ are the partial derivatives of $Y(r_t, \Theta_t)$ evaluated at the mean point $(\bar{r}, \bar{\Theta})$:

$$Y_r(\bar{r}, \bar{\Theta}) = \frac{\partial Y(r, \Theta)}{\partial r}\bigg|_{(r_t, \Theta_t)=(\bar{r}, \bar{\Theta})} < 0,$$

$$Y_\Theta(\bar{r}, \bar{\Theta}) = \frac{\partial Y(r, \Theta)}{\partial \Theta}\bigg|_{(r_t, \Theta_t)=(\bar{r}, \bar{\Theta})} > 0,$$

and where the signs of these partial derivatives come directly from equation (2.22). We can now rewrite equation (2.29) as follows:

$$\frac{Y_t - \bar{Y}}{\bar{Y}} = \frac{Y_r(\bar{r}, \bar{\Theta})}{\bar{Y}}(r_t - \bar{r}) + \frac{Y_\Theta(\bar{r}, \bar{\Theta})}{\bar{Y}}(\Theta_t - \bar{\Theta}).$$

Here again we are going to make use of the fact that $\ln(1 + x) \simeq x$ when x is close to 0 (see chapter 1, equation (1.3)), or equivalently $\ln(x) \simeq x - 1$ when x is close to 1. Thus we obtain the following approximation of the left-hand side of the above expression, when $Y_t/\bar{Y}$ is close to 1 (that is, when Y_t is close to its mean value $\bar{Y}$):

$$\frac{Y_t - \bar{Y}}{\bar{Y}} = \frac{Y_t}{\bar{Y}} - 1 \simeq \ln\left(\frac{Y_t}{\bar{Y}}\right) = \ln Y_t - \ln \bar{Y}.$$

By denoting $y_t = \ln Y_t$ (and therefore $\bar{y} = \ln \bar{Y}$), the expression of output can be rewritten in this way:

$$y_t = \bar{y} + \underbrace{\frac{Y_\Theta(\bar{r}, \bar{\Theta})}{\bar{Y}}(\Theta_t - \bar{\Theta})}_{=\theta_t} + \underbrace{\frac{Y_r(\bar{r}, \bar{\Theta})}{\bar{Y}}}_{=-\sigma<0}(r_t - \bar{r}).$$

such that θ_t is an increasing linear transformation of Θ_t.

AGGREGATE SUPPLY

There is a certain rate of interest on loans which is neutral in respect to commodity prices, and tends neither to raise nor to lower them. This is necessarily the same as the rate of interest which would be determined by supply and demand if no use were made of money and all lending were effected in the form of real capital goods.

—Knut Wicksell (1898)

In the preceding chapter, we studied the spending behaviors of various economic agents and concluded that aggregate demand responded negatively to a rise in the real interest rate. When coupled with the MP curve, which gave the value of the real interest rate targeted by the central bank, the IS curve gave rise to the AD curve—that is, a decreasing relation between output and inflation.

Now we are turning to the second block of our macroeconomic model, namely the *aggregate supply* block, which describes how firms respond to the fluctuations in the demand that they are facing. We will see that the supply behavior of firms generates at the aggregate level a second relation (this time increasing) between output and inflation—the *AS curve* (for aggregate supply). The short-term equilibrium will be situated at the intersection of AD and AS curves, as we will see in the next chapter.

To clarify things, let us take as the departure point for our analysis of aggregate supply the elementary fixed-price model that was already discussed in the preceding chapter (section 2.5.2). In that model, nominal prices are constant (by assumption) and firms produce the level of output that exactly serves the demand for goods and services that they are facing. In the short-term, this output level in turn determines the level of employment, according to a relation given by the inverse of the production function $F(L)$. Thus in the fixed-price model *aggregate supply, and hence employment, are entirely determined by aggregate demand.* We may summarize this causal chain as follows:

$$Y \quad \Rightarrow \quad Q \ (=Y) \Rightarrow \quad L \quad (=F^{-1}(Q)).$$

$\uparrow$ aggregate demand $\quad$ $\uparrow$ output $\quad$ $\uparrow$ employment

Now let us consider the exact opposite situation, in which nominal prices would be perfectly *flexible*. The flexibility of nominal prices implies that they do not, as such, affect the equilibrium: only *real* prices, in this case the *real wage* (i.e., the quantity of goods and services that one unit of labor can buy), matter from the point of view of households and firms. On the one hand, the optimal behavior of households determines labor supply, according to the usual condition of equality between the real wage and the marginal rate of substitution (MRS) between consumption and leisure. On the other hand, the real wage determines firms' marginal cost of production, and firms intensify their use of the labor input up to the point where this cost is equal to the marginal product of labor $\partial F(L)/\partial L$. The quantity of labor input then determines the quantity of output Q being produced, and thereby households' income and ultimately the quantity of goods that is demanded: *aggregate demand is entirely determined by aggregate supply.* We may summarize the logic of the flexible-price model as follows:

$$\text{MRS} = \text{real wage} = \partial F(L)/\partial L \Rightarrow \quad Q \ (=F(L)) \Rightarrow \quad Y.$$

$\underbrace{\qquad\qquad}$ labor supply $\quad$ $\underbrace{\qquad\qquad\qquad}$ labor demand $\quad$ $\uparrow$ output $\quad$ $\uparrow$ income, demand

This chapter offers an analysis of aggregate supply that is situated between these two extreme cases. This approach recognizes that in the short run aggregate demand partially determines aggregate supply, due to some rigidity in nominal prices. But it also recognizes that aggregate supply does not respond one for one to aggregate demand, because aggregate demand modifies the labor-market equilibrium and thereby the marginal cost of firms and their incentives to produce. The central assumption of the analysis is that nominal prices are at least *partially* rigid: some firms do adjust their nominal selling prices optimally after a macroeconomic shock, but others do not. This implies that the responses of output, employment, and inflation to variations in aggregate demand depend on the proportion of firms whose prices are adjusted optimally. This general model nests the two extreme cases discussed above. If we assume that no firm adjusts its price optimally after a macroeconomic shock, then the macroeconomic equilibrium works according to the logic of the fixed-price model in which "demand determines supply." On the other hand, if all firms adjust their prices optimally, then it is the logic of the flexible-price model (in which "supply determines demand"), that prevails.

As we will see, the existence of nominal price rigidities leads to the existence of an aggregate supply (AS) curve that links current inflation π_t to its past value π_{t-1} and to the *output gap*—that is to say, the difference between actual output (in log, y_t) and "natural" output (y_t^n), or the level that would prevail in the absence of nominal rigidities:

$$\mathbf{AS} : \pi_t = \pi_{t-1} + \kappa \left(y_t - y_t^n \right).$$

In what follows, we begin by analyzing the behavior of firms and then derive the labor-market equilibrium. Next we analyze aggregate supply in the absence of nominal rigidities—that is, in the so-called natural equilibrium. Finally, we introduce nominal price rigidities and derive the AS curve.[1]

3.1 FIRM BEHAVIOR

3.1.1 MONOPOLISTIC COMPETITION

When a firm sees the demand for its products vary (for example, because aggregate demand is fluctuating), how does it adjust its selling price and the quantity of goods it is producing? Aggregated at the level of the economy as a whole, these individual choices by firms about the quantities of goods put onto the market and the selling prices at which those goods are sold jointly determine *output* and *inflation*. To understand how this joint determination works, we must first study how individual firms make decisions about quantities and prices.

The first thing to note is that it is almost impossible to represent in a realistic and coherent way a firm's strategies regarding prices and quantities via a macroeconomic model featuring perfect competition—simply because in such an environment firms merely take prices as given. And so we will set aside this benchmark market structure and instead assume that firms operate under imperfect competition, and more precisely in an environment of *monopolistic competition*. Monopolistic competition is a market structure in which each firm is in a situation of local monopoly (for example, because the firm is the only one to produce the good that it is selling, or because it is the only one that is geographically present in a particular area, and so on), but where the various goods are partly substitutable from the point of view of the buyer (because consumers can avoid paying for an overly expensive

---

1. One precision is in order here: since in this chapter we are only analyzing the productive sector of an economy using domestic labor only (and not, for example, imported intermediate goods), the inflation rate that occurs in the AS curve is that for *domestically produced goods only* and is unaffected by changes in import prices. Whenever the economy is open to international trade, then we should expect (1) imported intermediate goods to affect the price of domestically produced goods, and (2) imported consumption goods to affect the consumer price index about which the central bank cares. For the sake of simplicity we abstract from these channels in the remainder of the book.

good by purchasing another one, or they can travel to buy a good outside the area they live in, and so forth). This partial substitutability implies that firms may enjoy some market power but that this power is not absolute.

The modeling of monopolistic competition here is as follows: Let us assume that there exists a large number N of different goods in the economy, with each good being produced and sold by a single firm in a situation of monopoly. Each firm $i \in \{1, \ldots, N\}$ produces its good by means of the production function:

$$Q_{i,t} = Z_t L_{i,t},\tag{3.1}$$

where $Q_{i,t}$ is the quantity produced by firm i at time t, $L_{i,t}$ the quantity of labor utilized by the firm and Z_t labor productivity at time t (assumed to be exogenous and common to all firms, hence nonindexed by i).[2] At this level of generality, Z_t potentially includes any factor that may alter the quantity of goods being produced at any given level of labor input (Z_t may be shifted by technological or organizational innovations, by the amelioration or deterioration of institutions, and so on).

Monopolistic competition shows up here through the assumption that the demand for good i in period t, noted in $Y_{i,t}$, is decreasing in the price of good i:

$$Y_{i,t} = Y_t \left(\frac{P_{i,t}}{P_t}\right)^{-\eta}, \eta > 1,\tag{3.2}$$

where $P_{i,t}$ is the nominal selling price (e.g., in US dollars) of firm i, P_t the price level (meaning the average of firms' nominal selling prices), and Y_t is aggregate demand (the sum of the demands for each good $Y_{i,t}$).

In simple words, equation (3.2) states that the market share of firm i, $Y_{i,t}/Y_t$ is decreasing in the *relative* price of good i, $P_{i,t}/P_t$. The parameter η measures the elasticity of the demand for good i with respect to its price: the higher η, the more the demand for this good $Y_{i,t}$ falls after an increase in its price $P_{i,t}$ (at any given price level P_t). Thus, an elevated value of η corresponds to a situation in which firms enjoy relatively little market power, since consumers may easily turn away from good i when its price increases. The limit case where $\eta \to \infty$ corresponds to a situation of perfect competition where a marginal increase of $P_{i,t}$ above P_t will trigger a collapse in the demand for good i.[3]

While in the real world the range N of different goods is large but finite, it turns out to be analytically convenient to work with a *continuous approximation* of this

---

2. Here we are abstracting from variations in the stock of capital. This is an acceptable simplification, to the extent that capital fluctuates much less than labor input over the business cycle (see chapter 1).

3. The condition $\eta > 1$ is necessary for the existence of an equilibrium (as $\eta \to 1$ firms enjoy so much market power that the selling price $P_{i,t}$ they charge becomes infinite).

range of goods. Formally, we will assume throughout that there exists an *infinity* of goods/firms, forming a continuum of length 1, with every firm (or equivalently the good it produces) being indexed by i, $0 \leq i \leq 1$ (think of i as the location of firm i on the interval $[0, 1]$). Under this continuous approximation aggregate demand is given by:

$$Y_t = \int_0^1 Y_{i,t}\mathrm{d}i;$$

that is, it is the continuous sum of all the demands addressed to each individual firm. Since in this representation, the "number" of firms is 1 (i.e., the length of the continuum), Y_t is both *aggregate* demand and the *average* individual demand addressed to firms. Similarly, total labor demand by firms $L_t^d = \int_0^1 L_{i,t}\mathrm{d}i$ is the same thing as average labor demand.

3.1.2   OPTIMAL SELLING PRICE

A seller in a monopoly situation faces the following dilemma: an elevated price increases the unit markup (the difference between the selling price and the marginal cost of production) but lowers the quantity demanded and hence the *market share* of the firm. The optimal selling price $P_{i,t}^*$ is that which strikes the best balance between these two forces and thereby maximizes profits.

Formally, firm i chooses its selling price $P_{i,t}$ to maximize[4]

$$\Pi_{i,t} = Q_{i,t}P_{i,t} - W_t L_{i,t},$$

where W_t is the nominal wage, under the constraints (3.1), (3.2) and $Q_i = Y_i$ (i.e., the firm produces only what it can sell).

Note that the firm maximizes $\Pi_{i,t}$ taking P_t and W_t as given; although the firm is in a monopoly situation with respect to its own produced good, it is atomistic relative to the size of the market (it is a point on a continuum of firms), which implies that $P_{i,t}$ does not influence P_t and $L_{i,t}$ does not influence W_t (P_t and W_t will be determined by the aggregation of the behaviors of all firms as to their selling prices and labor demands).

---

4. In general the firm maximizes the *present value* of real profits, that is (if the firm's horizon is infinite)

$$\sum_{k=0}^{+\infty} \left(\beta^F\right)^k \times \frac{\Pi_{i,t+k}}{P_{t+k}},$$

where $\beta^F < 1$ is the firm's discount factor and $\Pi_{i,t}/P_t$ its real profit at time t. In order to simplify the analysis, we are assuming here that $\beta^F = 0$, so that the firm is maximizing $\Pi_{i,t}/P_t$ —or equivalently $\Pi_{i,t}$ since the firm takes the average price level P_t as given.

Using the constraints in (3.1), (3.2), and $Q_i = Y_i$, we may restate the firm's maximization problem as follows:

$$\max_{P_{i,t}} \Pi_{i,t} = \underbrace{Y_t \left(\frac{P_{i,t}}{P_t} \right)^{-\eta}}_{\text{quantity sold}} \times \underbrace{\left(P_{i,t} - \frac{W_t}{Z_t} \right)}_{\text{nominal markup}}. \tag{3.3}$$

In this expression, the term W_t/Z_t is the *nominal marginal cost* of goods, meaning what it costs the firm, in terms of monetary units (for example in US dollars) to produce an additional unit of the good.[5] The nominal marginal cost is common to all firms because Z_t is so by assumption, and because the nominal wage W_t is determined on the labor market and hence is the same for all firms (see below). Firm i chooses the value of $P_{i,t}$ that maximizes $\Pi_{i,t}$, and this optimal price determines both its market share $(Y_{i,t}/Y_t)$ and its unit markup $(P_{i,t} - W_t/Z_t)$.

The objective function in equation (3.3) is strictly concave in $P_{i,t}$, hence the first-order condition gives the value of $P_{i,t}$ that maximizes $\Pi_{i,t}$:

$$\frac{\partial \Pi_{i,t}}{\partial P_{i,t}} = -\eta \frac{Y_t}{P_{i,t}} \left(\frac{P_{i,t}}{P_t} \right)^{-\eta} \left(P_{i,t} - \frac{W_t}{Z_t} \right) + Y_t \left(\frac{P_{i,t}}{P_t} \right)^{-\eta} = 0.$$

This equation gives the following optimal price:

$$\underbrace{P_t^*}_{\substack{\uparrow \\ \text{optimal nominal price}}} = \underbrace{(1+\mu)}_{\substack{\uparrow \\ \text{markup factor}}} \times \underbrace{\frac{W_t}{Z_t}}_{\substack{\uparrow \\ \text{nominal marginal cost}}},$$

where $\mu = 1/(\eta - 1) > 0$ is the optimal markup rate.

The optimal markup rate μ is constant here and thus independent of the quantity sold; this property comes from the fact that the elasticity of the demand for good i with respect to its price is itself constant (equal to $-\eta$) and thus independent of the level of the individual demand $Y_{i,t}$. Consequently, the optimal markup rate, and hence the optimal selling price, are the same for all firms, and therefore there is no index i for these two variables. Unsurprisingly, the optimal markup rate is decreasing in the price-elasticity of demand $(-\eta)$: the higher this elasticity (in absolute value), the less the firm can sell at a high price without losing market share, and thus the more it must compress its markup.

---

5. One unit of labor (one hour, for example) costs $\$W_t$ and allows the production of Z_t units of goods (see equation (3.1)). Therefore producing one unit of the good costs $\$W_t/Z_t$.

TABLE 3.1
Average markup rates, 1981–2004.

	Manufacturing	Services
United States	28%	36%
Euro area	18%	56%
France	15%	26%
Germany	16%	54%
Italy	23%	87%

Source: Christopoulou and Vermeulen (2010).

Table 3.1 below shows the average markup rates among European and US firms over the period 1981–2004 in both the services and manufacturing sectors (including construction). These markup rates can be large, which illustrates the relevance of our imperfectly competitive framework. From a quantitative perspective, these empirical markup rates may be used to calibrate the parameter η; that is, to give it a value such that the firm's optimal choice generates the markup rate that is observed empirically.

As explained in the two previous chapters, the macroeconomic model that we are using is solved in log-linear form. By shifting into log the equation for the optimal nominal price, we find:

$$p_t^* = \mu^* + w_t - z_t, \tag{3.4}$$

where

$$p_t^* = \ln P_t^*, \quad w_t = \ln W_t, \quad z_t = \ln Z_t, \quad \text{and} \quad \mu^* = \ln(1 + \mu).$$

Notice that when the optimal markup rate μ is sufficiently small we have $\mu^* = \ln(1 + \mu) \simeq \mu$ (see equation (1.3) in chapter 1). In other words, for a sufficiently small μ (i.e., a sufficiently large η), μ^* is a good approximation of the true optimal markup rate μ. In what follows, I will take the liberty of referring to μ^* as the "optimal markup rate" itself, without necessarily requiring it to be sufficiently small for the approximation $\mu^* \simeq \mu$ to be good.

Equation (3.4) implies that the firm would like to pass through to its selling price all variations in the nominal marginal cost $w_t - z_t$. The nominal marginal cost in turn depends on two variables, namely labor productivity z_t and the nominal wage w_t. Labor productivity z_t is exogenous (its variations will be one of the aggregate supply shocks considered in the next chapter), but the nominal wage w_t is endogenous—it is determined by the equality of demand and supply in the labor market.

3.2 LABOR MARKET EQUILIBRIUM

3.2.1 AGGREGATE LABOR DEMAND

The equilibrium wage equalizes the demand for and supply of labor in the economy. The aggregate demand for labor results from the labor demands of all firms. We know that a firm i that faces the demand $Y_{i,t}$ for its good produces exactly $Q_{i,t} = Y_{i,t}$. According to the production function (3.1), this implies that this firm expresses a demand for labor on the labor market equal to:

$$L_{i,t} = \frac{Y_{i,t}}{Z_t};$$

or, switching to logs and using equation (3.2):

$$
\begin{aligned}
l_{i,t} &= y_{i,t} - z_t \\
&= y_t - \eta\left(p_{i,t} - p_t\right) - z_t,
\end{aligned}
\tag{3.5}
$$

where p_t is the average price level (in log):[6]

$$p_t = \int_0^1 p_{i,t}\mathrm{d}i.$$

Equation (3.5) shows that, for a given level of aggregate demand y_t, the lower the selling price $p_{i,t}$ of firm i relative to the selling price of all other firms p_t and the greater the demand for the good it produces ($y_{i,t}$); hence the greater the demand for labor that the firm addresses to the labor market (since more labor is needed to produce and serve demand). The total demand for labor aggregates the labor demands of all firms $i \in [0, 1]$. Thus it is given by:

---

6. Note that, strictly speaking, $p_t = \int_0^1 \ln P_{i,t}\mathrm{d}i$ is the average of log-prices and not the log of the average price level $p_t = \ln(\int_0^1 P_{i,t}\mathrm{d}i)$. Nevertheless, these two price indices are approximately equal when the individual prices $P_{i,t}$ are close to each other. In this case equation (1.3) can be used to show that

$$\int_0^1 \ln\left(P_{i,t}/P_t\right)\mathrm{d}i \simeq 1,$$

and hence

$$\ln P_t \simeq \int_0^1 \ln P_{i,t}\mathrm{d}i.$$

We are assuming throughout that the economy always stays is in the vicinity of the symmetric equilibrium, where this approximation is valid.

$$l_t^d = \int_0^1 l_{i,t}\mathrm{d}i = y_t - \eta \underbrace{\left(\int_0^1 p_{i,t}\mathrm{d}i - p_t \right)}_{=0} - z_t$$

$$= y_t - z_t. \tag{3.6}$$

Equation (3.6) simply states that the dispersion in selling prices and output levels that may arise between firms does not affect *aggregate* labor demand. When there is some price dispersion, some firms sell at a price $p_{i,t}$ that is lower than the average price p_t, and thus reach an output level $q_{i,t}$ and labor demand $l_{i,t}$ that are themselves greater than that of the average firm; this effect is offset by the firms that sell at a price that is greater than p_t and thus produce less, and demand less labor, than the average firm. The aggregate demand for labor depends positively on output y_t (since more output requires more labor) but negatively on labor productivity z_t (since greater productivity reduces the quantity of labor necessary to produce a given quantity of output).

3.2.2 AGGREGATE LABOR SUPPLY

We will simply assume here that the total supply of labor in the economy (as supplied by all the households) takes the following form:

$$l_t^s = \xi(w_t - p_t - z_t), \quad \xi > 0. \tag{3.7}$$

The appendix to this chapter shows how this labor supply function can be derived from the optimal behavior of households once the disutility of labor is taken into account. Here we will merely content ourselves with providing an informal justification for this function, based on elementary microeconomic principles as well the empirical evidence on long-run labor supply. We know from the basic microeconomics of labor supply that the trade-off between greater leisure time and greater consumption (via a higher labor income) depends on the real wage. Now, the overall impact of the real wage on labor supply depends on the usual two suspects—namely the *substitution effect* and the *income effect*. According to the substitution effect a greater real wage raises the incentive to work; but the income effect works in the opposite direction, since a higher real wage allows attainment of higher consumption with a lower supply of labor. Equation (3.7) implies that when the rise in the real wage $w_t - p_t$ is due to a rise in labor productivity z_t, then the income and substitution effects associated with the greater real wage exactly offset each other, leaving labor supply unchanged. This property, which holds under certain restrictions on household preferences, can be justified by long-run considerations related to the balanced growth of the economy. Indeed, in the long run the growth of labor productivity brings along with it a growth in real wages of similar pace. If income effects dominated over substitution effects, then we ought to observe a rising trend

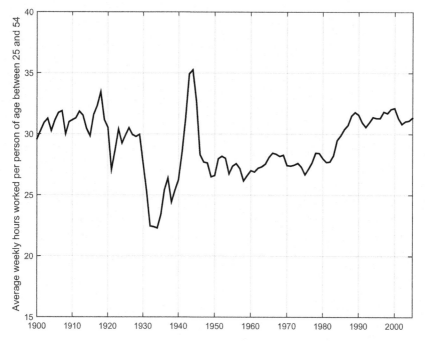

FIGURE 3.1
Labor supply in the long run. Average weekly hours worked per person aged between 25 and 54.
Source: Ramey and Francis (2009).

in leisure over time; that is, a falling trend in hours worked. Conversely, if the substitution effect dominated, then we would observe a secular growth in hours worked, as these additional hours are increasingly better paid. The evidence for the United States shows that hours worked display no such patterns; according to figure 3.1, the average number of hours worked per person aged between 25 and 54 in the United States is astoundingly stable between 1900 and 2005, despite the fact that real GDP has been multiplied by a factor of thirty over this period.

3.2.3 THE EQUILIBRIUM REAL WAGE AND THE MARGINAL COST OF PRODUCTION

The equilibrium real wage equalizes the total demand for labor in equation (3.6) with the total supply of labor in equation (3.7):

$$\underbrace{y_t - z_t}_{l_t^s} = \underbrace{\xi(w_t - p_t - z_t)}_{l_t^d},$$

which gives:

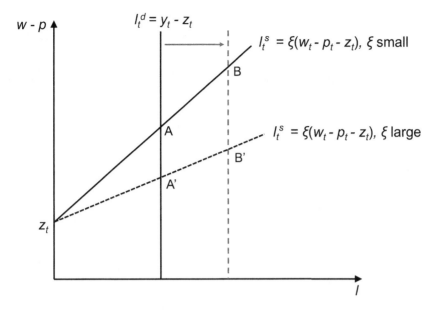

FIGURE 3.2
Labor market clearing and the equilibrium real wage. The less elastic the labor supply, the higher the real wage and the more it rises after an increase in output (at a given level of labor productivity).

$$w_t - p_t = \frac{y_t - (1 - \xi)\, z_t}{\xi}. \tag{3.8}$$

This equation may be interpreted as follows. At any given level of labor productivity z_t, an increase in output y_t generates a tension in the labor market that causes the equilibrium real wage to rise. This increase is weaker when the elasticity of labor supply ξ is large, since a high elasticity implies that a hike in labor demand is easily absorbed by an increasing supply. The adjustment of the equilibrium real wage after a variation in output y_t at any given labor productivity z_t is represented in figure 3.2, for two possible values of the labor-supply elasticity parameter ξ; the smaller this parameter, the greater the equilibrium real wage, and the more it rises after an increase in output.

3.3   THE NATURAL EQUILIBRIUM

Before studying the role of nominal rigidities, we must start by characterizing a benchmark equilibrium where nominal prices are *perfectly flexible*, which is customarily called the natural equilibrium. We may interpret this equilibrium as the one that would prevail after all the adjustments of nominal prices toward their optimal value have taken place. In the natural equilibrium, all firms set the optimal nominal price p_t^* in equation (3.4), which is therefore equal to the price level p_t:

$$p_t = \mu^* + w_t - z_t. \tag{3.9}$$

By using (3.9) to eliminate the real wage $w_t - p_t$ from equation (3.8), we find the natural level of output to be

$$y_t^n = z_t - \xi\mu^*. \tag{3.10}$$

By implication, the natural level of employment is given by (see equation (3.6)):

$$l^n = -\xi\mu^* \text{ (constant)}. \tag{3.11}$$

As is apparent from the latter equations, the natural equilibrium has four important properties:

- the natural equilibrium is perfectly symmetric, with all firms setting the same selling price (p_t^*), utilizing the same quantity of labor (l^n), and producing the same quantity of goods (y_t^n). This symmetry will not prevail in an equilibrium with nominal rigidities, since in that case firms face the same marginal cost of production but usually sell goods at different prices (and thus sell different quantities of those goods).

- as soon as the optimal markup rate μ^* is positive (so that firms effectively enjoy some market power), output y_t^n and employment l^n are smaller than what they would be under perfect competition (where $\mu^* = 0$). The reason for this is that the optimal strategy for a monopoly firm consists of rationing its supply of the good (and consequently its demand for labor) in order to raise its markup. The weaker the competition in the goods market, the greater the optimal markup μ^*, and therefore the more firms ration their production, and the smaller the resulting employment level l^n.

- The classical dichotomy prevails, meaning that both output y_t^n and employment l^n are entirely determined by *real* factors (labor productivity z_t as well as the degree of competition, which determines μ^*). Monetary policy and more generally any factor affecting aggregate demand without modifying z_t or μ^* have no effect on the natural equilibrium. This will no longer be true in the presence of nominal rigidities, where aggregate demand shocks and monetary policy will influence output and employment.

- The natural level of employment l^n does not depend on labor productivity z_t. This comes from the labor supply function that we have assumed (see equation (3.7)), which implies that the income and substitution effects associated with the rise in z_t exactly offset each other. This feature of the equilibrium is somewhat specific and would not survive under alternative labor supply functions.

3.4 EQUILIBRIUM WITH NOMINAL PRICE RIGIDITIES

3.4.1 INCOMPLETE PRICE ADJUSTMENT

The central assumption of the New Keynesian model used throughout this book is that *nominal prices are sticky in the short run*; that is, *they take time to fully adjust to changes in macroeconomic conditions*. By impeding the full and instantaneous adjustment of prices to macroeconomic shocks, nominal rigidities force a portion of the adjustments to be borne by real quantities (i.e., output and employment) rather than by prices. This situation typically results in excessively volatile business cycles, relative to what would happen in the hypothetical situation of full price flexibility (for example, employment is constant at $l^n = -\xi \mu^*$ under flexible prices but fluctuates under sticky prices).

The assumption that nominal prices are rigid is largely supported by empirical studies. Table 3.2 below reports the monthly frequency of changes of consumer prices (that is to say, the proportion of consumer prices that are modified each month) as well as the implicit mean and median duration of prices.[7] This table shows that the lifespan of a nominal price is of about a year, whereas we could expect much more volatile individual prices in the absence of nominal rigidities (think, for example, of stock market prices, which respond to news by the second).

A simple way of incorporating nominal price stickiness into our macroeconomic model is to suppose that only some firms adjust their selling prices optimally after a macroeconomic shock, while the other firms keep their selling prices unchanged or, more realistically, apply a simple indexation rule. In this spirit, we will assume that the dynamics of individual prices is as follows:

- In each period t, a fixed proportion $1 - \omega$ of firms, $0 \leq \omega \leq 1$, drawn at random from the population of firms, is able to set its selling price at its optimal level,

---

7. To summarize, in the United States, 21.5 percent of the consumer prices are changed every month; the average time between any two price changes for a particular good is of 11.7 months; and it takes 9.6 months for half of consumer prices to be changed.

TABLE 3.2
Nominal rigidities in consumer prices.

	Euro area (1996–2000)	United States (1998–2005)
Monthly frequency of price changes	15.1%	21.5%
Mean price duration	13.0 months	11.7 months
Median price duration	10.6 months	9.6 months

Sources: Alvarez et al. (2006); Nakamura and Steinsson (2008).

as given by equation (3.4):

$$p_{i,t} = p_t^* = \mu^* + w_t - z_t, \tag{3.12}$$

where z_t and w_t are, respectively, labor productivity and the equilibrium nominal wage in period t.

- The other firms (in proportion ω) do not set their selling price at the optimal level p_t^* but let it grow at a rate equal to the inflation rate of the preceding period $t-1$. Formally, these firms are choosing the nominal price

$$P_{i,t} = P_{i,t-1} (1 + \pi_{t-1}),$$

where $1 + \pi_{t-1} = P_{t-1}/P_{t-2}$ is the inflation factor between period $t-2$ and period $t-1$. This indexation of unoptimized prices is meant to capture the notion that the firms that do not optimize their price are still trying to keep up with the overall dynamics of the price level, which they observe with a lag. By taking the log of $P_i = P_{i,-1} (1 + \pi_{-1})$ and by using the approximation in equation (1.3) from chapter 1 (assuming π_{t-1} is sufficiently small), we obtain:

$$p_{i,t} \simeq p_{i,t-1} + \pi_{t-1}. \tag{3.13}$$

Under these assumptions, the (log) average price level p_t, which is the weighted average of optimized and indexed price, is given by

$$p_t = \underbrace{\omega \left(p_{t-1} + \pi_{t-1} \right)}_{\text{indexed prices}} + \underbrace{(1 - \omega) p_t^*}_{\text{optimized prices}}. \tag{3.14}$$

We recover the natural equilibrium when $\omega = 0$, so that all firms optimize their selling price in every period; in that case the average price level p_t reflects at every moment the variations in the marginal cost of production caused by macroeconomic shocks. Equation (3.14) implies that, whenever $\omega > 0$, the average price level is more inertial than in the natural equilibrium, since current business-cycle shocks are only partially reflected into changes in the average price level. In the extreme case where $\omega = 1$ such shocks are not transmitted at all and inflation is constant (since $\pi_t \simeq p_t - p_{t-1}$ according to equation (1.3), and equation (3.14) implies that $\pi_t = \pi_{t-1}$ when $\omega = 1$). Note that when $0 < \omega < 1$ the equilibrium is asymmetric; some firms sell their good at the optimal price while others sell it at an indexed price—which as such reflects past, rather than current, economic conditions. Consequently, under nominal rigidities, firms are typically not facing the same demand for goods, they do not choose the same levels of production and labor demand, and they do not earn the same profits.

3.4.2 THE AS CURVE

We are now in a position to derive the AS curve presented in the introduction of this chapter. For this derivation we will use equations (3.4), (3.8), and (3.14), which we restate here for clarity:

$$\textbf{optimal price}: p_t^* = \mu^* + w_t - z_t;$$

$$\textbf{real wage}: w_t - p_t = \frac{y_t - (1 - \xi)\, z_t}{\xi};$$

$$\textbf{average price level}: p_t = \omega\,(p_{t-1} + \pi_{t-1}) + (1 - \omega)\, p_t^*.$$

First of all, note that we can rearrange the expression of the average price level to rewrite it as follows:

$$p_t = p_{t-1} + \pi_{t-1} + \left(\frac{1 - \omega}{\omega}\right)(p_t^* - p_t),$$

or, in an equivalent manner (since $p_t - p_{t-1} \simeq \pi_t$):

$$\pi_t = \pi_{t-1} + \left(\frac{1 - \omega}{\omega}\right)(p_t^* - p_t), \tag{3.15}$$

where $p_t^* - p_t$ is the optimal (log) *real* price—that is, the optimal nominal price relative to the nominal price level. This formulation of the aggregate dynamics of prices shows that the greater the fraction of firms that adjust their prices optimally $(1 - \omega)$, the more variations in the optimal real price $(p_t^* - p_t)$ get passed through to the average price level (p_t) and thereby to the inflation rate (π_t).

The two other equations (that for the optimal price and that for the real wage) enable us to calculate $p_t^* - p_t$. By substracting p_t from the equation of the optimal price, and then by using the equation for the real wage to replace $w_t - p_t$ by its value, we obtain:

$$\underbrace{p_t^* - p_t}_{\text{optimal } \textit{real} \text{ price}} = \mu^* + (w_t - p_t) - z_t = \mu^* + \left(\frac{y_t - (1-\xi)\,z_t}{\xi} \right) - z_t \qquad (3.16)$$

$$= \frac{1}{\xi} (y_t - \underbrace{(z_t - \xi \mu^*)}_{=y_t^n})$$

$$= \frac{1}{\xi} \times \underbrace{(y_t - y_t^n)}_{\text{output gap}}.$$

Hence the optimal real price $p_t^* - p_t$ is related to the *output gap* $y_t - y_t^n$; that is, the difference between the actual (y_t) and natural (y_t^n) levels of output. The reason for this relation is as follows. The natural level of output y_t^n incorporates the real determinants of production—that is, labor productivity z_t and the degree of competition μ^*. In general, the actual level of output y_t differs from y_t^n because of fluctuations in aggregate demand and the presence nominal price rigidities. At a given y_t^n, an increase in output y_t generates a tension in the labor market (as firms demand more labor) and therefore generates an upward pressure on the real wage. The rise in the real wage $w_t - p_t$ mechanically brings about a rise in the real marginal cost $w_t - p_t - z_t$ faced by all the firms, which they would like (but may not be able) to pass through to their selling prices in order to maintain their markup at its optimal level (μ^*). The impact of the rise in real wage costs on the optimal selling price $p_t^* - p_t$ is all the higher when the elasticity of labor supply ξ is low, since a low elasticity implies that a sharp rise in wages (and therefore in the unit cost of production) is required for firms to attract the additional labor force needed to produce more.

It is essential to note that this effect of actual output on the real marginal cost and the optimal selling price takes place only for variations of y_t *relative to* y_t^n. When the rise in y_t is accompanied by that of y_t^n (for example, because the optimal markup rate μ^* drops after competition has become more severe, or because labor productivity z_t has increased), then the impact of the rise of y_t on the equilibrium real wage $w_t - p_t$ is partially offset, if not completely eliminated, by the rise in y_t^n (formally, the effect of w_t on p_t^* in equation (3.12) is offset by the fall in $\mu^* - z_t$).

By using equation (3.16) to replace $p_t^* - p_t$ by its value in equation (3.15), we obtain the *aggregate supply curve*, or AS curve for short:

$$\textbf{AS}: \pi_t = \pi_{t-1} + \kappa \left(y_t - y_t^n \right), \qquad (3.17)$$

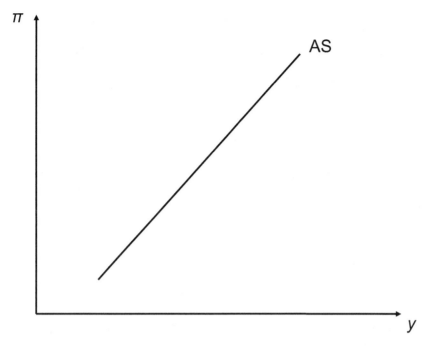

FIGURE 3.3
The AS curve. At a given level of labor productivity, a high level of output tightens the labor market, which pushes up the equilibrium real wage and hence firms' real marginal cost of production. The firms that adjust their selling price optimally pass through this higher cost to their selling price, which is inflationary.

with

$$\kappa = \frac{1 - \omega}{\xi \omega} \geq 0.$$

The AS curve is an increasing relation between the *output gap* and the *variation of inflation*. Inflation in period t thus responds to two forces. On the one hand, an increase in actual output y_t relative to natural output y_t^n tightens the labor market and results in a greater equilibrium real wage and therefore a greater unit production cost for the firms; the firms that adjust their prices optimally pass along this rise in the cost of production to their selling price, which ultimately results in higher inflation. On the other hand, the firms that do *not* adjust their prices optimally after a hike in the marginal cost just let them grow at the rate of past inflation π_{t-1}, which is why the latter variable appears in the AS curve. The increasing relation between π_t and y_t, at any given π_{t-1} and y_t^n, is represented in figure 3.3. The AS curve is also often referred to as the Phillips curve—a term that will also occasionally be used in remainder of the book.

Two important properties of the AS curve above are worth discussing here. First, provided that the central bank is able to avoid hyper-inflations—that is, economic paths where inflation explodes asymptotically—then *actual output and natural output coincide in the long run*. Indeed, if the long-run inflation rate is finite and equal to π_∞, then we have $\pi_{t+k} = \pi_{t-1+k} = \pi_\infty$ as $k \to \infty$ and thus $y_\infty = y^n_\infty$. This is consistent with the *natural rate hypothesis* on which modern macroeconomics is built since the work of Friedman (1968), Phelps (1970), and Lucas (1972) and according to which output necessarily returns to its natural level in the long run. The hypothesis implies that there is no trade-off between inflation and output in the long run (i.e., no way to "buy" a higher level of output at that horizon) even if the central bank is willing to tolerate high average inflation. Note that the hypothesis does not require the central bank to adopt any form of inflation targeting (see chapter 2), since long-run inflation need not be the same as a preannounced target (if any). It just requires the central bank not to let the inflation rate explode asymptotically. Although the natural rate hypothesis has been criticized, and accordingly alternative formulations of the AS curve have been proposed (some of them are reviewed below), it remains the natural benchmark for business-cycle and macroeconomic policy analysis.

The second important property of the AS curve relates to the short-run dynamics of inflation. Loosely speaking, the output gap reflects transitory imbalances between aggregate demand and supply. As we will see in chapter 6, in many situations the right thing for the central bank to do is to adjust the real interest rate in a way that corrects for such imbalances—that is, in a way that closes the output gap. The main difficulty facing the central bank in this task is that the natural level of output y^n_t that enters the output gap is not observable; it is a theoretical concept with no *direct* empirical counterpart. Of course, equation (3.10) above gives us a formula for the output gap, so one could in principle reconstruct it using data on labor productivity, markups, and some evidence on labor supply elasticities. But what if the data is flawed with measurement errors, or if the theory is too simple to capture all important determinants of natural output? Then the measurement of the imbalances between demand and supply will itself be flawed and provide a poor guide to policymakers. But the reassuring thing is that, according to the AS curve, one need not worry about all these empirical and theoretical approximations; whatever the macroeconomic shocks that move output and the output gap, all the potential imbalances between aggregate demand and supply show up as changes in inflation. Hence, in principle *it is sufficient to examine the path of inflation to make appropriate monetary policy decisions*. Of course, things can be more complicated because not all macroeconomic shocks are optimally countered by simply closing the output gap.[8] However, many such shocks are, and hence in many cases inflation provides

---

8. This point will be discussed further in chapter 6.

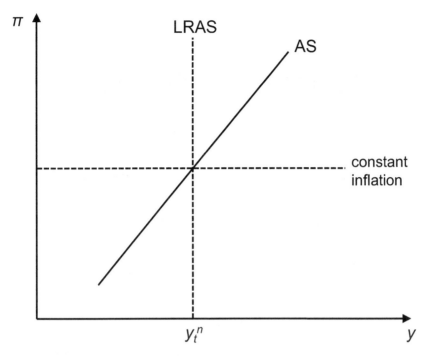

FIGURE 3.4
The long-run AS (LRAS) curve and the constant-inflation curve. When all prices are optimized, the AS curve is vertical, which corresponds to its position in the long run; when all prices are indexed, inflation is constant and the AS curve is horizontal.

a sufficient statistics for monetary policy decisions. Such is the ultimate justification for the regime of inflation targeting that so many central banks have adopted nowadays.

Let us conclude our analysis of the AS curve by looking at two limit cases: full optimization of prices ($\omega = 0$) and full indexation of prices ($\omega = 1$). When prices are all adjusted optimally (a situation that corresponds to the natural equilibrium), then the AS curve is vertical at $y_t = y_t^n$. We can interpret this situation as the one that would prevail in the long run, once all firms have adjusted their prices optimally (so that $\omega = 0$). For this reason, we call the corresponding AS curve the *LRAS curve*, for long-run aggregate supply curve. Conversely, when all prices are indexed ($\omega = 1$), then inflation is constant at $\pi_t = \pi_{t-1} = \ldots = \pi_0$. These two extreme cases are represented in figure 3.4.

An important question, to which we will return in the next chapter, is to know how the economy moves from the AS curve, which applies to the short run, to the LRAS curve. If we assume that in each period a fraction ω of firms, drawn at random from the population of firms, can adjust their selling prices optimally, then the

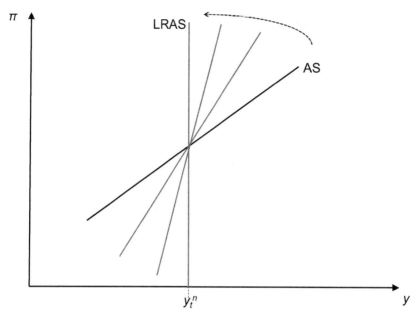

FIGURE 3.5
The transition from the AS curve to the LRAS curve. As time passes, the fraction of firms having adjusted their price optimally increases; hence the slope of the AS curve also increases. In the long run, the AS curve becomes the (vertical) LRAS curve.

proportion of firms that have been able to adjust their prices optimally at one moment or another increases over time to reach asymptotically the value of 1. Indeed, after a shift in the macroeconomic equilibrium occurring in period t, the fraction of firms that adjust their price optimally is $1 - \omega$. In period $t + 1$, the fraction of firms having adjusted their price optimally either in period t or in period $t + 1$ is $1 - \omega^2$ (since ω^2 is the proportion of firms that have *indexed* their prices in *both* period t and $t + 1$). In $t + 2$, the same fraction is $1 - \omega^3$, and so forth. The proportion $1 - \omega^n$ is increasing in n—implying that the slope of the AS curve increases with the time horizon—and tends toward 1 as $n \to \infty$—so that the AS curve ultimately becomes vertical. The rotation of the AS curve toward the LRAS curve is represented in figure 3.5.

3.4.3 THE NATURAL RATE OF INTEREST

The quotation from Knut Wicksell at the beginning of this chapter refers to the value of the interest rate "which is neutral in respect to commodity prices, and tends neither to raise nor to lower them." The representation of aggregate supply that we have just developed makes it possible to explicitly derive the value of this natural interest rate. Let us assume that the average price level p_t was stable between period $t - 2$ and period $t - 1$, so that $\pi_{t-1} = 0$. The real interest rate in period t that is neutral in respect to commodity prices is the one that ensures the stability of the average price level between period $t-1$ and period t, so that $\pi_t = 0$. And therefore, according to the AS curve, it is the real interest rate that closes the current output gap—meaning that it equalizes actual output y_t with its natural level y_t^n. Then, from the IS curve (see equation (2.24)), the *natural interest rate* in period t is given by:

$$r_t^n = \bar{r} + \frac{1}{\sigma}\left(\theta_t - y_t^n\right).$$

Intuitively, the natural interest rate is the one that eliminates any imbalance that might arise between aggregate supply and demand and would thereby jeopardize price stability. For example, if business cycle shocks led to an excess of aggregate demand (y_t) relative to aggregate supply (y_t^n), then the natural interest rate rises to resorb the excess level of aggregate demand and maintain the inflation rate at zero (so that prices remain stable).[9] Now recall from section 3.3 that the natural equilibrium is the hypothetical equilibrium that would prevail if prices were perfectly flexible. By definition, in the natural equilibrium output y_t *is* equal to its natural level y_t^n at every point in time. Therefore, the natural rate of interest can equally be defined as *the real interest rate that would prevail in the hypothetical flexible-price economy*. In the natural equilibrium any shock to aggregate demand, causing it to temporarily depart from supply, is promptly corrected by the endogenous adjustment of the natural interest rate. For example, a negative aggregate demand shock ($d\theta_t < 0$) causing aggregate demand to fall short of aggregate supply ($dy_t < dy_t^n = 0$) is promptly corrected by a fall in the natural rate (dr_t^n) that again aligns aggregate demand and supply. Therefore, in an economy with nominal rigidities the central bank's failure to align aggregate demand with supply is, equivalently, a failure to align the actual real interest rate r_t with its natural counterpart r_t^n. We will return to these considerations in chapter 6, which is devoted to the implementation and optimality of monetary policy.

3.5 EMPIRICAL EVALUATION OF THE AS CURVE

We have seen that it was the *output gap* $y_t - y_t^n$ (and not output y_t in itself) that tightened the labor market and therefore generated inflationary pressures on wages and prices. Can we verify empirically the existence of a relation like the AS curve? The main difficulty here comes from the fact that the natural level of output is a

---

9. The expression for r_t^n features a *real* interest rate (that which occurs in the IS curve), while Wicksell seemed to have had in mind a *nominal* interest rate. However, if r_t^n is implemented at every point in time, then inflation is zero in every period; hence the nominal and the real natural rates are the same ($i_t^n = r_t^n$).

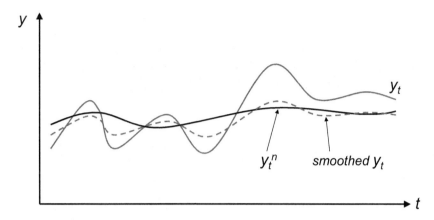

FIGURE 3.6
Natural output versus smoothed output. A smoothed version of output does not permit, in general, recovering the natural level of output.

theoretical concept (the output level that would prevail *if* prices were flexible), and so, as already mentioned, it is not directly observable—only *actual* macroeconomic variables are (π_t, π_{t-1}, and y_t here). Two solutions are possible to overcome this difficulty. The first is statistical and consists of assuming that the natural level of output y_t^n, which by definition is only affected by fluctuations in aggregate supply, is correctly approximated by a smoothed version of actual output y_t. This approach, however, can be misleading about the true position of the economy in the business cycle. Figure 3.6 illustrates this point: actual output y_t fluctuates around natural output y_t^n, but the smoothed version of y_t (for example, as constructed with the HP filter—see chapter 1) is only slightly (if not negatively) correlated with y_t^n. A poor estimate of y_t^n mechanically contaminates the estimate of the output gap $y_t - y_t^n$ and thus of the inflation rate π_t predicted by the model. For concreteness, suppose that for some reason labor productivity drops, causing an abrupt drop in natural output y_t^n, with actual output y_t likewise heading downward after the shock but in a more inertial way. A smoothed version of y_t would overestimate y_t^n and thus underestimate $y_t - y_t^n$ and the associated inflationary pressures.[10]

An alternative way of measuring the output gap, based on macroeconomic theory (rather than being purely statistical), consists of using other (observable) variables that are in principle systematically linked to the output gap. In this spirit, Galí,

10. This is the interpretation offered by Orphanides and Williams (2013) of the Great Inflation of the 1970s. In their account, the monetary authorities at the time underestimated the inflationary pressure generated by the oil price shocks, and so they did not readily adopt the sort of contractionary monetary policy that would have been required to stabilize inflation.

Gertler, and López-Salido (2001) argue that the output gap is systematically linked to the *real marginal cost* faced by firms in the economy. Indeed, by using equations (3.8) and (3.10), we can write the output gap like this:

$$y_t - y_t^n = \underbrace{\xi\left(w_t - p_t\right) + (1-\xi)z_t}_{=y_t \text{ (by eq. (3.8))}} - \underbrace{(z_t - \xi\mu^*)}_{=y_t^n \text{ (by eq. (3.10))}}$$

$$= \xi\mu^* + \xi \times \underbrace{(w_t - p_t - z_t)}_{\text{real marginal cost}}.$$

Intuitively, at any given productivity level z_t, a demand-driven expansion (and therefore an increase of $y_t - y_t^n$) is manifested by a tighter labor market, which causes the real wage $w_t - p_t$, and hence firms' real marginal cost to rise. Conversely, at a given level of output y_t, a positive productivity shock (an increase in z_t) reduces the real marginal cost while at the same time causing natural output y_t^n to increase.

By replacing the output gap by the real marginal cost in the AS curve (equation (3.17)), we obtain

$$\pi_t = \pi_{t-1} + \kappa\xi\mu^* + \kappa\xi(w_t - p_t - z_t).$$

Figure 3.7 illustrates the joint evolution of firms' real marginal cost and inflation in the euro area since 1970.

3.6   ALTERNATIVE FORMULATIONS OF THE AS CURVE

The AS curve that we have constructed is simple, easy to derive from first principles (namely, monopolistic competition and staggered nominal price setting), and provides a good guide in many policy situations of interest. For these reasons it plainly fulfills the objective of conceptual clarity that we argued in chapter 1 to be the hallmark of a good piece of macroeconomic theory. However, one should again not get confused about the correct way to interpret this theory. Its goal is to capture in a simple way the main forces that affect inflation fluctuations in a world with nominal rigidities. The price-setting mechanism that we postulated in section 3.4 turns out to be quite well suited for this purpose. This form of nominal rigidity does not, however, capture *all* potentially important dimensions of the data, and for this reason it is useful to consider alternative price or wage-setting mechanisms that may generate the same—or possibly slightly different—AS curves. We briefly discuss these mechanisms here, occasionally referring to material in the following chapters.

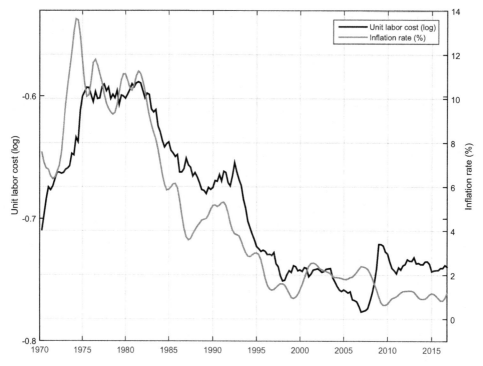

FIGURE 3.7
Unit labor cost and inflation in the euro area.
Sources: AWM database and the author's calculations.

3.6.1 ALTERNATIVE PRICE-SETTING MECHANISMS

3.6.1.1 PARTIAL INDEXATION TO PAST INFLATION

The first and somewhat obvious departure from our baseline AS curve comes from recognizing that price-indexing firms may not adjust their nominal selling price as much as past inflation would require—a phenomenon known as partial indexation. This occurs if price-indexing firms set the nominal price $p_{i,t} = p_{i,t-1} + \phi\pi_{t-1}$, where $0 \leq \phi \leq 1$ (so that we recover our baseline assumption of full indexation when $\phi = 1$). It is easy to show, going through the same steps as in section 3.4, that the AS curve then becomes

$$\mathbf{AS} : \pi_t = \phi\pi_{t-1} + \kappa \left(y_t - y_t^n\right).$$

Estimates of AS curves of this form consistently give $\phi < 1$, suggesting a muted role for past inflation in the determination of current inflation (Blanchard 2016, 2018). Taken at face value, this result may seem to reject the natural rate hypothesis, since in principle it then becomes possible for a dovish central bank to permanently raise output above its natural level through a policy of high (but stable) inflation.

Indeed, suppose that the central bank aims—and manages—to maintain inflation at some target $\bar{\pi} > 0$ in the long run. Then, according to the latter AS curve above, the relation between trend inflation $\bar{\pi}$ and the long-run value of the output gap $y_\infty - y_\infty^n$ is given by

$$y_\infty - y_\infty^n = \frac{(1 - \phi)}{\kappa}\bar{\pi}.$$

Thus, if ϕ is below 1 then it seems that the central bank would have a cheap way of permanently raising output above its natural level. This reasoning is wrong, however; it neglects the fact that firms are likely to include trend inflation in their price-setting process, in addition to past inflation, should trend inflation effectively persist. Exercise 3.7.1 studies a price-setting process that is consistent with the presence of positive trend inflation and generalizes the AS curve accordingly.

3.6.1.2 THE ACCELERATIONIST PHILLIPS CURVE

As explained in chapter 1, our maintained assumption throughout the book regarding the way in which private agents form their expectations is that they have *perfect foresight*—a property that results from the assumptions that information is being used optimally and that no aggregate shock will ever occur after the current period. Now suppose instead that firms form *static* expectations—that is, they anticipate an inflation rate for the next period equal to the inflation rate of the current period; formally, $\pi_{t,t+1}^e = \pi_t$, where $\pi_{t,t+1}^e$ is the expectation formed in period t about the level of inflation that will prevail in period $t+1$. It is shown in chapter 6 that such expectations, coupled with a price-setting mechanism with *predetermined nominal prices*—that is, where *all* firms can freely reset their nominal price optimally one period in advance—generate exactly the same AS curve as in equation (3.17) above. Intuitively, under static expectations and predetermined prices the backward-lookingness of the AS curve comes from the inertia in inflation expectations, rather than from the staggered nature of nominal price adjustments. The AS curve with such a foundation is commonly referred to as the accelerationist Phillips curve, a tribute to Milton Friedman's (1968) presidential address to the American Economic Association. Friedman showed that a central bank facing such naïve agents could persistently raise employment above its natural level by engineering an ever increasing inflation rate—or equivalently an ever *accelerating* average price level. Of course, the same is true of our perfect-foresight AS curve with price-indexing firms. We will discuss these issues in detail in chapter 6.

3.6.1.3 THE NEW CLASSICAL PHILLIPS CURVE

The *New Classical Phillips curve*, also examined in chapter 6, is a variant of the AS curve that arises when (1) nominal prices are predetermined (rather than adjusted in a staggered manner), and (2) macroeconomic shocks occurring in future periods are *not* assumed away, so that we must depart from the mere perfect-foresight assumption when dealing with agents' expectations. In chapter 6 we show how the assumption of perfect foresight can be generalized into that of *rational expectations*, according to which agents optimally use the mathematical expectations of a random macroeconomic variable (e.g., inflation) as the best predictor of that variable. The resulting AS curve takes the form:

$$\text{NCPC}: \pi_t = \mathbb{E}_{t-1}\left(\pi_t\right) + \kappa\left(y_t - y_t^n\right),$$

where $\mathbb{E}_{t-1}\left(\pi_t\right)$ is the rational expectation formed in period $t-1$ about the value of time-t inflation—formally, it is the conditional expectation of π_t given the information set available in period $t-1$. This formulation of the AS curve fully takes into account the fact that macroeconomic variables must in general be predicted in advance and in an environment of uncertainty about future economic conditions. The New Classical Phillips curve is well suited for a medium- to long-run analysis of inflation—a horizon at which we expect prices to be relatively flexible and where agents have had the time to learn the joint distribution of macroeconomic variables.

3.6.1.4   THE NEW KEYNESIAN PHILLIPS CURVE

One important limitation of the price-setting mechanism postulated in section 3.4 is that it is not forward looking; the firms that index their nominal selling price only look at *past* inflation, while the firms that optimize this price only look at *current* profits. In reality firms are forward looking in that they make decisions about pricing, production, and hiring, taking into account the consequences of their current actions on *future* profits. Formally, this concern for the future shows up if we assume that the firms that do set their nominal selling price optimally maximize the *present value of their current and future profit flows* (rather than their current profit only) and form rational expectations. It can be shown that under such assumptions the AS curve has the following form:

$$\text{NKPC}: \pi_t = \left(\frac{\phi}{1+\beta\phi}\right)\pi_{t-1} + \left(\frac{\beta}{1+\beta\phi}\right)\mathbb{E}_t\left(\pi_{t+1}\right) + \left(\frac{\kappa}{1+\beta\phi}\right)\left(y_t - y_t^n\right),$$

where $0 \le \phi \le 1$ and $0 \le \beta < 1$. This specification nests, as special cases, both our simpler AS curve ($\phi = 1$, $\beta = 0$) and a purely forward-looking equation wherein only future inflation (and the output gap) affects current inflation ($\phi = 0$).

The New Keynesian Phillips curve implies that current inflation responds to three factors, two of which we already know and understand: the output gap $y_t - y_t^n$ and past inflation π_{t-1}. The new determinant of current inflation is (rationally expected) *future inflation* $\mathbb{E}_t\left(\pi_{t+1}\right)$. To understand why future inflation shows up here, recall that firms operate in an environment of monopolistic competition wherein the optimal selling price is that which strikes the best balance between raising the firm's markup—which calls for increasing the price—and broadening the firm's market share—which calls for lowering it. In the absence of nominal rigidities firms would all set the same nominal selling price (as given by equation (3.12)) at every point in time, and the equilibrium would be perfectly symmetric. There is a cost to departing from this symmetric flexible-price equilibrium. A firm that sells below the average price sells more but gets a relatively low markup and ultimately suffers from a lower profit; and conversely, a firm that sells above the average price gets a high markup but sells too little and similarly gets a relatively low profit. Now, recall that under our hypothesized price-setting mechanisms firms only reoptimize their selling price infrequently (with a probability of $1 - \omega$ in every period). Consequently, a firm that resets its price in the current period and is forward looking takes into account the fact it will probably not reset this price optimally for some time. But because departing from the average price level is costly, such a firm sets its own selling price in a way that will best track the expected evolution of the price level—not only the current price level. Consequently, if this firm expects high inflation in the future, it will raise its current selling price—else the price it sets right now will likely turn out to be too low in the future—and the other way around. Aggregating this behavior over all price-resetting firms implies that high expected inflation raises the selling price of all price-optimizing firms, which in turn raises current inflation.

There have been numerous empirical evaluations of the New Keynesian Phillips curve since the pioneering work of Galí and Gertler (1999) and Galí, Gertler, and López-Salido (2001). These studies tend to confirm the fact that expected inflation $\mathbb{E}_t(\pi_{t+1})$—and not only past inflation π_{t-1}—affect current inflation π_t. Abstracting from this forward-looking term, however, greatly simplifies the analysis of the business cycle, and most of the mechanisms that we discuss in the book would remain valid should this term be incorporated.[11]

3.6.2 NOMINAL WAGE RIGIDITIES

While our analysis thus far has focused exclusively on nominal rigidities in *goods* prices, other nominal prices may be rigid as well—notably the nominal price of labor, and namely the *nominal wage*. Barattieri, Basu, and Gottschalk (2014) find that the probability of experiencing a nominal wage change is of about 25 percent every quarter in the United States, while most wage changes occur upon changing jobs; this implies that there is substantial nominal wage rigidity on the job. Le Bihan, Mortornes, and Heckel (2012), Sigurdsson and Sigurdardottir (2011), and Lünnemann and Wintr (2009) find similar evidence of significant nominal wage rigidity in France, Iceland, and Luxembourg, respectively.

---

11. See Galí (2008) and Woodford (2003) for exensive treatments of the business-cycle implications of the New Keynesian Phillips curve.

3.6.2.1   HOUSEHOLDS AS MONOPOLISTIC LABOR SUPPLIERS

There are at least two ways of introducing nominal wage rigidity in place of—or in addition to—the nominal price rigidity considered in section 3.4. The first way, which is the subject of Exercise 3.7.2 at the end of the chapter, consists of treating the labor market exactly in the same way as we treated the goods market in the preceeding sections. To be more specific, this approach posits that every household is the monopolistic supplier of a particular labor type and may thus charge a *wage markup*—just as our firms were assumed to be monopolistic suppliers of particular good types and could extract a price markup as a result. The relevant markup here is over the marginal rate of substitution between consumption and leisure; that is, the household's own subjective valuation of consumption goods relative to leisure time. Now if those monopolistic households only infrequently optimize the nominal wage at which they sell their labor and simply index their own wage growth based on past nominal wage growth when they do not optimize, then the AS curve has exactly the same form as equation (3.17) above—except that it now features *wage inflation* instead of price inflation:

$$\mathbf{AS} : \pi_t^W = \pi_{t-1}^W + \kappa^W \left(y_t - y_t^n \right),$$

where $\kappa^W \geq 0$ is a constant and π_t^W is nominal wage inflation:

$$\pi_t^W = \frac{W_t - W_{t-1}}{W_{t-1}} \simeq w_t - w_{t-1}.$$

Such nominal wage rigidities are a substitute to nominal price rigidities in the following sense: if nominal wages are set in this way, while nominal prices are reoptimized by all firms in every period (i.e., $\omega = 0$), then nominal price inflation has *exactly* the same form as in equation (3.17). The reason for this is that firms in this scenario set their nominal selling price in every period by just applying a constant markup over the nominal marginal cost of production (see equation (3.4) above), which here is just the nominal wage minus labor productivity. If one aggregates this constant markup pricing behavior at the level of the economy as a whole, we get that the average price level p_t in the economy is just an upward translation (of size $\mu^* - z_t$) of the average nominal wage w_t. This in turn implies that (up to a labor productivity shock) price inflation and wage inflation are the same ($\pi_t = \pi_t^W - \Delta z_t$), and hence price inflation is also described by a equation of the form of (3.17).

3.6.2.2   NOMINAL WAGE RIGIDITIES INSIDE THE BARGAINING SET

Finally, in chapter 5 we provide yet another possible microfoundation for an AS curve that resembles equation (3.17) above, but again based on nominal wage stickiness rather than price stickiness. The framework that we develop in chapter 5 takes more seriously the concrete functioning of the labor market and notably the fact that it is made of *bilateral relationships* between workers and employers. Such bilateral (and hence inherently noncompetitive) relationships imply that there is in general a full range of potential wages upon which the firm and the worker can agree. Any wage that lies above the subjective cost of working for the worker, while remaining sufficiently low for the firm to extract a positive surplus from the relationship, is a potential "equilibrium wage." This indeterminacy of the bilaterally efficient wage inside the bargaining set of the worker and the firm means that the wage is ultimately given by a *self-fulfilling custom*: the nominal wage that actually prevails is simply what both parties expect it to be, usually on the basis of what it used to be (Hall 2005). This custom and associated wage expectations may involve a substantial amount of nominal stickiness, as is suggested by the data. Nominal wage stickiness in turn implies that aggregate shocks that hit the price level affect the real wage and hence change the firms' incentives to produce. We explore and discuss this possibility in chapter 5.

3.7 EXERCISES

3.7.1 PRICE INDEXATION TO TREND INFLATION

Assume that the aggregate supply block is exactly the same as in this chapter except for one modification: among the firms that do not reset their price optimally, only a fraction ϕ of them indexes their price growth to past inflation, while the remaining fraction indexes their price growth to trend inflation $\bar{\pi}$. Going through the same steps as in section 3.4, show that the AS curve now takes the form:

$$\mathbf{AS}: \pi_t = \phi \pi_{t-1} + (1 - \phi)\,\bar{\pi} + \kappa \left(y_t - y_t^n\right).$$

Is this AS curve consistent with the natural rate hypothesis? Is this AS curve consistent with the evidence presented in Blanchard (2016, 2018)?

3.7.2 NOMINAL WAGE RIGIDITIES

Consider the following macroeconomic model. There is no investment, government spending, or net exports, so private consumption is the only component of aggregate demand. There is a continuum of firms i, $0 \le i \le 1$, operating under monopolistic competition—firm i is the sole producer of good i and faces the demand function

$$Y_{i,t} = Y_t \left(\frac{P_{i,t}}{P_t}\right)^{-\eta}, \eta > 1,$$

where $Y_{i,t}$ is the demand for good i, Y_t aggregate demand, $P_{i,t}$ the nominal price of good i, and P_t the average price level. Firm i produces a quantity of goods $Q_{i,t}$ using a quantity of labor $L_{i,t}$ as per the production function

$$Q_{i,t} = L_{i,t}.$$

Thus, the total demand for labor in the economy is given by

$$L_t^d = \int_0^1 L_{i,t} \mathrm{d}i.$$

The labor utilized by firms is supplied by a continuum of length 1 of households, which are indexed by j, $0 \le j \le 1$. The labor supply of each household is specialized, such that a household is in a monopoly situation over the type of labor it supplies. But this monopoly power is limited by the partial substitutability of those different labor types from the point of view of the firms. This substitutability is manifested as follows: when the total demand for labor by the firms is L_t^d, the demand for specialized labor j is given by

$$L_{j,t}^d = L_t^d \left(\frac{W_{j,t}}{W_t} \right)^{-\theta}, \theta > 1,$$

where $W_{j,t}$ is the nominal wage paid to household j, and W_t the average nominal wage.

Household j maximizes in each period the utility function

$$u\left(C_{j,t}, L_{j,t}\right) = C_{j,t} - \frac{1}{2}L_{j,t}^2,$$

where $C_{j,t}$ the consumption of household j and $L_{j,t}$ its labor supply. Household j's budget constraint is given by

$$P_t C_{j,t} = W_{j,t} L_{j,t}.$$

In what follows, lowercase letters refer to the logarithms of the corresponding capital letters. We assume that we are always close to the symmetric equilibrium, such that (in first approximation) the log of the average nominal price is equal to the average of log nominal prices, and the same for the nominal wage:

$$p_t \simeq \int_0^1 p_{i,t} \mathrm{d}i, \ w_t \simeq \int_0^1 w_{i,t} \mathrm{d}i, \text{ with } p_t = \ln P_t \text{ and } w_t = \ln W_t.$$

Finally, we distinguish between price inflation π_t and wage inflation π_t^w. Recall that in first approximation, and for small variations in nominal prices and wages, we have:

$$\pi_t = \frac{P_t - P_{t-1}}{P_{t-1}} \simeq p - p_{-1} \ \text{ and } \ \pi_t^w = \frac{W_t - W_{t-1}}{W_{t-1}} \simeq w_t - w_{t-1}.$$

1. Compute the optimal nominal price P_t^*. Show that $p_t^* = \ln P_t^*$ is given by

$$p_t^* = \mu^* + w_t,$$

where μ^* is a constant to be determined. Provide an interpretation of this relation.

2. Show that the optimal nominal wage W_t^* at which any household j wishes to sell its labor satisfies the following first-order condition:

$$\frac{W_t^*}{P_t} = \left(\frac{\theta}{\theta - 1} \right) L_t^d,$$

and explain this equation intuitively. Infer from this result that, in the vicinity of symmetric equilibrium, we have

$$w_t^* - p_t = v^* + y_t, \ \text{ with } v^* = \ln \left(\frac{\theta}{\theta - 1} \right),$$

and provide an interpretation of this relation.

3. Suppose that nominal prices and nominal wages are perfectly flexible. Show that the natural level of output y_t^n is constant and given by

$$y_t^n = -\mu^* - v^*,$$

and explain this result intuitively.

4. Now suppose that nominal prices are perfectly flexible but that nominal wages are partially rigid. More precisely, in each period a proportion $1 - \tau$ of the households is free to set the nominal wage at which it rents out its labor to the firm at the optimal level w_t^*. The other households adopt the following indexation rule:

$$w_{j,t} = w_{j,t-1} + \pi_{t-1}^w.$$

(a) Show, by using the preceding relations, that the optimal relative wage (in log) is given by

$$w_t^* - w_t = y_t - y_t^n,$$

and provide an interpretation for this result.

(b) Infer from this that wage inflation π_t^w evolves as follows:

$$\pi_t^w = \pi_{t-1}^w + \left(\frac{1-\tau}{\tau}\right)(y_t - y_t^n).$$

(c) Show that $\pi_t = \pi_t^w$, so that price inflation is described by the same dynamics as wage inflation.

3.7.3 MENU COSTS AND MULTIPLICITY OF EQUILIBRIA

Consider the following static model of monopolistic competition with nominal rigidities in the goods market.

3.7.3.1 FIRMS

Firms form a continuum of length 1. Each firm i, $0 \leq i \leq 1$, maximizes its real profit Π_i and faces the demand function

$$Y_i = Y (P_i/P)^{-2},\tag{3.18}$$

where Y_i, $0 \leq i \leq 1$, is the demand addressed to firm i; P_i the nominal selling price of good i; P the average price level; and Y aggregate demand. Firms operates with the production function $Q_i = L_i$, with Q_i the output of firm i and L_i the quantity of labor utilized. The households own the firms and hence recuperate all their profits.

3.7.3.2 HOUSEHOLDS

Households form a continuum of length 1. Since all households are identical, we are studying the behavior of the representative household, whose utility function is given by

$$U = C - \frac{1}{3} (L)^{3/2},\tag{3.19}$$

where C is the consumption of the representative household and L its labor supply. The representative household works for the firms at the nominal wage W. At the same time, it recuperates the whole amount of profits generated by the firms. The representative household's budget constraint is therefore

$$PC = P\int_0^1 \Pi_i di + WL.\tag{3.20}$$

In this problem we will concentrate exclusively on *symmetric* equilibria; that is, those in which firms adopt the same behavior in equilibrium. In such equilibria all firms make the same profit, such that we have $\int_0^1 \Pi_i di = \Pi_i$.

3.7.3.3   THE CENTRAL BANK

The central bank controls the quantity of money in circulation M. All payments must be made with money, so aggregate demand is given by:

$$Y = M/P. \tag{3.21}$$

3.7.3.4   EQUILIBRIUM

In this economy, the sole component of spending is household consumption. Therefore we necessarily have:

$$Y = C.$$

1. Using equations (3.18), (3.19), and (3.20), compute the optimal labor supply of the representative household L^*, as well as the real optimal selling price P^*/P, as a function of the real wage W/P.

2. Compute the natural equilibrium of this economy. What is the average price level P in the natural equilibrium?

3. Assume that firms have set their prices anticipating that the quantity of money in circulation would be $M_0 = 1$. Once these prices have been set, however, an expansionary monetary policy shock occurs and the central bank sets $M_1 = 2 > M_0$ instead of the expected M_0.

(a) Compute the levels of output, employment, the real wage, and profits that prevail in the economy if none of the firms adjust their selling price after the monetary shock.

(b) Compute the profit that a dissident firm would earn, on this equilibrium, by adjusting its price in an optimal way after the shock.

(c) Compute the profit that firms would make if they all adjusted their prices optimally after the monetary shock.

(d) Compute, on this second equilibrium, the profit of a dissident firm that would instead keep its price unchanged.

(e) Prove that the incentive of a firm to adjust is selling price after the monetary policy shock is higher when the other firms also adjust their prices optimally.

4. Suppose that a firm must pay a "menu cost" $Z > 0$ to readjust its selling price optimally after the monetary shock. Show that:

- when $Z < \frac{1}{\sqrt{2}} - (2 - \sqrt{2})$, the only Nash equilibrium is one in which all firms adjust their prices. (As a reminder, a Nash equilibrium is a profile of actions on the part of all players, none of whom has an interest in deviating unilaterally; in the present case, an equilibrium with price adjustment is a Nash equilibrium if no firm individually finds it worthwhile to keep its price unchanged when all the others adjust their prices.);

- when $Z > 1/2$, the only Nash equilibrium is one where no firm adjusts its price after the shock;

- when $1/\sqrt{2} - 2 + \sqrt{2}) \leq Z \leq 1/2$, the two equilibria above are Nash equilibria.

5. Prove that the representative household prefers the fixed-price equilibrium and explain why.

3.8   APPENDIX: OPTIMAL LABOR SUPPLY

This appendix shows how the labor supply function that has been postulated in this chapter (in equation (3.7)) can be derived from the optimal choices of the households under suitable assumptions about their preferences over consumption and leisure time. To do this we are going to generalize the intertemporal utility of household j that we studied in chapter 2 (equation (2.3)) in a manner to make endogenous the choice of labor supply L_t^j. To be more specific, assume that household j maximizes

$$\mathcal{U}_t^j = \sum_{k=0}^{n} \left(\frac{1}{1+\rho} \right)^k \left[\ln C_{t+k}^j - \xi (L_{t+k}^j)^{\frac{1}{\xi}} \right], \ 0 < \xi \leq 1,$$

under the usual intertemporal budget constraint (see equation (2.5)). The fact that $0 < \xi \leq 1$ implies that the marginal disutility of labor $(L_t^j)^{\frac{1-\xi}{\xi}}$ is either constant ($\xi = 1$) or increasing ($\xi < 1$) in L_t^j, and all the more so when ξ is small (this is why the parameter ξ determines the elasticity of labor supply in equation (3.7)).

The Lagrangian function corresponding to this problem is:

$$\mathcal{L}_t = \mathcal{U}_t + \Lambda_t^j \left\{ A_{t-1}^j (1 + r_{t-1}) + \sum_{k=0}^{n} \frac{\frac{W_{t+k}}{P_{t+k}} L_{t+k}^j - T_{t+k}^j}{\Pi_{m=0}^{k-1} (1 + r_{t+m})} - \sum_{k=0}^{n} \frac{C_{t+k}^j}{\Pi_{k=m}^{k-1} (1 + r_{t+m})} \right\}.$$

The first-order conditions associated with the choices of C_t^j and L_t^j are, for any t, given by

$$\frac{\partial \mathcal{L}_t}{\partial L_t^j} = -(L_t^j)^{\frac{1}{\xi}-1} + \Lambda_t^j \frac{W_t}{P_t} = 0 \text{ and } \frac{\partial \mathcal{L}_t}{\partial C_t^j} = \frac{1}{C_t^j} - \Lambda_t^j = 0.$$

By combining these two first-order conditions to eliminate Λ^j, we find:

$$(L_t^j)^{\frac{1}{\xi}-1} = \frac{W_t}{P_t} \frac{1}{C_t^j}. \tag{3.22}$$

Equation (3.22) states that the household increases its hours worked L_t^j up to the point where one additional unit of labor brings as much in terms of utility of consumption (the right-hand side of the equation) as it costs in terms of disutility of labor (the left-hand side of the equation).[12] More precisely, an additional unit

---

12. Note that the optimality condition in equation (3.22) is verified whether the household is Ricardian or Keynesian in its consumption behavior (see chapter 2).

of labor supplied reduces the utility of the household by $(l^j)^{\frac{1}{\xi}-1}$. This unit of labor earns W_t US dollars (for example), while each US dollar permits buying $1/P_t$ units of goods, and finally each unit of goods consumed increases the utility of the household by $1/C_t^j$. In particular, an elevated real wage W_t/P_t encourages labor supply, whereas a high consumption level C_t^j implies a low marginal utility of consumption, which discourages labor supply. By turning equation (3.22) into log we obtain:

$$l_t^j = \frac{\xi}{1-\xi}(w_t - p_t - c_t^j). \tag{3.23}$$

We assume here that private consumption is the sole component of aggregate demand, so that there are neither net exports nor investment nor government expenditure. If in addition we assume that all households are identical and form a continuum of length 1, then the total supply of labor l_t^s is given by equation (3.23), while the total consumption of goods is $c_t^j = y_t = z_t + l_t^s$, with $c_t = \ln C_t$. In this case, equation (3.23) can be rewritten as:

$$
\begin{aligned}
l_t^s &= \frac{\xi}{1-\xi}(w_t - p_t - y_t) \\
&= \frac{\xi}{1-\xi}(w_t - p_t - z_t - l_t^s) \\
&= \xi(w_t - p_t - z_t),
\end{aligned}
$$

which corresponds to equation (3.7).

PART II

BUSINESS CYCLES

AS-AD EQUILIBRIUM AND THE PROPAGATION OF MACROECONOMIC SHOCKS

Accordingly we find, that, in every kingdom into which money begins to flow in greater abundance than formerly, every thing takes a new face: labour and industry gain life; the merchant becomes more enterprising, the manufacturer more diligent and skilful, and even the farmer follows his plough with greater alacrity and attention. To account, then, for this phenomenon, we must consider, that though the high price of commodities be a necessary consequence of the increase of gold and silver, yet it follows not immediately upon that increase; but some time is required before the money circulates through the whole state, and makes its effect be felt on all ranks of people. At first, no alteration is perceived; by degrees the price rises, first of one commodity, then of another; till the whole at last reaches a just proportion with the new quantity of specie which is in the kingdom. In my opinion, it is only in this interval or intermediate situation, between the acquisition of money and rise of prices, that the increasing quantity of gold and silver is favourable to industry.

—David Hume (1752)

In order to understand this passage from David Hume, we have to return to the context of monetary institutions in the eighteenth century. At that time, pieces of precious metals were used as units of account, circulated as means of payment, and also served as a store of value. A monetary shock occurred when, after gold or silver (obtained in exchange for exported goods or more directly coming from newly exploited mines) was imported, the quantity of coins in circulation suddenly increased. Hume describes in this passage the effects of such a shock on prices (nominal effects) and on quantities (real effects), and he supports the idea that the quantity of money is neutral in the long run but not in the short run. In modern monetary systems, where instead of gold and silver coins, fiat money issued by the banking system circulates as means of payment, a monetary shock is simply a facilitated access to credit from which economic agents may benefit, thanks to more attractive interest rates.

In this chapter, we are using the AS-AD model derived in the last two chapters for the purpose of studying the propagation of macroeconomic shocks. In doing so, we are interested not only in aggregate demand shocks like the monetary shocks studied by David Hume, but also in aggregate supply shocks (productivity, shocks, commodity price shocks, deregulation shocks, and so forth). Whenever this is possible we will compare the implications of the AS-AD model with the available empirical evidence.

4.1 MACROECONOMIC EQUILIBRIUM

4.1.1 AS-AD EQUILIBRIUM

In chapter 2 we saw how the aggregation of the spending behaviors of private agents (households, firms, and the rest of the world) interacted with the behavior of policy makers (the government and the central bank) to generate an aggregate demand curve (or *AD curve*), meaning a decreasing relation between output and inflation:

$$\mathbf{AD}: y_t = \theta_t - \sigma\gamma\,(\pi_t - \bar{\pi})\,, \quad \sigma, \gamma \geq 0. \tag{4.1}$$

This relation is decreasing due to the automatic component of monetary policy. When inflation rises above its target, the central bank attempts to raise the real interest rate so as to bring inflation back to its target (and conversely). In the (y, π) plane, the AD curve has a slope $-1/\sigma\gamma$, and it is shifted by all the aggregate demand shocks that move θ_t (that is, the determinants of Θ_t in equation (2.23)).

Chapter 3 was devoted to the construction of the *AS curve*—namely an increasing relation between changes in inflation and the output gap:

$$\mathbf{AS}: \pi_t = \pi_{t-1} + \kappa\,\left(y_t - y_t^n\right)\,, \quad \kappa \geq 0. \tag{4.2}$$

The AS curve is increasing since, at any given level of natural output y_t^n, a higher actual level of output y_t tightens the labor market, with the effect of increasing the equilibrium real wage and thereby pushing up firms' selling prices. The AS curve is parameterized by y_t^n. When labor productivity z_t rises, or when there is more competition so that μ^* falls, the output-inflation tradeoff is improved, and one can enjoy higher output or lower inflation or both. It is also parameterized by π_{t-1}: higher inflation in the past pushes up current inflation due to the indexation of some selling prices on past inflation.

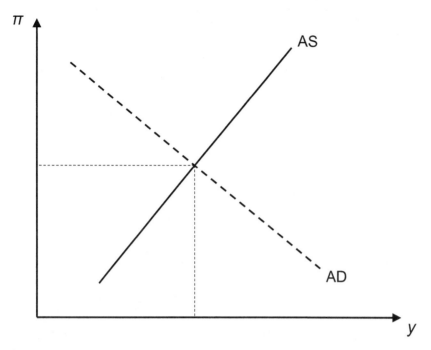

FIGURE 4.1
The AS-AD equilibrium. The AD curve (chapter 2) and the AS curve (chapter 3).

The short-run macroeconomic equilibrium is located at the intersection of the AS and AD curves, as is represented in figure 4.1. The location of the two curves, which in the short run are parameterized by $(\theta_t, \pi_{t-1}, y_t^n)$, determines the equilibrium values of (y_t, π_t). However, π_{t-1} is not determined in period t, but in period $t-1$. Therefore, the aggregate shocks that shift the AS and AD curves in period t are shifts to θ_t (the aggregate demand shocks) and y_t^n (the aggregate supply shocks).

We may solve the preceding AS-AD system so as to compute the equilibrium in period t (y_t, π_t) as a function of the aggregate demand and supply shocks of period t:

$$y_t = \text{constant} + \left(\frac{1}{1 + \sigma \gamma \kappa} \right) \theta_t + \left(\frac{\sigma \gamma \kappa}{1 + \sigma \gamma \kappa} \right) y_t^n, \tag{4.3}$$

$$\pi_t = \text{constant} + \left(\frac{\kappa}{1 + \sigma \gamma \kappa} \right) \theta_t - \left(\frac{\kappa}{1 + \sigma \gamma \kappa} \right) y_t^n. \tag{4.4}$$

This representation explicitly features the shock multipliers (i.e., the terms in brackets), which summarize how the equilibrium is shifted by the underlying macroeconomic shocks.

4.1.2 LONG-RUN EQUILIBRIUM

Once an aggregate shock has occurred, toward which equilibrium does the economy return in the long run? At this time horizon, all aggregate shocks have vanished and all nominal prices have been optimally adjusted. Therefore, the long-run level of output (y_∞) is equal to the natural level of output at the same horizon (y_∞^n):

$$y_\infty = y_\infty^n = z_\infty - \xi \mu^*.$$

At this horizon the real interest rate is necessarily equal to its average value, so we have $r_\infty = \bar{r}$. From the IS curve (equation (2.24)) and the absence of shock at that horizon we have

$$\theta_\infty = y_\infty.$$

The logic of the long-run equilibrium is the opposite to that of the short-run equilibrium. In the short run, the real interest rate determines aggregate demand, possibly giving rise to transitory imbalances between supply and demand that materialize in the form of inflationary or deflationary pressures. But in the long run, where prices are flexible, there cannot be any such imbalances and it is precisely the equality between demand and supply that determines the market-clearing interest rate r_∞. This interest rate is the average real interest rate $\bar{r}$ around which its current value r_t fluctuates.

Another way of understanding the logic of the long-run equilibrium is to examine what would happen if, for example, the central bank attempted to lower the long-run real interest rate by adopting a permanently expansionary monetary policy. Doing so requires being a little more explicit about how the central bank manipulates the real interest rate. We will see in chapter 6 that what the central bank controls (yet indirectly) is not the real interest rate but the *nominal* interest rate i_t. Now, from the Fisher equation we have $r_\infty = i_\infty - \pi_\infty$. The market-clearing interest rate r_∞ is given by the equality of aggregate demand and supply in the long-run, while i_∞ is set by the central bank. Something has to give—and it is inflation:

$$\pi_\infty = i_\infty - r_\infty.$$

Put differently, whatever the nominal interest rate set by the central bank, in the long-run inflation adjusts until the implied real interest rate clears the goods market. It follows that, for the central bank to honor a given inflation target $\bar{\pi}$, the average value of the nominal interest rate must be

$$\bar{i} = r_\infty + \bar{\pi}.$$

The MP curve that we postulated in chapter 2 implicitly incorporates those long-run constraints. Given an inflation target $\bar{\pi}$, the central bank sets the average nominal interest at the level $\bar{\imath}$, which results in an average inflation rate consistent with the target.

In the remainder of this chapter we study the propagation of business-cycle shocks occurring in period t, assuming that the economy is in long-run equilibrium (and inflation at its target $\bar{\pi}$) in period $t-1$:

$$y_{t-1} = y_{t-1}^n = \theta_{t-1} = z_\infty - \xi\mu^*,$$

and

$$\pi_{t-1} = \bar{\pi}.$$

4.2 Effect of an Aggregate Demand Shock

4.2.1 Theoretical Impact

Figure 4.2 illustrates the effect of a transitory aggregate demand shock ($d\theta_t > 0$ with $d\theta_\infty = 0$) on the short-run equilibrium.[1] The shock shifts the AD curve to the right, which causes a shift of the equilibrium from point A to point B along the AS curve. The new equilibrium is associated with higher levels of output and inflation.

Intuitively, the causal chain that leads to the new equilibrium after the shock may be described as follows. The increase in the aggregate demand for goods ($\theta_t \uparrow$) generates an increase in output ($y_t \uparrow$), so that firms express a higher demand for labor on the labor market ($l_t^d \uparrow$). Since labor supply is elastic, it rises ($l_t^s = l_t^d \uparrow$), but the tightening of the labor market caused by the rise in labor demand has triggered an increase in the real wage ($w_t - p_t \uparrow$) and hence an increase in firms' real unit cost of production ($w_t - p_t - z_t \uparrow$). The firms that optimize their selling price pass along this higher cost to their selling price ($p_t \uparrow$), which ultimately generates a rise in inflation ($\pi_t \uparrow$). The impact of the shift of the AD curve depends on the slope of the AS curve. The higher this slope—either because the fraction of firms that readjust their prices optimally ($1 - \omega$) is greater, or because the elasticity of labor supply (ξ) is smaller—the greater the effect on inflation, and the lower the effect on output. The northwest and northeast panels of figure 4.3 show the instantaneous impact of the aggregate demand shock in the two extreme cases, where $\omega = 1$ and where $\omega = 0$. In the first case, all prices are indexed so that inflation remains unchanged at $\pi_{t-1} = \bar{\pi}$ after an aggregate demand shock, whereas the effect on output y_t is maximal. In the second case, all prices are optimized and we recover the natural equilibrium: the aggregate demand shock has no effect on output and it affects only inflation.

What happens in the medium run, after the initial aggregate demand shock has taken place but before the complete reversion of (y_t, π_t) toward their long-run

---

1. See chapter 2 for a description of the underlying macroeconomic shocks leading to shifts in θ_t.

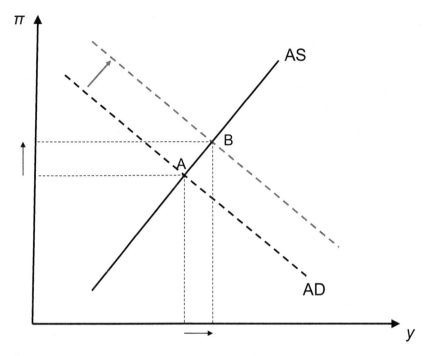

FIGURE 4.2
Impact of an aggregate demand shock. An expansionary demand shock shifts the AD curve to the right, which displaces the equilibrium along the AS curve; output and inflation both rise.

equilibrium values? In the preceding chapter we saw how the fraction of optimized prices increased over time after a macroeconomic shock, causing the AS curve to rotate counterclockwise toward the LRAS curve. At the same time, the reversion of θ_t triggers a gradual return of the AD curve toward its initial position. The joined movements of the AS and AD curves over time generate a hump-shaped dynamics of inflation and output after the initial aggregate demand shock, as shown in figure 4.4. Note that this hump-shaped dynamics characterizes all macroeconomic variables that underlie the AS and AD blocks, and whose dynamic adjustments are left implicit here. For example, at a given level of labor productivity, the hump-shaped dynamics of output after an aggregate demand shock generates a similar dynamic for the real wage (since $w_t - p_t = (y_t - (1 - \xi)z_t)/\xi$, from equation (3.8)) and hence for the real marginal cost ($w_t - p_t - z_t$). The effects of a negative aggregate demand shock are the mirror image: upon impact, the plunge in the demand for goods triggers a drop in output and hence in the demand for labor. This in turn generates a drop in real wages that is ultimately passed through to prices and inflation. As this negative shock dissipates, output and inflation gradually recover.

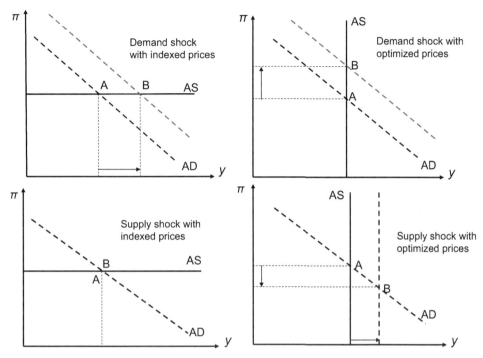

Figure 4.3
Impact of macroeconomic shocks with fully indexed versus fully optimized prices. When all prices are indexed, so that inflation is constant, the effect of an aggregate demand shock on output is maximized, but an aggregate supply shock has no effect. When all prices are optimized, an aggregate demand shock has no effect on output, but an aggregate supply shock raises it.

What happens when the persistence of the aggregate demand shock increases, so that θ_t reverts more slowly to its long-run value θ_∞? This persistence implies that, in the (y, π) plane, the AD curve takes longer to come back to its initial position before the shock. At the same time, the AS curve rotates toward the LRAS as it did previously. Consequently, output returns to its natural level at a pace close to the one that prevailed in the case of a transitory shock, whereas the rise in inflation is both larger and more persistent. Figure 4.5 illustrates this dynamics in the case of a very persistent aggregate demand shock.

4.2.2 Effect of a Monetary Policy Shock

The analysis above applies in principle to any aggregate demand shock, whatever its origin. Therefore we expect to observe the same dynamics for every kind of aggregate demand shock considered in chapter 2 (a trade shock—whether on world output y_t^w or on the future value of the real exchange rate q_{t+1}, bad news about the future productivity of investment z_{t+1}, or other types of disruption). Are the predicted

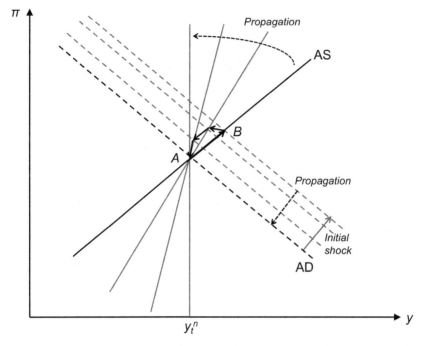

FIGURE 4.4
Adjustment dynamics after a transitory aggregate demand shock. After the shock, the AD curve gradually returns to its initial position, whereas the AS curve pivots toward the LRAS curve. In each period, equilibrium is found at the intersection of the AD and AS curves.

effects of a transitory aggregate demand shock, as per the AS-AD model, confirmed by empirical observations? In order to verify this, empirical studies have principally concentrated on a kind of demand shock that has been relatively well identified empirically: a *monetary policy shock*—that is, a transitory and unanticipated drop in the real interest rate. This translates into an exogenous drop in r_t at a given level of the inflation gap $\pi_t - \bar{\pi}$ in the MP curve and is thus formally equivalent to an exogenous rise in θ_t in the AD curve (to put it simply, an expansionary monetary policy shock is a type of positive aggregate demand shock). According to equations (4.3), (4.4), and (3.7), and also taking into account the aggregate production function ($y_t = z_t + l_t$), the immediate impact of this shock on output, employment, inflation, and the real wage is given by:

$$dy_t = dl_t = \left(\frac{1}{1 + \sigma\gamma\kappa}\right) d\theta_t > 0,$$

$$d\pi_t = \left(\frac{\kappa}{1 + \sigma\gamma\kappa}\right) d\theta_t > 0,$$

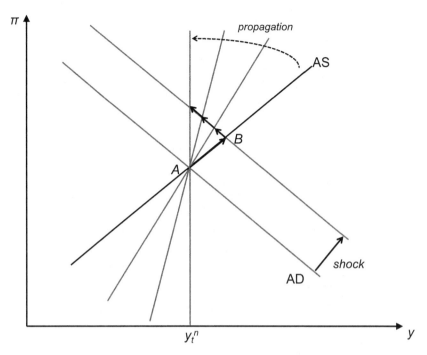

FIGURE 4.5
Adjustment dynamics after a very persistent aggregate demand shock. Output gradually returns to its natural level, but inflation is lastingly higher.

and

$$d\left(w_t - p_t\right) = \left(\frac{1}{\xi\left(1 + \sigma\gamma\kappa\right)}\right) d\theta_t > 0.$$

Over time, these variables gradually revert to their long-run value following the counterclockwise rotation of the AS curve (toward the LRAS curve) and the reversion of the AD curve towards its initial position. Christiano, Eichenbaum, and Evans (2005) have studied empirically the dynamics of macroeconomic variables after such a monetary policy shock in the United States. Their analysis confirms the response predicted by the model—that is, an initial rise in inflation, output, real wages, and employment followed by a gradual reversion to the mean. This outcome is the modern version of David Hume's quote that opens this chapter.

4.3 EFFECT OF AN AGGREGATE SUPPLY SHOCK

4.3.1 THEORETICAL IMPACT

An *aggregate supply shock* is a shock to the natural level of output y_t^n, meaning to z_t or μ^* (we are assuming throughout that the elasticity of labor supply ξ does not vary over time). Therefore a positive aggregate supply shock produces a downward shift of the AS curve in the (y, π) plane. Figure 4.6 shows that a transitory aggregate supply shock generates both a rise in output and a drop in inflation.

We may intuitively explain these adjustments as follows. At a given real wage $w_t - p_t$, a positive aggregate supply shock causes the optimal nominal price $p_t^* = w_t - p_t - z_t + \mu^*$ to fall (see chapter 3), by lowering either the optimal markup rate (μ^*) or the real marginal cost ($w_t - p_t - z_t$). The new optimal price is implemented by all firms that reoptimize their prices, which generates a drop in the price level and hence a decline in inflation ($\pi_t \downarrow$). The lowering of π_t pushes the monetary authority to adopt an expansionary monetary policy ($r_t \downarrow$), in accordance with the MP curve, which stimulates aggregate demand and output ($y_t \uparrow$). The effect of the shock on y_t is all the more pronounced when the slope of the AD curve in the (y, π)

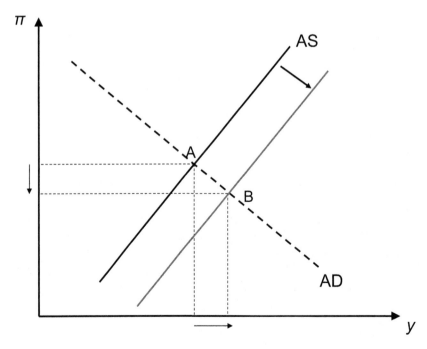

FIGURE 4.6

Impact of a transitory aggregate supply shock. A favorable supply shock shifts the AS curve downward, which moves the equilibrium along the AD curve; output rises and inflation falls.

plane (meaning $-1/\sigma\gamma$) is small in absolute value. To expand a little, the effect of the shock is greater when:

- the sensitivity of the real interest rate to inflation (γ) is high, such that the central bank responds to the disinflation triggered by the shock with a strong stimulus to aggregate demand;

- the sensitivity of aggregate demand to the interest rate (σ) is high, so that the monetary stimulus effectively stimulates demand and output.

The southwest and southeast quadrants of figure 4.3 illustrate the effect of a transitory aggregate supply shock on inflation and output in the two extreme cases mentioned above—namely, fully optimized ($\omega = 0$) versus fully indexed ($\omega = 1$) prices. In the former case there is no impact on output or inflation (graphically, the aggregate supply shock shifts a horizontal line to the right), while in the latter case, the effect of the shock is maximal. The former outcome is key and can be understood as follows. When prices are all indexed, aggregate supply is entirely determined by aggregate demand, and hence an aggregate supply shock is without any effect on output in the short run. It follows that at a given level of aggregate demand, an aggregate supply shock that increases labor productivity *necessarily leads firms to use less labor*. Now let us examine the bearing of this outcome outside the limit case of the full rigidity in nominal prices.

4.3.2 Effect of a Productivity Shock

When all prices are indexed rather than optimized, then aggregate demand fully determines aggregate supply, and thus a higher level of productivity reduces the need for labor input. In other words, a shock that raises productivity reduces employment. Is this outcome a by-product of extreme nominal rigidities? Even more importantly, is it observed in the data?

Galí and Rabanal (2005) and Basu, Fernald, and Kimball (2006) evaluated empirically the effect of rising productivity on output and employment in the United States over the period 1948–2002. They found that a rise in productivity generates:

- in the short run, an increase in output but a transitory drop in employment;

- in the longer run, a gradual reversion of employment towards its level before the shock.

The AS-AD model offers a natural explanation for these effects. In the long run, we know that employment is at its natural level, which is independent of z_t (see equation (3.11) in chapter 3):

$l^n = -\xi\mu^*$.

As a consequence, if actual employment l_t deviates from l^n in the short run, it must necessarily return to it in the long run. What happens in the shorter run? The shock on z_t does not modify θ_t (see equation (2.23), which summarizes the determinants of θ_t), but only y_t^n ($= z_t - \xi\mu^*$). According to equation (4.3), the variation in current output induced by the productivity shock is given by:

$$dy_t = \left(\frac{\sigma\gamma\kappa}{1+\sigma\gamma\kappa}\right) dy_t^n$$

$$= \left(\frac{\sigma\gamma\kappa}{1+\sigma\gamma\kappa}\right) dz_t > 0.$$

On the other hand, since in the aggregate we have $y_t = z_t + l_t$, the variation of employment in the short run is given by:

$$dl_t = dy_t - dz_t$$

$$= -\left(\frac{1}{1+\sigma\gamma\kappa}\right) dz_t \leq 0,$$

with a strict inequality as soon as we depart from the natural equilibrium. Thus the AS-AD model generates exactly the short-run effects of productivity shocks on employment and output as documented by Galí and Rabanal (2005) and Basu, Fernald, and Kimball (2006). The explanation for this phenomenon is that in the presence of nominal rigidities, short-run output is, at least marginally, constrained by demand. In this context, an increase in productivity permits serving this demand with less labor input, and hence equilibrium employment must fall. The negative effect of the productivity shock on employment is all the more pronounced when:

- nominal rigidities (ω) are significant, such that aggregate supply is strongly constrained by aggregate demand;

- the responsiveness of monetary policy to inflation (γ) is weak, such that the central bank does not aggressively counter the disinflation triggered by the shock with an active demand stimulus;

- the reaction of private demand to monetary policy (σ) is weak, such that the drop in the real interest rate set by the central bank that follows upon the productivity shock has little effect on aggregate demand.

4.4 Nominal Rigidities and the Nature of Business-Cycle Fluctuations

4.4.1 A Decomposition of Output

The economy described up to now carries two distinct distortions relative to a situation of perfect competition. First of all, *imperfect competition* implies that there is underproduction (and thus underutilization of labor input), and this is true even in the flexible-price, natural equilibrium (see equations (3.10) and (3.11)). On top of this inefficient level of output and of employment, *nominal price rigidities* slow down the reversion of actual output y_t toward its natural level y_t^n after a macroeconomic shock.

Now we are going to break down output y_t so as to clearly separate the effects of these two distortions, which will enable us to better understand how macroeconomic shocks are propagated over the business cycle. To do so, let us return to the expression for natural output given by equation (3.10):

$$y_t^n = z_t - \xi \mu^*.$$

If the firms in the economy were operating under *perfect competition*, then the markup μ^* would be zero, so that natural output would be at its maximum possible value y_t^{cp} (where *cp* stands for competitive):

$$y_t^{cp} = z_t,$$

By using these last two expressions, we see that we may decompose output y_t as follows:

$$y_t = \underbrace{y_t^{cp}}_{\text{efficient output}} - \underbrace{\xi \mu^*}_{\text{monopolistic distortion}} + \underbrace{(y_t - y_t^n)}_{\text{output gap}}.$$

This breakdown of output shows that its fluctuations may be traced back to three factors. Shocks to labor productivity will in general affect output because they change efficient output. The monopolistic distortion $\xi \mu^*$ implies that the economy always produces below efficient output, even when prices are perfectly flexible; hence changes in the degree of competition (μ^*) will also affect actual output. Finally, the presence of nominal rigidities implies that output y_t will in general differ from natural output y_t^n after a macroeconomic shock. Figure 4.7 illustrates graphically this decomposition. Under the assumption that the competitive distortion $\xi \mu^*$ is acyclical (the degree of competition being little modified at the business-cycle

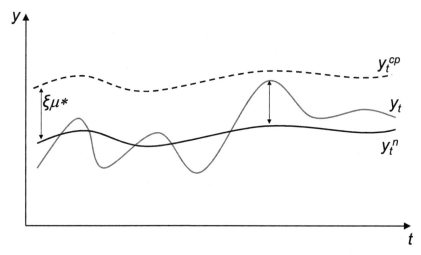

FIGURE 4.7
The nature of macroeconomic fluctuations. The natural level of output is lower than the output level that would prevail in a competitive market. Aggregate supply shocks cause natural output to vary, while both demand and supply shocks cause the output gap to vary.

frequency), this distortion translates output downward relative to its efficient level. Cyclical fluctuations in actual output y_t come from those of efficient output y_t^{cp} (due to aggregate supply shocks) as well as those of the output gap (due to aggregate demand and supply shocks under nominal rigidities).

4.4.2 THE CYCLICALITY OF MARKUPS
Another way of understanding the nature of fluctuations in the presence of nominal rigidities is to examine the behavior of the average markup rate in the economy. We show below that the short-run equilibrium model developed so far implies that the average markup rate in the economy is *procyclical* in response to aggregate supply shocks but *countercyclical* in response to aggregate demand shocks. While the countercyclicality of average markups is somewhat model-specific and need not hold in all specifications of aggregate supply—as the next chapter illustrates—this property sheds light on both the internal workings of the model and the way it can be evaluated in the data.

The cyclicality of the average markup results from the reaction of the marginal cost of production to aggregate supply and demand shocks. While a favorable productivity shock lowers the marginal cost of production, a favorable aggregate demand shock increases it, in a context in which some firms cannot completely pass through a higher production cost to their selling price. To see this most clearly, let us formally study the behavior of the average markup rate in the economy. We know that a proportion $1 - \omega$ of firms sell at the optimal price and are thus able to extract the optimal markup rate μ^* even after a macroeconomic shock. The other firms do not adjust their prices optimally but follow an indexation rule (see equation (3.13)). For these latter firms, the *ex post* markup (meaning the nominal selling price minus the nominal marginal cost) is *endogenous* and given by:

$$\tilde{\mu}_{i,t} = p_{i,t} - w_t + z_t$$
$$= p_{i,t-1} + \pi_{t-1} - w_t + z_t.$$

We have assumed that the firms that do not adjust their prices optimally are drawn at random from the population of firms. Consequently, the average markup rate of these firms is given by:

$$\tilde{\mu}_t = p_{t-1} + \pi_{t-1} - w_t + z_t.$$

The average markup rate in the economy as a whole ($\bar{\mu}_t$) is the weighted average of the markup rates of firms that optimally adjust their prices and those of firms that adopt the indexation rule:

$$\bar{\mu}_t = (1 - \omega)\mu^* + \omega\tilde{\mu}_t.$$

One may show (and this is the purpose of Exercise 4.5.3) that the previous expression implies:

$$\bar{\mu}_t \quad = \quad \mu^* \quad - \quad \frac{\omega}{\xi}\left(y_t - y_t^n\right). \tag{4.5}$$

$$\underset{\text{average markup rate}}{\uparrow} \qquad \underset{\text{optimal markup rate}}{\uparrow} \qquad \underbrace{}_{\text{impact of the output gap}}$$

In the natural equilibrium (which is such that $y_t = y_t^n$ for all t), the markup of all firms is equal to the optimal markup μ^*, which is therefore the economywide markup (whatever the macroeconomic shocks that hit the economy). In the presence of nominal rigidities, output y_t generally differs from natural output y_t^n and the average markup $\bar{\mu}_t$ is decreasing in the output gap $y_t - y_t^n$. For example, after a positive aggregate demand shock that raises $y_t - y_t^n$, the labor market tightens, which leads to a hike in the real wage. The firms that optimize their selling price are able to maintain their markup at μ^*, but the other firms undergo a compression of their markups that pulls down the average markup rate $\bar{\mu}_t$. On the other hand, a positive aggregate supply shock raises y_t^n but typically leads (in the presence of nominal rigidities) to a delayed adjustment of y_t, so that the output gap $y_t - y_t^n$ falls. This shock reduces the marginal production cost of all firms, including those that do not adjust their price optimally, which see their realized markup increase. In that case, since the markup of firms that do optimize their prices is μ^*, the average markup rate must necessarily increase.

4.5 EXERCISES

4.5.1 RESPONSE OF THE EXCHANGE RATE TO AN AGGREGATE DEMAND SHOCK

Consider the following (static) macroeconomic model, which summarizes the behavior of a small open economy operating under a floating exchange rate regime, but with *imperfect* capital mobility:

IS : $y = \theta + b - kr$;

MP : $r = r^W + \gamma \left(p - \bar{p}\right)$;

XM : $b = \mu(y^W - y) + \sigma \left(e + p^W - p\right)$;

BP : $b = \phi(r^W - r)$.

In those expressions y is aggregate demand (equal to output in equilibrium), b net exports, r the real interest rate, p the average price level, $\bar{p}$ its (constant) target value, and e the nominal exchange rate. The world interest rate is r^W, and y^W and p^W denote respectively output and the price level in the rest of the world. All these variables are in logarithm, except for r and r^W, which are expressed in levels. The assumption of a small open economy implies that y^W, p^W, and r^W are not affected by the shocks that hit the domestic economy. Thus we consider them as constant and we will adopt the normalization $y^W = p^W = 0$. The constant parameters k, γ, μ, σ, and φ are all positive, and θ is an exogenous demand shock that shifts aggregate demand independently of net exports. Finally, we assume (without loss of generality) that $\bar{p} = 0$. Equation XM determines net exports, and equation BP the balance of payments; net exports are necessarily equal to private capital outflows, which depend on the real interest rate differential $r^W - r$ and on the degree of capital mobility $\varphi \geq 0$.

Domestic output is produced by a continuum of firms i, $0 \leq i \leq 1$, endowed with the production function $Q_i = L_i$, where L_i is the quantity of labor utilized by firm i. Each firm faces the demand function

$$Y_i = Y \left(P_i/P\right)^{-2} ,$$

where P_i is firm i's selling price (in level), $P = e^p$, and $Y = e^y$. Labor is supplied by the representative household according to the labor supply function

$$L^s = 2W/P,$$

where W is the nominal wage. Once again, we assume that the economy stays in the vicinity of the symmetric equilibrium, such that the average of log prices is approximately equal to the log of the average price:

$$p \simeq \int_0^1 p_i di.$$

1. Use equations IS and BP to write the relation between the real interest rate r and aggregate demand y, and explain how and why this relation depends on the capital mobility parameter φ.

2. Compute and explain intuitively the effect of an aggregate demand shock $d\theta > 0$ on output y, the price level p, the real interest rate r, net exports b, the nominal exchange rate e, and the real exchange rate (denoted ϵ) when prices are fixed at $p = \bar{p}$.

3. Assume henceforth that prices are partially rigid. All firms have set the price p_{-1} in the period before the shock, and only a fraction $(1 - \omega)$ adjust their selling price optimally after the current shock $d\theta$. The other firms adopt the usual indexation rule $p_i = p_{i,-1} + \pi_{-1}$, where π_{-1} is the inflation rate between the previous two periods.

(a) Compute the optimal selling price of a firm p^* as a function of the nominal wage (in log) w, and derive from this the natural level of output y^n.

(b) Write down and explain the aggregate supply relation that links output y to the change inflation $\pi - \pi_{-1}$.

(c) Show that in the general case where $0 \leq \omega \leq 1$ an aggregate demand shock $d\theta > 0$ generates a nominal appreciation if and only if:

$$\phi\gamma > \sigma + \mu \left(\frac{\omega}{1 - \omega} \right).$$

Explain this result intuitively.

4.5.2 Effect of Energy Prices on Natural Output

Suppose that the production function of firm i is given by

$$Q_{i,t} = \sqrt{E_{i,t} L_{i,t}},$$

where $E_{i,t}$ and $L_{i,t}$ are respectively the quantity of energy and labor used in the production of good i in period t. The *real* price of energy (i.e., in terms of units of goods) is assumed to be exogenous and given by $\tilde{P}_t^E$. The total cost associated with the use of $L_{i,t}$ units of labor and $E_{i,t}$ units of energy is thus given by

$$C_{i,t} = \frac{W_t}{P_t} L_{i,t} + \tilde{P}_t^E E_{i,t},$$

where W_t is the nominal wage and P_t the nominal price level.

Finally, household labor supply is given by

$$L_t^s = \sqrt{W_t/P_t}.$$

In this problem, we are interested in the way in which variations of $\tilde{P}_t^E$ modify the optimal composition of inputs, the real marginal cost of firms, and ultimately the natural level of output.

1. Show that the cost minimization problem of the firm gives

$$\frac{E_{i,t}}{L_{i,t}} = \frac{W_t/P_t}{\tilde{p}_t^E},$$

and explain this result. Derive from this that the real marginal cost of production (in log) is

$$\psi_t = \frac{1}{2}\left(w_t - p_t + \tilde{p}_t^E\right) + \ln 2,$$

and provide an intuitive explanation of this expression.

2. Using you answers to question 1, show that the demand for labor by firm i is given by

$$l_{i,t} = y_{i,t} - \frac{1}{2}\left(w_t - p_t - \tilde{p}_t^E\right).$$

Derive the total demand for labor l_t^d and show that the equilibrium real wage is given by

$$w_t - p_t = y_t + \frac{1}{2}\tilde{p}_t^E.$$

Why is the equilibrium real wage increasing in energy prices?

3. Show that the AS curve has the same form as that derived in chapter 3 (section 3.4), except that the natural level of output is now given by

$$y_t^n = -2\left(\mu^* + \ln 2\right) - \frac{3}{2}\tilde{p}_t^E,$$

and discuss this result.

4.5.3   Computation of the Economywide Markup

Derive equation (4.5) from the expression for $\tilde{\mu}_t$ and the analysis of chapter 3, section 3.4.

4.5.4   Propagation of Aggregate Shocks with a Financial Accelerator

Consider the following macroeconomic model. The AS and MP curves are given by:

$$\mathbf{AS}: \pi_t = \pi_{t-1} + \kappa \left(y_t - y_t^n \right), \quad \kappa \geq 0;$$

$$\mathbf{MP}: r_t = \bar{r} + \gamma \left(\pi_t - \bar{\pi} \right), \quad \gamma \geq 0.$$

Suppose that households lend to banks at the real interest rate r_t, but that firms borrow from banks at the real interest rate $r_t^b > r_t$. The intermediation margin $r_t^b - r_t$ covers the various costs associated with lending to firms (such as evaluating and verifying their solvency, checking the quality of their investments, and so on) and the perceived risk of the firm going bankrupt. Since this risk is higher in recession than in expansion, the intermediation margin is decreasing in the level output y_t. This margin is also decreasing in the efficiency of the banking sector, denoted as β. To be more specific, we assume here that:

$$r_t^b - r_t = \alpha - \beta - v.y_t, \quad \beta > 0, \; 0 < v < 1.$$

Finally, assume that consumption demand is insensitive to the real interest rate, so that only investment demand is sensitive to it. Thus the IS curve is given by:

$$\mathbf{IS}: y_t = \theta_t - \sigma^F r_t^b, \quad 0 < \sigma^F < 1.$$

Analyze the response of the economy to transitory aggregate supply (y_t^n) and financial (β) shocks and explain the propagation mechanisms at work.

UNEMPLOYMENT FLUCTUATIONS

At any moment of time, there is some level of unemployment which has the property that it is consistent with equilibrium in the structure of real wage rates. At that level of unemployment, real wage rates are tending on the average to rise at a "normal" secular rate, i.e., at a rate that can be indefinitely maintained so long as capital formation, technological improvements, etc., remain on their long-run trends. A lower level of unemployment is an indication that there is an excess demand for labor that will produce upward pressure on real wage rates. A higher level of unemployment is an indication that there is an excess supply of labor that will produce downward pressure on real wage rates. The "natural rate of unemployment," in other words, is the level that would be ground out by the Walrasian system of general equilibrium equations, provided there is imbedded in them the actual structural characteristics of the labor and commodity markets, including market imperfections, stochastic variability in demands and supplies, the cost of gathering information about job vacancies and labor availabilities, the costs of mobility, and so on.

—Milton Friedman (1968)

Fluctuations in unemployment, along with fluctuations in output and inflation, are the most tangible manifestation of the business cycle. And they are also undoubtedly the most costly socially. In a recession, an increase in unemployment reflects two underlying phenomena, whose relative importance may vary from one country to another. First, a growing number of employees lose their jobs (either due to outright firing or a nonrenewal of a short-term contract), and second, those who are unemployed tend to remain unemployed longer (due to the freeze in hiring). The two phenomena have painful consequences for the people affected. Empirical studies show that the dismissal of an employee translates into not only a permanent income loss (a person who has lost his or her job spends years recovering the salary earned previously, not to mention running the risk of long-term unemployment), but also an increased employment instability, a degraded state of health (including a higher mortality rate), and worse prospects for the dismissed employee's children.[1] The drop in recruitment that is observed during a recession is also costly. Apart from putting a brake on the return to employment of people having lost their jobs, it slows down the integration of newcomers into the labor market (primarily the young), with long-lasting consequences for their careers and income prospects. Entering into the active population at a bad time in the business cycle therefore reverberates on one's whole professional life.

In the three preceding chapters, we have studied macroeconomic fluctuations and their impact on employment, but there was no discussion of *involuntary unemployment* per se, since each household freely adjusted its working time as a function of the real wage offered by the firms. This representation of the labor market is a useful abstraction, especially thanks to its simplicity. It is inadequate, however, if one is trying to understand the dynamics of unemployment, and how it depends on the underlying worker flows across different employment statuses (employment versus unemployment).

This chapter is organized into three sections. The first introduces the main concepts necessary to understand worker flows and presents some empirical data on the breadth and cyclicality of these flows. The second section develops a theory of involuntary unemployment according to which unemployment depends on the worker flows resulting from firms' job creation as well as the regular destruction process of existing employment relationships. The representation of the labor market that we will use throughout the chapter will be that of a market with *search and matching*, in which the unemployed and employers seek each other and, unless they are exceptionally lucky, do not find each other immediately.[2] Unlike the usual Walrasian market (such as the market for hours worked in chapter 3), the fact that one has to invest time and resources to form employment relationships implies that there may coexist unsatisfied supplies and demands on both sides of the market (with unemployed workers on one side and unfilled vacancies on the other side). Finally, section 5.3 integrates this theory of involuntary unemployment into the aggregate supply block of the AS-AD model. This will enable us to study the impact of aggregate supply and demand shocks on worker flows and equilibrium unemployment.

---

1. See Davis and Von Wachter (2011) for a review of the empirical literature on the impact of job loss.

2. The representation of the labor market as a search-and-matching market was developed by Peter Diamond, Dale Mortensen, and Christopher Pissarides, who received the Nobel Prize in Economic Sciences in 2010 for this work. See Mortensen and Pissarides (1994, 1999) for a complete formulation of the model.

5.1 THE DYNAMICS OF UNEMPLOYMENT AND WORKER FLOWS: EMPIRICAL ASPECTS

5.1.1 UNEMPLOYMENT RATE AND WORKER FLOWS

According to the International Labour Organization (ILO), an unemployed person is an individual who is *without work, currently available for work, and seeking work*. Figure 5.1 illustrates the diverse trajectories of unemployment from one OECD country to another.[3]

To understand the dynamics of unemployment and to apply the appropriate macroeconomic policies, it is not enough to consider variations in employment from one period to another, meaning the *net* worker flow between employment and unemployment. We have to examine the *gross* worker flows, as they result from all the individual transitions between employment and unemployment in the economy. These gross flows are one order of magnitude larger than the net flow. As an example, over the year 2012 the number of unemployed workers in the United States fell by 200,000 on average every month, but this net flow hides the fact that *in an average month, about 3,200,000 unemployed workers found jobs while 3,000,000 lost theirs*. The scope of and variations in gross worker flows thus represent a macroeconomic phenomenon of first-order importance, which would be disguised by a representation of the labor market centered on the mere variation in employment (the net flow).

We may summarize the importance of gross worker flows between different statuses in the labor market by two rates—namely the entry rate into, and the exit rate from, unemployment. The *entry rate into unemployment* over a certain period of time (for example, one month) is given by:

$$s_t = \frac{\text{flow of employed workers falling into unemployment during period } t}{\text{employment at the beginning of period } t}.$$

In summary, the monthly entry rate into unemployment is the average probability of an individual who is currently employed falling into unemployment during the coming month. Symmetrically, we define the *exit rate from unemployment* (or in an equivalent way, the *job-finding rate*) as follows:

$$f_t = \frac{\text{flow of unemployed workers finding a job during period } t}{\text{unemployment at the beginning of period } t}.$$

3. Note that the United States and United Kingdom have not always shown the performances that they show today with respect to unemployment. The United Kingdom had an unemployment rate higher than that of the countries of continental Europe until the middle of the 1990s and the United States, until the middle of the 1980s.

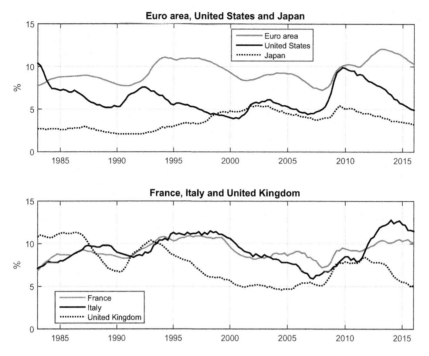

FIGURE 5.1
Unemployment rates.
Sources: Eurostat and AWM database.

This rate therefore corresponds to the average probability that an individual who is currently unemployed will find a job during the coming month. Since the labor market is heterogeneous, we may further disaggregate the rates of entry and exit in order to focus on specific categories of the population (say, depending on the qualification). Nevertheless, in the context of our macroeconomic analysis we are going to focus on *average* rates of transition across employment statuses, which is acceptable as a first approximation. Finally, note that alongside the rates of entry into and exit from unemployment, we find similar rates of entry into and exit from the active population (i.e., the sum of employed workers and those seeking a job). Here we are ignoring the latter type of transitions, for the reason that the rate of participation in the labor market is much less cyclical than the unemployment rate (see chapter 1).[4]

4. This is not substantiated everywhere and all the time. In the United States the participation rate in the labor market dropped sharply in 2008–2009, reflecting the rapid increase in the number of discouraged workers—meaning those who stopped actively looking for a job and who thereby were no longer counted as unemployed.

In what follows, we will denote as u_t the unemployment rate at the end of period t, so that the unemployment rate at the start of period t is u_{t-1}. By definition, the gross entry flow into unemployment—meaning the number of individuals losing their jobs in the course of period t—is given by $s_t(1 - u_{t-1})$. Symmetrically, the gross exit flow from unemployment—meaning the number of unemployed workers finding a job in the course of period t—is given by $f_t u_{t-1}$. The relation that ties the transition rates f_t and s_t to the gross flows $s_t(1 - u_{t-1})$ and $f_t u_{t-1}$, and then to the net entry flow into unemployment $\Delta u_t = u_t - u_{t-1}$, is given by:

$$\underbrace{u_t - u_{t-1}}_{\text{net entry flow}} = \underbrace{\underset{\uparrow}{s_t} \times \underset{\uparrow}{(1 - u_{t-1})}}_{\text{gross entry flow}} - \underbrace{\underset{\uparrow}{f_t} \times \underset{\uparrow}{u_{t-1}}}_{\text{gross exit flow}}. \qquad (5.1)$$

entry rate · employment · exit rate · unemployment

This equation shows that, at any given unemployment level at the start of period t (u_{t-1}), the dynamics of gross flows ($s_t(1 - u_{t-1})$, $f_t u_{t-1}$) and of unemployment (u_t) are entirely summarized by the transition rates f_t and s_t. Thus from an empirical standpoint, these transition rates offer a natural synthetic measure of the dynamics of the labor market.

Using $\bar{f}$ and $\bar{s}$ to denote the mean transition rates in the labor market, equation (5.1) implies that the mean unemployment rate is given by

$$\bar{u} = \frac{\bar{s}}{\bar{s} + \bar{f}}. \qquad (5.2)$$

Figure 5.2 shows the average values of the monthly rates of entry into, and exit from, unemployment in a sample of developed countries over the last forty years. The cluster of points is concentrated around a positively sloped straight line, since at any given average unemployment rate $\bar{u}$, equation (5.1) shows that an elevated value for the average exit rate $\bar{f}$ should be associated with an elevated value of the average entry rate $\bar{s}$ (such that the gross entry and exit flows offset each other). If all the countries in the sample shared the same unemployment rate $\bar{u}$, they would be located along a straight line in the (f, s) plane. But since average unemployment rates differ from one country to another, the pairs $(\bar{f}, \bar{s})$ form a cluster of points and not a straight line, with countries with high average unemployment rates being found north of countries with relatively lower average unemployment rates.

Figure 5.2 illustrates in a spectacular way an important dimension of the degree of rigidity of labor markets—that is, the mobility of the labor force between jobs. In southern Europe as well as in France and Germany, this mobility is low; employed individuals have little chance of losing their jobs but will spend time finding a new job if they do lose theirs. At the extreme opposite, the labor market is very flexible

FIGURE 5.2
Average monthly rates of entry into and exit from unemployment.
Source: Elsby, Hobijn, and Sahin (2013).

in the United States, with very high rates of entry into and exit from unemployment. By comparing the extreme points of the cluster, we see that the monthly probability of losing one's job is *eight times higher* in the United States than in Italy, but the probability of finding a new job is *ten times higher*! As a result, the average unemployment rate is much lower in the United States.

The measurement of the average entry and exit rates and their comparison between countries provides valuable information about the organization of labor markets and their relative rigidity—and possibly about the structural employment policies that would have to be conducted to make these markets more flexible.[5] However, in what follows we are going to focus on the *cyclical* dimension of worker flows and unemployment, in line with our study of macroeconomic fluctuations in previous chapters. The dynamic behavior of the transition rates will inform us about the relative contributions of the entry flow into, and exit flow from, unemployment to the cyclicality of the unemployment rate.

Figure 5.3 shows the evolution of the rates of entry into and exit from unemployment in the United States, Japan, France, and the United Kingdom from 1980 to 2015. The rate of exit from unemployment is (unsurprisingly) one order of

5. Flexibility is *not* synonymous with macroeconomic efficiency; since the reallocation of the labor force is costly (in terms of posting vacancies, training workers, etc.) and the functioning of the market is imperfect, there can (at least in principle) be some excess turnover relative to the social optimum.

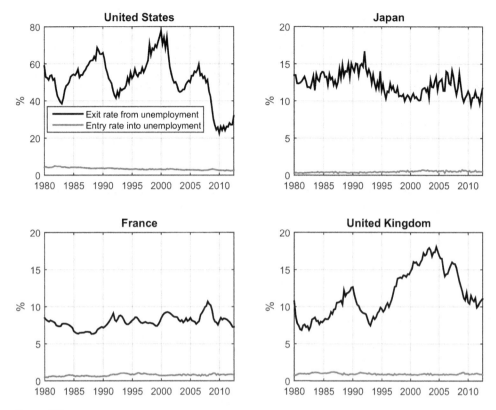

FIGURE 5.3
Monthly rates of entry into and exit from unemployment.
Source: Barnichon and Garda (2016).

magnitude above the rate of entry into unemployment. The employment level is in effect itself one order of magnitude above the level of unemployment, and the gross flows of entry and exit must necessarily almost offset each other, so that the resulting net flow be small relative to the underlying gross flows. The example of the United States illustrates the procyclical nature of the exit rate from unemployment, but to a lesser extent we also observe this procyclicality in the other countries. In France, the rate of entry into unemployment fluctuates just as significantly; we see in the figure that it shifted for example from 0.6 percent per month 1990 to 1 percent in 1993—almost a doubling. Elsby, Hobijn, and Sahin (2013) calculated the relative contributions of the cyclicality of the rates of entry into unemployment (s_t) and exit from unemployment (f_t) to the cyclicality of the unemployment rate (u_t) in a large number of OECD countries. They found that fluctuations in the unemployment rate are largely explained by those of the exit rate f_t. The relative contribution of the two transition rates may nevertheless vary substantially from one country to another. In the Anglo-Saxon countries, cyclical fluctuations of unemployment are dominantly explained by fluctuations in the exit rate from unemployment; in other words, in a recession unemployment increases not so much because firms fire more employees but mostly because they stop hiring new employees (so that those who are unemployed remain unemployed longer). In continental Europe and the Scandinavian countries, the contributions of f_t and of s_t to the cyclicality of unemployment are more balanced, with about 60 percent of the fluctuations in unemployment explained by those of f_t.

5.1.2   A STATIC APPROXIMATION OF THE UNEMPLOYMENT RATE

Before going any further, let us use our analysis of worker flows to arrive at an approximation for the unemployment rate that will prove useful for what follows. We are going to show that, under conditions that are empirically verified, the unemployment rate can be approximated by the following relation:

$$u_t \simeq \frac{s_t}{s_t + f_t}. \tag{5.3}$$

In other words, in a first approximation we may use for calculating the *actual* unemployment rate at any point in time an expression similar to that for the *average* unemployment rate (see equation (5.2) above). The measurement of the unemployment rate according to equation (5.3) (rather than (5.1)) is static—it only shows the current variables f_t and s_t and not the lagged variable u_{t-1}. Its simplicity will greatly facilitate the theoretical analysis of worker flows in the following section.

Under what conditions is the approximation (5.3) valid? Intuitively, it can only be valid if the past unemployment rate u_{t-1} has little influence on the current rate u_t, relative to the other determinants of u_t—namely f_t and s_t. We are going to see that this is precisely the case *when the gross flows are large relative to the net flow* $\Delta u_t = u_t - u_{t-1}$. In effect, a simple manipulation of equation (5.1) allows expressing current unemployment in the following form:

$$u_t = \underbrace{\frac{s_t}{f_t + s_t}}_{\text{negligible}} - \left(\frac{1 - f_t - s_t}{f_t + s_t} \right) \Delta u_t.$$

The second term on the right-hand side of the equation is of the same order of magnitude as the net flow of entry into unemployment Δu_t. The first term on the right-hand side—$s_t/(s_t + f_t)$—is equal to $s_t(1 - u_{t-1})/(f_t + \Delta u_t)$. When the net flow of entry into unemployment Δu_t is negligible relative to the gross flow of entry into unemployment $s_t(1 - u_{t-1})$, then the second term on the right-hand side of the equation becomes negligible but not the first term (which is of the order of $s_t(1 - u_{t-1})$), so that we have $u_t \simeq s_t/(f_t + s_t)$. This approximation is empirically satisfactory for all

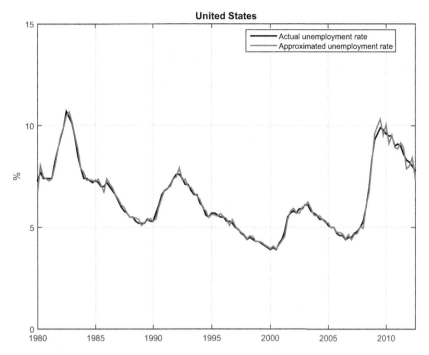

FIGURE 5.4
The static approximation of the unemployment rate.
Sources: Barnichon and Garda (2016) and the author's calculations.

the countries under consideration because gross worker flows are always one order of magnitude larger than net entry flows. Figure 5.4 illustrates the precision of this static approximation for the US economy.

5.1.3 THE BEVERIDGE CURVE

The AS-AD model studied in the preceding chapters enabled us to speak of employment but not really of unemployment—and certainly not of involuntary unemployment—since households freely chose their working time given the current real wage. The labor market was *Walrasian*—meaning that the labor supply curve emanating from household behavior intersected the labor demand curve generated by firm behavior, and the intersection of these curves determined both the economy-wide real wage and aggregate employment. An important feature of the Walrasian equilibrium is that once the equilibrium price (here, wage) is determined, then finding a trading counterpart (a worker, a firm) poses no difficulty—trade is immediate and without uncertainty about the nature of what is exchanged. This simplified representation of market processes, which is useful and satisfactory in many situations, becomes inadequate as soon as we take a closer look at the labor market and the determinants of unemployment. Indeed, the labor market is characterized by strong heterogeneities (of both potential employees and firms), while the information (about job vacancies, about the quality of workers, and so on) that is dispersed among the parties circulates only slowly and imperfectly. Consequently, workers and firms may spend a lot of time finding each other, and when they do, they form bilateral employment relationships that are costly to break since they will not be quickly re-formed.

A market that is characterized by the costly formation (in terms of time, physical resources, and so on) of bilateral relationships is called a *search-and-matching market*. The essential property of such a market is that *there generally exists rationed agents on both sides of the market* (which by construction is impossible in a Walrasian market). Thus, on the labor market, the unemployed and vacant jobs permanently coexist.[6] Throughout the cycle, the number of unemployed workers and the number of vacant jobs vary in opposite directions; in recessions there are few vacancies and many unemployed workers, and vice versa in expansions.

The decreasing relation between the unemployment rate and the number of vacancies over the business cycle is called the *Beveridge curve*. Figure 5.5, borrowed from Elsby , Michaels, and Ratner (2015), shows the Beveridge curve in the United States from the 1960s to the year 2013. In all subperiods under consideration there is a clear northwest-southeast movement of the equilibrium depending on the phase of the business cycle. The economy moves northwest when the economy is in expansion (so that firms have many openings available and unemployment is low) and southeast when it is in a recession (i.e., when firms have fewer openings available and consequently unemployment is high).

5.2 SEARCH, MATCHING, AND EQUILIBRIUM UNEMPLOYMENT

The analytical framework of the preceding chapters offers a rather general representation of the macroeconomic equilibrium but it does not permit a close analysis of the dynamics of unemployment and worker flows. In order to remedy this, this section develops a theory of unemployment that incorporates the specificities of the labor market that were stressed section 5.1. The analysis will rely on a formal presentation of this market as a search-and-matching market (Mortensen and Pissarides, 1994, 2000). This theory explicitly makes equilibrium unemployment dependent on the underlying worker flows and hence on the transition rates f_t and s_t. In particular, the rate of exit from unemployment f_t is made endogenous to the recruiting effort by firms (as measured by the number of vacancies that firms open up) and to the effectiveness of the matching process. In this way, any

---

6. Another typical example of a search-and-matching market is the housing market, in which there permanently coexist houses for sale and individuals seeking to buy a house.

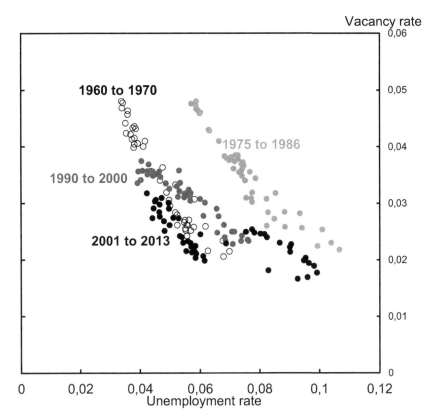

FIGURE 5.5
The Beveridge curve in the United States.
Source: Elsby, Michaels, and Ratner (2015).

macroeconomic shock that reduces the firm's expected profits from an employment relationship discourages new job openings and translates into a lower exit flow from unemployment. Although it is possible to extend this framework of analysis in order to produce endogenous fluctuations of the entry rate into unemployment s_t, here we will consider s_t as exogenous (but potentially time varying), for simplicity's sake.

5.2.1 MATCHING THE UNEMPLOYED TO VACANT JOBS

Let us assume that there exists a large number of households in the economy, which are all active and have one unit of (indivisible) labor to be supplied on the labor market. We will adopt the normalization that these households form a continuum of length 1, such that the number of unemployed workers is equal to the unemployment rate. In addition, we will ignore two possible sources of fluctuations in employment: variations in the participation rate in the labor market, and variations in hours worked per worker. These simplifications are acceptable to the extent that the participation rate and the number of hours worked per worker vary much less over the business cycle than does the unemployment rate (see chapter 1).

On the side of firms, we will assume that there exists a continuum of length 1 of firms indexed by i, where $0 \leq i \leq 1$. Thus, the economywide unemployment rate u_t is given by

$$u_t = 1 - \int_0^1 N_{i,t} \, di.$$

where $N_{i,t}$ is employment in firm i and in period t.

The worker flows operate in the following manner. At the start of period t, there are u_{t-1} unemployed workers (inherited from period $t-1$) and $1 - u_{t-1}$ employed workers. The unemployed are searching for jobs under our maintained assumption that that the real wage W_t/P_t offered by firms is higher than the unemployment benefit b. On the other hand, an exogenous fraction s_t of existing employment relationships gets destroyed in the course of period t.

Firm i opens $v_{i,t}$ vacancies in the course of the period. The total number of vacancies in the economy at time t is therefore given by

$$v_t = \int_0^1 v_{i,t} \, di. \tag{5.4}$$

Following the approach of Mortensen and Pissarides (1994), we will assume that the number of new employment relationships M_t created during period t is given by a matching function that takes the form

$$M_t = u_{t-1}^\alpha v_t^{1-\alpha}, \ 0 < \alpha < 1. \tag{5.5}$$

This matching function is not derived from an explicit and detailed modelling of how the labor market functions; instead, it is a reduced form that we expect to be able to summarize the essential features of the labor market.[7] The three important properties of the matching function (5.5) are the following:

- The number of new employment relationships that are created during period t (M_t) is increasing in both the number of job seekers (u_{t-1}) and in the number of vacancies (v_t). For any given number of vacancies, a high number of job seekers augments the number of potential candidates for each job, which

7. Recall that producer theory summarizes the production of goods by a production function, rather than describing in detail how the combination of inputs operates. The matching function plays exactly the same role in unemployment theory.

facilitates recruitment from the firms' point of view; symmetrically, for any given number of unemployed workers, a greater number of vacancies augments the probability that each of the unemployed will find a job.

- The matching function is concave in each of these arguments. The effect of one additional job seeker or one additional vacancy on the total number of matches goes down as the number of job seekers or vacancies increases; thus, job vacancies become harder and harder to fill as the extent of economywide job creation intensifies.

- The matching function has constant returns to scale, which in first approximation is consistent with the empirical observation of worker flows (see Petrongolo and Pissarides 2001). This property implies that a simultaneous doubling of the numbers of vacancies and job seekers would double the number of matches.

The exit rate from unemployment f_t is the ratio of the number of unemployed workers who find a job during the period over the number of job seekers (that is, to the number of unemployed workers at the start of the period). Thus we have

$$f_t = \frac{M_t}{u_{t-1}} = \left(\frac{v_t}{u_{t-1}} \right)^{1-\alpha}. \tag{5.6}$$

Symmetrically, the *hiring rate* of firms, λ_t, is defined as the proportion of vacancies in the economy that are filled during the period. The hiring rate is given by

$$\lambda_t = \frac{M_t}{v_t} = \left(\frac{v_t}{u_{t-1}} \right)^{-\alpha}. \tag{5.7}$$

The ratio v_t/u_{t-1} (the number of vacancies per unemployed person) is an index of *labor market tightness*. When v_t/u_{t-1} is high, which is the case during economic booms, the labor market is tight. The unemployed easily find a job (f_t is high) but firms have a hard time recruiting (λ_t is low). Conversely, in a recession, when v_t/u_{t-1} is low, then firms that wish to hire easily manage to do so (because there are many job seekers), whereas the unemployed have more difficulty in finding a job (because there are relatively few vacancies). By using equations (5.6) and (5.7) to eliminate v_t/u_{t-1}, we see that there exists a decreasing relation between λ_t and f_t:

$$\lambda_t = f_t^{-\frac{\alpha}{1-\alpha}}, \tag{5.8}$$

which reflects the fact that the periods when firms have a hard time hiring are precisely those when the unemployed easily find a job (and vice versa).

Modeling the exit flow from unemployment by means of the matching function in equation (5.5) naturally generates a theoretical Beveridge curve—that is, a decreasing relation between the number of unemployed workers (or equivalently, the unemployment rate) and the number of vacancies. In effect, since the gross exit flow from unemployment is $u_{t-1}^{\alpha} v_t^{1-\alpha}$ ($= f_t u_{t-1}$, by definition), we may write the net entry flow into unemployment as follows:

$$\Delta u_t = s_t (1 - u_{t-1}) - u_{t-1}^{\alpha} v_t^{1-\alpha}.$$

Since, as discussed above, the net worker flow Δu_t is negligible relative to the gross flows, we have $u_t \simeq u_{t-1}$ and thus $s_t (1 - u_t) \simeq u_t^{\alpha} v_t^{1-\alpha}$. This allows us to rewrite the preceding equation as:

$$v_t \simeq \left[\frac{s_t (1 - u_t)}{u_t^{\alpha}} \right]^{\frac{1}{1-\alpha}}.$$

This relation, represented in figure 5.6, gives the number of vacancies v_t that would have to be opened in the course of period t in order to sustain an unemployment rate of u_t, given the rate of job destruction s_t. The level of the Beveridge curve depends on s_t—a higher entry rate into unemployment implies that more vacancies must be available in the economy in order to sustain a given level of unemployment.

5.2.2   FIRM BEHAVIOR

Now let us describe the behavior of firms, notably with regard to their recruitment efforts. We will suppose (as in chapter 3) that firm i produces goods by means of the production function

$$Q_{i,t} = Z_t N_{i,t},$$

where $N_{i,t}$ is the number of employees in the firm after time t worker flows (hiring and separation) have taken place. Z_t is labor productivity, which is exogenous and common to all firms.

The rate of entry into unemployment s_t is, from the firms' standpoint, the probability of separating from an employee. We will therefore also use the term "separation rate" for s_t. On average, firm i loses $s_t N_{i,t-1}$ employees during period t, where $N_{i-1,t}$ is its level of employment at firm i at the beginning of period t (before worker flows have taken place). On the other hand, the firm opens $v_{i,t}$ vacancies in the course of period t, of which a share λ_t (which is the hiring rate) will be filled. Thus total employment in the firm after worker flows have taken place is given by

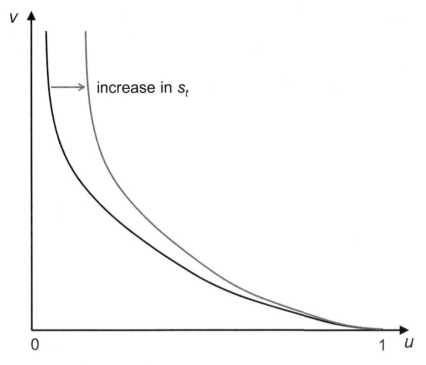

Figure 5.6
The theoretical Beveridge curve. The matching model generates a decreasing relation between the number of vacancies and the number of unemployed workers. This relation is shifted by shocks to the entry rate into unemployment.

$$N_{i,t} = \underbrace{(1 - s_t) \times N_{i,t-1}}_{\text{surviving employment relationships}} + \underbrace{\lambda_t \times v_{i,t}}_{\text{new employment relationships}}. \tag{5.9}$$

Let us be explicit here about the meaning of the last term in the equation, because it plays a central role in the theory of unemployment. The hiring rate λ_t depends on the *total* number of vacancies $v_t = \int v_{i,t} di$ (see equation (5.6)). Nevertheless, since firm i is small (in fact, atomistic) relative to the size of the economy as a whole (which contains a continuum of firms), its individual choice of $v_{i,t}$ does not affect v_t and therefore does not affect λ_t. Accordingly, at the individual level, each firm i considers the (linear) relation between the number of vacancies that it opens ($v_{i,t}$) and its current level of employment ($N_{i,t}$) as given; however, in equilibrium it is the vacancies opened by *all* firms ($v_t = \int v_{i,t} di$) that determine λ_t jointly with u_{t-1} (by equation (5.7)).[8]

---

8. The variable λ_t therefore has the same status as a market price under perfect competition—individual agents take λ_t as given, but it is the actions of all the agents that determine its equilibrium value.

The firm optimally chooses the number of vacancies to open, taking into account the expected costs and benefits that this choice implies. On the side of benefits, each filled vacancy generates, by definition, an output of Z_t. The firm faces two types of costs. The first cost is the real wage W_t/P_t, to be paid to every employed individual during the period of employment. The second cost is a *unit search cost* $c > 0$, which must be paid on each vacancy until it is filled. This cost, assumed to be constant for simplicity, synthesizes everything that the search for a workers implies for the firm—describing and advertising the job, reading and studying resumes, interviewing applicants, and so forth. If this cost were zero, then firms would all choose $v_{i,t} = \infty$ (as soon as $Z_t > W_t/P_t$), and there would be no unemployment.

As in chapter 3, we denote $\Pi_{i,t}$ as the nominal profit of firm i at time t, such that its real profit is $\Pi_{i,t}/P_t$. This last term is given by the sold output ($Z_t N_{i,t}$) net of wages payments ($W_t N_{i,t}/P_t$ in real terms) and of the search costs ($c v_{i,t}$):

$$\frac{\Pi_{i,t}}{P_t} = \underbrace{\left(Z_t - \frac{W_t}{P_t} \right)}_{\text{payoff per employee}} \times \underset{\underset{\text{number of employees}}{\uparrow}}{N_{i,t}} - \underbrace{c \times v_{i,t}}_{\text{total cost of vacancies}} .$$

In all generality, the firm chooses the value of $v_{i,t}$ that maximizes the present value of its real profits, meaning that the firm solves

$$\max_{\{v_{i,t+k}\}_{k=0}^{\infty}} \sum_{k=0}^{\infty} \left(\frac{1}{1+\rho^E} \right)^k \frac{\Pi_{i,t+k}}{P_{t+k}},$$

where $\rho^E > 0$ is the firm's discount rate, under the constraints given by equation (5.9):

$$N_{i,t+k} = \left(1 - s_{t+k} \right) N_{i,t-1+k} + \lambda_{t+k} v_{i,t+k}, \quad k = 0, 1, 2 \ldots$$

This general formulation of the firm's problem takes into account the fact that the vacancies it opens in period t may generate profit not only in period t but also in the succeeding periods, due to the persistence of employment relationships (as soon as $s_t < 1$). Here we will ignore these future benefits for the sake of simplicity. In other words, we will assume here that $\rho^E = \infty$, so that the firm simply chooses in each period t the value of $v_{i,t}$ that maximizes $\Pi_{i,t}/P_t$.

Using the constraint in equation (5.9) to eliminate $N_{i,t}$ from the expression of $\Pi_{i,t}/P_t$, and under the assumption that $\rho^E = \infty$, the firm's problem can be rewritten as follows:

$$\max_{v_{i,t}} \left(\left(Z_t - \frac{W_t}{P_t} \right) \lambda_t - c \right) v_{i,t} + \left(Z_t - \frac{W_t}{P_t} \right) (1 - s_t) N_{i,t-1}.$$

This formulation of the firm's problem summarizes the expected costs and benefits associated with each vacancy. The last term features the stock of employment inherited from the preceding period ($N_{i,t-1}$) as well as aggregate variables that are beyond the control of the individual firm (Z_t, W_t/P_t and s_t). Thus this term does not affect the optimal choice of $v_{i,t}$ by the firm; only the first term does. On the one hand, each vacancy opened by the firm requires paying the search cost c with certainty (that is, with probability 1). On the other hand, if the vacancy is filled, which occurs with probability λ_t, it then generates a benefit Z_t and a cost W_t/P_t. The net expected gain associated with a vacancy is therefore $(Z_t - W_t/P_t)\lambda_t$. As the program is linear in $v_{i,t}$, its solution is the following:

- If $(Z_t - W_t/P_t)\lambda_t - c > 0$, then the net expected profit from a vacancy exceeds the search cost and firm i chooses $v_{i,t} = \infty$.

- If $(Z_t - W_t/P_t)\lambda_t - c < 0$, then the search cost exceeds the expected benefit and so firm i chooses $v_{i,t} = 0$.

- If $(Z_t - W_t/P_t)\lambda_t - c = 0$, then the expected profit and the search cost exactly offset each other, such that firm i becomes indifferent to its choice of $v_{i,t}$.

With a linear program like this, the possibility of corner solutions (here, $v_{i,t} = \infty$ and $v_{i,t} = 0$) implies that one cannot consider the individual optimum of the firm independently of the equilibrium, which determines the value of λ_t. In the present case, equilibrium is given by a *free-entry condition*. At the individual level, each firm continues to open vacancies as long as the expected benefit exceeds the search cost, but ceases doing so when the net benefit is zero or negative. At the aggregate level, the recruitment rate λ_t depends on the behavior of all firms since, from equation (5.4) and (5.7),

$$\lambda_t = \left(\frac{\int v_{i,t} di}{u_{t-1}} \right)^{-\alpha}.$$

The free-entry equilibrium is reached when the expected net profit from a vacancy exactly offsets the search cost, so that no firm has an incentive to change the number of vacancies that it has posted. Thus, in equilibrium the hiring rate λ_t should satisfy

$$\underbrace{\left(Z_t - \frac{W_t}{P_t}\right) \times \lambda_t}_{\text{expected net benefit from a vacancy}} = \underset{\underset{\text{unit vacancy cost}}{\uparrow}}{c} \qquad (5.10)$$

and it is the $v_{i,t}$s of all the firms that adjust until this equality holds.[9] Using equation (5.8) we can rewrite the free-entry condition (5.10) as follows:

$$f_t = \left(\frac{Z_t - W_t/P_t}{c}\right)^{\frac{1-\alpha}{\alpha}}. \qquad (5.11)$$

This expression implies that the exit rate from unemployment *is increasing in the surplus earned by firms on each employment relationship* (the benefit Z_t minus the wage cost W_t/P_t) but *decreasing in the cost of a vacancy*. In effect, the matching process described above implies that f_t depends positively on the recruitment effort by firms as a whole (by equation (5.6)). This recruitment effort is all the more sustained when the unit cost of vacancies is low and when the net profit associated with one unit of labor in the firm is high.

5.2.3 WAGE SETTING

Equation (5.11) allows us to calculate the exit rate from unemployment in the economy as a function of c, α, and Z_t. We have assumed that c and α were constant parameters and that labor productivity Z_t was exogenous (although potentially subject to shocks, just as in chapter 4). But we have not yet said anything about the real wage W_t/P_t, which plays a central role in firms' incentives to hire and hence affects the level of, and fluctuations in, unemployment.

How is the real wage determined? In a competitive Walrasian labor market such as that postulated in chapter 3, the answer to this question is clear: the real wage is the one that equalizes the total supply of and demand for labor, and thus it is determined in equilibrium jointly with the aggregate quantity of labor. At this equilibrium, every economic agent considers the real wage as given. Specifically, a firm that would try to offer a wage lower than the equilibrium wage would see the other firms competing for its employees; ultimately the firm would have to align its

9. By inverting the expression of λ_t, we see that in the free-entry equilibrium we have

$$v_t = \int_0^1 v_{i,t} \mathrm{d}i = u_{t-1} \left(\frac{1}{\lambda_t}\right)^{\frac{1}{\alpha}} = u_{t-1} \left(\frac{Z_t - W_t/P_t}{c}\right)^{\frac{1}{\alpha}},$$

The free-entry condition determines the total number of vacancies v_t in the economy but not its distribution across firms (which is consistent with the fact that, by construction, in the equilibrium with free entry any particular firm is indifferent as to the specific number of vacancies that it opens).

own wages with the equilibrium wage, or else it would lose all its employees. Symmetrically, a firm that would pay a wage higher than the equilibrium wage would not cover its production cost and would go bankrupt.

In a matching market the wage is set completely differently for two reasons. First, the employment relationships that result from the matching process are bilateral, and hence the wage is bilaterally negotiated rather than determined by the economywide demand for and supply of labor. Second, an employment relationship cannot be broken without going through a search phase and therefore an income loss, for both parties. Hence the firm and the worker have a mutual interest in maintaining their relationship, and there is a whole set of wages—and not a unique one as in a Walrasian market—that is consistent with this mutual interest. To be more specific, the negotiated real wage W_t/P_t must be sufficiently high for the employee to have an interest in keeping its job (rather than resigning and receiving the unemployment benefits $b > 0$), and at the same time it must be sufficiently low for the firm to have an interest in keeping the employee (so W_t/P_t cannot be higher than Z_t). Any real wage W_t/P_t, such that $b \leq W_t/P_t \leq Z_t$, satisfies this criterion of *bilateral efficiency* and therefore constitutes a potential equilibrium wage.

Let us begin by considering the determination of the real wage and unemployment in the absence of nominal wage or price rigidities; that is, in the *natural* equilibrium. This equilibrium is the analogue of the natural equilibrium of chapter 3, except that the wage is negotiated between the parties and is not determined in a Walrasian market. We will assume that in the natural equilibrium the real wage is proportional to labor productivity:

$$\frac{W_t^n}{P_t} = \gamma Z_t, \tag{5.12}$$

where γ, $0 < \gamma < 1$, is assumed to be sufficiently close to 1 so that $W_t^n/P_t > b$. Note that in a Walrasian market the real wage would necessarily be proportional to productivity, with a coefficient of proportionality of 1 (since the real wage would be equal to the marginal product of labor [here, Z_t] at all times). The wage process specified in equation (5.12) preserves this property of the Walrasian wage while permitting a coefficient of proportionality below 1.

By definition, the assumption that the real wage in the natural equilibrium is proportional to labor productivity implies a perfect indexation of the nominal wage W_t^n to the price level P_t (i.e., $W_t^n = (\gamma Z_t) P_t$). Although this property may be verified in the long run, in the short run nominal wages are more rigid and inertial than the price level, notably because many wage contracts are long-term contracts specified in nominal terms. A simple and realistic way of introducing nominal wage rigidity is to consider a *delayed* indexation of the nominal wage upon the price level. More specifically, we will assume that the nominal wage

W_t is indeed indexed to a benchmark price, as is the case in the natural equilibrium; however, this benchmark price is not the current price level (P_t), but an indexed version of this price based on the past price level and the past inflation rate ($P_{t-1}(1 + \pi_{t-1})$). By replacing P_t by $P_{t-1}(1 + \pi_{t-1})$ in equation (5.12), we obtain the nominal wage:

$$W_t = \gamma Z_t P_{t-1}(1 + \pi_{t-1}).$$

As already discussed in chapter 3, nominal wage rigidity provides an alternative foundation for the AS curve (i.e., the increasing relation between the output gap and the variation of inflation), relative to nominal price rigidity. Because the two forms of nominal rigidity are substitutes, we completely abstract from nominal price rigidity in the remainder of the chapter.[10]

The nominal wage above implies that the *real* wage is given by:

$$\frac{W_t}{P_t} = \gamma Z_t \frac{1 + \pi_{t-1}}{P_t / P_{t-1}} = \gamma Z_t \left(\frac{1 + \pi_{t-1}}{1 + \pi_t} \right)$$

$$\simeq \gamma Z_t (1 + \pi_{t-1} - \pi_t). \tag{5.13}$$

where we are using equation (1.3) from chapter 1 to move from the first to the second line (under the assumption that π_{t-1} and π_t are small).

Equation (5.13) shows that in the presence of nominal rigidities the real wage is decreasing in the difference between the past and the current inflation rates. Intuitively, past inflation determines the perceived price trend and hence the benchmark price that serves to index the nominal wage; if a macroeconomic shock leads the price level P_t to rise above this benchmark price (so that realized inflation at time t turns out to be greater than its value at time $t - 1$), then the current real wage W_t/P_t falls mechanically.

5.2.4 THE NATURAL RATE OF UNEMPLOYMENT

The natural real wage γZ_t permits us to calculate the natural rate of exit from unemployment f_t^n (via equation (5.11)) and thereby the *natural rate of unemployment* u_t^n (via equation (5.3)). For the former we find

$$f_t^n = \left(\frac{(1 - \gamma) Z_t}{c} \right)^{\frac{1-\alpha}{\alpha}},$$

---

10. Exercise 5.4.1 at the end of the chapter studies a version of the search-and-matching model with nominal price rigidities.

and, for the latter,

$$u_t^n = \frac{s_t}{s_t + f_t^n} = \left[1 + \frac{1}{s_t}\left(\frac{(1-\gamma)Z_t}{c}\right)^{\frac{1-\alpha}{\alpha}}\right]^{-1}. \tag{5.14}$$

The natural rate of unemployment u_t^n is that which would prevail in the absence of nominal rigidities, and hence it only depends on *real* factors (recall Friedman's quote at the beginning of the chapter). More specifically, it depends positively on the separation rate s_t (which raises the flow of individuals going from employment to unemployment), on the unit search cost c (which deters firms from opening vacancies), and on the level of the real wage, as parameterized by γ (which reduces the net profit per employee accruing to the firm: $Z_t - W_t/P_t$). On the other hand, the natural rate of unemployment depends negatively on labor productivity Z_t, inasmuch as the latter boosts firms' incentives to hire.

5.2.5   THE ACTUAL RATE OF UNEMPLOYMENT

In the presence of nominal wage rigidities, the real wage is given by equation (5.13) rather than equation (5.12). It follows that the exit rate from unemployment is given by

$$f_t = \left[\frac{(1-\gamma(1+\pi_{t-1}-\pi_t))Z_t}{c}\right]^{\frac{1-\alpha}{\alpha}}. \tag{5.15}$$

The effect of current inflation π_t (relative to past inflation π_{t-1}) on the exit rate from unemployment f_t works through the real wage W_t/P_t. An increase in π_t reduces the real wage, which increases the net profit per labor unit $Z_t - W_t/P_t$ and therefore encourages firms to create more jobs.

The unemployment rate that results from this exit rate (at any given job-loss rate s_t) is given by

$$u_t = \frac{s_t}{s_t + f_t} = \left[1 + \frac{1}{s_t}\left[\frac{(1-\gamma(1+\pi_{t-1}-\pi_t))Z_t}{c}\right]^{\frac{1-\alpha}{\alpha}}\right]^{-1}. \tag{5.16}$$

The unemployment rate depends not only on the variables and parameters that affected the natural rate of unemployment (equation (5.14)), but also on the variation in inflation $\Delta\pi_t = \pi_t - \pi_{t-1}$, due to the effect of $\Delta\pi_t$ on the real wage and hence on the incentive to create jobs.

5.3 MACROECONOMIC EQUILIBRIUM

5.3.1 ASU-AD EQUILIBRIUM AND THE IMPACT OF MACROECONOMIC SHOCKS

We now are in a position to integrate unemployment and worker flows into the macroeconomic equilibrium. The aggregate demand block is not modified by the modeling of the labor market above, so it is still given by the usual AD curve (see chapters 2 and 4):

$$\textbf{AD} : y_t = \theta_t - \gamma\sigma\,(\pi_t - \bar{\pi})\,.$$

To assess the impact of macroeconomic shocks on unemployment, output, and inflation, we must complement the AD curve with an aggregate supply relation derived from the working of the labor market. To get to this relation, note first that total output results from the output of all the firms in the economy so that we have:

$$Y_t = Z_t \int_0^1 N_{i,t}\mathrm{d}i = Z_t N_t$$
$$= Z_t\,(1 - u_t)\,.$$

By taking logs and considering small variations of u_t in the vicinity of $u_t = 0$, we see that (see equation (1.3)):

$$y_t = z_t + \ln\,(1 - u_t) \simeq z_t - u_t.$$

Finally, by using the expression for u_t in equation (5.16), we obtain the following ASU curve:

$$\textbf{ASU} : y_t = z_t - \left[1 + \frac{1}{s_t}\left[\frac{(1 - \gamma\,(1 + \pi_{t-1} - \pi_t))\,\mathrm{e}^{z_t}}{c}\right]^{\frac{1-\alpha}{\alpha}}\right]^{-1}$$
$$= y(\underset{+}{\pi_t - \pi_{t-1}},\ \underset{+}{z_t},\ \underset{-}{s_t}),$$

which we call the ASU curve for *aggregate supply with unemployment*. The ASU curve establishes an increasing relation between output y_t and inflation π_t—a relation that is parameterized by past inflation π_{t-1} as well as by two types of aggregate shocks: to productivity z_t and to the rate of job destruction s_t. The positive relation between y_t and π_t comes from the fact that a hike in inflation π_t (above its past value π_{t-1}) reduces the real wage (due to nominal wage rigidities), which stimulates job creation and therefore increases output. The effect of labor productivity z_t is dual.

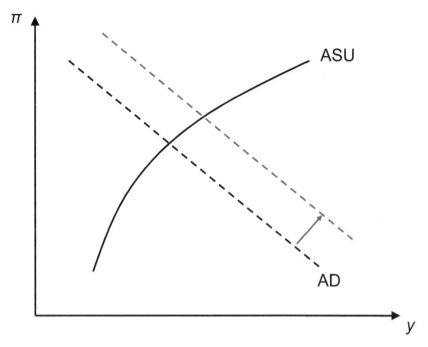

FIGURE 5.7
Impact of an aggregate demand shock in the ASU-AD model. An aggregate demand shock shifts the AD curve, which moves the equilibrium along the ASU curve.

On the one hand, a favorable productivity shock directly increases output at any given level of employment; on the other hand, the shock raises firms' surplus from a match. These two effects induce a downward shift of the ASU curve in the (y, π) plane after a hike in labor productivity. Finally, an increase in the destruction rate s_t (sometimes called a job reallocation shock) has a negative effect on output since it reduces the quantity of employment in period t. The macroeconomic equilibrium with unemployment, and the way it is shifted by aggregate supply and demand shocks, are represented in figures 5.7 and 5.8.

Let us start by studying the propagation of an *expansionary aggregate demand shock* (a hike in θ_t), which shifts the AD curve northeast in figure 5.7. As in the case of the basic AS-AD model in chapter 4, it is the fact that the ASU curve has positive but finite slope that allows a demand shock to influence output rather than to be passed through solely to inflation. The propagation mechanism of the shock is the following: the hike in demand generates inflationary pressures ($\pi_t \uparrow$), which, given nominal wage rigidities, contributes to lowering the real wage ($W_t/P_t \downarrow$). This drop in the real wage raises the firm surplus associated with an additional hiring ($Z_t - W_t/P_t \uparrow$), which boosts aggregate vacancy openings ($v_t \uparrow$). These vacancies contribute to tightening the labor market ($v_t/u_{t-1} \uparrow$), so that the exit rate from unemployment increases

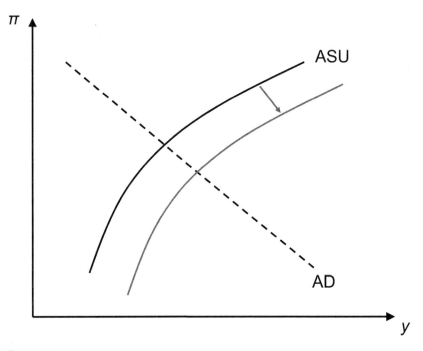

FIGURE 5.8
Impact of a productivity shock in the ASU-AD model. A productivity shock shifts the ASU curve, which moves the equilibrium along the AD curve.

($f_t \uparrow$) while the hiring rate falls ($\lambda_t \downarrow$). At any given separation rate s_t, the increase in f_t generates a drop in the equilibrium rate of unemployment ($u_t = s_t/(s_t + f_t) \downarrow$).

An *expansionary productivity shock*, such as represented in figure 5.8, is manifested by a downward shift of the ASU curve and hence by a shift of the equilibrium along the AD curve that raises output and reduces inflation. As stressed above, the productivity shock has two effects on output: one via the production function, and the other through the incentive to create jobs (via the term $Z_t - W_t/P_t$). Does this imply that the shock raises employment? Not necessarily, because the real wage also adjusts to the shock. Indeed, the shift of the ASU curve exerts a downward pressure on inflation ($\pi_t \downarrow$) which, given nominal wage rigidities, leads to an increase in the real wage ($W_t/P_t \uparrow$). The ultimate effect on unemployment depends on whether $Z_t - W_t/P_t$ ultimately rises or fall—that is, on how strong the response of W_t/P_t to the Z_t shock is. Thus, employment may increase or decrease after a productivity shock depending on the values of the parameters.

Finally, the ASU curve opens the door to a new type of shock relative to those considered in previous chapters: a shock on the separation rate s_t. An exogenous increase in s_t (not represented graphically) shifts the ASU curve upward and thus generates an economic contraction and excess inflation. The direct effect of the rise in s_t is to increase unemployment, but the hike in the inflation rate reduces the real wage, which stimulates job creation (via the effect on the firm surplus $Z_t -$ W_t/P_t). Thus, although unemployment increases, the effect of the rise in s_t on u_t is attenuated by nominal wage rigidities.

5.3.2 BACK TO THE CYCLICALITY OF MARKUPS

The ASU curve is an increasing relation between output and inflation, just like the basic AS curve studied in chapters 3 and 4. Moreover, these two aggregate supply curves shift in the same way after a productivity shock. Thus, from a purely descriptive point of view, the responses of output and inflation to aggregate demand or productivity shocks are qualitatively the same whether one uses the AS curve or the ASU curve (we get a joint increase in y_t and π_t in the case of an expansionary aggregate demand shock, but an increase in y_t and a drop in π_t in the case of an expansionary productivity shock). Nevertheless, beyond this surface resemblance, the ways in which these aggregate shocks propagate are different depending on which representation of aggregate supply is adopted. One manifestation of this difference between the two mechanisms is the cyclicality of markups and, more precisely, the response of the average markup rate to aggregate demand shocks. We saw in the previous chapter (section 4.2) that the AS curve (as derived in chapter 3) implied a countercyclical response of the average markup to aggregate demand shocks. The explanation for this countercyclicality lay in the procyclical behavior of the real marginal cost—after an increase in aggregate demand, the tension exerted on labor input led to a rise in the marginal cost of production, which firms passed through to their selling price if those firms could do so. However, firms that were constrained by nominal price rigidities (that is, firms that applied an indexation rule rather than implementing the optimal selling price), underwent a contraction in their markup that pulled downward the average, economywide markup. In the present chapter, on the contrary, nominal wage rigidities imply that the real wage, and thus the average unit cost of production faced by firms, falls after an expansionary aggregate demand shock (due to the rise in the price level in the face of an inertial nominal wage). Consequently, the average markup in the economy increases after such a shock. Formally, the average markup $\bar{\mu}_t^u$ is the proportional gap between the nominal selling price and the unit cost of production:

$$\bar{\mu}_t^u = \frac{P_t - W_t/Z_t}{W_t/Z_t}.$$

By using equation (5.13), we see that we may rewrite $\bar{\mu}_t^u$ as follows:

$$\bar{\mu}_t^u = Z_t \frac{P_t}{W_t} - 1 = \frac{1}{\gamma \left(1 + \pi_{t-1} - \pi_t\right)} - 1.$$

Thus, any aggregate shock that generates a hike in the current rate of inflation π_t above the past rate of inflation π_{t-1}, which is precisely the case with an expansionary aggregate demand shock, generates a rise in the average markup. This effect on the markup is thus the opposite of that obtained in the previous chapters under the assumption of nominal *price* rigidities.

Do empirical observations unambiguously determine which theory of aggregate supply is the more pertinent in practice—the one in chapter 3, based on monopolistic competition between firms and nominal price rigidities, or the one in this chapter, based on a non-Walrasian labor market with nominal wage rigidities? Not quite. Examination of the dynamics of nominal prices and wages reveals that the two adjust over time in an inertial way, such that there is no direct evidence specifically favoring one particular form of nominal rigidity. Empirical estimates of the response of the average markup to aggregate demand shocks, which in principle would settle the debate, is no more conclusive either: certain empirical studies reach the conclusion that demand shocks generate a procyclical response of unit production costs and a countercyclical response of markups, which lends credence to the aggregate supply mechanism of chapter 3; however, other studies produce the opposite result, which leans toward the mechanism described in this chapter.[11] If an empirical consensus is difficult to establish, this is probably because the two mechanisms, which are both plausible *a priori*, play out simultaneously in practice and are manifested more or less strongly according to the period under consideration and the data used in the estimation. In the rest of this book we will use the supply mechanism described in chapter 3 without making it interact with that described in this chapter. This choice is guided by the search for simplicity of exposition, and not by the belief that one of the two supply mechanisms would be intrinsically more important than the other.

5.4 EXERCISES

5.4.1 LABOR-MARKET MATCHING AND NOMINAL PRICE RIGIDITIES

In this problem we study the determination of equilibrium unemployment when labor market frictions interact with nominal price rigidities. The economy is populated by a continuum of size 1 of active households, each supplying one (indivisible) labor unit on the market, as well as a continuum of size 1 of firm i, with $0 \le i \le 1$. At the start of period t, u_{t-1} unemployed workers are seeking a job, while firms open v_t vacancies. The matching of the unemployed and vacancies is not instantaneous; the number of matches in period t M_t is given by

---

11. See Bils et al. (2018), Gu and Prasad (2018), and Nekarda and Ramey (2013) for recent contributions to this empirical debate.

$M(u_{t-1}, v_t) = \alpha \sqrt{u_{t-1} v_t}, \ \alpha > 0.$

At the same time, a fraction s_t of the population employed in period $t - 1$ loses jobs and so cannot work in period t.

Each firm i produces with the production technology $Q_{i,t} = N_{i,t}$, where $N_{i,t}$ is employment in firm i in period t. Firm i faces the demand function

$$Y_{i,t} = Y_t \left(\frac{P_{i,t}}{P_t} \right)^{-\eta}, \ \eta > 1,$$

where $P_{i,t}$ the selling price of good i and P_t the price level.

The firm may adjust its current employment level by opening $v_{i,t}$ vacancies, knowing that each vacancy costs c units of goods, while the probability of filling a vacancy is given by the hiring rate λ_t (which is endogenously determined in equilibrium). Finally, let us assume that the bargaining of workers and firms over the real wage implies that the real wage W_t/P_t is an increasing (linear) function of the exit rate from unemployment, denoted f_t:

$$W_t/P_t = \beta f_t, \ \beta > 0,$$

where W_t is the nominal wage. Aggregate demand is given by

$$y_t = \theta_t - \sigma \pi_t, \ \sigma > 0,$$

where θ_t is a demand parameter and π_t the inflation rate. Finally, we will make use of equation (5.3) to express current unemployment as a function of the current transition rates:

$$u_t \simeq \frac{s_t}{s_t + f_t}.$$

1. Explain the role and properties of the matching function and provide an interpretation of the wage function. Compute the exit rate from unemployment f_t and the hiring rate λ_t as a function of the ratio v_t/u_{t-1}, and then explain those expressions intuitively.

2. Let $N_{i,t-1}$ be the number of employees in firm i at the end of period $t - 1$, which is taken as given in period t when hiring decisions are made. Express $N_{i,t}$ as a function of $N_{i,t-1}$.

3. Compute the optimal selling price of firm i and discuss the expression obtained.

4. Compute the natural rate of unemployment—that is, the unemployment rate in the absence of nominal rigidities.

5. Now suppose that firms face nominal price rigidities. More precisely, at time t a fraction $1 - \omega$ of firms may optimally adjust their prices after a macroeconomic shock, while the other firms adopt the indexation rule

$$p_{i,t} = p_{i,t-1} + \pi_{t-1}.$$

Show that inflation is given by:

$$\pi_t = \pi_{t-1} + \frac{1 - \omega}{\omega} \left(\ln f_t - \ln f_t^n \right),$$

where f_t^n is the exit rate from unemployment in the natural equilibrium. Explain this relation.

6. How do the unemployment and inflation rates respond to an aggregate demand shock $d\theta_t > 0$ and to a labor reallocation shock $ds_t > 0$?

5.4.2   HYSTERESIS AND UNEMPLOYMENT

Consider an economy whose firms operate under monopolistic competition, as described in chapter 3. There is a continuum of length 1 of firms, indexed by i, $0 \leq i \leq 1$. The demand addressed to firm i in period t is given by (all the variables are expressed in logarithm)

$$y_{i,t} = y_t - \eta \left(p_{i,t} - p_t \right), \eta > 1,$$

where y_t is aggregate demand, p_t the price level, and $p_{i,t}$ the selling price of firm i. Aggregate demand is a function of economywide real balances:

$$y_t = m_t - p_t,$$

where m_t is the quantity of money, which is controlled by the central bank.
The production function of firm i is written as

$$y_{i,t} = n_{i,t},$$

where $n_{i,t}$ is the number of employees at this firm at time t. Since the number of firms is normalized to 1, total output and employment are $y_t = \int_0^1 y_{i,t} di$ and $n_t = \int_0^1 n_{i,t} di$, respectively. Nominal prices are perfectly flexible, so at every point in time firm i sets its selling price according to the usual markup rule (see chapter 3):

$$p_{i,t} = w_{i,t} + \mu^*,$$

where $w_{i,t}$ is the nominal wage in firm i. All firms are symmetric in period $t-1$ (i.e., $w_{i,t-1} = w_{t-1}$ and $n_{i,t-1} = n_{t-1}$ for all i).

1. Determine the labor demand of firm i as a function of the nominal wage at the firm ($w_{i,t}$) and the aggregate variables (m_t, p_t).

2. Assume that total labor supply at time t is $\bar{n}_t$. Show that the competitive nominal wage of period t is given by

$$w_t = m_t - \bar{n}_t - \mu^*,$$

and provide a brief discussion of this result.

3. Now assume that in every firm i, the nominal wage $w_{i,t}$ is set in period $t-1$ by a local labor union in a way to ensure that firm i will find it worthwhile to reemploy in period t its entire workforce $n_{i,t-1}$. When setting that wage (denoted $\bar{w}_{i,t}$) in period $t-1$, the union expects the money supply of period t to be m_t^e. Show that in period $t-1$ the union at firm i chooses the following wage:

$$\bar{w}_{i,t} = m_t^e - n_{i,t-1} + \mu^*.$$

(Hint: use the expected variables $n_{i,t}^e$ and p_t^e and exploit the fact that $p_t^e = \bar{w}_{i,t} + \mu^*$ since firms are symmetric.)

4. In period t the money supply is m_t, which is possibly different from what unions expected. Show that total employment at time t is given by:

$$n_t = n_{t-1} + \left(m_t - m_t^e \right),$$

and discuss this result.

5.4.3 PRODUCTIVITY AND UNEMPLOYMENT

Consider the following economy. Workers form a continuum of length 1, so that the number of unemployed workers is equal to the unemployment rate. Symmetrically, firms form a continuum of length 1, with every firm indexed by i, $0 \le i \le 1$. Firm i produces a specialized good in quantity $Q_{i,t}$ by means of the production function

$$Q_{i,t} = Z_t N_{i,t},$$

where Z_t is labor productivity (common across firms) and $N_{i,t}$ is employment at firm i. Every firm i is the sole supplier of good i and, as a result, is able to charge a markup over marginal cost. As a result, the optimal real price of firms is given by:

$$\frac{P_t^*}{P_t} = (1 + \mu^*) \left(\frac{c}{\lambda_t} + \frac{W_t}{P_t} \right) \frac{1}{Z_t}, \tag{5.17}$$

where P_t^* is the optimal nominal price, P_t the price level, μ^* the optimal markup rate, c the unit cost of a vacancy, λ_t the hiring rate, and W_t the nominal wage.

It is assumed that the real wage W_t/P_t that is negotiated between a worker and a firm upon a match is affected by the state of the labor market, in the following way:

$$\frac{W_t}{P_t} = f_t^2,$$

where f_t is the exit rate from unemployment. This rate, as well as the hiring rate λ_t, are the outcome of a search-and-matching process whereby unemployed workers (in number u_{t-1}) and vacant jobs (in number v_t) give rise to the following number of matches:

$$M_t = u_{t-1}^{2/3} v_t^{1/3},$$

Unemployment at the end of period t is given by

$$u_t = \frac{s}{s+f_t},$$

where s, $0 < s < 1$, is the entry rate into unemployment and assumed to be exogenous and constant.

From the aggregation of the production of all firms, total output is given by:

$$y_t \simeq z_t - u_t,$$

where y_t is log output and z_t is log labor productivity. Finally, aggregate demand is given by

$$\mathbf{AD}: y_t = -\pi_t,$$

where (by the usual approximation (1.3)):

$$\pi_t = \frac{P_t - P_{t-1}}{P_{t-1}} \simeq \ln P_t - \ln P_{t-1}.$$

We will assume throughout that

$$\frac{1}{2} < z < 1.$$

5.4.3.1 AGGREGATE SUPPLY

1. Provide an intuitive explanation of equation (5.17).

2. Express the job-finding and hiring rates f_t and λ_t as a function of the ratio v_t/u_{t-1} and explain intuitively the relations between those three variables.

3. Express the optimal real price P_t^*/P_t as a function of the job-finding rate f_t, labor productivity Z_t, as well as the constants c and μ^*, and provide a brief discussion of this result.

4. Compute the values of f_t and λ_t in the natural equilibrium (denoted f_t^n and λ_t^n); that is, in the absence of nominal price rigidities. Infer that in this case the optimal real price can by written as

$$P_t^*/P_t = \left(f_t/f_t^n\right)^2$$

and provide an interpretation of this result.

5. Now assume that, following a macroeconomic shock, only a fraction $1-\omega$, $0 \leq \omega \leq 1$, of the firms are able to reset their price optimally, while the other firms apply the indexation rule $P_{i,t} = P_{i,t-1}(1+\pi_{t-1})$. In first approximation the log price level satisfies:

$$p_t = \omega\left(p_{t-1} + \pi_{t-1}\right) + (1-\omega)p_t^*,$$

where $p_t = \ln P_t$ and $p_t^* = \ln P_t^*$. Infer from this an expression for aggregate supply that ties current inflation to labor market conditions (as summarized by f_t and f_t^n) as well as to past inflation π_{t-1} and explain your result intuitively.

5.4.3.2 AGGREGATE DEMAND

Using the AD curve, the expression for aggregate output, as well as that for the unemployment rate, show that:

$$f_t = \frac{s}{z_t + \pi_t} - s$$

and explain intuitively the impact of z_t and π_t on f_t.

5.4.3.3 IMPACT OF A PRODUCTIVITY SHOCK

1. Assume that the economy is in natural equilibrium until time $t-1$, where labor productivity was equal to its long-run value $\bar{z}$ and inflation was at its target $\bar{\pi} = 0$. At time t a productivity shock of size $dz = z_t - \bar{z} > 0$ occurs. What is the effect of this shock on f_t in the natural equilibrium and in the equilibrium with full price indexation (i.e., such that $\omega = 1$).? Provide an interpretation of your results.

2. Compute the response of f_t to the productivity shock in the vicinity of $(z_t = \bar{z}, \pi_t = 0)$ as a function of ω. Can a productivity improvement raise unemployment?

PART III

CONVENTIONAL MACROECONOMIC POLICIES

CHAPTER 6

MONETARY POLICY

Let us assume that the monetary authority tries to peg the "market" rate of unemployment at a level below the "natural" rate ... . [I]t will tend initially to lower interest rates and in this and other ways to stimulate spending .... To begin with, much or most of the rise in income will take the form of an increase in output and employment rather than in prices. People have been expecting prices to be stable, and prices and wages have been set for some time in the future on that basis. It takes time for people to adjust to a new state of demand. Producers will tend to react to the initial expansion in aggregate demand by increasing output, employees by working longer hours, and the unemployed, by taking jobs now offered at former nominal wages .... The simultaneous fall ex post in real wages to employers and rise ex ante in real wages to employees is what enabled employment to increase. But the decline ex post in real wages will soon come to affect anticipations. Employees will start to reckon on rising prices of the things they buy and to demand higher nominal wages for the future .... Even though the higher rate of monetary growth continues, the rise in real wages will reverse the decline in unemployment, and then lead to a rise, which will tend to return unemployment to its former level .... In order to keep unemployment at its target level, ... the monetary authority would have to raise monetary growth still more .... The "market" rate can be kept below the "natural" rate only by inflation. And, as in the interest rate case, too, only by accelerating inflation.

—Milton Friedman (1968)

Chapter 6 is devoted to monetary policy, starting from its implementation in the (very) short run and proceeding to its consequences in the medium run (for macroeconomic stability) and in the long run (for trend inflation). We have already touched on monetary policy several times. In chapter 2 was introduced the *MP curve*, which summarized the behavior of the central bank and notably the systematic response of the real interest rate (r_t) to deviations of inflation from its target ($\pi_t - \bar{\pi}$). We saw that this reaction corresponded to a regime of *inflation targeting*, which has been more or less explicitly adopted by the majority of central banks in the developed countries for twenty-some years. Coupled with the IS curve, the MP curve allowed us to construct the *AD curve*, which summarized the behavior of aggregate demand. Together with the AS curve, the AD curve determines the short-run macroeconomic equilibrium and in particular the responses of output, employment, inflation, and interest rates to macroeconomic shocks (see chapters 4 and 5). Monetary policy played an essential role in all these adjustments, notably because it affected the slope of the AD curve and hence the response of the economy to aggregate shocks.

The purpose of this chapter is to push the study of monetary policy in three directions. First, we will be interested in the way in which the central bank effectively affects the real interest rate r_t. As we saw in chapter 2, this interest rate, which influences private decisions about consumption, savings, and investment, is not directly controlled by the central bank but rather is targeted by it. Thus there is a path that runs from the instrument of the central bank (the short-term nominal interest rate) to the target (the longer-term real interest rate). The purpose of the first section of this chapter will be to clarify this path. We will also take this opportunity to present the *Taylor rule*, which summarizes the link between the short-term nominal interest rate and some macroeconomic indicators, as well as the *Taylor principle*, the violation of which may lead to a loss of control by the central bank over inflation.

When we introduced the MP curve in chapter 2, our perspective was fundamentally descriptive. It was a matter of representing the behavior of the central bank in an empirically accurate way, at least as a first approximation. In the second section of this chapter, we will adopt the complementary *normative* perspective on monetary policy. Instead of describing the behavior of the real interest rate by means of the MP curve, we will ask what *should* the real interest be in light of a social welfare criterion to be maximized. This approach will allow us to better understand the fundamental trade-offs that the central bank faces—for example, when it must buffer a macroeconomic shock or else implement a disinflationary policy. We will see that there are subtle differences between the optimal monetary policy (which maximizes welfare) and concrete monetary policy (as described by the MP curve) and we will discuss the bearing of this observation.

The third section of the chapter turns to the study of monetary policy in the longer run. At the long horizon, economic agents seek to anticipate monetary policy trends, potential regime changes, and the central bank's incentives to stabilize inflation. Therefore we will modify the AS curve to incorporate the expectations of private agents about future inflation, and we will show how the nature of these expectations modifies the equilibrium and the effectiveness of monetary policy. We will also overview the Lucas critique (Lucas 1976), which shows that neglecting the way private agents adjust their expectations and actions following changes in economic policy may lead to serious policy mistakes. Finally, we will see that the very structure of interactions between the citizens and a democratic central bank that reflect their preferences may be the source of excessive inflation, and we will contemplate several potential solutions to this inflation bias.[1]

One precision is in order at this stage. In the present chapter we will assume that the central bank is always able to freely implement whatever real interest rate it deems adequate. This more or less corresponds to what happens in normal times, and this is why we call it *conventional* monetary policy. Starting in 2008 (and as early as in 1995 in Japan), a number of major central banks lost their ability to influence the real interest rate, because the short-term nominal interest rates that they use as an instrument reached their lowest possible value (close to zero) and could not go any lower. Consequently, the real interest rate has been excessively high and could no longer provide the adequate degree of monetary accommodation in the face of contractionary macroeconomic shocks. We will study the dynamics of this liquidity trap in detail in Part IV of this book, and we will see that it requires the implementation of *unconventional* monetary policies that are quite different from the conventional policy examined in the present chapter.

6.1 MONETARY POLICY IMPLEMENTATION

We saw in chapter 2 that the central bank can manipulate aggregate demand by influencing the real interest rate, which affects the spending behavior of private agents (households, firms, and the rest of the world). However, the central bank does not directly control the real interest rate; its *instrument*, meaning the interest rate that it does control directly, is the *short-term nominal interest rate*. The bank determines the evolution of the latter by intervening on the wholesale market for interbank liquidity and by fixing the interest rate on reserves. In the present section, we go back up the path that runs from the real interest rate (which affects private demand) to these very short-term operations. At this stage, we are ignoring credit risk for simplicity and thus assume that the face interest rate of a loan or a bond is always repaid. We will introduce credit risk and the implied *credit spread* in chapter 8 in the context of the financial crisis of 2008.

6.1.1 INFLATION EXPECTATIONS AND THE FISHER EQUATION

Let us begin by noticing that, according to the Fisher equation (equation (2.2)), implementing a certain value of the real interest rate is equivalent to implementing a value of the nominal interest rate of the same maturity, conditional upon knowledge of inflation expectations:

$$\mathbf{FE} : r_t = i_t - \pi_{t+1},$$

---

1. The theory of the inflation bias was meant to explain the Great Inflation of the 1970s. In Part III of the book we will study a symmetric *deflation* bias that is arguably more topical than the inflation bias.

where i_t is the nominal interest rate and π_{t+1} expected inflation (equal to realized inflation under our assumption of perfect foresight, as discussed in chapter 1). Thus, a central bank that targets a certain value of r_t and knows π_{t+1} (thanks to survey data or forecasting models) may in an equivalent manner target the value of i_t consistent with r_t and π_{t+1}. In this spirit, we may rewrite the MP curve (equation (2.27)) as follows:

$$\mathbf{MP} : i_t = \bar{r} + \gamma \, (\pi_t - \bar{\pi}) + \pi_{t+1}. \tag{6.1}$$

The central bank does not directly control the nominal interest rate i_t but instead controls a series of (very) short-term nominal interest rates—that is, the interest rates on the interbank market in which banks lend overnight the excess reserves they hold on their accounts with the central bank (we describe these procedures farther down). Now we will show how the control of the short-term nominal interest rate on the interbank market, joint with an effective communication about its future path, permit the central bank to manipulate the nominal longer-term interest rate i_l. To achieve this manipulation the central bank takes advantage of an arbitrage relation between interest rates of different maturities—the so-called *term structure of interest rates*.

6.1.2   THE TERM STRUCTURE OF INTEREST RATES

Let us now examine in more detail what these arbitrage operations are, expressing the various interest rates in *annualized* terms in order to be able to compare them.[2] To be concrete, let us put ourselves in the position of an investor wishing to invest \$1 on a two-year horizon, and let us assume that there are bonds with only two possible maturities—three months and two years. The investor may therefore on today's date (noted as s)

- buy a two-year bond at the nominal (annualized) rate i_s^{2y} percent, which will yield in two years the following guaranteed amount:

  $\$(1 + i_s^{2y})^2$.

- or buy a succession of shorter-maturity bonds (say, three-month bonds), which after successive reinvestments over two years will yield:

  $\$ \left(1 + i_s^{3m}\right)^{\frac{1}{4}} \times \left(1 + i_{s+3m}^{3m}\right)^{\frac{1}{4}} \times \left(1 + i_{s+6m}^{3m}\right)^{\frac{1}{4}} \dots \times \left(1 + i_{s+21m}^{3m}\right)^{\frac{1}{4}},$

---

2. For example, a three-month bond costing \$10 and yielding \$10.10 in three months time pays an interest rate of 1 percent using the bond's own maturity, but of $(1.01)^4 - 1 = 4.06$ percent in annualized terms. In effect, if the \$10 were systematically reinvested at the same interest rate over a whole year, they would yield $10 \times (1.01)^4 = \$10.406$, or \$10 in capital and \$0.406 in interest (so that the annual interest rate is indeed \$0.406/\$10 = 4.06 percent).

where i_s^{3m} is the current value of the nominal (annualized) interest rate at the three-month maturity, i_{s+3m}^{3m} the expectation formed today of the three-month maturity nominal interest rate that will prevail in three months time, i_{s+6m}^{3m} the expectation formed today of the three-month maturity nominal interest rate that will prevail in six months' time, etc. Since each year carries four quarters and the horizon is two years, this strategy implies one initial investment and seven reinvestments.

If there is no barrier to arbitrage and if investors are risk-neutral, then the expected returns on the two investment strategies should be equal. For interest rates that are sufficiently small, we have $\ln(1 + i) \simeq i$ (see equation (1.3)), so that we may write this equality of expected returns as follows:

$$i_s^{2y} \simeq \frac{1}{8}\left(i_s^{3m} + \sum_{j=1}^{7} i_{s+j\times 3m}^{3m}\right).$$

Since investors are in general not risk-neutral, and since holding long-maturity bonds carries a risk relative to holding short-maturity bonds, market equilibrium requires that the former pay a *term premium* relative to the latter. The term premium compensates the investor not for the credit risk (which we are assuming away here), but rather for the *interest-rate risk* associated with holding long-term bonds. Indeed, fluctuations in short-term interest rates generate arbitrage operations that cause fluctuations in the equilibrium price of already issued bonds of longer maturities; for example, if the interest rate on short bonds rises, the trading price of an already issued long-term bond must drop so that its yield to maturity also rises. This means that an investor who buys a long-maturity bond but who might want to sell it before maturity is exposed to the fluctuations of its resale price triggered by changes in the short-term interest rate. This interest-rate risk on long-term bonds explains why in practice even long-term bonds that carry no credit risk whatsoever (for example, ten-year government bonds from creditworthy governments) carry a positive term premium relative to the average of short-term interest rates. It follows that, in our example, the interest rate on a bond maturing in two years will be

$$i_s^{2y} \simeq \underbrace{\frac{1}{8}\left(i_s^{3m} + \sum_{j=1}^{7} i_{s+j\times 3m}^{3m}\right)}_{\text{forward average of short-term interest rates}} + \underbrace{\varphi^{3m,2y}}_{\uparrow \\ \text{term premium}},$$

where $\varphi^{3m,2y} \geq 0$ is the term premium on two-year bonds (assumed to be constant here for simplicity). The reasoning above may be generalized to the whole range of maturities. In principle term premia cannot be negative since they compensate investors for bearing a specific source of risk.[3] Therefore, term premia necessarily increase with the maturity of the bonds.

The central bank controls only very short-term nominal interest rates on the interbank market. But it may use the term structure of interest rates to influence longer-term nominal interest rates, by adequately setting the current short-term rate and communicating about the path the future short-term rates that it plans to implement. Suppose that the central bank is trying to influence the one-year nominal interest rate i_s^{1y} via the control of overnight interest rates. Assuming that the communication about the path of future short-term interest rates is credible, by the term structure of interest rates the central bank must choose a sequence $\{i_{s+j\times 1d}^{1d}\}_{j=0}^{365}$ (which is the overnight interest rate, every day of the year starting from the current day s) that will satisfy:

$$\sum_{j=0}^{365} i_{s+j\times 1d}^{1d} = 365 \times (i_s^{1y} - \varphi^{1d,1y}), \quad \varphi^{1d,1y} \text{ given.}$$

In what follows I compactly summarize the determinants of the nominal interest rate i_t (the one that occurred above in the Fisher equation) by writing it as follows:

$$i_t = \tilde{\imath}_t + \varphi, \tag{6.2}$$

where $\tilde{\imath}_t$ is the (forward) average of short-term nominal interest rates set by the central bank between the current period and the horizon $t + 1$, and φ the term premium on bonds of long maturity, meaning one period in our AS-AD model (which might be interpreted, say, as a year). In an equivalent way, the real interest rate at this maturity can be written:

$$r_t = \tilde{\imath}_t + \varphi - \pi_{t+1}. \tag{6.3}$$

Note that the central bank cannot use short-term nominal interest rates to influence longer-term nominal interest rates unless two conditions are satisfied. First of all, the decisions of the central bank about the path of future short-term interest rates much be sufficiently predictable. If this were not the case, then market expectations

---

3. Things are not so simple in the real world, because some investors may purchase bonds for other reasons than the mere arbitrage between yields of different maturities. For example, pension funds may by regulation be forced to hold high-quality, long-maturity bonds, with the effect of taking down the term premium on these bonds, and may even produce a negative term premium. We abstract from these complications here.

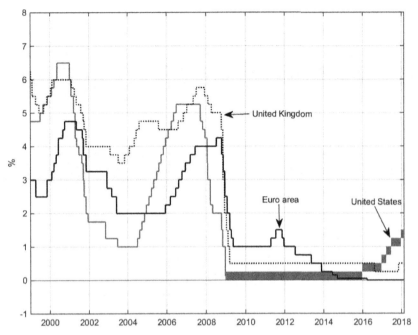

FIGURE 6.1
Short-term interest rate targets. Interest rates on Main Refinancing Operations (euro area), targeted Fed funds rate (United States), and Official Bank Rate (United Kingdom).
Sources: European Central Bank, US Federal Reserve, Bank of England.

about the future values of short-term nominal interest rates would be unstable, and hence their forward average would be equally unstable. Figure 6.1 shows that between 1999 and 2008, the short-term nominal interest rates targeted by the US Federal Reserve and the European Central Bank were effectively everything except erratic. They responded in a gradual and coherent way (in short, predictably) to macroeconomic conditions and only rarely took bond investors by surprise. After 2008, short-term nominal interest rates approached or hit their zero lower bound—a problem that we will examine in detail in Part IV of the book.

The second condition for the control of the short-term nominal interest rate to successfully influence longer-term nominal interest rates is that the term premium φ be relatively stable. It is so empirically when we compare securities of different maturities that bear no credit risk (for example, when we compare rates on the Bund, the German long-term public debt bonds, and the anticipated path of the interbank nominal interest rates in the eurozone, called the "Eonia"). Term premia may vary significantly in times of financial turmoil but we leave this aspect aside until Part IV of the book.

6.1.3 THE INTEREST RATE ON RESERVES AND THE INTEREST RATE IN THE INTERBANK MARKET

The central bank adjusts its instrument—the short-term nominal interest rates—and communicates (more or less explicitly) about the future path of this instrument in such a way as to manipulate the longer-term nominal interest rates i_t and thereby the real interest rate r_t. What follows is an outline of the operational procedures used by central banks to set the short-term nominal interest rates at the desired value.

Every single day, the banks perform for their clients a multitude of operations, which by the end of the day generate liquidity imbalances across banks—some banks are in surplus while some are in deficit. These debts may be settled in two ways: either by an interbank loan, with the banks in surplus granting a short-term loan of their excess reserves to the banks in deficit, or by an outright payment in reserve money, meaning by debiting the account that the bank in deficit holds with the central bank and by crediting the same amount to the bank in surplus. The short-term nominal interest rate is the rate at which banks lend to each other in the very short run on the interbank market in order to finance these transitory liquidity needs.

The equilibrium interest rate on the interbank market results from banks' portfolio choices, which determine the *demand* for reserve money, and from the open-market operations of the central bank, which determine the *supply* of reserve money. The demand for reserve money by the banks is determined by two factors—the state of the business cycle and the opportunity cost of reserves:

- The greater economic activity, the more it gives rise to transactions between the clients of the various banks and the larger are the transitory liquidity imbalances among banks to be cleared. Therefore it takes more reserve money in the economy to settle these imbalances. The demand for reserve money is thus an increasing function of output y.[4]

- The greater the opportunity cost of holding reserve money, the less banks are willing to hold it. The opportunity cost of reserves is the difference between, on the one hand, what the loan of these reserves to other banks would yield, namely the overnight (say) interest rate on the interbank market (denoted i^M); and, on the other hand, the overnight interest rate that the central bank pays on the reserves that the banks hold with it (denoted i^R). An important distinction between these two rates is that i^M is a *market rate* (the overnight interest rate that clears the interbank market), whereas i^R is *exogenously set* by the central bank. At any given interest rate on reserves i^R, the market interest rate i^M

---

4. This is reminiscent of the "demand for money for transaction purpose" in monetary theory, which states that households need more money to pay for their transactions when there are more of them (which occurs when output is higher). Here it is the banks rather than the housholds that express this demand, and it is a demand for *reserve money*, rather than for bank deposits and currency. But the logic underlying the two money demands is similar.

necessarily satisfies $i^M \geq i^R$. If this were not the case, then no bank would agree to lend its excess reserve to other banks while the liquidity demand by banks incurring a transitory liquidity shortage would be positive; i^M would thus rise up to the point of making interbank loans by those banks that were holding excess reserves attractive again (that is, up to the point where $i^M \geq i^R$). The greater the gap $i^M - i^R$, the more the banks have an interest in lending their reserve money to the other banks rather than keeping it with the central bank and hence the greater the opportunity cost of holding onto those reserves.

We may summarize these two determinants of the demand for reserves by the following *demand for reserve money* function:

$$R^d = R^d(\underbrace{i^M - i^R}_{-}, \underset{+}{y}).$$

On the supply side, the central bank perfectly controls the aggregate quantity of reserve money in the economy R^s by its open-market operations—meaning the operations of purchasing (or selling) financial assets to banks against credit (or debit) of their reserve account. The equilibrium interest rate i^M is the one that equalizes the demand and supply of reserve money, given output y and the interest rate on reserves i^R. We derive from the equilibrium on the interbank market ($R^s = R^d$) the determinants of i^M:

$$R^s = R^d(\underbrace{i^M - i^R}_{-}, \underset{+}{y}) \;\Rightarrow\; i^M = i^M(\underset{+}{i^R}, \underset{+}{y}, \underset{-}{R^o}) \geq i^R. \tag{6.4}$$

Thus, to increase the short-term nominal interest rate i^M, the central bank can either increase the interest rate on reserves i^R (which, at any given value of R^s, shifts both i^R and i^M upward), or else contract the quantity of reserves R^s (which raises the opportunity cost of reserves $i^M - i^R$ and hence raises i^M at any given value of i^R)— or even do both. In practice, the monetary policy committee meets regularly and makes simultaneous decisions about i^R (which the central bank sets) and i^M (which it targets).[5] In the very short run, y can be considered as exogenous and constant; conditionally on (i^R, y), the central bank thus adjusts R^s in such a way as to attain the desired value of i^M. Figure 6.2 shows the joint evolution of the interest rate on reserves (formally called the deposit facility interest rate) and the interbank market

5. For example, in the euro area interest-rate decisions are made every six weeks by the Council of the Governors of the European Central Bank, and in the United States they are made about once a month by the Federal Open Market Committee.

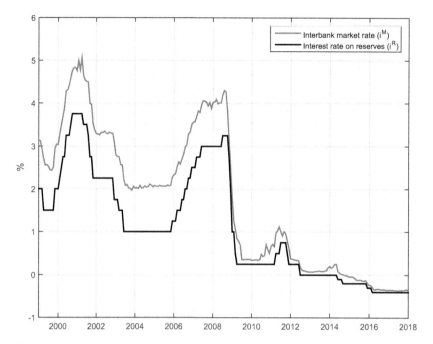

FIGURE 6.2
Interest rate on the interbank market (EONIA) and interest rates on reserves in the euro area.
Source: European Central Bank.

interest rate (Euro OverNight Index Average, or EONIA for short) in the euro area since 1999.[6,7] Starting in 2008, the strong increase in reserve money in the euro area brought together i^M and i^R, as implied in equation (6.4).

6.1.4 THE TAYLOR RULE

It is common to represent (and estimate empirically) the behavior of the central bank not in the form of the MP curve, which features the real interest rate, but instead in the form of an *instrument rule* linking the short-term nominal interest rate i^M to the

---

6. In the United States the interbank market interest rate is called the effective federal (or fed) funds rate (EFFR). The Federal Reserve was only allowed to pay interest rate on reserves (the interest rate on excess reserves, or IOER) in October 2008. Before that time, i^R was just zero.

7. There is a third short-term interest rate, at which banks may borrow directly from the central banks in case of emergency without going through the interbank market. This rate (noted as i^E) is fixed by the central bank at a level necessarily higher than i^R—otherwise the banks would borrow an unlimited amount at rate i^E and then deposit it back at the rate i^R. The equilibrium interbank market rate i^M cannot be higher than i^E. Otherwise banks would borrow large amounts from the central bank at rate i^E and lend them to the other banks at the rate i^M; i^M would then adjust until $i^M \leq i^E$. Therefore we must necessarily have $i^R \leq i^M \leq i^E$; in other words, the equilibrium interest rate on the interbank market is bracketed by the other two. i^E is called the discount rate in the United States and the interest rate on the marginal lending facility in the euro area.

gap between inflation and its target, and to an empirical measure of the output gap. This idea goes back John Taylor (1993), who showed that such a rule tracked the behavior of the federal funds rate (the interbank market interest rate in the United States) between 1987 and 1992 very well.[8] The original version of the Taylor Rule took the form

$$i_t^M = 2 + \pi_t + \frac{1}{2}(\pi_t - 2) + \frac{1}{2}\left(y_t - \tau_t^y\right), \tag{6.5}$$

with $i_t^M(\%)$ the average value over the quarter of the federal funds rate (expressed in annualized terms), π_t (%) the year-on-year inflation rate,[9] 2 (%) the inflation target, y_t quarterly real GDP (in log), and τ_t^y its linear trend over the sample. Since Taylor's article, any description of monetary policy that makes the short-term nominal interest rate appear as a dependent variable is called a Taylor rule, whatever the variables are that appear on the right-hand side of the equation (which may be the nominal exchange rate, the unemployment rate, stock prices, real-estate prices, just to mention a few). These Taylor rules were commonly used to describe the behavior of central banks until 2008.[10]

Although the representation of the behavior of the central bank in the form of a Taylor rule used to be very popular, we should not exaggerate its scope: the Taylor rule does not reveal the objectives of the central bank and should therefore be interpreted more as a statistical regularity than as a proper reaction function. In fact we know that it is the real interest rate r_t that determines the spending behaviors of private agents and not the short-term nominal interest rate i_t^M. Thus it is r_t that the central bank tries to influence by its monetary policy, and we have seen that r_t depends on a entire path of short-term nominal interest rates, not only the current rate. If the Taylor rule seems to establish a direct empirical link between the business cycle (i.e., the cyclical variations in inflation and output) and the short-term nominal interest rate, this is simply because movements in the latter are very correlated with those of longer-term nominal interest rates, due to the inertia of short-term nominal interest rates and the term structure of interest rates.

The main reason for the popularity of Taylor rule is, precisely, that *it helps central banks communicate about the path of short-term nominal interest rates.*

8. See Taylor (1999) for a complete and integrated discussion of the Taylor Rule and the Taylor principle discussed in the following section.

9. The year-on-year inflation rate at a given quarter is the rate of growth of the price level between the current quarter and the same quarter of the preceeding year.

10. Figure 6.1 shows that after 2008 the short-term nominal interest rates in the eurozone and in the United States (as well as in many other countries) reached the "zero lower bound," so that the Taylor rule ceased being a good description of their behavior. As of December 2015 the US Federal Reserve is no longer constrained by the zero lower bound, but it is still unclear whether a Taylor rule is adequately capturing its policy stance or will do so in the future.

Indeed, an important challenge with the real interest rate in terms of monetary policy communication is that it is only indirectly manipulated by the central bank, and somewhat imperfectly due to variations both in expected inflation and in future short-term nominal interest rates. By contrast, the short-term nominal interest rate is directly controlled by the central bank and is immediately observable by all. This confers a clear advantage in terms of transparency and accountability. The central bank cannot claim to have targeted a short-term nominal interest rate that is different from the one that everybody observes on the interbank market; by contrast, it could pretend to be targeting a real interest rate that is different from the one that it is actually aiming at, and then assert that aggregate shocks or expectational errors explain the gap between the targeted rate and the observed rate. The central bank might (for example) claim to be targeting a high real interest rate in order to counter nascent inflationary pressures while actually targeting a low real interest rate in order to boost employment, and then pretend that the difference between the announcement and the outcome is due to aggregate shocks and is thus beyond its responsibility. This type of deception is not possible when the central bank advertises and explains its decisions over short-term nominal interest rates, and this is precisely what Taylor rules help it do.

6.1.5 THE TAYLOR PRINCIPLE

In chapter 2, we made an assumption that seemed natural, but in fact was far from innocuous, about the MP curve. We assumed that it was such that a rise in inflation relative to its target led (automatically) to an *increase* in the real interest rate implemented by the central bank (the parameter γ of the MP curve was assumed to be nonnegative). Since the real interest rate is itself the difference between the nominal interest rate and the rate of (expected) inflation, this condition requires that the nominal interest rate respond sufficiently strongly to inflation (to be more precise, to a linear combination of current inflation and expected future inflation, specifically the term $\gamma \pi_t + \pi_{t+1}$ of equation (6.1)). Finally, since the AS curve implies that inflation is persistent, which shows up in the fact that the AS curve of period $t+1$ — "AS(t+1) curve" henceforth—features current inflation ($\pi_{t+1} = \pi_t + \kappa(y_{t+1} - y_{t+1}^n)$), we may rewrite equation (6.1) as follows:

$$i_t = (\bar{r} - \gamma \bar{\pi}) + (1 + \gamma)\pi_t + \kappa \left(y_{t+1} - y_{t+1}^n\right).$$

At any given future anticipated output gap (the term $\kappa(y_{t+1} - y_{t+1}^n)$), the condition $\gamma > 0$ is equivalent to a condition about the response of i_t to π_t, or, namely, that *the nominal interest rate must respond more than one-for-one to inflation*. This condition, called the Taylor principle, is necessary for macroeconomic stability (at least within our AS-AD model). When the Taylor principle is not satisfied, the economy may find itself trapped in the following vicious circle: high inflation today generates high inflation tomorrow (because of the persistence of inflation; see the AS(t+1) curve), which reduces the real interest rate today (by the Fisher equation), which boosts aggregate demand (by the IS curve), which in turn raises current inflation (by the AS curve), and so on. To see this, let us suppose (for the clarity of the example and with no loss of generality) that natural output (y_t^n) and the demand parameter (θ_t) are constant over time and normalized to zero.[11] In this case the equilibrium is described by the following system, for $t = 0, 1, \ldots$:

AD : $y_t = -\gamma\sigma\,(\pi_t - \bar{\pi})$;

AS : $\pi_t = \pi_{t-1} + \kappa y_t$.

By replacing y_t by its value in the AS curve and then by factorizing the terms in $\pi_t - \bar{\pi}$, we obtain

$$\pi_t = \pi_{t-1} - \sigma\gamma\kappa\,(\pi_t - \bar{\pi})$$
$$= \bar{\pi} + \Gamma\,(\pi_{t-1} - \bar{\pi}), \quad \text{with} \quad \Gamma = \frac{1}{1 + \gamma\sigma\kappa}.$$

When $\gamma > 0$, meaning when the Taylor principle is satisfied, we have $0 < \Gamma < 1$, which implies that the dynamics of inflation is stable; any deviation of π_t from $\bar{\pi}$ is self-correcting (because the reaction of i_t is sufficiently strong to raise r_t and thus to cause y_t and π_t to drop). On the other hand, when $\gamma < 0$, then we have $\Gamma > 1$ and the dynamics of inflation becomes unstable; any deviation of π_t from $\bar{\pi}$ gets amplified over time.[12]

We may represent graphically the stability of the equilibrium in the (y, π) plane, according to whether the Taylor principle is verified or not (see figures 6.3 and 6.4). Since $\theta_t = 0$ for all t by assumption, the AD curve does not depend on t; it is an unmoving straight line in the (y, π) plane, of pivot point $(0, \bar{\pi})$, and of negative slope when the Taylor principle holds $(\gamma > 0 \Leftrightarrow \Gamma < 1)$ but positive slope when it does not $(\gamma < 0 \Leftrightarrow \Gamma > 1)$. Let us assume that some shock in period $t - 1$ has caused inflation to deviate from its target, so that $\pi_{t-1} = \hat{\pi} > \bar{\pi}$, while output y_t was at its natural level $y_{t-1}^n = 0$. The AS curve is thus given by $\pi_t = \pi_{t-1} + \kappa y_t = \hat{\pi} + \kappa y_t$, meaning it is a straight line with slope $\kappa > 0$ and intercept $\hat{\pi} > 0$. When the Taylor principle holds, the intersection of the AS and AD curves necessarily occurs at a level of inflation π_t *lower* than $\hat{\pi}$ (see figure 6.3). Intuitively, the automatic reaction of r_t to $\pi_t - \bar{\pi}$ is sufficiently strong to cause a contraction in aggregate demand and output, with

---

11. Since $y_t^n = z_t - \xi\mu^*$ (see chapter 3), normalizing y_t^n to 0 amounts to normalizing z_t to $\xi\mu^*$. In the long run we necessarily have $\theta_\infty = y_\infty$ (see chapter 4), and hence the assumption $\theta_t = 0$ simply means that there is no demand shock in the short run.

12. We are assuming here that $\gamma < 0$ but $\gamma > -1/\sigma\kappa$, so that $\Gamma > 0$. The condition $\gamma > -1/\sigma\kappa$ is always verified for realistic values of γ, σ, and κ.

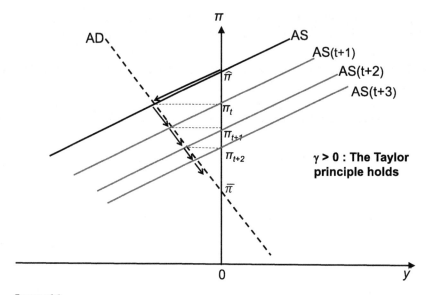

FIGURE 6.3
The stability of inflation when the Taylor principle holds. When the central bank conforms to the Taylor principle, any deviation of inflation from its target is self-correcting.

the effect of stabilizing inflation. Current inflation π_t then determines the intercept of the AS(t+1) curve (we have $\pi_{t+1} = \pi_t + \kappa y_{t+1}$). The equilibrium of period $t+1$ thus has a level of inflation π_{t+1} which in its turn strictly lower than π_t, and so on; inflation converges asymptotically toward its target $\bar{\pi}$. In contrast, when the Taylor principle is not satisfied, the intersection between the AS and AD curves necessarily occurs at a level of inflation π_t *greater* than $\hat{\pi}$ (see figure 6.4); intuitively, the hike in inflation leads to a drop in the real interest rate r_t (because the nominal interest rate does not react sufficiently strongly to inflation), which raises aggregate demand and thereby strengthens the initial inflationary pressures. Since $\pi_t > \pi_{t-1} = \hat{\pi}$, the AS(t+1) curve is an upward translation of the AS curve, whose intersection with the AD curve generates a rate of inflation π_{t+1} in turn higher than π_t, and so on; inflation gradually diverges from its target $\bar{\pi}$.

The violation of the Taylor principle, perhaps due to a poor understanding of the long-term effects of monetary policy, is the most plausible explanation for the loss of control over inflation in the 1970s—the so-called Great Inflation.[13] For

---

13. Since chapter 3 we have known that in the long run output is equal to its natural level and hence independent of inflation. So it is illusory to think that one could durably stimulate the economy at the cost of high inflation. Yet this impossibility was not evident, either to economists or to central bankers, in the 1960s and early 1970s. Further along in this chapter we will tackle another possible explanation of the Great Inflation, related to the incentives of the central bank. Oil price shocks (in 1973, then in 1979) are

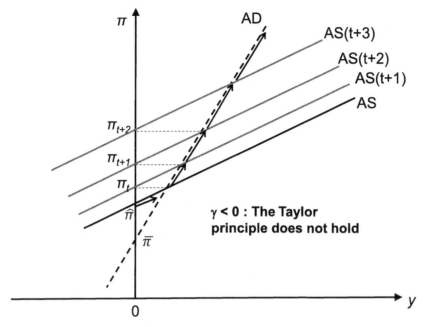

FIGURE 6.4
The instability of inflation when the Taylor principle does not hold. When the central bank does not conform the Taylor principle, any deviation of inflation from its target leads to a divergence in the path of inflation.

example, Clarida, Gali, and Gertler (2000) show empirically that US monetary policy did not conform to the Taylor principle in the 1970s, precisely when inflation was taking off, not until the Volcker shock of August 1979. Starting at this date, the new president of the Federal Reserve, Paul Volcker, adopted a monetary regime that did conform with the Taylor principle, which led to a gradual stabilization of inflation in the 1980s.[14] To illustrate this idea, figure 6.5 superimposes the path of inflation in the United States upon the dynamic described above, assuming that $\Gamma = 1.27 > 1$ before 1980, and then $\Gamma = 0.75 < 1$ after 1980 (with an inflation target of $\bar{\pi} = 2$ percent).[15]

also sometimes advanced to explain the Great Inflation. However, oil prices soared in the 2000s without any noticeable effect on inflation, which throws doubt on this explanation.

14. Bernanke (2013, Lecture 2) provides a brief history of monetary policy from the end of World War II to the eve of the Great Recession.

15. The value of Γ does not independently identify the parameters γ, σ, and κ. The simulation assumes that $\sigma\kappa = 1/2$ and uses for each regime the value of γ that best brings together empirical inflation and theoretical inflation.

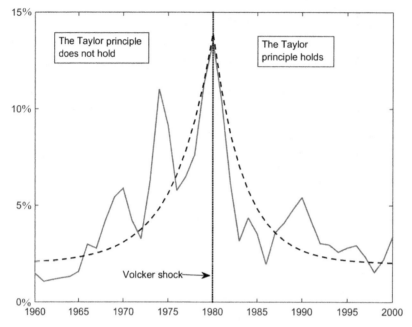

FIGURE 6.5
Inflation and the Volcker shock in the United States.
Sources: BLS and the author's calculations.

6.2 OPTIMAL MONETARY POLICY

Until now, we have summarized the behavior of the central bank by means of the MP curve, which determined the real interest rate r_t as a function of deviations of inflation π_t from its target $\bar{\pi}$. This approach is satisfactory from an empirical point of view in the sense that it correctly represents, at least as a first approximation, the actual behavior of central banks. However, it remains rather vague about precisely why the central banks behave in this specific way. In chapter 2, we justified the MP curve by the general notion that in an inflation-targeting regime, the central bank leans against the wind—which means that it seeks to stabilize inflation around its target— and so it raises the real interest rate so as to reduce private demand when inflation is above its target, and vice versa. This naturally raises the following question: if the central bank really wishes to align inflation with its target, why does it do so gradually rather than immediately (all at once) in a single period? Similarly, we saw in chapter 4 that after an aggregate supply shock, the slope of the MP curve (γ), which determined the (generally finite) slope of the AD curve, implied a simultaneous variation in inflation and output. Why should the central bank act in a way that lets *both* variables move after the shock, rather than letting only one of them take the full hit?

To answer these questions, we have to move from the positive approach to monetary policy adopted so far to a *normative* analysis. In order to do this, instead of describing the behavior of the real interest rate by means of an MP curve, we are going to derive its optimal value as the solution to a problem of maximization of social welfare by the central bank. This approach will enrich our understanding of monetary policy by highlighting the fundamental trade-offs that any central bank faces. We will notably see that the MP curve is not only a good empirical description of actual monetary policy; it also corresponds, in a number of situations, to the optimal monetary policy. But we will also examine a situation in which the MP curve does *not* correspond to the optimal policy, and we will discuss the scope and limits of this result.

6.2.1   THE LOSS FUNCTION OF THE CENTRAL BANK

How can we determine the optimal choice of real interest rate by the central bank among all the possible values it can take? To answer this question, we have to posit a *social welfare function* that the central bank seeks to maximize, or in an equivalent way a *social loss function* that it seeks to minimize. This loss function is meant to capture the main objectives of the central bank and hence the potential trade-offs that it faces in situations of conflict between objectives. We generally think of the central bank as trying to stabilize inflation while limiting output fluctuations. A classic loss function that incorporates these two objectives penalizes quadratic deviations of output y_t and inflation π_t from some target values $\bar{y}$ and $\bar{\pi}$:

$$L\left(y_t, \pi_t\right) = \lambda \left(y_t - \bar{y}\right)^2 + (\pi_t - \bar{\pi})^2, \tag{6.6}$$

where $\lambda \geq 0$ is a constant. This loss function has two important properties. It penalizes the deviations of the relevant variables from their respective targets in a symmetric way, and the marginal penalty is increasing in the size of the deviations from the targets (by the convexity of the loss function). These two properties of the loss function (symmetry and increasing marginal penalty) imply that the central bank has an incentive to bring the two variables back toward their respective targets as soon as they deviate from them. Nevertheless, the central bank possesses only one choice variable—namely the real interest rate r_t—to achieve this goal, and so there may be a *monetary policy trade-off* between stabilizing inflation and stabilizing output (for example, when getting π_t closer to $\bar{\pi}$ also leads to taking y_t further away from $\bar{y}$). The parameter λ, which measures the weight of output stabilization relative to inflation stabilization in the central bank's objective, regulates this trade-off. In the extreme case where $\lambda = 0$, the central bank worries only about stabilizing inflation, and so we have $\pi_t = \bar{\pi}$ at every point in time, whatever the value of y_t. Conversely, when $\lambda \to \infty$ the central bank is indifferent to inflation and so we have $y_t = \bar{y}$ at every point in time. Apart from these two extreme cases, meaning when $0 < \lambda < \infty$, it is possible to have at the same time $\pi_t \neq \bar{\pi}$ and $y_t \neq \bar{y}$.

The AS curve implies that inflation is persistent. Inflation today (π_t) affects inflation tomorrow (π_{t+1}). The AS(t+1) curve is indeed given by

$$\textbf{AS(t+1)}: \pi_{t+1} = \pi_t + \kappa \left(y_{t+1} - y_{t+1}^n \right).$$

The persistence of inflation implies that the decisions taken by the central bank in period t in general influence the deviation of inflation from its target in period $t+1$ (i.e., $\pi_{t+1} - \bar{\pi}$), and then in period $t+2$, etc. The fact that the current decisions of the central bank influence future equilibrium outcomes introduces a new trade-off, not between the stabilizations of inflation and of output around their targets within a given period, but between *present* and *future* stabilization of these variables around their targets. Representing the choices of the central bank among all the options that it has therefore requires the specification of an *intertemporal loss function*, which is the present value of current and future losses:

$$L_t^I = L\left(y_t, \pi_t\right) + \beta L\left(y_{t+1}, \pi_{t+1}\right) + \beta^2 L\left(y_{t+2}, \pi_{t+2}\right) + \dots$$

$$= \sum_{k=0}^{\infty} \beta^k L\left(y_{t+k}, \pi_{t+k}\right), \quad 0 \leq \beta < 1. \tag{6.7}$$

The parameter β is the central bank's discount factor, which determines the relative weight of future losses (the $L(y_{t+k}, \pi_{t+k})$, for $k = 1, 2, \dots$) relative to the current loss ($L(\pi_t, y_t)$). The fact that $0 \leq \beta < 1$ ensures that the sum in (6.7) is finite, and thus the minimization problem is well defined. In the special case where $\beta = 0$ so that $L_t^I = L(\pi_t, y_t)$, the central bank does not care about the effects of its present actions on *future* outcomes. But in general it does grant them some importance, which will affect its current choices. The optimal monetary policy problem consists, then, of selecting the sequence of real interest rates $\{r_{t+k}\}_{k=0}^{\infty} = \{r_t, r_{t+1}, r_{t+2}, \dots\}$ that minimizes L_t^I, which we can express formally as

$$\{r_{t+k}\}_{k=0}^{\infty} = \arg\min L_t^I, \quad \pi_{t-1} \text{ given.}$$

This formulation of the problem of the central bank considers the real interest rate r_t as its choice variable. But in an equivalent way we might pose the problem in terms of the optimal choice of y_t or of π_t. In effect—according to the IS curve—r_t determines y_t (conditionally on θ_t, which is exogenous), while y_t—according to the AS curve—in turn determines π_t (conditionally on y_t^n, which is also exogenous, and π_{t-1}, which is predetermined). Thus it is equivalent, when it comes to minimizing the intertemporal loss L_t^I, to choosing optimally the sequences $\{r_{t+k}\}_{k=0}^{\infty}$, $\{y_{t+k}\}_{k=0}^{\infty}$, or $\{\pi_{t+k}\}_{k=0}^{\infty}$. To summarize this formally, we have

$$\min_{\{r_{t+k}\}_{k=0}^{\infty}} L_t^I = \min_{\{y_{t+k}\}_{k=0}^{\infty}} L_t^I = \min_{\{\pi_{t+k}\}_{k=0}^{\infty}} L_t^I.$$

In practice, it is often more convenient to solve $\min_{\{\pi_{t+k}\}_{k=0}^{\infty}} L_t^I$ (with π_{t-1} given), and then to infer $\{y_{t+k}\}_{k=0}^{\infty}$ (via the AS curve), and finally $\{r_{t+k}\}_{k=0}^{\infty}$ (via the IS curve). This is precisely what we are going to do next, where we study two classic optimal policy problems—the optimal pace of disinflation and the optimal reaction of the central bank to macroeconomic shocks.

6.2.2 Optimal Disinflation
In the 1970s the central banks of many countries lost control of inflation—an episode that was later called the Great Inflation (see figure 6.5 above, for the United States). Recognizing that high inflation rates disturb the economy without bringing any lasting benefits in terms of employment or output, central banks engaged at the start of the 1980s in vigorous *disinflation* policies, which were associated with sharp recessions (just as the AS curve predicts). To the extent that disinflation brings both benefits (the gradual realignment of inflation to its target) and costs (a temporary recession), does there exist an optimal pace of disinflation, which would best balance these benefits and costs?

6.2.2.1 The Speed of Disinflation and the Adjustment of Output
Before answering this question, let us first study the impact of the *speed* of the disinflation on equilibrium outcomes, taking this speed as given (later on we will compute the *optimal* speed of disinflation according to the central bank's preferences). To simplify the analysis as much as possible, let us assume here that the natural level of output y_t^n is constant and normalized to zero.[16] Thus the AS curve becomes

$$\textbf{AS}: \pi_t = \pi_{t-1} + \kappa y_t.$$

Let us further assume that in period $t-1$ inflation was high at $\pi_{t-1} = \hat{\pi} > 0$, whatever the reason (bad aggregate shock, bad policy, and so forth). Starting in period t, the central bank chooses to target zero inflation in the long run and to gradually adjust current inflation toward its target at the speed Ω, with $0 \leq \Omega \leq 1$. That is, starting in period t we have:

$$\pi_{t+k} = \Omega \pi_{t+k-1}, \; 0 \leq \Omega \leq 1, \; \text{for } k = 0, 1, 2, \ldots$$

The lower the Ω, the faster the adjustment to the new inflation target. If $\Omega = 0$, then we have $\pi_t = 0$, so the adjustment to the new target is instantaneous. Conversely,

---

16. In other words, we are normalizing z_t to $\xi\mu^*$ since $y_t^n = z_t - \xi\mu^*$ (see chapter 3).

when $\Omega = 1$, then $\pi_t = \pi_{t-1}$, and no adjustment ever takes place. The dynamics of inflation implies that the inflation rate in period t is given by $\pi_t = \Omega \pi_{t-1} = \Omega \hat{\pi}$. In period $t+1$ the inflation rate will be of $\pi_{t+1} = \Omega \pi_t = \Omega^2 \hat{\pi}$, and so forth. To summarize, the inflation rate both before and after the deflationary shock is given by

$$
\pi_{t+k} = \begin{cases} \hat{\pi} & \text{for } k = \dots, -2, -1 \\ \Omega^{k+1}\hat{\pi} & \text{for } k = 0, 1, 2, \dots \end{cases} \tag{6.8}
$$

What path of output does this inflation dynamics generate? The AS curve implies that until period $t-1$, output was given by $\kappa^{-1}(\hat{\pi} - \hat{\pi}) = 0$. In period t it is given by

$$
y_t = \kappa^{-1}(\pi_t - \pi_{t-1}) = -\kappa^{-1}(1 - \Omega)\hat{\pi} < 0.
$$

In period $t \mid 1$, it will be

$$
y_{t+1} = \kappa^{-1}(\pi_{t+1} - \pi_t) = -\kappa^{-1}(1 - \Omega)\Omega\hat{\pi} < 0.
$$

and so on. To summarize, output before and after the implementation of the disinflation policy is given by:

$$
y_{t+k} = \begin{cases} 0 & \text{for } k = \dots, -2, -1 \\ -\kappa^{-1}(1 - \Omega)\Omega^k\hat{\pi} < 0 & \text{for } k = 0, 1, 2, \dots \end{cases} \tag{6.9}
$$

This expression implies that output *falls* sharply at the moment the disinflation policy is implemented and then gradually returns, at rate Ω, to its long-term value $(= 0)$. The initial drop has size $\kappa^{-1}(1 - \Omega)\hat{\pi}$, which means that it is all the higher when initial inflation $\hat{\pi}$ is high and when the adjustment of inflation to its target is rapid. So there is a trade-off here: *the greater the initial fall in output, the less durable it is.*

The response of y_t to the disinflation policy suggests that a large short-run output loss is somehow offset in the longer term by a more rapid reversion of y_t toward $\bar{y}$. We may measure the total cost of the disinflation by calculating the implied cumulative output loss. It is given by:

$$
-\sum_{k=0}^{\infty} y_{t+k} = \underbrace{-\kappa^{-1}(\Omega - 1)\hat{\pi}}_{y_t} + \underbrace{\kappa^{-1}(\Omega - 1)\Omega\hat{\pi}}_{y_{t+1}} + \underbrace{\kappa^{-1}(\Omega - 1)\Omega^2\hat{\pi}}_{y_{t+2}} + \dots
$$

$$
= -\kappa^{-1}(\Omega - 1)\left(1 + \Omega + \Omega^2 + \dots\right)\hat{\pi} = \frac{\hat{\pi}}{\kappa}.
$$

This expression implies that the cumulative output loss is *independent of the speed of the disinflation* (as measured by Ω); that is, the two effects—on the *size* and on the *durability* of the output loss—exactly offset each other. As a consequence, the cumulative output loss depends only on the size of the disinflation to be achieved $\hat{\pi} - \bar{\pi}$ ($= \hat{\pi}$ since $\bar{\pi} = 0$ here, by assumption) and on the response of inflation to output κ (i.e., the slope of the AS curve), with is decreasing in the degree of nominal price rigidity (see chapter 3). The reason why κ affects the cumulative output loss is that, when prices are more flexible, the size of the recession that is necessary to take them down is lower. Therefore, the more prices are flexible, the lower the cost of the disinflation.

The ratio of the cumulative output loss (in log) to the size of the disinflation— in other words, the quantity of output that has to be sacrificed for inflation to go back down to target—is called the *sacrifice ratio*. Here it is given by

$$S = -\frac{\sum_{k=0}^{\infty} y_{+k}}{\hat{\pi}} = \frac{1}{\kappa} = \frac{\xi \omega}{1 - \omega},$$

where we recall that $\xi > 0$ is the elasticity of labor supply and $1 - \omega$ the fraction of firms that optimally adjust their prices (see chapter 3). The more elastic the labor supply, and the greater the degree of nominal rigidities, then the more costly is the disinflation episode in terms of output loss.

Several empirical studies have tried to measure sacrifice ratios across countries that at one time or another engaged in disinflation policies. Empirically, this ratio is calculated over a given window of time and relative to some GDP trend (in short, the GDP trend that supposedly would have occurred had the disinflation policy not occurred). By using our usual approximation (see equation (1.3)), the sacrifice ratio generated by a fall in inflation from its value in period t (π_t) to its value in period $t + T$ (π_{t+T}) is given by:

$$S_{t+T} = \frac{-\sum_{k=0}^{T} \left(y_{t+k} - y_{t+k}^{\tau} \right)}{\pi_{t+T} - \pi_t} \simeq \frac{-\sum_{k=0}^{T} \left(\frac{Y_{t+k} - Y_{t+k}^{\tau}}{Y_{t+k}^{\tau}} \right)}{\pi_{t+T} - \pi_t},$$

which is to say that S_{t+T} is the ratio of the cumulative proportional GDP loss (relative to its trend) to the achieved drop in the inflation rate—or, to put it more simply, the *cumulative GDP loss generated by a 1 percent reduction in the inflation rate*. Ball (1994) has surveyed a large number of disinflation episodes in the world and calculated the corresponding sacrifice ratios. Table 6.1 reproduces part of his results. The table confirms that the sacrifice ratio is (almost) always positive. It is also relatively stable from one disinflation episode to another within the same country but

TABLE 6.1
Empirical sacrifice ratios.

Country	Disinflation period	T (quarters)	$\pi_{t+T} - \pi_t$ (%)	S_{t+T}
France	1974T2–1974T4	10	2.98	0.0363
	1981T2–1986T4	23	10.42	0.0240
Germany	1965T4–1967T3	7	2.43	0.1024
	1973T1–1977T3	18	4.23	0.1054
	1980T1–1986T3	26	5.95	0.1423
United Kingdom	1961T2–1963T3	9	2,10	0.0764
	1975T1–1978T2	13	9.71	0.0347
	1980T2–1983T3	13	11.12	0.0117
	1984T2–1986T3	9	3.03	0.0347
United States	1969T4–1971T4	8	2.14	0.1175
	1974T1–1976T4	11	4.00	0.0957
	1980T1–1983T4	15	8.83	0.0733

Source: Ball (1994).

very variable from one country to another. This may reflect the fact that different countries have different degrees of price rigidity and labor supply elasticity.

Before we proceed, it is important to stress here that the output loss associated with the disinflation policy is a direct consequence of the assumed shape of the AS curve, and more specifically of the importance it gives to past inflation. Consequently, alternative specifications of the AS curve that mute down this backward-looking term would mechanically reduce the associated output loss. Take, for example, the New Keynesian Phillips curve discussed in section 3.6 of chapter 3. In the extreme case of a purely forward-looking curve ($\phi = 0$), we would have $\pi_t = \beta\pi_{t+1} + \kappa y_t$ ($0 \le \beta < 1$), implying that a sharp and unexpected disinflation going straight from $\pi_{t-1} = \hat{\pi} > 0$ to $\pi_t = \pi_{t+1} = \ldots = 0$ would be costless in terms of output. In the more realistic case where $\alpha < 1$, disinflation would still be costly in terms of output but less than under our baseline AS curve.

6.2.2.2 THE OPTIMAL SPEED OF DISINFLATION

The preceding analysis studied the macroeconomic impact of disinflation taking its speed (determined by the coefficient Ω) as given. We now show how this parameter is actually determined by an optimal decision on the part of the central bank, taking into account its objective—the minimization of the intertemporal loss L_t^I —and constraint—namely the AS curve, which determines the set of equilibrium outcomes (y_t, π_t) that can possibly be attained given past inflation π_t. Recall that inflation, until period $t - 1$, is $\hat{\pi} > 0$, while starting in period t the central bank targets zero inflation. Moreover, we will assume that the target level of output $\bar{y}$ is the natural level of output; that is, zero by our normalization. Thus, the intertemporal loss function of the central bank is given by

$$L_t^I = (\lambda y_t^2 + \pi_t^2) + \beta \left(\lambda y_{t+1}^2 + \pi_{t+1}^2\right) + \beta^2 \left(\lambda y_{t+2}^2 + \pi_{t+2}^2\right) + \ldots, \ \lambda \geq 0, \ 0 \leq \beta < 1,$$

The central bank solves $\min_{\{\pi_{t+k}\}_{k=0}^\infty} L_t^I$ under the constraints:

AS(t+k) $: \pi_{t+k} = \pi_{t+k-1} + \kappa y_{t+k}$, for $k = 0, 1, \ldots$, with $\pi_{t-1} = \hat{\pi}$ given.

To solve this plan, let us invert the AS(t+k) curve $(y_{t+k} = \kappa^{-1}(\pi_{t+k} - \pi_{t+k-1}))$ and introduce this expression of y_t into L_t^I. The problem of the central bank can then be rewritten as follows:

$$\min_{\{\pi_{t+k}\}_{k=0}^\infty} L_t^I = \{[\lambda \kappa^{-2} (\pi_t - \pi_{t-1})^2 + \pi_t^2] + \beta[\lambda \kappa^{-2} (\pi_{t+1} - \pi_t)^2 + \pi_{t+1}^2]$$

$$+ \beta^2[\lambda \kappa^{-2} (\pi_{t+2} - \pi_{t+1})^2 + \pi_{t+2}^2] + \ldots \}.$$

The central bank chooses the inflation levels π_{t+k}, $k = 0, 1, \ldots$ that satisfy the first-order conditions of the minimization problem. We obtain, for $k = 0, 1, \ldots$:

$$\frac{\partial L_t^I}{\partial \pi_{t+k}} = \beta^k \left\{2\lambda \kappa^{-2} \left(\pi_{t+k} - \pi_{t+k-1}\right) + 2\pi_{t+k} - 2\beta \lambda \kappa^{-2} \left(\pi_{t+k+1} - \pi_{t+k}\right)\right\} = 0.$$

These conditions can be rewritten as follows:

$$\pi_{t+k} = \frac{\pi_{t+k-1} + \beta \pi_{t+k+1}}{1 + \beta + \kappa^2/\lambda}, \ k = 0, 1, \ldots \tag{6.10}$$

Thus, the optimal inflation rate in period $t+k$ depends on inflation in the preceding period $(t+k-1)$ as well as inflation in the following period $(t+k+1)$—which will itself be chosen in period $t+k+1$ in an optimal way as a function of the inflation rates in periods $t+k$ and $t+k+2$, and so on.

We begin by analyzing the simplest scenario in which $\beta = 0$, and we will then generalize the analysis to the case where $\beta > 0$ (but this will not substantially modify the trade-offs that are in play).

Case where $\beta = 0$. When $\beta = 0$, the preceding expression gives:

$$\pi_{t+k} = \left(\frac{\lambda}{\lambda + \kappa^2}\right) \pi_{t+k-1}, \ k = 0, 1, \ldots$$

Since the inflation rate was $\hat{\pi}$ in period $t-1$, we obtain:

$$\pi_{t+k} = \begin{cases} \hat{\pi} & \text{for } k = \dots -3, -2, -1; \\ \Omega^{k+1}\hat{\pi} & \text{for } k = 0, 1, 2, \dots, \text{ with } \Omega = \frac{\lambda}{\lambda+\kappa^2} \in [0, 1). \end{cases}$$

Thus, the adjustment of inflation to its target $\bar{\pi} = 0$ is gradual *even though the central bank's objective is not intertemporal* (since $\beta = 0$). Inflation inertia comes here exclusively from the *intratemporal* tradeoff between the stabilization of π_t (toward $\bar{\pi} = 0$) and that of y_t (toward $\bar{y} = 0$); an excessively abrupt alignment of π_t to $\bar{\pi} = 0$ would trigger too severe a recession, which is penalized by the term λy_t^2 in the loss function.

The optimal path of inflation predicts a geometric convergence toward the inflation target; this is exactly the same dynamics of adjustment as the one described in the preceding section, except that the speed of disinflation (Ω) is no longer exogenous but now solves the optimal disinflation problem. As a consequence, Ω determines the evolution of y_t and thus the way in which the costs of the disinflation in terms of output are spread out over time. Disinflation is all the slower as Ω rises; that is, when λ is high and κ is low. In effect, the higher the λ, the more importance the central bank gives to the stabilization of output around its target $\bar{y} = 0$, relative to the disinflation motive. Thus, an increase in λ leads the central bank to defer in time the output cost of the disinflation.[17] In the limit case where $\lambda = \infty$, the central bank worries only about stabilizing output, and we have $\Omega \to 1$—the disinflation takes an infinite amount of time. Conversely, when $\lambda = 0$, meaning when the central bank is indifferent to output variations, then $\Omega = 0$: the disinflation is instantaneous. The effect of κ on Ω is also intuitive. When κ is low, meaning when nominal rigidities are strong, the response of inflation to the output gap is limited; it thus takes a sharper drop in output to attain a given level of disinflation, and this high output cost reduces the optimal speed of disinflation. In the limit when $\kappa = 0$, so that prices are fully indexed and hence insensitive to output, then it would take an infinitely large drop in output to lower inflation; in this case, the optimal policy is to maintain a constant rate inflation ($\Omega = 1$), despite the zero inflation target. Conversely, when all prices are fully flexible ($\kappa = \infty$), the cost of disinflation in terms of output is zero, and it becomes optimal to attain the target $\bar{\pi} = 0$ instantaneously (i.e., $\Omega = 0$).

Case where $\beta > 0$. Now let us consider the general case where β is not zero. The difficulty here comes from the presence of *future* inflation in the expression for current optimal inflation. The first-order condition associated with the choice of π_{t+k} gives (6.10), which implies that the elements of the optimal sequence $\{\pi_{t+k}\}_{k=0}^{\infty}$ are

17. This is true whenever $\beta < 1$ and not only when $\beta = 0$.

imbricated in a more complex way than when $\beta = 0$. Nevertheless, the problem of optimal disinflation can be solved easily by using the so-called method of undetermined coefficients.

The method requires two steps. The first step consists of conjecturing the general form of the solution. An informed conjecture is that even when $\beta > 0$, the solution to the optimal disinflation problem is still of the form:

$$\pi_{t+k} = \Omega \pi_{t+k-1}, \ k = 0, 1, \ldots$$

where Ω, $0 \leq \Omega \leq 1$, is the coefficient to be determined. The second step is to identify the coefficient Ω and to show that the implied inflation dynamics solve all the first-order conditions associated with the optimal policy problem. To do so, we first rewrite equation (6.10) in the following form:

$$\left(1 + \beta + \kappa^2/\lambda\right) \pi_{t+k} = \pi_{t+k-1} + \beta \pi_{t+k+1}, \text{ for } k = 0, 1, \ldots$$

Our conjecture was that $\pi_{t+k} = \Omega \pi_{t+k-1}$ starting from $k = 0$, which implies that $\pi_{t+k+1} = \Omega \pi_{t+k} = \Omega^2 \pi_{t+k-1}$. By using these expressions, we may rewrite the first-order conditions as follows:

$$\left(1 + \beta + \kappa^2/\lambda\right) \Omega \pi_{t+k-1} = \pi_{t+k-1} + \beta \Omega^2 \pi_{t+k-1}, \text{ for } k = 0, 1, \ldots$$

or, after factorizing,

$$\left[\beta \Omega^2 - \left(1 + \beta + \kappa^2/\lambda\right) \Omega + 1\right] \times \pi_{t+k-1} = 0, \ \ k = 0, 1, \ldots$$

Since $\pi_{t+k-1} \neq 0$ for all $k \geq 0$ under our conjecture, the term between square brackets must be equal to zero. And if it is, then *all* the first-order conditions (for $k = 0, 1, \ldots$) associated with the optimal policy problem are satisfied. Thus, if there exists a root $\Omega \in [0, 1]$ to the second-order polynomial in the square brackets, then this is a solution to our optimal policy problem. We may easily show that there exists a unique solution inside the interval $[0, 1]$, namely:[18]

$$\Omega = \frac{1}{2\beta}\left[1 + \beta + \frac{\kappa^2}{\lambda} - \sqrt{\left(1 + \beta + \frac{\kappa^2}{\lambda}\right)^2 - 4\beta}\right]. \tag{6.11}$$

18. The other root of this polynomial is greater than 1 and so cannot be the solution to the optimal disinflation problem.

In this calculation we assumed that $\beta \neq 0$. However, it may be shown that $\lim_{\beta \to 0} \Omega = \frac{\lambda}{\lambda + \kappa^2}$, so that the parameter Ω is continuous in β over the closed interval $[0, 1]$.[19] We may also show that $\partial \Omega / \partial \beta < 0$; an increase in β causes Ω to fall—that is, it increases the speed of the disinflation. The reason is the following: by lowering current inflation π_t, the central bank facilitates the task for tomorrow, since output tomorrow $y_{t+1} = \kappa^{-1} (\pi_{t+1} - \pi_t)$ is negatively linked to π_t. A central bank that values the future takes account of this effect, which leads it to reduce current inflation in a more aggressive way than if it ignored the future. Finally, λ and κ have the same effect on Ω as in the case where $\beta = 0$—Ω increases with λ and decreases with κ, for the reasons already discussed.

The OP Curve. Here again, a graphical representation of macroeconomic adjustments in the (y, π) plane proves to be useful and intuitive. Let us first of all notice that, starting in period t, inflation and output are entirely determined by the following two relations (for $k = 0, 1, \ldots$):

Optimal disinflation : $\pi_{t+k} = \Omega \pi_{t+k-1}$;

AS(t+k) : $\pi_{t+k} = \pi_{t+k-1} + \kappa y_{t+k}$.

By eliminating π_{t+k-1}, we find the following relation between inflation and output:

$$\textbf{OP} : \pi_{t+k} = - \left(\frac{\kappa \Omega}{1 - \Omega} \right) y_{t+k}.$$

We call this curve the *OP curve*, for optimal policy. The OP curve is independent of k since the relation between π_{t+k} and y_{t+k} is the same for any k. It passes through the point $(0, 0)$ and is decreasing in the (y, π) plane. As long as inflation π_{t+k} is higher than its target $(= 0)$, disinflation is still underway and hence output y_{t+k} is lower than its target $(= 0)$. The OP curve and the gradual adjustment of (y_{t+k}, π_{t+k}) along this curve are represented in figure 6.6. In period $t - 1$ (that is, on the eve of the implementation of the disinflation), inflation is high at $\pi_{t-1} = \hat{\pi}$. In period t, the AS curve is given by $\pi_t = \pi_{t-1} + \kappa y_t$, thus it is a straight line with slope $\kappa > 0$ and intercept $\pi_{t-1} = \hat{\pi} > 0$. The optimal policy is implemented in period t, and hence the (y_t, π_t) pair is now to be found not only on the AS curve but also on the OP curve. The equilibrium is shifted along the AS curve, in the southwest direction, up to the OP curve, so that we observe a fall in both output and inflation in period t.

---

19. The proof requires the application of the L'Hospital rule for derivates. As a reminder, the rule runs as follows: let $f(x)$ and $g(x)$ be two differentiable functions on the interval $]-\delta, \delta[$ and both such that $g(x) \neq 0$ and $g'(x) \neq 0 \; \forall x \neq 0$. If $\lim_{x \to 0} f(x) = 0$ and $\lim_{x \to 0} g(x) = 0$ but $\lim_{x \to 0} f'(x) / g'(x)$ is finite, then $\lim_{x \to 0} f(x) / g(x) = 1$.

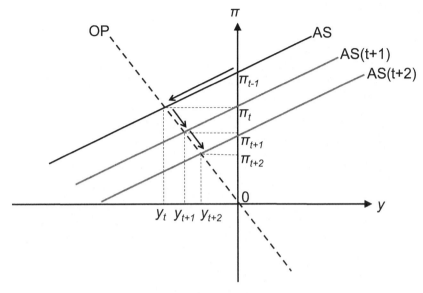

FIGURE 6.6
The OP curve and the optimal speed of disinflation. In every period, the equilibrium is found at the intersection of the AS curve and the OP curve.

What happens after that? Current inflation π_t determines the intercept of the AS(t+1) curve— $\pi_{t+1} = \pi_t + \kappa y_t$. The equilibrium of period $t+1$—that is, the (y_{t+1}, π_{t+1}) pair—is found at the intersection of the OP curve and the AS(t+1) curve, and hence inflation continues to fall while output starts recovering. Then π_{t+1} determines the intercept of the AS(t+2) curve, whose intersection with the OP curve gives (y_{t+2}, π_{t+2}), and so on. The dynamics goes on like this and leads to a gradual convergence of (y_t, π_t) toward the point $(0, 0)$.

We saw above that the disinflation was all the more costly *in the short run* when it was rapid, as this cost is being compensated in the longer run by a faster reversion of y_t toward $\bar{y}$ $(=0)$. The speed of disinflation could in turn be explained by the relative preference of the central bank for output stabilization. The more the central bank wishes to stabilize output (i.e., λ is high), the slower the disinflation (Ω is high), but the more limited the fall of output at the moment this policy is implemented. Figure 6.7 shows two disinflationary dynamics (constructed in the same way as in figure 6.6), according to whether λ is high or low. When λ is high, the slope of the OP curve is itself high in absolute value. The initial output drop is small, but the gradual shift of the equilibrium along the OP curve is slow. Conversely, when λ is small, the slope of the OP curve is itself small in absolute value; disinflation is then abrupt, but the convergence toward the long-run equilibrium is rapid.

Up to now we have characterized optimal monetary policy in terms of inflation and output, leaving implicit the path of r_t that effectively implements the optimal

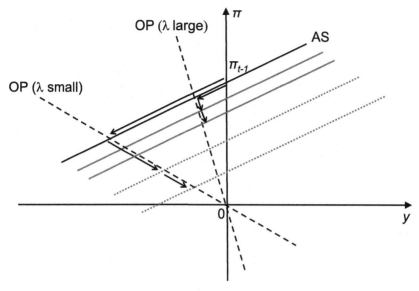

FIGURE 6.7
The optimal speed of disinflation according to society's preferences. When society grants a lot of importance to stabilizing output, the slope of OP is high in absolute value, and the disinflation is slow.

policy. But we can explicitly calculate this path by inverting the IS curve. Abstracting from aggregate demand shocks (which are studied in the next section), we have

$$\textbf{IS(t+k)}: r_{t+k} = \bar{r} - \frac{y_{t+k}}{\sigma}.$$

When disinflation takes place at an optimal pace Ω, output y_{t+k} is given by equation (6.9) above. The optimal real interest rate is therefore given by

$$r_{t+k} = \bar{r} + \left(\frac{1-\Omega}{\kappa\sigma}\right)\Omega^k \hat{\pi}.$$

Thus the optimal disinflation policy is implemented by raising r_t above $\bar{r}$ at time t, and then by gradually reducing r_t as π_t approaches its target.

6.2.3 OPTIMAL STABILIZATION

We turn now to a second classic problem of optimal monetary policy, which is in fact a generalization of the previous problem of optimal disinflation: the optimal *stabilization* of macroeconomic shocks. In other words, here we will complement the *descriptive* analysis of the effects of macroeconomic shocks undertaken in chapter 4 (where monetary policy was summarized by the MP curve) with a *normative* analysis of the ideal reaction that the central bank ought to have, if it adopted a welfare criterion of the type described above (equations (6.6) and (6.7)).

6.2.3.1 THE STABILIZATION OF AGGREGATE DEMAND SHOCKS

Let us begin by analyzing the optimal reaction to aggregate demand shocks, setting aside aggregate supply shocks for the time being. We thus assume that natural output y_t^n is zero at all times and, as before, that the period loss function is $L(y_t, \pi_t) = \lambda y_t^2 + \pi_t^2$ (i.e., both targets are zero). The central bank chooses r_t in each period, and the equilibrium (y_t, π_t) is then completely determined by the IS and AS curves, conditional upon the current aggregate demand shock θ_t and the chosen value of r_t:

$$\textbf{IS}: y_t = \theta_t - \sigma\,(r_t - \bar{r}),$$

$$\textbf{AS}: \pi_t = \pi_{t-1} + \kappa y_t.$$

Starting off, we assume that in period $t-1$ the economy was in long-run equilibrium so that $y_{t-1} = \pi_{t-1} = 0$ (i.e., both variables are at their targets). In this case the monetary policy that minimizes L_t^I is trivial. Suppose that r_t in the IS curve adjusts in each period to exactly offset all the movements of θ_t, in such a way that y_t remains constant at $\bar{y} = 0$; formally, this requires setting $dr_t = \sigma^{-1} d\theta_t$, such that $dy_t = 0$. This response to aggregate demand shocks fully and permanently stabilizes y_t (at its target $\bar{y} = 0$). By virtue of the AS curve, this policy also fully and permanently stabilizes π_t (at $\bar{\pi} = 0$). Thus, *there is no trade-off between the stabilization of π_t and that of y_t around their respective targets*—the central bank can align them to their targets instantaneously and simultaneously in every period. This property, known by the name of "divine coincidence" (after Blanchard and Galí 2007) comes from the fact that aggregate demand shocks induce a perfect positive correlation between y_t and π_t. As a consequence, a monetary policy that stabilizes one of the two variables mechanically stabilizes the other (and thus minimizes L_t^I).

In the case where the economy was *not* in long-run equilibrium $(y_{t-1}, \pi_{t-1}) = (0, 0)$ in period $t-1$, the optimal policy consists of gradually adjusting (y_t, π_t) toward $(0, 0)$ according to the dynamics described by the solution to the problem of optimal disinflation. Optimal output starting in period t is then given by

$$y_{t+k} = -\kappa^{-1}\,(1 - \Omega)\,\Omega^k \pi_{t-1}, \quad k = 0, 1, 2, \ldots$$

and hence the optimal path of the real interest rate, which we find by inverting the IS curve, is given by

$$r_{t+k} = \bar{r} + \frac{\theta_{t+k} - y_{t+k}}{\sigma}$$

$$= \bar{r} + \frac{\theta_{t+k}}{\sigma} + \frac{(1 - \Omega)\,\Omega^k}{\kappa\sigma}\pi_{t-1}$$

Such a real interest rate path takes y_t closer and closer to 0 (since $0 < \Omega < 1$), while completely neutralizing the aggregate demand shocks that might occur in the course of this adjustment (via the term θ_{t+k}/σ). This policy asymptotically and deterministically takes (y_t, π_t) toward $(0, 0)$.

6.2.3.2 THE STABILIZATION OF AGGREGATE SUPPLY SHOCKS

Now let us now turn to the optimal central bank response to aggregate *supply* shocks. To do so, let us assume that natural output y_t^n is not constant but time varying due to *markup shocks*—that is, shocks to the optimal markup rate of firms. Recall from chapter 3 that natural output is given by $y_t^n = z_t - \xi \mu^*$. We are assuming here that $y_{t+k}^n = 0$ at all times, except in period t where it is shifted by μ^*, so that $y_t^n \neq 0$; this aggregate supply shock thus has no persistence at all.[20]

The AS curve of period $t+k$ is given by

$$\textbf{AS(t+k)}: \pi_{t+k} = \pi_{t+k-1} + \kappa(y_{t|k} - y_{t+k}^n), \quad k = 0, 1, \ldots$$

The central bank minimizes L_t^I under the constraints given by the AS(t+k) curves, for $k = 0, 1, \ldots$, and taking π_{t-1} as given. The problem of the central bank may be rewritten as follows:

$$\min_{\{\pi_{t+k}\}_{k=0}^{\infty}} L_t^I = \lambda[\kappa^{-1}(\pi_t - \pi_{t-1}) + y_t^n]^2 + \pi_t^2 + \beta \left\{\lambda[\kappa^{-1}(\pi_{t+1} - \pi_t) + y_{t+1}^n]^2 + \pi_{t+1}^2\right\}$$

$$+ \beta^2 \left\{\lambda[\kappa^{-1}(\pi_{t+2} - \pi_{t+1}) + y_{t+2}^n]^2 + \pi_{t+2}^2\right\} + \ldots, \quad \text{with } \pi_{t-1} \text{ given.}$$

The first-order conditions $\partial L^I/\partial \pi_{t+k} = 0$, for $k = 0, 1, \ldots$, give

$$\beta^k \left\{\lambda[\kappa^{-1}\left(\pi_{t+k} - \pi_{t+k-1}\right) + y_{t+k}^n] + \kappa \pi_{t+k}\right\}$$

$$- \beta^{k+1} \left\{\lambda[\kappa^{-1}\left(\pi_{t+k+1} - \pi_{t+k}\right) + y_{t+k+1}^n]\right\} = 0.$$

Since $y_{t+k}^n = 0$ for all $k \geq 1$ (by assumption), these first-order conditions can be rewritten as:

For $k = 0: \left(1 + \beta + \kappa^2/\lambda\right)\pi_t - \pi_{t-1} - \beta \pi_{t+1} + \kappa y_t^n = 0;$ \hfill (6.12)

for $k \geq 1: \left(1 + \beta + \kappa^2/\lambda\right)\pi_{t+k} - \pi_{t+k-1} - \beta \pi_{t+k+1} = 0.$ \hfill (6.13)

---

20. Exercise 6.4.1 at the end of the chapter studies the optimal policy response to *persistent* markup shocks. The reason we take the markup rather than labor productivity as the underlying source of supply shock is that (for reasons that are beyond the scope of this book) it is usually *not* desirable to smooth the impact of productivity shocks on output.

Just as for the problem of optimal disinflation, we begin by studying the simple case where $\beta = 0$, and then we will rely on the undetermined coefficients method to solve the case where $\beta > 0$.

Case where $\beta = 0$. In the special case where $\beta = 0$, the first-order conditions give:

$$\pi_t = \Omega\pi_{t-1} - \Omega\kappa y_t^n \text{ and } \pi_{t+k} = \Omega\pi_{t+k-1} \text{ for } k \geq 1, \text{ with } \Omega = \frac{\lambda}{\lambda + \kappa^2} \qquad (6.14)$$

Here again, as long as $\lambda < \infty$, the optimal policy after a deviation of inflation π_t from its target $\bar{\pi} = 0$ implies a gradual convergence of π_t toward 0 (since $0 \leq \Omega < 1$). This is for the exact same reason as with the optimal disinflation problem. Bringing π_t toward its target reduces the central bank's loss but leads y_t to move away from its own target in the short run. It is thus preferable to adjust π_t gradually and not at once—except of course in the extreme case where $\lambda = 0$. What differs from the basic optimal disinflation problem is the way current inflation responds to the aggregate supply shock. Suppose that $(y_{t-1}, \pi_{t-1}) = (0, 0)$, but that a favorable aggregate supply shock (an increase in the degree of competition that lowers the optimal markup μ^*) raises natural output y_t^n above 0. Holding current output unchanged at $y_t = 0$, this shock would reduce current inflation (by the AS curve) and hence cause it to deviate from its target, thereby generating a loss for the central bank (in the amount π_t^2). Since the loss function is convex in y_t and π_t, and since the AS curve is linear, the central bank finds it worthwhile to mute down the deviation of inflation from its target in exchange for an increase in the deviation of output from its target. We may formally establish this result as follows. Let us call $\check{\pi}$ (< 0) the inflation rate that would prevail if output were maintained at $y_t = 0$ after the aggregate supply shock. By marginally raising π_t above $\check{\pi}$ (hence by bringing π_t closer to its target), the central bank reduces its loss by the amount

$$\left. \frac{\partial \pi_t^2}{\partial \pi_t} \right|_{\pi_t = \check{\pi}} = 2\check{\pi}.$$

This marginal increase in π_t, however, generates a marginal rise in y_t, of the amount $\partial y_t/\partial \pi_t = \kappa^{-1}$ (see the AS curve). This increases the loss of the central bank by

$$\kappa^{-1} \left. \frac{\partial \left(\lambda y_t^2\right)}{\partial y_t} \right|_{y_t = 0} = \kappa^{-1} \times 2\lambda \times 0 = 0.$$

This latter result comes from the fact that at $y_t = 0$ a marginal variation in y_t has no impact on the loss, precisely because the y_t^2 term in the loss function is flat at $y_t = 0$. We are thus comparing a strictly positive gain with a zero cost, and hence the central bank always finds it worthwhile to move away from the outcome $(\pi_t, y_t) = (\check{\pi}, 0)$. Put differently, the central bank always finds it worthwhile to adjust its policy so that part of the improvement in competition is manifested as a rise in output. We might perform the opposite reasoning in the case of a negative aggregate supply shock (which leads, in an optimal way, to a rise in π_t and a fall in y_t). The optimum is reached when the marginal gains and losses exactly balance each other, which gives us the coefficient $-\Omega\kappa$ before the term y_t^n in equation (6.14). The more concerned the central bank is about stabilizing output (high λ), the more it will make inflation absorb the aggregate supply shock (i.e., $-\Omega\kappa$ is high in absolute value), and vice versa.

Case where $\beta > 0$. Let us now solve the problem of optimal stabilization of aggregate supply shocks when $\beta > 0$; that is, when the central bank takes into account the effect of its current policy on future outcomes. Here again, this problem can be solved using the method of undetermined coefficients. An informed conjecture is that the solution to the problem is of the same form as when $\beta = 0$:

$$\pi_t = \Omega\pi_{t-1} - \Omega\kappa y_t^n, \text{ and } \pi_{t+k} = \Omega\pi_{t+k-1} \text{ for } k \geq 1,$$

where Ω is the coefficient to be determined. Substituting the conjecture for $k \geq 1$ into the first-order conditions in equation (6.13) and factorizing, we get

$$\left[\left(1 + \beta + \kappa^2/\lambda\right)\Omega - 1 - \beta\Omega^2\right]\pi_{t+k-1} = 0.$$

The coefficient Ω that solves the polynomial inside the square brackets and satisfies the condition $0 \leq \Omega \leq 1$ is the same as in equation (6.11) above. It is straightforward to check that this value of Ω and the conjecture $\pi_t = \Omega\pi_{t-1} - \Omega\kappa y_t^n$ also solve the first-order condition (6.12). Therefore, the general solution to the optimal stabilization problem is given by equation (6.14), with Ω given by equation (6.11) instead of $\lambda/\left(\lambda + \kappa^2\right)$.

Back to the OP curve. The OP curve previously constructed can also be applied to a situation with aggregate shocks. To see this, let us rewrite the expressions that determine (y_{t+k}, π_{t+k}), for $k = 0, 1, \ldots$ as follows:

Optimal stabilization: $\pi_{t+k} = \Omega\pi_{t+k-1} - \kappa\Omega y_{t+k}^n$ (with $y_{t+k}^n = 0$ for $k > 1$)

$$\textbf{AS(t+k)}: \pi_{t+k} = \pi_{t+k-1} + \kappa\left(y_{t+k} - y_{t+k}^n\right)$$

These two expressions give us

$$\Omega \pi_{t+k} = \Omega \pi_{t+k-1} + \kappa \Omega \left(y_{t+k} - y_{t+k}^n \right)$$

$$= \left(\Omega \pi_{t+k-1} - \kappa \Omega y_{t+k}^n \right) + \kappa \Omega y_{t+k}$$

$$= \pi_{t+k} + \kappa \Omega y_{t+k}$$

or, combining the two:

$$\mathbf{OP} : \pi_{t+k} = - \left(\frac{\Omega \kappa}{1 - \Omega} \right) y_{t+k}$$

In other words, we obtain exactly the same OP curve as in the economy without aggregate shocks. In the (y, π) plane, the equilibrium is always located at the intersection of the AS(t+k) curve and the OP curve. Aggregate demand shocks are fully neutralized and have no effect on the equilibrium (by virtue of the divine coincidence). Aggregate supply shocks shift the AS curve and consequently shift the equilibrium (y_{t+k}, π_{t+k}) along the OP curve. The translation of the equilibrium depends on the slope of the OP curve and thus on the weight of the output stabilization objective (λ) in the central bank's loss function (*via* its effect on Ω). Figure 6.8 illustrates this point for two values of λ. When λ is high, the slope of the OP curve is high in absolute value, so that an aggregate supply shock brings about a small variation in output but a large variation in inflation. In the limit, when $\lambda = \infty$, the OP curve is vertical and only inflation reacts to the shock. Conversely, when λ is low, so that the slope of OP curve is low in absolute value, then it is output that reacts strongly to the shock, while inflation respond little.

6.2.4   ARE ACTUAL MONETARY POLICIES OPTIMAL?

To review, in chapter 2 we advanced the idea that the MP curve, according to which the central bank adjusted the real interest rate as a function of deviations of inflation from its target, was a relatively accurate description (at least as a first approximation) of concrete monetary policies. The MP curve was written as:

$$\mathbf{MP} : r_t = \bar{r} + \gamma \left(\pi_t - \bar{\pi} \right), \quad \gamma > 0,$$

where $\bar{r}$ is the average real interest rate and $\bar{\pi}$ the inflation target. We then used the MP curve to complement the IS curve and construct the AD curve, which established a decreasing relation between output and inflation. Finally, we used the AD curve in chapters 4 and 5 to understand the way in which macroeconomic shocks (whether aggregate supply or demand shocks) propagate to the equilibrium (y_t, π_t). In these

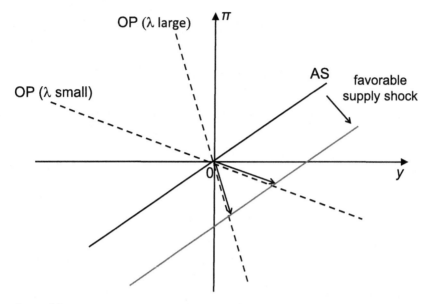

FIGURE 6.8
The optimal adjustment to an aggregate supply shock. When society grants a lot of importance to stabilizing output, the slope of the OP curve is high in absolute value and output varies little, but inflation varies a lot, after an aggregate supply shock.

developments, the existence and form of the MP curve played an central role in the propagation and stabilization of macroeconomic shocks.

In the present chapter, we have taken a different view on monetary policy by trying to compute what the real interest rate r_t *ought to be* if the central bank behaved in an optimal way with respect to a certain social welfare function. We have deduced from this analysis that any optimal outcome ought to be found along the OP curve, which is a decreasing relation between y_t and π_t (just as in the AD curve, which the OP curve replaces).

Since y_t is systematically linked to r_t (via the IS curve), we may derive the level of r_t that implements the optimal stabilization of aggregate shocks. Inverting both the IS and the OP curves gives us:

$$r_t = \bar{r} - \frac{y_t - \theta_t}{\sigma}, \quad y_t = -\left(\frac{1-\Omega}{\kappa\Omega}\right)\pi_t. \tag{6.15}$$

so that we can rewrite the expression of the real interest rate as follows:

$$r_t = \bar{r} + \gamma^*\left(\pi_t - \bar{\pi}\right) + \frac{\theta_t}{\sigma}, \tag{6.16}$$

where

$$\gamma^* = \frac{1 - \Omega}{\sigma \kappa \Omega} > 0 \ \text{ and } \ \bar{\pi} = 0. \tag{6.17}$$

We observe here that equation (6.16), which summarizes the *optimal* response of the real interest rate to aggregate shocks, closely resembles the ad hoc MP curve posited in chapter 2. Does this imply that the MP curve effectively describes what central bank should be doing, and not only what they actually do?

To answer this question, let us start with the dimension in which the two interest-rate rules (the optimal interest-rate rule and the ad hoc MP curve) are most similar, namely in the way they describe the monetary policy response to aggregate *supply* shocks. When monetary policy is described by the MP curve, the latter becomes embodied in the AD curve of the AS-AD model analyzed in chapter 4. There we have seen that a contractionary aggregate supply shock, for example, leads to a response of both output (downward) and inflation (upward). Intuitively, the direct effect of the shock is to push up inflation, and the central bank responds to the resulting inflationary pressures by raising the real interest rate so as to lower aggregate demand. Provided that the parameter γ in the ad hoc MP curve is positive but finite, both inflation and output move (i.e., both variables share the burden of adjustment to the shock). This response turns out to be fully consistent with the *optimal* response to the contractionary supply shock. Indeed, starting from a situation where both inflation and output are on target, the aggregate supply shocks can only move them in opposite direction. The convexity of the loss function then implies that it cannot be optimal for the central bank to have only one of the two equilibrium variables (inflation or output) bear the full burden of adjustment. Indeed, as discussed above, it is always preferable to deviate even marginally from such an extreme outcome and instead opt for an interior response where *both* output and inflation vary (inflation upward and output downward), provided of course that the parameter λ in the loss function is positive but finite. This endogenous adjustment of (y_t, π_t) is qualitatively the same as that under a simple MP curve. To summarize, the *MP curve adequately describes the optimal monetary policy response to aggregate supply shocks*. In this sense the key parameter in the MP curve (namely the elasticity parameter γ) can be rationalized by some underlying social preferences toward output versus inflation stabilization. The weight λ in the loss function determines the composite parameter Ω and thereby the optimal value of γ—namely γ^* in equation (6.16).

Things are not as simple with regard to aggregate *demand* shocks. According to the MP curve, the interest rate should rise after a positive shock to aggregate demand in order to counter the associated inflationary pressures (see chapter 4). However, and again provided that γ in the MP curve is positive but finite, those inflationary pressures are never completely neutralized and thereby both inflation and output rise after the shock. This is inconsistent with the optimal interest rate response to the same shock. Indeed, from equations (6.16) and (6.17), the optimal interest-rate response to an aggregate demand shock of size $d\theta_t$ is $dr_t = d\theta_t/\sigma$. But then, equation (6.15) implies that $dy_t = d\pi_t = 0$. That is, the optimal monetary policy response to an aggregate demand shock consists of *varying the real interest rate sufficiently strongly so as to fully neutralize the impact of the shock on output and inflation.* Thus the real interest rate will move as much as necessary to ensure that output and inflation never leave their targets.

If we accept the notion that the MP curve offers a satisfying representation of the behavior of central banks in practice, then our normative analysis suggests that central banks are adequately responding to aggregate supply shocks but are underreacting to demand shocks, relative to what would be optimal. However, there may be specific reasons, not captured by our simple AS-AD framework, why central banks are not willing to let real interest rates vary as much as necessary to fully and instantaneously neutralize aggregate demand shocks. For example, doing so may require abrupt changes in the policy rate that would destabilize other asset prices. Either that, or any cost to interest-rate changes would make at least *some* smoothing of the real interest rate desirable and could (at least in principle) reconcile the MP curve with the optimal policy.

6.3 EXPECTATIONS AND THE CREDIBILITY AND EFFECTIVENESS OF MONETARY POLICY

The presidential address given by Milton Friedman to the American Economic Association (from which the paragraph at the beginning of the chapter is taken) inaugurated a major methodological turning point in economics by emphasizing the role of the expectations of economic agents (about inflation, output, government decisions, and so on) and the ways in which these expectations influence the effectiveness and optimality of economic policies. The worries expressed by the American economist on this occasion contained an acute premonition: at the time of his writing, inflation was barely beginning to take off in the United States, and it would take several more years for it to reach double-digit rates (see figure 6.5). However, Milton Friedman already perceived the risk of a loss of control over inflation by the central bank as soon as it went about lowering the unemployment rate below its natural level. The heart of the problem, Friedman tells us, lies in the formation of expectations, and more specifically the way in which households adjust their expectations as a function of the monetary policy they expect the central bank to follow. The central bank may be willing to adopt an expansionary monetary policy that takes private agents by surprise, and thereby generates a realized (i.e., *ex post*) rate of inflation higher than what was anticipated (*ex ante*); but the central bank cannot do so in a systematic way, for then households would adjust their inflation expectations and would consequently modify the nominal wage they demand from their employers—with the result of neutralizing the effect of *ex post* inflation on real wages.

The present section studies the way in which the expectations of economic agents about future monetary policy influence its credibility and effectiveness. To do so, we are going to set aside provisionally some assumptions made in chapter 3 about the way that prices are formed. There we considered that firms could either adjust their prices in an optimal manner once macroeconomic shocks were known, or else simply index their selling price to past inflation. This assumption is satisfying for a short-run analysis of macroeconomic shocks, in which we consider that one period in the model corresponds to a quarter or a year. But it is less satisfying when we consider longer time horizons, as firms try to anticipate monetary trends when setting prices. Taking into account these expectations of future monetary policy and the way they affect current prices requires postulating a price-setting mechanism that differs from that in chapter 3, and that is how we begin.

6.3.1 THE AS CURVE WITH PREDETERMINED PRICES

The price-setting mechanism that we will use in this section is the following:

1. At the end of period $t-1$, all firms freely set the selling price that will prevail in period t, depending on the labor cost they expect for period t. So prices are determined one period in advance (thus, they are predetermined). The selling price they choose is simply the optimal price implied by these expectations. We know (from equation (3.4)) that the optimal selling price for period t is $p_t^* = \mu^* + w_t - z_t$. From the standpoint of period $t-1$, these values are expected; hence every firm sets the price $p_{t-1,t}^{*e} = \mu^* + w_{t-1,t}^e - z_{t-1,t}^e$, where $w_{t-1,t}^e$ and $z_{t-1,t}^e$ are the expectations formed in period $t-1$ about the nominal wage and labor productivity (both in log) that will prevail in period t. Since all firms set this price, agents' expectations formed in period $t-1$ about the price level of period t are given by

$$p_{t-1,t}^e = \int_0^1 p_{t-1,t}^{*e} \mathrm{d}i = \mu^* + w_{t-1,t}^e - z_{t-1,t}^e.$$

Note that here firms modify their prices in an optimal way (for the following period) at the end of *every* period—unlike in the price-setting mechanism posited in chapter 3.

2. In period t the actual values of (w_t, z_t) are revealed, and in general they differ from their expected values $(w_{t-1,t}^e, z_{t-1,t}^e)$ due to the occurrence of macroeconomic shocks or changes in economic policies that were not (possibly because they could not) be fully anticipated as of period $t-1$. After the information about these new

economic conditions is revealed, a fraction $1 - \omega$ of the firms, with $0 \leq \omega \leq 1$, adjusts their prices optimally and thus choose $p_t^* = \mu^* + w_t - z_t$. By contrast, the other firms maintain their selling prices unchanged at $p_{t-1,t}^e = \mu^* + w_{t-1,t}^e - z_{t-1,t}^e$. It follows that the price level in period t, after the optimal price adjustment by only a fraction $1 - \omega$ of the firms has taken place, is given by

$$p_t = \omega p_{t-1,t}^e + (1 - \omega) p_t^*,$$

which may be restated in terms of the optimal *relative* price $p_t^* - p_t$ as follows:

$$p_t = p_{t-1,t}^e + \left(\frac{1 - \omega}{\omega} \right) (p_t^* - p_t).$$

The rest of the aggregate supply block is similar to that in chapter 3. In particular, the natural level of output is given by $y_t^n = z_t - \xi \mu^*$, and the labor-market equilibrium generates the real wage:

$$w_t - p_t = \frac{y_t - (1 - \xi) z_t}{\xi}.$$

By using these expressions, the price level p_t may be written (the steps in the calculation are similar to those in section 3.4 of chapter 3):

$$
\begin{aligned}
p_t &= p_{t-1,t}^e + \left(\frac{1 - \omega}{\omega} \right) (\mu^* + w_t - p_t - z) \\
&= p_{t-1,t}^e + \left(\frac{1 - \omega}{\omega} \right) \left(\mu^* + \frac{y_t - (1 - \xi) z_t}{\xi} - z_t \right) \\
&= p_{t-1,t}^e + \left(\frac{1 - \omega}{\omega \xi} \right) (y_t - y_t^n),
\end{aligned}
$$

or, by adding $-p_{t-1}$ to both sides of this equation:

$$\mathbf{AS} : \pi_t = \pi_{t-1,t}^e + \kappa \left(y_t - y_t^n \right), \quad \kappa = \frac{1 - \omega}{\omega \xi},$$

where

$$\pi_{t-1,t}^e = p_{t-1,t}^e - p_{t-1} \simeq \frac{p_{t-1,t}^e - p_{t-1}}{p_{t-1}}$$

is the expectation formed in period $t - 1$ about the inflation rate of time t.

The fundamental difference between this AS curve and the one we previously used is that here it is the *expectation of current inflation* $\pi^e_{t-1,t}$, and not past inflation π_{t-1}, that determines the intercept of the curve. Hence if inflation were perfectly anticipated (such that $\pi_t = \pi^e_{t-1,t}$), then output would necessarily be at its natural level (i.e., $y_t = y^n_t$). In effect, in this situation all firms will effectively have set (at time $t-1$) their prices at the optimal level for time t, a situation which is equivalent to one of perfect price flexibility. By contrast, y_t deviates from y^n_t as soon as realized inflation (π_t) is different from what was expected ($\pi^e_{t-1,t}$), either because unforeseen aggregate shocks occurred in the meantime or because inflation expectations were biased (we will come back to this point further on). In this case, firms fixed, in period $t-1$, prices that ultimately proved to be inadequate in period t. However, only a fraction of firms can optimally readjust their prices, whereas all the others respond to demand at an unchanged selling price. For example, if aggregate demand in period t turns out to be higher than expected, then the firms that do not increase their prices respond to this demand by increasing their production, causing y_t to rises. By contrast, if all firms adjusted their prices when faced with the new demand conditions, then the price level would increase to the point of completely eliminating the initial effect of the aggregate demand shock on output. In this situation, output would remain at its natural level y^n_t.

The AS curve above links the output gap $y_t - y^n_t$ to an expectational error $\pi_t - \pi^e_{t-1,t}$. The way in which expectations are formed thus plays an essential role in the determination of the equilibrium.

6.3.2 THE FORMATION OF EXPECTATIONS

Economic agents always have an interest in forming the best possible expectations about the future. Not doing so would lead to deviating from the individual optimum, which would necessarily be costly in terms of profits or utility. However, there are two obstacles to the formation of perfectly accurate expectations about future economic conditions:

1. All relevant information is generally not available at the time when expectations are formed; for example, agents form their inflation expectations $\pi^e_{t-1,t}$ for period t before the time t conditions of aggregate demand (θ_t) and supply (y^n_t) are perfectly known.

2. Information processing and the computation of the optimal choices involve certain physical and cognitive costs; if these costs are too high, then agents may prefer to save on them, even if this entails some departures from the optimal choices.

The first obstacle is ubiquitous but poses no particular conceptual difficulty. Even if they do not know the future perfectly (or even very badly), agents can always use the information they do have for the best when forming their expectations. It is this idea that lies at the foundation of the so-called *rational expectations*, which we discuss in more detail below. The second obstacle is more problematic because it leaves the economist with an open Pandora's box. If agents do not best use the information they possess, what do they do instead? The answer to this question necessarily is somewhat arbitrary, since it requires making particular assumptions about the effectiveness with which private agents exploit whatever information they have. Let us explore the implications of two such assumptions here, before we turn to rational expectations.

6.3.2.1 CONSTANT EXPECTATIONS

When expectations are constant ($\pi_{t-1,t}^e = \bar{\pi}$), the AS curve above becomes:

$$\mathbf{AS} : \pi_t = \bar{\pi} + \kappa \left(y_t - y_t^n \right).$$

This assumption corresponds to an extreme form of bounded rationality. It is unrealistic for two reasons. First of all, it implies that agents could recurrently observe $\pi_t > \pi_{t-1,t}^e$ (or the opposite) and yet not adjust their expectations $\pi_{t-1,t}^e$. This would be an extreme violation of individual rationality. Second, the assumption of constant expectations implies that the central bank might permanently raise y_t above y_t^n (by permanently lowering r_t) without causing a significant drift in inflation. As discussed earlier in the book, both the theory and the evidence cast doubt on this property. Theoretically, this monetary might is at odds with the natural rate hypothesis. And empirically, the experience of the Great Inflation of the 1970s suggests that the central bank may easily lose control of inflation when monetary policy is overly expansionary.

6.3.2.2 STATIC EXPECTATIONS

Static expectations take the form $\pi_{t-1,t}^e = \pi_{t-1}$; agents take account of macroeconomic conditions but with a one-period lag. Under this assumption, we find exactly the same AS curve as that derived in chapter 3, but with an alternative theoretical foundation (the inertia of expectations, rather than the indexation of prices):

$$\mathbf{AS} : \pi_t = \pi_{t-1} + \kappa \left(y_t - y_t^n \right).$$

This AS curve is sometimes called "accelerationist" since it implies that it is theoretically possible to durably raise y_t above y_t^n but at the cost of an *ever-increasing inflation rate*—meaning an acceleration of the price level. By contrast, under constant expectations it was possible to persistently maintain $y_t > y_t^n$ with a *constant* (and not rising) inflation rate. The accelerationist view is exactly the one described by Friedman in the epigraph to this chapter. The worry that he expressed at the time is justified, since maintaining $y_t - y_t^n > 0$ (say, at a constant value $\overline{y - y^n}$)

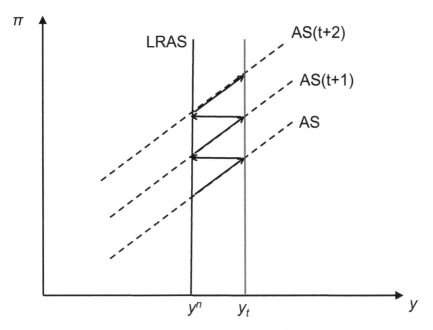

FIGURE 6.9
Friedman's accelerationism. Static expectations produce inertia in the adjustment of inflation expectations; the central bank may thus durably raise output above its natural level, at the price of ever-increasing inflation.

would inevitably lead to an explosion of inflation. Indeed, we would have

$$\pi_t = \pi_{t-1} + \kappa \left(\overline{y} - y^n\right)$$
$$\pi_{t+1} = \pi_t + \kappa \left(\overline{y} - y^n\right) = \pi_{t-1} + 2\kappa \left(\overline{y} - y^n\right)$$
$$\vdots$$
$$\pi_{t+k} = \pi_{t-1} + k\kappa \left(\overline{y} - y^n\right) \underset{k \to \infty}{\to} \infty.$$

We might represent this situation graphically by using AS and LRAS curves (see figure 6.9). In period t the AS curve is given by $\pi_t = \pi_{t-1} + \kappa \left(y_t - y_t^n\right)$ (since $\pi_{t-1,t}^e = \pi_{t-1}$), and its intercept is thus $\pi_{t-1} - \kappa y_t^n$. The central bank then lowers the real interest rate r_t so as to raise $y_t - y_t^n$ to the level $\overline{y} - y^n$, which leads to a shift (northeast) of the equilibrium (y_t, π_t) along the AS curve. The equilibrium value of π_t determines the intercept of the AS(t+1) curve (i.e., $\pi_{t-1} + \kappa \left(\overline{y} - y^n\right) - \kappa y_t^n$), which is located above the intercept of the AS curve. The central bank then shifts the equilibrium along the AS(t+1) curve, which raises the intercept of the AS(t+2) curve further up, and so on. In the long run, the LRAS curve is vertical at $y_t = y_t^n$, but the succession of equilibrium outcomes (y_{t+k}, π_{t+k}) is located to the right of the LRAS curve—the central bank successfully maintains an expansionary policy, but loses control of inflation.

6.3.2.3 RATIONAL EXPECTATIONS

Under static expectations, and under the monetary policy that we have just considered, private agents are systematically mistaken ($\pi_t \neq \pi_{t-1,t}^e$ for all t), and the expectational bias $\pi_t - \pi_{t-1,t}^e = \kappa \left(\overline{y - y^n}\right)$ is not reduced even when it is observed repeatedly *ex post*. It is reasonable to think that if private agents truly observed this situation over and over again, they would be led to gradually reduce—and even eliminate completely—such expectational errors. Let us push this argument further: if the monetary policy under consideration were perfectly known by the agents, why would they not adjust *immediately* their inflation expectations, in order to align them with the *equilibrium* path of inflation, rather than go through a phase of systematic underestimation of the inflation rate? After all, if agents knew the true economic model (in the present case, the AS curve and the monetary policy adopted by the central bank), they would have no reason to make any systematic errors, or even simply persistent ones, in forecasting inflation. It is this simple idea that lies at the root of the so-called rational expectations hypothesis.

Formally, rational expectations are a generalization of the notion of perfect foresight to the case where the economy is periodically hit by random aggregate shocks. As discussed in chapter 1, perfect foresight follows from the knowledge of the economic model itself, in a situation where there are no aggregate shocks between the time when expectations are formed and the moment when equilibrium outcomes are realized. In the context of our model, if there are no aggregate shocks and agents perfectly know current and future monetary policy (meaning the path of π_t), then we have $\pi_{t-1,t}^e = \pi_t$ and hence $y_t = y_t^n$.

We are moving from perfect foresight to rational expectations when we add aggregate shocks between the formation of expectations and the realization of the equilibrium. Formally, the inflation rate that is rationally anticipated for period $t+1$, taking account of all information available in period t, is given by

$$\pi_{t,t+1}^e = \mathbb{E}_t\left(\pi_{t+1}\right).$$

where $\mathbb{E}_t\left(x_{t+1}\right)$ is the expectation of variable x_{t+1} conditional on all the information available in period t (which is called the information set of period t). In the same way we will note as $\mathbb{E}_{t+j}\left(x_{t+k}\right), j, k \in \mathbb{Z}$, the expectation formed in period $t+j$ about the realization of variable x in period $t+k$. For example, if the period corresponds to a year, $\mathbb{E}_{t-1}\left(\pi_{t+2}\right)$ is the expectation formed last year, conditional on the information available then, of the inflation rate that will prevail in two years' time from now.

The AS curve features $\pi^e_{t-1,t}$; that is, the expectation formed in period $t-1$ about the inflation rate of period t. Under rational expectations the AS curve becomes

$$\mathbf{AS} : \pi_t = \mathbb{E}_{t-1}(\pi_t) + \kappa \left(y_t - y^n_t \right),$$

which is known as the *New Classical Phillips curve* after its discovery and promotion by prominent economists such as Robert Lucas and Thomas Sargent in the late 1970s and early 1980s.

Agents who form rational expectations best use the information they possess and commit no persistent forecasting errors. Let us illustrate this point by comparing the equilibrium outcomes that would be obtained with a noisy version of the accelerationist monetary policy described above, according to whether expectations are rational or static. More precisely, we will assume that the central bank applies (in every period) the following inflation path:

$$\pi_t = \mu + \pi_{t-1} + \varepsilon_t, \ \mu > 0, \ \mathbb{E}_{t-1}(\varepsilon_t) = 0.$$

where ε_t reflects the imperfect control of inflation by the central bank.

Under static expectations, we would have $\pi^e_{t-1,t} = \pi_{t-1}$, and thus:

$$\underbrace{\pi_t - \pi^e_{t-1,t}}_{\text{forecasting error}} = \pi_t - \pi_{t-1} = \mu + \varepsilon_t,$$

and

$$\underbrace{y_t - y^n_t}_{\text{output gap}} = \kappa^{-1} \left(\pi_t - \pi^e_{t-1,t} \right) = \kappa^{-1} \left(\mu + \varepsilon_t \right).$$

Hence when expectations are static, the forecasting error gravitates around $\mu > 0$ and the output gap around $\kappa^{-1}\mu > 0$. Nevertheless, these expectations imply that agents are not using the information they have in the best possible way, since a systematic expectational bias (of size μ) persistently remains.

By contrast, under rational expectations, we have:

$$\pi^e_{t-1,t} = \mathbb{E}_{t-1}(\pi_t)$$

$$= \mathbb{E}_{t-1}(\mu + \pi_{t-1} + \varepsilon_t)$$

$$= \mu + \pi_{t-1},$$

so that:

$$\underbrace{\pi_t - \pi_{t-1,t}^e}_{\text{forecasting error}} = \varepsilon_t,$$

and thus, ultimately:

$$\underbrace{y_t - y_t^n}_{\text{output gap}} = \kappa^{-1}\left(\pi_t - \pi_{t-1,t}^e\right) = \kappa^{-1}\varepsilon_t.$$

Therefore, under rational expectations, the forecasting error and the output gap are both zero-mean white noise processes. Firms rationally expect the path of inflation and incorporate it *ex ante* into their pricing decisions, which neutralizes any systematic (and hence predictable) effect of inflation on output. Only the share of inflation that it is impossible to anticipate (the white-noise policy shock ε_t) may cause π_t to deviate from $\pi_{t-1,t}^e$ and thus y_t from y_t^n.

This property is very general and does not depend on the (simplistic) monetary policy that we have just considered. Suppose, for example, that the central bank is trying to implement an inflation rate that depends in a complex way on the past levels of inflation and output as well as on the cumulative noise in the control of inflation:

$$\pi_t = g\left(\pi_{t-1}, \pi_{t-2}, \ldots, y_{t-1}, y_{t-2}, \ldots\right) + \varepsilon_t + a_1\varepsilon_{t-1} + a_2\varepsilon_{t-2} + \ldots$$

Since π_{t-1}, $\pi_{t-2},\ldots,$ y_{t-1}, $y_{t-2},\ldots$ are known in period $t-1$ and since $\mathbb{E}_{t-1}\left(\varepsilon_t\right) = 0$, we still have:

$$\mathbb{E}_{t-1}\left(\pi_t\right) = g\left(\pi_{t-1}, \pi_{t-2}, \ldots, y_{t-1}, y_{t-2}, \ldots\right) + a_1\varepsilon_{t-1} + a_2\varepsilon_{t-2} + \ldots,$$

and hence:

$$\pi_t - \mathbb{E}_{t-1}\left(\pi_t\right) = \varepsilon_t \text{ and } y_t - y_t^n = \kappa^{-1}\varepsilon_t.$$

Thus, the output gap is a white noise process, even though the monetary policy rule is complex and generates inflation persistence. This is because *forecasting errors are not persistent*, for if they were, then they would be promptly corrected by those who made them.

6.3.3 THE LUCAS CRITIQUE

Given that the structure of all econometric models consists of optimal decision rules of economic agents, and that optimal decision rules vary systematically with changes in the structure of series relevant to the decision maker, it follows that any change in policy will systematically alter the structure of econometric models. [This] implies that comparisons of the effects of alternative policy rules using current macroeconometric models are invalid.

—Robert Lucas (1976)

Rational expectations limit the power of economic policy in a very precise sense: they limit the ability of monetary and fiscal authorities to affect the equilibrium by hoping to systematically surprise private agents. The Lucas critique, which is summarized in the quote above, aims to draw all the methodological implications of this proposition. Before this critique, economists viewed economic models as a set of stable relations (the "laws" of the economy) whose parameters could be estimated by appropriate econometric methods. These relations could then be used to simulate the effects of economic policies, just as one would simulate the effect of a shock on a physical system. This approach is mistaken, Lucas tells us, because the statistical regularities observed by econometricians depend on economic choices (about savings, labor supply, and so on) made by private agents, and these choices are bound to be modified after a change in economic policy— the nature and implications of which private agents can understand. The statistical regularities that econometricians consider as given, therefore, are fated to be modified after a change in economic policy. This implies that what is observed before the policy change is no longer any sort of guide for evaluating the consequences of this change.

Let us illustrate this statement very precisely with the aid of a simple example. Suppose that $y_t^n = 0$ and that the monetary policy followed by the central bank is accelerationist and noisy:

Policy Rule: $\Delta \pi_t = \mu + \varepsilon_t$.

Since $\pi_t - \mathbb{E}_{t-1}(\pi_t) = \pi_t - \pi_{t-1} - \mathbb{E}_{t-1}(\pi_t - \pi_{t-1})$, we may rewrite the AS curve as follows:

AS: $y_t = \kappa^{-1} [\Delta \pi_t - \mathbb{E}_{t-1}(\Delta \pi_t)]$.

These two equations (the monetary policy rule and the AS curve) constitute the *true* economic model. Over time, the successive realizations of shocks ε_t generate time series for y_t and π_t. Since $\Delta \pi_t - \mathbb{E}_{t-1}(\Delta \pi_t) = \varepsilon_t$, under the monetary policy under consideration those time series are

$$y_t = \kappa^{-1}\varepsilon_t,$$

$$\Delta\pi_t = \mu + \varepsilon_t.$$

Let us assume that the central bank is contemplating a change in the monetary policy rule—specifically a shift from μ to $\mu' > \mu$. The central bank (obviously) knows its own policy rule but it does not exactly know how the economy works, and in particular it does not know the exact form and parameters of the AS curve. So it wishes to estimate it beforehand in order to measure the likely effects on output of a shift from μ to μ'. To do so, the central bank, which senses (correctly) that there exists a relation between $\Delta\pi_t$ and y_t, asks its econometricians to perform the following linear regression:

$$y_t = \alpha + \beta\Delta\pi_t + \varkappa_t,$$

where α and β are the coefficients to be estimated and $\varkappa_t$ is the residual. Given the time series observed until period T, namely $\{y_t\}_{k=0}^T$ and $\{\pi_t\}_{t=0}^T$ (which were generated by the true economic model), the least-square coefficients of this regression are

$$\hat{\beta} = \frac{\text{cov}\left[y_t, \Delta\pi_t\right]}{\text{var}\left[\Delta\pi_t\right]} = \frac{\mathbb{E}\left[\kappa^{-1}\varepsilon_t \times \varepsilon_t\right]}{\text{var}\left[\varepsilon_t\right]} = 1/\kappa > 0,$$

$$\hat{\alpha} = \mathbb{E}\left(y_t\right) - \hat{\beta}\mathbb{E}\left(\Delta\pi_t\right) = 0 - \hat{\beta}\mu = -\mu/\kappa,$$

where $\mathbb{E}(x)$ is the mean of x. From this regression the central bank will conclude that the systematic relation between y_t and $\Delta\pi_t$ is given by

$$y_t = \hat{\alpha} + \hat{\beta}\Delta\pi_t.$$

Everything has seemed to work fine up to now—except for the following problem. The central bank, considering that the relation $\hat{\alpha} + \hat{\beta}\Delta\pi_t$, with $\hat{\beta} > 0$, is a stable relation between $\Delta\pi_t$ and y_t, will naturally conclude that a permanent increase in $\Delta\pi_t$, obtained by a rise in μ, *will raise y_t in all periods*. However, such an attempt would be doomed to failure as soon as private agents understand the new monetary policy rule. In effect, the shift from μ to $\mu' > \mu$ implies that $\mathbb{E}_{t-1}(\Delta\pi_t) = \mu'$ and not $\mathbb{E}_{t-1}(\Delta\pi_t) = \mu$. Now, since $\hat{\alpha} = -\mu/\kappa$, the new statistical relation between the variables after the policy change will be given by

$$y_t = \hat{\alpha}' + \hat{\beta}\Delta\pi_t, \text{ with } \hat{\alpha}' = -\mu'/\kappa,$$

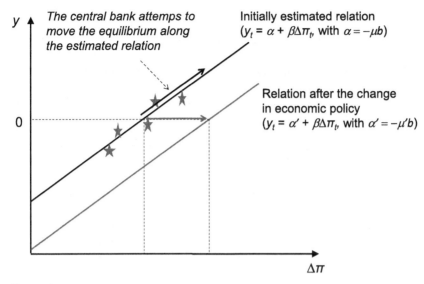

The central bank attemps to move the equilibrium along the estimated relation

Initially estimated relation ($y_t = \alpha + \beta\Delta\pi_t$, with $\alpha = -\mu b$)

Relation after the change in economic policy ($y_t = \alpha' + \beta\Delta\pi_t$, with $\alpha' = -\mu' b$)

FIGURE 6.10

The Lucas critique. When authorities try to exploit an existing statistical relation for the purpose of economic policy, this relation breaks down.

and not $y = \hat{\alpha} + \hat{\beta}\Delta\pi$ with $\hat{\alpha} = -\mu/\kappa$. By changing its monetary policy rule (from μ to μ'), the central bank has also changed the statistical relation between variables, since the intercept of the relation between y_t and $\Delta\pi_t$ moves from $\hat{\alpha}$ to $\hat{\alpha}' < \hat{\alpha}$. The estimated relation from before the policy change is thus no guide at all for simulating the impact of an increase of μ over y_t. By seeking to exploit the fact that $\hat{\beta} > 0$ to stimulate y_t, *the central bank did not perceive that the parameter $\hat{\alpha}$ is endogenous to its own economic policy and not exogenous and constant.*

The endogenous modification of the statistical relation between y_t and $\Delta\pi_t$ after the change in monetary policy is represented in figure 6.10. The stars represent the series of (y_t, π_t) pairs initially used to estimate the relation between y_t and π_t. Observing that the slope of this relation is positive, the central bank tries to durably increase y_t via an increase in $\Delta\pi_t$; that is, by shifting the equilibrium *along the estimated AS curve*. However, as soon as agents understand this policy and modify their expectations accordingly (by anticipating $\mathbb{E}_{t-1}(\Delta\pi_t) = \mu'$ rather than $\mathbb{E}_{t-1}(\Delta\pi_t) = \mu$), then *the intercept of the AS curves shifts downward* (from $-\mu/\kappa$ to $-\mu'/\kappa$). In the end, we still have $y_t = b\varepsilon_t$ (as the true model of the economy *necessarily* implies), but $\Delta\pi_t$ is now higher on average. Put differently, the downward shift of the AS curve exactly cancels the effect of the rise in $\Delta\pi_t$. The new cluster of points generated by the economic model and its aggregate shocks will still be situated around $y_t = 0$, but at a higher level of $\Delta\pi_t$ (the horizontal arrow on the figure represents the translation of this cluster).

6.3.4 THE INFLATION BIAS

The study of the supply behavior of firms, as done in chapter 3 as well as in this chapter, implies that there exists no output-inflation tradeoff in the long run. It is not possible for the monetary authority to boost output durably while at the same time keeping inflation at a prespecified target. In other words, the LRAS (long run aggregate supply) curve is vertical (i.e., the natural rate hypothesis holds). However, before the monetary policy regime of inflation targeting became widespread in the 1990s, it frequently occurred that *ex post* inflation was lastingly higher than that it was announced to be *ex ante* by the central bank, or in any case manifestly higher than what was socially desirable (see figure 6.5 for the United States).

The theory of the inflation bias was developed in the late 1970s and the early 1980s to explain why central banks, even with the best intentions in the world, might not be capable of resisting the temptation of inflation. The heart of the problem does not lie in the objective function of the central bank *per se*, but rather in the structure of interactions between the central bank and private agents, in a context in which the latter form their expectations rationally. According to this theory, the central bank is always tempted to exploit the form of the AS curve (whose slope κ is positive and finite) by adopting an expansionary policy that raises output at the expense of a higher inflation rate, once private sector expectations have been formed. However, private agents, who rationally anticipate this policy, form inflation expectations *ex ante* accordingly, and in so doing they neutralize from the start the impact of the expansionary policy on output. Ultimately, the central bank will have created inflation with no benefit in terms of output.

To understand the source of the inflation bias, let us start with the rational-expectations AS curve, in inverted form:

$$\mathbf{AS} : y_t = \kappa^{-1} \left(\pi_t - \mathbb{E}_{t-1} \left(\pi \right) \right) + y_t^n, \tag{6.18}$$

where natural output is assumed to be a white noise process with mean zero and positive variance:

$$\mathbb{E}_{t-1} \left[y_t^n \right] = 0 \text{ and } \mathbb{E}_{t-1} \left[\left(y_t^n \right)^2 \right] > 0 \text{ constant.}$$

Equation (6.18) shows that the central bank cannot raise y_t above y_t^n unless it manages to surprise private agents; that is, to act in such a way that $\pi_t > \mathbb{E}_{t-1} \left(\pi_t \right)$.

We will assume, to simplify the analysis but with no loss of generality, that the economy lasts only two periods: time $t - 1$, when expectations about the time t variables are formed, and time t, when monetary policy is implemented and the equilibrium is realized. The loss function of the central bank is given by:

$$L\left(\pi_t, y_t\right) = \lambda \left(y_t - \bar{y}\right)^2 + \pi_t^2, \text{ with } \lambda, \bar{y} \geq 0. \tag{6.19}$$

The instantaneous loss $L(\pi_t, y_t)$ implies that the central bank is aiming at zero inflation but at an output level that is potentially higher than average natural output $(= \mathbb{E}_{t-1}\left[y_t^n\right] = 0)$. For example, $\bar{y}$ may corresponds to the efficient level of output; that is, the one that would prevail if prices were flexible and competition were perfect. We saw at the end of chapter 4 that this effective output level is strictly higher than natural output as soon as competition is imperfect (we had $y_t^{cp} = z_t > y_t^n = z_t - \xi \mu^*$). To the extent that the central bank maximizes society's welfare, there is in principle no disagreement between them about which objectives to pursue.[21] However, as we are going to show, despite this convergence of objectives, the central bank does not manage to maximize social welfare, because it cannot resist the (vain) temptation to boost output at the cost of higher inflation.

6.3.4.1   OPTIMAL RULE

Let us consider first, as a benchmark case, a situation where monetary policy decisions are not freely decided by the central bank in period t, but instead obey a *strict rule* (potentially contingent on the aggregate supply shock y_t^n) that has been optimally chosen at time $t - 1$. An informed conjecture about this optimal rule is that it has the form

$$\pi_t = a + b y_t^n, \tag{6.20}$$

where a and b are parameters to be determined. Since $\mathbb{E}_{t-1}\left[y_t^n\right] = 0$ by assumption, under this rule expected inflation is constant at

$$\mathbb{E}_{t-1}\left(\pi_t\right) = a + b\mathbb{E}_{t-1}\left(y_t^n\right) = a,$$

while, by the AS curve, output is given by

$$y_t = \left(1 + \frac{b}{\kappa}\right) y_t^n. \tag{6.21}$$

Society chooses *ex ante* (in period $t - 1$) the optimal rule (i.e., the parameters a and b) that it will apply in period t. Hence, it solves

---

21. The theory of the inflation bias is thus distinct from theories based on political-economy considerations, which stress that monetary policy is determined by politicians whose interests may differ from those of society.

$$\min_{a,b} \mathbb{E}_{t-1}\left[L\left(\pi_t, y_t\right)\right],$$

under the constraints (6.20) and (6.21). Substituting the constraints into the objective, we may reformulate the objective of the central bank as follows:

$$\min_{a,b} \mathbb{E}_{t-1}\left[\lambda\left(\left(1+b/\kappa\right)y_t^n - \bar{y}\right)^2 + \left(a+by_t^n\right)^2\right].$$

The first-order conditions with respect to a and b are given by

$$\frac{\partial \mathbb{E}_{t-1}\left[L_t\right]}{\partial a} = 2\left(a + b\mathbb{E}_{t-1}\left[y^n\right]\right) = 0,$$

$$\frac{\partial \mathbb{E}_{-1}\left[L_t\right]}{\partial b} = 2\mathbb{E}_{t-1}\left[\lambda\left(\left(1+\frac{b}{\kappa}\right)y_t^n - \bar{y}\right)\frac{y_t^n}{\kappa} + \left(a+by_t^n\right)y_t^n\right] = 0.$$

Since $\mathbb{E}_{t-1}\left[y_t^n\right] = 0$, the first equation gives $a = 0$. By developing the second equation and recalling that $\mathbb{E}_{t-1}[(y_t^n)^2] > 0$, we obtain

$$b = -\frac{\kappa}{1 + \kappa^2/\lambda}.$$

Thus the optimal policy rule is

$$\pi_t = -\left(\frac{\kappa}{1+\kappa^2/\lambda}\right)y_t^n, \tag{6.22}$$

and it implies an output level of

$$y_t = \left(\frac{1}{1+\lambda/\kappa^2}\right)y_t^n.$$

Since $\mathbb{E}_{t-1}\left[y_t^n\right] = 0$, the optimal policy rule implies that the conditional mean of π_t is also zero; *average* inflation $(= \mathbb{E}\left(\pi_t\right))$ is thus effectively aligned with the inflation target $(= 0)$. However, since the conditional mean of output y_t is also zero, average output $(= 0)$ is *below* its target $(\bar{y} > 0)$. This is not surprising—we know that under rational expectations the central bank cannot on average raise output above its natural level. The optimal rule fully incorporates this constraint and focuses on the optimal stabilization of aggregate supply shocks. The burden of the supply shock y_t^n is then optimally spread between y_t and π_t, for the reasons explained in the previous section.

6.3.4.2   OPTIMAL DISCRETIONARY POLICY

In practice, monetary policy in not set in stone at the beginning of time but is chosen in every period by the central bank. Monetary policy is discretionary and not automatic. We now show that the structure of interactions between private agents and the central bank (when the former have rational expectations and the latter is freely choosing its policy in every period) does not permit attaining the same optimal outcome as under the fixed rule computed above. Instead, it is a suboptimal outcome that prevails, in which not only is output y_t systematically below its target $\bar{y}$ (which is inevitable, due to the AS curve), but moreover inflation π_t is systematically above its target $\bar{\pi} = 0$ (which might in principle be avoided). There is thus a welfare loss relative to the optimal rule.

Under discretion the central bank minimizes $L(\pi_t, y_t)$ in period t, taking inflation expectations $\mathbb{E}_{t-1}(\pi_t)$ as given and the AS curve (equation (6.18)) as a constraint. It thus solves

$$\min_{\pi_t} L_t = \lambda \left[\kappa^{-1} (\pi_t - \mathbb{E}_{t-1}(\pi_t)) + y_t^n - \bar{y} \right]^2 + \pi_t^2, \quad \text{with } \mathbb{E}_{t-1}(\pi_t) \text{ given.}$$

The first-order condition is written as

$$\frac{\partial L_t}{\partial \pi_t} = 2\lambda \left(\kappa^{-1} (\pi_t - \mathbb{E}_{t-1}(\pi_t)) + y_t^n - \bar{y} \right) \kappa^{-1} + 2\pi_t = 0,$$

which gives the best inflation response by the central bank to private sector inflation expectations $\mathbb{E}_{t-1}(\pi_t)$:

$$\pi_t = \frac{\kappa \left(\bar{y} - y_t^n \right) + \mathbb{E}_{t-1}(\pi_t)}{1 + \kappa^2 / \lambda}$$

The greater inflation expectations $\mathbb{E}_{t-1}(\pi_t)$, the greater the optimal inflation response π_t by the central bank. Indeed, the greater $\mathbb{E}_{t-1}(\pi_t)$, the lower the expectational surprise $\pi_t - \mathbb{E}_{t-1}(\pi_t)$ if actual inflation π_t does not follow, and hence the lower output y_t (by the AS curve) and the greater the loss $(y_t - \bar{y})^2$. In addition, π_t is increasing in $\bar{y}$. At any given level of inflation expectations $\mathbb{E}_{t-1}(\pi_t)$, the AS curve defines an increasing relation between y_t and π_t, that the central bank seeks to exploit in order to reach $\bar{y}$.

The preceding equation is the *reaction function* of the central bank, which describes its optimal strategy (the choice of π_t) given the expectations formed by private agents ($\mathbb{E}_{t-1}(\pi_t)$). For their part, private agents anticipate rationally as of period $t-1$ the behavior that the central bank will adopt in period t. Thus they form the following expectations:

$$\mathbb{E}_{t-1}\left[\pi_t\right] = \mathbb{E}_{t-1}\left[\frac{\kappa\left(\bar{y} - y_t^n\right) + \mathbb{E}_{t-1}\left(\pi_t\right)}{1 + \kappa^2/\lambda}\right],$$

which, after gathering the terms in $\mathbb{E}_{t-1}\left(\pi_t\right)$, gives:

$$\mathbb{E}_{t-1}\left[\pi_t\right] = \frac{\lambda\bar{y}}{\kappa} > 0.$$

By introducing this expression back into the reaction function of the central bank and then using the AS curve, we obtain the equilibrium values of inflation and output:

$$\pi_t = \frac{\lambda\bar{y}}{\kappa} - \left(\frac{\kappa}{1 + \kappa^2/\lambda}\right) y_t^n \text{ and } y_t = \left(\frac{1}{1 + \lambda/\kappa^2}\right) y_t^n. \tag{6.23}$$

By comparing the optimal discretionary monetary policy (equation (6.23)) and the optimal monetary policy rule (equation (6.22)), we see that the response to the aggregate supply shock y_t^n is exactly the same, the only difference being the *inflation bias* (of size $\lambda\bar{y}/\kappa$) that appears in the discretionary case. The inflation bias comes from the fact that, once expectations are formed, the central bank is enticed to exploit the AS curve and thus to stimulate output (in order to get it closer to its target $\bar{y}$) at the cost of a higher inflation. However, since this policy is perfectly anticipated by private agents as of time $t-1$, it turns out to be self-defeating (since only inflation *surprises* can push output up). Three parameters affect the incentives of the central bank to raise y_t and thus affect the size of the inflation bias—the output target ($\bar{y}$), the preference for output stabilization (λ), and the response of output to inflation in the AS curve (κ^{-1}).

The inflation bias generates a systematic deviation of inflation from target, which unambiguously lowers society's welfare (relative to the optimal rule) *even though the central bank and private agents share the same preference* (by assumption). Therefore it is the sequence of the game (namely the fact that the central bank plays after agents have formed their expectations), and this sequence alone, that is the source of this inefficiency. If the central bank had the ability to commit to its future policy, rather than minimize its loss function sequentially, it would choose to tie its hand to the optimal rule; private agents would then adjust their beliefs accordingly and so the inflation bias would disappear. Thus it is *the inability of the central bank to credibly commit* (in period $t-1$) *to its future policy* (in period t) that is responsible for the inefficiency of discretionary monetary policy. Economic theory refers to this situation as one of *time inconsistency of the optimal plan*, after the pioneering work of Kydland and Prescott (1977). In our case, the optimal plan *ex ante*, meaning the levels of inflation and output that would be obtained if the optimal rule were applied, is not time-consistent, since the central bank seeks to deviate from the plan *ex post*, once private agents' expectations have been formed.[22]

Is it possible to eliminate, or at least reduce, the inflation bias? One extreme solution would consist of constitutionalizing monetary policy in a way that would withdraw any discretionary power from the central bank. However, this solution appears inappropriate, since it would also eliminate any flexibility and thus any possible adaptation to changes in the economic environment. Another solution, which we will now examine, is to delegate monetary policy to an independent central bank—one that does not necessarily share the average preferences of society toward inflation and output stabilization. In fact, the existence of an inflation bias is the main theoretical justification for the movement toward central bank independence that started in the 1980s.

6.3.4.3   CENTRAL BANK INDEPENDENCE AND THE OPTIMAL DEGREE OF CONSERVATISM

Society's preferences vis-á-vis inflation and output, summarized by the parameter λ of the loss function, should be understood as *average* preferences, once the heterogeneous preferences of society's members (that is, the citizens of a country) have been aggregated. Until now, we have assumed that the central banker in charge of monetary policy merely shared these average preferences. Another way of interpreting this assumption is to say that the central banker was not independent—whatever his or her *own* personal preferences, he or she behaved as a representative of society. We will now study the alternative configuration, in which the central banker decides himself or herself about monetary policy (that is, by following his or her own preferences) *after having been appointed by society*. We already know that a society choosing a central banker who shares its average preferences is not doing *a priori* good service, since this central banker will generate exactly the inflation bias that was previously described. Is it possible to appoint a central banker whose behavior would perform better?

This problem amounts to optimally choosing *ex ante* the preferences of the central banker, then letting him or her choose the inflation rate of period t. Formally, society should choose the value of λ that minimizes the social loss $\mathbb{E}_{t-1}[\lambda \left(y_t - \bar{y}\right)^2 + \pi_t^2]$, knowing that the central banker thus appointed will choose a level of inflation *ex post* that will depend on λ. We know from equation (6.23) above that a central banker conducting the optimal discretionary policy and having preferences toward inflation and output stabilization parameterized by $\hat{\lambda}$ will choose the following levels of output and inflation:

$$\pi_t = \frac{\hat{\lambda}\bar{y}}{\kappa} - \frac{\kappa y_t^n}{1 + \kappa^2/\hat{\lambda}}, \quad y_t = \frac{y_t^n}{1 + \hat{\lambda}/\kappa^2}. \tag{6.24}$$

---

22. In the present case, the inability of the central bank to commit to its future policy generates excess inflation. In chapter 9 we will study an alternative macroeconomic configuration, wherein the same inability generates excess *deflation* instead.

Society chooses $\hat{\lambda}$ optimally, meaning that it solves $\min_{\hat{\lambda}} \mathbb{E}_{t-1}\left(L\left(y_t, \pi_t\right)\right)$ with y_t and π_t given by (6.24). Hence, we may reformulate society's problem as follows:

$$
\min_{\hat{\lambda}} \lambda \mathbb{E}_{t-1}\left[\left(\frac{y_t^n}{1+\hat{\lambda}/\kappa^2}-\bar{y}\right)^2\right]+\mathbb{E}_{t-1}\left[\left(\frac{\hat{\lambda}\bar{y}}{\kappa}-\frac{\kappa y_t^n}{1+\kappa^2/\hat{\lambda}}\right)^2\right].
$$

The first-order condition gives:

$$
\frac{\partial \mathbb{E}_{t-1}\left(L\left(y_t, \pi_t\right)\right)}{\partial \hat{\lambda}}=-2\lambda \mathbb{E}_{t-1}\left[\left(\frac{y_t^n}{1+\hat{\lambda}/\kappa^2}-\bar{y}\right)\frac{y_t^n}{\left(1+\hat{\lambda}/\kappa^2\right)^2\kappa^2}\right]
$$

$$
+2\mathbb{E}_{t-1}\left[\left(\frac{\hat{\lambda}\bar{y}}{\kappa}-\frac{\kappa y_t^n}{1+\kappa^2/\hat{\lambda}}\right)\left(\frac{\bar{y}}{\kappa}-\frac{\kappa^3 y_t^n}{\left(1+\kappa^2/\hat{\lambda}\right)^2\hat{\lambda}^2}\right)\right]=0.
$$

After developing and then eliminating all the terms in $\mathbb{E}_{t-1}\left[y_t^n\right]\,(=0)$, we see that the optimal preference parameter satisfies the following expression:

$$
\underbrace{\frac{\bar{y}^2\hat{\lambda}}{\mathbb{E}_{t-1}[\left(y_t^n\right)^2]}}_{G\left(\hat{\lambda}\right)}=\underbrace{\frac{\lambda-\hat{\lambda}}{\left(1+\hat{\lambda}/\kappa^2\right)^3}}_{D\left(\hat{\lambda}\right)}.
$$

The two sides of this equation are functions of $\hat{\lambda}$. The left-hand side ($G(\hat{\lambda})$) is a straight line with intercept zero and positive slope; the right-hand side ($D(\hat{\lambda})$) is a decreasing function that takes the value $\lambda > 0$ at $\hat{\lambda} = 0$ and the value 0 at $\hat{\lambda} = \lambda$. This implies that there exists a unique interior solution $\hat{\lambda}$, $0 < \hat{\lambda} < \lambda$, to the problem of the optimal choice of central banker (see figure 6.11). This choice implies that *it is optimal for society to appoint a central banker who gives less importance than it does itself to output stabilization* (Rogoff 1985). Such a central banker is called "conservative" in reference to the way in which central bankers are often perceived by the public and politicians (who often blame them for granting too much importance to inflation and not enough to the level of economic activity). The delegation of monetary policy to a conservative central banker enables partly resolving the inflation bias, which becomes:

$$
\mathbb{E}_{t-1}\left[\pi_t\right]=\frac{\hat{\lambda}\bar{y}}{\kappa}<\frac{\lambda\bar{y}}{\kappa}.
$$

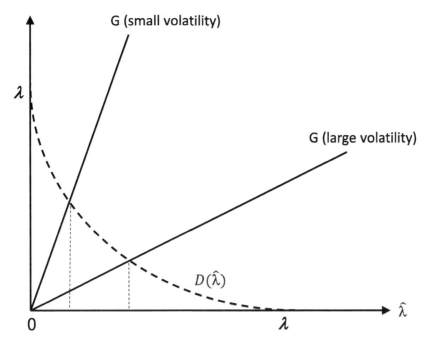

FIGURE 6.11
The optimal degree of monetary conservatism. When society grants a lot of importance to stabilizing output, it chooses a central banker who is not conservative, and average inflation tends to be high.

Why is the optimal solution inside the interval $(0, \lambda)$? The reason is because the reduction in the expected loss $\mathbb{E}_{t-1}\left(L\left(y_t, \pi_t\right)\right)$ brought about by the reduction of the inflation bias must be balanced against the loss implied by the fact that a conservative central banker does not react to macroeconomic *shocks* in the way that society would wish. Since the level of output chosen by the conservative central banker is $y_t = (1 + \hat{\lambda}/\kappa^2)^{-1} y_t^n$ (see equation (6.23)), the variance in output is given by

$$\mathbb{E}_{t-1}\left[y_t^2\right] = \frac{\mathbb{E}_{t-1}\left[\left(y_t^n\right)^2\right]}{1 + \hat{\lambda}/\kappa^2}.$$

This variance is thus higher than society would wish it to be (since $\hat{\lambda} < \lambda$). Put differently, a conservative central banker who puts less weight than society on output stabilization achieves lower inflation (which is good) but excess output volatility (which is bad). The first effect dominates but never to the point of making it desirable to appoint a central banker who would completely eliminate the inflation bias. In the absence of aggregate supply shocks (i.e., if we had $\mathbb{E}_{t-1}[(y_t^n)^2] = 0$), then only the beneficial effect linked to correcting the inflation bias would be present, and we would have $\hat{\lambda} = 0$; graphically, the $G(\hat{\lambda})$ line would be vertical and would cut the $D(\hat{\lambda})$ curve at the point $(0, \lambda)$. As the variance of aggregate shocks $\mathbb{E}_{t-1}[(y_t^n)^2]$ increases, the $G(\hat{\lambda})$ line rotates in a clockwise direction and the central banker appointed by society becomes less and less conservative (see figure 6.11).

From an empirical point of view, the notion of independence as applied to central banks is not only polysemic but also a matter of degree. Alesina and Summers (1993) constructed an aggregate index of central bank independence for a sample of OECD countries, based on underlying indices of political independence (understood as the capacity of the central bank to define its own objectives without undergoing the influence of political power) and economic independence (i.e., the freedom the central bank has in the use of its instruments). In line with the theory of delegation developed above, they found that a more independent central bank produces less average inflation and less inflation volatility. On the other hand, they did not find any significant effects on output volatility, which suggests that the real cost of inflation stability is relatively low. Grilli, Masciandaro, and Tabellini (1991) obtained similar results.

6.4 EXERCISES

6.4.1 OPTIMAL POLICY WITH PERSISTENT AGGREGATE SUPPLY SHOCKS

Consider the problem of optimal stabilization of aggregate supply shocks in section 6.2.3.2, assuming that $\beta > 0$ while the shocks are persistent. More precisely, natural output now follows the process

For $k < 0 : y_{t+k}^n = 0$;

for $k = 0 : y_t^n > 0$;

for $k > 0 : y_{t+k}^n = \vartheta y_{t+k-1}^n$, with $0 < \vartheta < 1$.

Use the method of undetermined coefficients to show that the optimal path of inflation in response to the shock is, for all $k \geq 0$,

$$\pi_{t+k} = \Omega \pi_{t+k-1} + \Gamma y_{t+k}^n;$$

with Ω given by equation (6.11) and

$$\Gamma = -\frac{\kappa \Omega (1 - \beta \vartheta)}{1 + \beta \vartheta \Omega} < 0.$$

6.4.2 INFLATION AND REPUTATION

Could a soft central banker have an interest in passing himself off as tough? To answer this question, consider the following model of optimal monetary policy, inspired by Backus and Drifill (1985). There are two periods, $t = 1, 2$. Inflation and output in period t are linked by the relation

$$\mathbf{AS} : \pi_t = \pi^e_{t-1,t} + b^{-1} y_t, \; b > 0, \tag{6.25}$$

where π_t is realized inflation at time t, $\pi^e_{t-1,t}$ its anticipated level (as of time $t-1$), and y_t is output.

The preferences of private agents about the levels of output and inflation are represented by the period utility function

$$U_t = y_t - \frac{a}{2} \pi_t^2, \; a > 0, \tag{6.26}$$

and the intertemporal utility

$$W = U_1 + \beta U_2, \; 0 < \beta < 1. \tag{6.27}$$

Suppose that the central banker freely chooses in a discretionary manner the inflation rate that is realized in both period. But there is uncertainty about the identity of the central banker. A central banker of type 1 shares the preferences of private agents. A central banker of type 2 is extremely conservative and always chooses $\pi_1 = \pi_2 = 0$. We denote by p, $0 \le p \le 1$, the probability that the central banker private agents face is of type 1. We are asking ourselves whether a central banker of type 1 may have an interest in exploiting this uncertainty in order to pass himself off as a type 2 banker in period $t = 1$.

1. Discuss equations (6.25) and (6.26), notably by explaining the role of the parameters a, b, and β.

2. Suppose that $p = 1$, so that the central banker is of type 1 with certainty. Compute the levels of inflation π_1 and π_2 that maximize the total utility of the central banker. Derive from this the levels of output y_1 and y_2 and the realized value of the intertemporal utility W.

3. Now consider the case where $p < 1$. The central banker turns out to be of type 1, but private agents do not know that. Therefore at the start of period 1 (i.e., before the central bank has chosen π_1), private agents think that the central banker is of type 1 with probability p. Once π_1 is chosen, agents may revise their beliefs about the type

of central banker they are facing. For example, if the central banker chooses $\pi_1 \neq 0$, he or she is directly identified as being of type 1 (since a type 2 central banker always chooses $\pi_1 = 0$). However, the central banker also has the option not to reveal his or her type by choosing $\pi_1 = 0$ in period $t = 1$.

(a) Explain intuitively why the central banker always plays $\pi_2 = b/a$, but may have an interest in playing $\pi_1 = 0$.

(b) Suppose that the central banker effectively chooses $\pi_1 = 0$. What are expected inflation $\pi_{1,2}^e$, realized output y_2, and second period utility U_2?

(c) Taking $\pi_{0,1}^e$ as given, compute the total utility of the central banker according to whether he or she chooses $\pi_1 = b/a$ or $\pi_1 = 0$. Compare the associated intertemporal losses and infer that the central banker plays tough at time 1 if and only if

$$\beta > \frac{1}{2(1-p)}.$$

Provide an intuitive explanation for this result.

6.4.3 PUBLIC DEBT AND THE TEMPTATION OF INFLATION

The real value of government bonds may erode in the absence of indexation on inflation. In this context, can the central bank resist the temptation to use inflation in order to reduce the real cost of public debt? To answer this question, assume that the government must borrow a real amount d of public debt from investors at the start of the period, with this debt being reimbursed at the end of the period. Agents are risk neutral and require a real interest rate of $\check{r}$ on all their investments. Taking into account their inflation expectations, from the Fisher equation investors require a nominal interest rate

$$i = \check{r} + \pi^e,$$

where π^e is expected inflation. The *ex post* return on government bonds, which is also the real cost of debt for the government, depends on *realized* inflation π:

$$r = i - \pi.$$

Thus, the real value of public debt to reimburse at the end of the period is given by

$$\tilde{d} = d(1+r).$$

Finally, suppose that the loss function of the central bank is of the form

$$L(\pi, \tilde{d}) = \left(\frac{a}{2}\right) \pi^2 + \tilde{d}.$$

1. Give an interpretation of the loss function $L(\pi, \tilde{d})$. Show that the real value of the debt depends on the gap between realized inflation and anticipated inflation and explain intuitively why.

2. Suppose that the central bank announces an inflation target π^* at the start of the period and is able to commit to honor its promise *ex post*. Compute the optimal value of π^* and the associated loss for the central bank, L^*.

3. Suppose that investors believe that the central bank is going to implement the inflation rate π^* calculated in question 2, whereas in reality it can renege on its commitment in the course of the period. What inflation rate does the central bank choose in this case, and what is its loss? Provide an interpretation of your results.

4. Based on questions 2 and 3, find a measure of the temptation that the central bank has to betray its initial promise.

5. Now suppose that investors do not believe the promises of the central bank about the inflation rate but seek to infer this rate from the incentives of the central bank. Compute the inflation rate that prevails in this case, as well as the loss suffered by the central bank. Explain intuitively why the corresponding equilibrium is inefficient.

6.4.4   SELF-FULFILLING INFLATION EXPECTATIONS

Consider the following game between the central bank and the private sector. At time $t-1$ private agents form rational expectations about time t inflation—that is, $\mathbb{E}_{t-1}(\pi_t)$. At time t the central bank chooses the monetary policy that minimizes its loss function, which is given by:

$$L_t = \lambda y_t^2 + \pi_t^2,$$

where y_t is (log) output (natural output is constant and normalized to zero). Realized inflation π_t follows from this monetary policy.

The AS curve is of the New Classical type:

$$AS : \pi_t = \mathbb{E}_{t-1}(\pi_t) + \kappa y_t, \quad \kappa > 0.$$

In period $t-1$ the central bank promises zero inflation for period t. However, it operates under discretion and hence may renege on its promise when the time comes. If it does, it runs an expansionary monetary policy that pushes inflation up to the value $\pi_t = \pi^* > 0$. The private sector contemplates this possibility as of time $t-1$ and assigns a probability θ, $0 \leq \theta \leq 1$, to this scenario. Show that if $\lambda > \kappa^2$, then both $\theta = 0$ and $\theta = 1$ are Nash equilibria, and provide an intuitive explanation for this result.

FISCAL POLICY

Broadly speaking, therefore, an increase of output cannot occur unless by the operation of one or other of three factors. Individuals must be induced to spend more out of their existing incomes; or the business world must be induced, either by increased confidence in the prospects or by a lower rate of interest, to create additional current incomes in the hands of their employees, which is what happens when either the working or the fixed capital of the country is being increased; or public authority must be called in aid to create additional current incomes through the expenditure of borrowed or printed money. In bad times the first factor cannot be expected to work on a sufficient scale. The second factor will come in as the second wave of attack on the slump after the tide has been turned by the expenditures of public authority. It is, therefore, only from the third factor that we can expect the initial major impulse.

—John Maynard Keynes (1933)

Between the middle of the 1980s and the crisis of 2008, fiscal policy, which is the second main dimension of macroeconomic stabilization (alongside monetary policy), seemed to have fallen into disuse. In the United States during this period, monetary policy had from every standpoint fulfilled the objectives that had been assigned to it—specifically the joint stabilization of inflation and output. This period corresponds to the so-called Great Moderation, which was a period when both macroeconomic and monetary volatility were historically low. The dominant explanation for this was the effective control of aggregate demand by the major central banks. In this context, why resort to fiscal policy, which is redundant at best and at worst harmful due to the tax distortions it creates? On the other side of the Atlantic, in the eurozone, the run-up to the single currency under the conditions of the Maastricht criteria, followed by the Stability and Growth Pact that began in 1999, strongly reduced the capacity of member-states to conduct activist fiscal policies.[1] Again, therefore, fiscal policy seemed bound to have the passenger seat in macroeconomic stabilization.

This perception of the role of fiscal policy, and the comprehension of its mechanisms, has somewhat evolved in recent years, after the Great Moderation gave way to the Great Recession, and faith in the omnipotence of monetary policy burned out. When the economy is in a deep recession characterized by a liquidity trap and therefore conventional monetary policy is rendered inoperative, fiscal policy naturally recovers its legitimacy and may even gain in effectiveness. We will study this dynamic in more detail in Part IV of the book. But first one must understand the effects of fiscal policy *in normal times*, within the framework of conventional macroeconomic policy. This is the first and main objective of this chapter.

The second objective of the chapter is methodological. We solve here a version of the AS-AD model used in chapters 2 to 4 that is simplified in a certain number of dimensions, but enriched in the fundamental dimension of *intertemporal general equilibrium*. The study of fiscal policy, as we shall see, only makes sense within that analytical framework, which ensures that any dollar spent by the government (be it in the form of government spending or lower taxes) is at one moment or another financed by private agents. A dynamic general equilibrium analysis also ensures that all the effects of the government's financing needs on the behavior of private agents are taken into account. In particular, it takes account of the fact that expansionary fiscal policies may arouse an opposite reaction on the part of private spending, while at the same time modifying the labor supply of the households. Only a explicit general-equilibrium version of the AS-AD model can correctly account for all these effects at work.

The chapter is organized in five sections. Section 7.1 discusses the *Ricardian equivalence theorem*, according to which the timing of lump-sum taxes does not matter (for example, financing a tax cut by issuing some public debt that will be repaid later has no effect on the equilibrium). The theorem holds under quite restrictive conditions but provides a sound benchmark against which the effects of real-world fiscal policies can be studied. Section 7.2 spells out the general-equilibrium foundations of the AS-AD model in the presence of a government, once we move away from the conditions of Ricardian equivalence. Section 7.3 uses the AS-AD framework to study the macroeconomic impact of changes in *government spending*—the government-spending multiplier—while section 7.4 examines the effects of changes in two prominent taxes—namely the *income tax* and the *value-added tax* (VAT).

---

1. The Stability and Growth Pact stated that the member countries of the European Union should not let their fiscal deficit grow larger than 3 percent of GDP.

7.1 Ricardian Equivalence

7.1.1 The Government Budget Constraint

When studying fiscal policy, the first thing to review is the government budget constraint. Let us call $\tilde{B}_t$ the quantity of *nominal* public debt in period t and $B_t = \tilde{B}_t / P_t$ its *real* amount—that is, the nominal debt divided by the price level P_t. In the same way, we denote by $\tilde{T}_t^{tot}$ the total nominal fiscal revenue and $T_t^{tot} = \tilde{T}_t^{tot} / P_t$ its real value. Finally, let us denote the real value of government spending by G_t. The nominal (e.g., in US dollars) government budget constraint in period t is given by

$$\underbrace{\tilde{B}_t - \tilde{B}_{t-1}}_{\text{change in public debt}} = \underbrace{\underbrace{i_{t-1}\tilde{B}_{t-1}}_{\text{nominal debt burden}} + \underbrace{P_t G_t - \tilde{T}_t^{tot}}_{\text{primary deficit}}}_{\text{fiscal deficit}},$$

where i_{t-1} is the nominal interest rate from period $t-1$ to period t (see chapter 2).

By dividing each side of this equation by the price level P_t, then by factorizing the terms in $\tilde{B}_{t-1}$, and finally by recalling that the real interest rate between $t-1$ and period t is given by $1 + r_{t-1} = (1 + i_{t-1}) / (P_t / P_{t-1})$, we see that the government budget constraint in *real* terms is given by

$$B_t = (1 + r_{t-1}) B_{t-1} + G_t - T_t^{tot}. \tag{7.1}$$

Equation (7.1) shows that fiscal policy in period t influences the evolution of public debt and may thus constrain *future* fiscal policies. The solvency of the government requires—just like the solvency of households does (see chapter 2)—that its *intertemporal budget constraint* (IBC) be satisfied. In one way or another, the path of fiscal revenues as of period t (i.e., $\{T_{t+k}^{tot}\}_{k=0}^{\infty}$), must be such that, taking account of both the total debt burden (interest and capital) of the current period $((1 + r_{t-1}) B_{t-1})$ and the path of government spending $(\{G_{t+k}\}_{k=0}^{\infty})$, equation (7.1) be satisfied *in all periods starting from period t*.

The government IBC is constructed iteratively from the period budget constraint in equation (7.1), by appropriately using it to eliminate the stock variable B_t in every period.[2] Let us begin by writing the budget constraint (7.1) in periods t and $t +1$ as follows:

---

2. This is exactly what we did in chapter 2 to construct the household's IBC—namely by using the period budget constraints of the household so as to successively eliminating asset wealth A_t.

$$B_t = (1 + r_{t-1}) B_{t-1} + G_t - T_t^{tot},$$

$$\frac{B_{t+1}}{1 + r_t} - \frac{G_{t+1}}{1 + r_t} + \frac{T_{t+1}^{tot}}{1 + r_t} = B_t.$$

Using the second equation to eliminate B_t from the first equation, we obtain

$$T_t^{tot} + \frac{T_{t+1}^{tot}}{1 + r_t} + \frac{B_{t+1}}{1 + r_t} = (1 + r_{t-1}) B_{t-1} + G_t + \frac{G_{t+1}}{1 + r_t}.$$

By repeating this operation—that is, by using the period budget constraint (7.1) in period $t + 2$ to eliminate B_{t+1}, then using the same constraint in period $t + 3$ to eliminate B_{t+2}, and so on—we obtain:

$$\underbrace{\sum_{k=0}^{\infty} \frac{T_{t+k}^{tot}}{\Pi_{m=0}^{k-1} (1 + r_{t+m})}}_{\text{present value of fiscal revenues}} + \underbrace{\lim_{n \to \infty} \frac{B_{t+n}}{\Pi_{m=0}^{n-1} (1 + r_{t+n})}}_{=?} \tag{7.2}$$

$$= \underbrace{B_{t-1} (1 + r_{t-1})}_{\text{debt burden inherited from the past}} + \underbrace{\sum_{k=0}^{\infty} \frac{G_{t+k}}{\Pi_{m=0}^{k-1} (1 + r_{t+m})}}_{\text{present value of government spending}}.$$

We assume, realistically, that public debt is nonnegative—that is, $B_t \geq 0$ for all t (so that the government is not a creditor of the private sector). Moreover, we assume that the following condition always hold:

No-Ponzi condition: $\lim_{n \to \infty} \dfrac{B_{t+n}}{\Pi_{m=0}^{n-1} (1 + r_{t+m})} \leq 0.$ \hfill (7.3)

This condition requires that the government does not engage in a Ponzi scheme—which is a strategy consisting of fully and indefinitely rolling over the existing public debt without ever collecting taxes to pay it back. If this condition were not imposed, the government could finance *any* level of government spending by issuing government bonds and simply letting public debt explode asymptotically without ever having to reimburse it. If that were possible, the government would effectively escape any budget constraint. Let us take the following extreme example to illustrate this point. Imagine that the government inherits no public debt in period t (that is, $B_{t-1} (1 + r_{t-1}) = 0$ in equation (7.2)) and does not plan to—perhaps because it is unable to—collect any tax any time in the future (so that $T_{t+k}^{tot} = 0$ for all $k \geq 0$). Nevertheless, this government contemplates the possibility of a one-shot government spending G_t in period t but will never spend again afterward (so that $G_{t+k} = 0$ for all $k \geq 1$). Under these assumptions, the IBC in equation (7.2) becomes

$$\lim_{n \to \infty} \frac{B_{t+n}}{\Pi_{m=0}^{n-1} (1 + r_{t+m})} = G_t.$$

We would expect that, without any fiscal revenue in the present or the future, the government would have no choice but to set $G_t = 0$. However, this is not true if Ponzi schemes are allowed. Indeed, if the government spends G_t, then from its period t budget constraint (equation (7.1)) we have $B_t = G_t$. That is, government spending is fully by debt. But since the government has no revenue in period $t+1$, its debt in that period will become $B_{t+1} = (1 + r_t) B_t = (1 + r_t) G_t$ (again from equation (7.1), and the fact that $G_{t+1} = 0$). In the same way, in period $t+2$ public debt becomes $B_{t+2} = (1 + r_{t+1}) B_{t+1} = (1 + r_{t+1}) (1 + r_t) G_t$, and so on until period n, when public debt has reached the level:

$$B_{t+n} = \Pi_{m=0}^{n-1} (1 + r_{t+m}) G_t.$$

By pursuing this Ponzi scheme until the end of time (for $n \to \infty$), the previous equality implies

$$\lim_{n \to \infty} \frac{B_{t+n}}{\Pi_{m=0}^{n-1} (1 + r_{t+m})} = G_t.$$

The latter expression is just a restatement of the government IBC in our example. In other words, we have just shown that the Ponzi strategy, if allowed, makes it possible to reach *any* level of government spending G_t in period t while still satisfying the government IBC. The No-Ponzi condition in equation (7.3), which should be understood as a constraint on the dynamics of public debt imposed by the government's creditors, is precisely designed to exclude this possibility. Moreover, since we have assumed public debt to be nonnegative, the limit term in equation (7.2) cannot itself be negative. Together with the No-Ponzi condition, this implies that

$$\lim_{n \to \infty} \frac{B_{t+n}}{\Pi_{m=0}^{n-1} (1 + r_{t+m})} = 0.$$

Thus, the IBC in equation (7.2) simply states that the present value of taxes must be equal to the existing debt burden *plus* the present value of government spending.

7.1.2   A MISTAKEN INTUITION

At the start of the nineteenth century, the British economist David Ricardo wondered whether it was equivalent to finance a given amount of public deficit either by issuing public debt, which would generate some interest burden, or by raising taxes so as to keep the budget balanced. He arrived at the conclusion that in principle the two options should be equivalent in terms of public finances (since any public debt must someday be reimbursed), but nevertheless he remained skeptical about his own conclusion (Ricardo [1820] 1888). Following Ricardo's skepticism—from the early nineteenth century to the contribution of Barro (1974)—economists considered that a tax cut that was financed by issuing government bonds (at any given level of government spending) was *not* neutral. In this view, a tax cut stimulated private consumption (thanks to the increase in disposable income) but it partially crowded out investment (due to the greater debt level and induced rise in the real interest rate), ultimately leading to a rise in output, which was somewhat mitigated by the rise in the interest rate. According to this view, the way in which one finances a given volume of government spending is anything but neutral, since replacing current taxes with debt (and hence future taxes) effectively increases output.

The steps of this intuition—which we will show to be mistaken—are as follows. First, let us aggregate the time t budget constraints of all the households j (equation (2.4) in chapter 2) and use letters without the superscript j to denote aggregate variables:

$$C_t + \underbrace{A_t - A_{t-1}}_{\text{net financial savings } S_t} = \underbrace{A_{t-1} r_{t-1} + (W_t/P_t) L_t - T_t}_{\text{disposable income}},$$

$\uparrow$
consumption

where T_t is the aggregate lump-sum tax collected from the households (recall from chapter 2 that T_t^j was the lump-sum tax paid by household j).

Let us likewise consider the budget constraint of the government in period t, assuming that T_t is its only source of revenue. In this case we simply have, from equation (7.1) above,

$$B_t = (1 + r_{t-1}) B_{t-1} - T_t + G_t.$$

A customary intuition about the effects of a tax cut (conveyed, for example, by the basic IS-LM model overviewed in chapter 2) is the following. At G_t unchanged, we have $dB_t = -dT_t > 0$; in other words, public debt increases by the same amount as the tax cut. On the household side, this cut increases disposable income, which liberates resources for consumption and savings—at an unchanged income before tax, we have $dC_t + dS_t = -dT_t > 0$. We expect that this windfall gain will be divided in one way or another between more consumption and more savings, so that $dC_t > 0$ and $dS_t > 0$. Moreover, provided that $dC_t > 0$, we have $dS_t < dB_t$; that is, the rise in households' net financial savings is not sufficient to match the increase in public debt. In a hypothetical flexible-price world, the (natural) interest rate would rise until the desired savings of the households match the borrowing needs of the government, and this greater natural rate would somewhat mitigate the initial impact of the higher consumption demand. In a world with nominal rigidities, though, in the short and medium run the real interest rate is determined by monetary policy. At an unchanged real interest rate, the rise in consumption demand would raise output and inflation (since it is an aggregate demand shock), and the resulting higher level of output would generate the additional income that households need to buy all the newly issued public debt. If the central bank raised the real interest rate in order to dampen the nascent inflationary pressures, then this rise in output would be somewhat mitigated. But either way, it seems that the tax cut will have raised output and employment (i.e., the tax cut will have been anything but neutral).

7.1.3 THE RICARDIAN EQUIVALENCE THEOREM

As intuitive as it may be, this description of the macroeconomic adjustment to a tax cut is *not* what would happen under the conditions of the *Ricardian equivalence theorem*. Under such conditions, households simply save the *full* windfall gain associated with the tax cut, so that we have $dC_t = 0$ and thus $dS_t = dB_t (= -dT_t)$. As a result, there is no increase in aggregate demand, output, or inflation. By way of consequence, the central bank need not change the real interest rate to maintain inflation close to target. The *only* modification to the macroeconomic equilibrium before the tax cut is a rise in public debt that is *exactly matched by a rise in household savings*. To fully understand this neutrality result, one must explicitly analyze how households respond to variations in the path of taxes that they expect to face.

7.1.3.1 HOUSEHOLD BEHAVIOR

For simplicity we examine the logic of the Ricardian equivalence theorem under a set of assumptions that is somewhat more stringent than necessary:[3]

- All households are identical and Ricardian in the sense of chapter 2 (hence the name). Since households are identical we can study the behavior of a representative household that stands for any household in the economy. That this household is Ricardian means that it never faces a binding debt limit, and so its consumption-saving choices are entirely governed by its preferences and intertemporal budget constraint.

- All households are (equally) taxed in a lump-sum way, as described by their period budget constraint above. Hence the government fiscal revenue is just the aggregate lump-sum tax: $T_t^{tot} = T_t$ for all t.

---

3. To be clear, this set of assumption is sufficient but not necessary for the Ricardian equivalence theorem to hold (for example, households need not be identical for the theorem to hold).

- All households live indefinitely; that is, their horizon n in equations (2.3) and (2.5) tends to infinity. This assumption makes sense if we adopt a dynastic perspective on household choices. Indeed, even if a particular generation is bound to die, it may care about its offsprings and maximize their intertemporal utility jointly with its own. This next generation may also value the intertemporal utility of the following one, which is thus indirectly taken care of by the current generation, and so on. It may formally be shown that the consumption-saving choices of such an altruistic household caring about its offsprings is adequately represented by an intertemporal utility function with an infinite horizon. Crucially, this implies that the horizon of the household is in fact the same as that of the government (which was also assumed to be infinite in section 7.1).

It is tempting to readily extend the consumption function for the Ricardian household, which is given by equation (2.10), to the case where $n \to \infty$. Since $\rho > 0$, the term $(1/(1+\rho))^{n+1}$ in that equation tends to zero as $n \to \infty$, so this would give us

$$C_t = \frac{\rho}{1+\rho} \left[A_{t-1} (1 + r_{t-1}) + \sum_{k=0}^{n} \frac{(W_{t+k}/P_{t+k}) L_{t+k}^s}{\Pi_{m=0}^{k-1} (1 + r_{t+m})} - \sum_{k=0}^{\infty} \frac{T_{t+k}}{\Pi_{m=0}^{k-1} (1 + r_{t+m})} \right]. \quad (7.4)$$

While this turns out to be the correct consumption function, an important caveat is in order here. The consumption function in equation (2.10) was derived under the assumption that n was *finite*, which implied that asset wealth A_{t+n} was zero at the end of the household's lifetime. The argument there was that it would be suboptimal to keep any asset wealth before dying (hence $A_{t+n}^j \leq 0$), while at the same time nobody would lend to someone who is about to leave the economy (hence $A_{t+n}^j \geq 0$). The successive elimination of the A_{t+k}s, $k \geq 0$, led therefore to their disappearance from the IBC. However, when $n \to \infty$ there is no final level of asset wealth that could be made to equal zero; successively eliminating the A_{t+k} from the period budget constraints (equation (2.4)) now gives rise to a limit term in the household's IBC:

$$\mathbf{IBC} : \sum_{k=0}^{\infty} \frac{C_{t+k}}{\Pi_{m=0}^{k-1} (1 + r_{t+m})} + \underbrace{\lim_{n \to \infty} \frac{A_{t+n}}{\Pi_{m=0}^{n-1} (1 + r_{t+m})}}_{= ?}$$

$$= A_{t-1} (1 + r_{t-1}) + \sum_{k=0}^{\infty} \frac{\frac{W_{t+k}}{P_{t+k}} L_{t+k}^s - T_{t+k}}{\Pi_{m=0}^{k-1} (1 + r_{t+m})}.$$

Without knowing what the limit term $\lim_{n\to\infty} A_{t+n}/[\Pi_{m=0}^n (1+r_{t+n})]$ is, we cannot know how the IBC effectively constrains household choices. We will now show that this limit term *must* be equal to zero, using two (symmetric) arguments.

The first argument is that this limit *cannot be negative*. This follows from the very same *No-Ponzi condition* that we imposed on the government earlier on, and which for the representative Ricardian household is given by

No-Ponzi condition :
$$A_t = \lim_{n\to\infty} \frac{A_{t+n}}{\Pi_{m=0}^{n-1} (1+r_{t+m})} \geq 0. \tag{7.5}$$

This condition follows from the fact that lenders would never let the household engage in a Ponzi scheme; that is, a strategy of borrowing in order to consume and then rolling over the debt forever without ever making a dent in one's labor income. Without assumption (7.5), a household could finance whatever level of current consumption without ever working—that is, it would effectively escape any budget constraint—just as the government could finance any level of spending without raising taxes, if Ponzi schemes were allowed. To see this clearly, let us take again an extreme example, namely that of a household that never works (such that $W_{t+k}L_{t+k}^s/P_{t+k}=0$ for all $k \geq 0$) and holds no asset wealth at the beginning of period t (i.e., $A_{t-1}(1+r_{t-1})=0$). This household wishes to borrow in order to consume $C_t > 0$ in period t, but will never consume again later, so that $C_{t+k}=0$ for all $k \geq 1$. Under these assumptions, the IBC above becomes

$$C_t + \lim_{n\to\infty} \frac{A_{t+n}}{\Pi_{m=0}^{n-1} (1+r_{t+m})} = 0. \tag{7.6}$$

If Ponzi schemes were allowed, then the household could reach whatever level of desired consumption in period t, despite having no asset at that time and earning no labor income at time t or any time later. The household would do so by permanently rolling over whatever debt that was issued to finance time t consumption. Indeed, if the household borrows to consume C_t, then from the budget constraint in period t we have $A_t = -C_t < 0$. But since the household has no wage income at time $t+1$ (by assumption), its asset wealth in that period becomes $A_{t+1} = A_t (1+r_t) = -(1+r_t) C_t$. In the same way, in period $t+2$ the asset wealth becomes $A_{t+2} = A_{t+1}(1+r_{t+1}) = -(1+r_t)(1+r_{t+1}) C_t$, and so on until period n when the household's debt has become

$$A_{t+n} = -\Pi_{m=0}^{n-1} (1+r_{t+m}) C_t \quad (<0).$$

By pursuing this Ponzi scheme until the end of time (for $n \to \infty$) we observe that

$$\lim_{n \to \infty} \frac{A_{t+n}}{\Pi_{m=0}^{n-1} (1 + r_{t+m})} = -C_t,$$

which is simply the IBC in our example (equation (7.6)). In other words, we have just shown that the Ponzi strategy, if allowed, makes it possible to reach *any* level of consumption in period t while satisfying the IBC. Assumption (7.5), which excludes this possibility, is the infinite-horizon equivalent of the finite-horizon condition discussed in chapter 2, in which a lender would not extend credit to a household who is about to die.

The second argument that will determine the limit term in the IBC is that this limit *cannot be positive* if consumption is chosen optimally. This is called the transversality condition and is written formally as:

Transversality condition : $A_t = \lim_{n \to \infty} \dfrac{A_{t+n}}{\Pi_{m=0}^{n-1} (1 + r_{t+m})} \leq 0.$ \hfill (7.7)

To understand this condition intuitively, suppose that the real interest rate r_{t+k}, $k \geq 0$, is constant at $\bar{r}$ and that condition (7.7) is violated because A_t is a positive constant rather than being equal to zero:

$$\lim_{n \to \infty} \frac{A_{t+n}}{(1 + \bar{r})^n} = A > 0.$$

A can be positive and finite only if, at least asymptotically, A_{t+n} and $(1 + \bar{r})^n$ grow at the same rate (otherwise this limit would be either infinite or zero). Since the growth rate of the denominator is $\bar{r}$ (by the mere definition of a growth rate), asset wealth A_{t+n} would have to grow exactly at the rate of $\bar{r}$. Now, the only way to have total wealth growing at a rate equal to the real interest rate is to *always reinvest all interests on assets without ever consuming them*. This behavior cannot be optimal since it is always preferable to depart from it (at least marginally) in order to increase consumption at one point in time or another. More generally, any consumption path that does not satisfy (7.7) would imply that some wealth is permanently and fully reinvested, which cannot be optimal. This condition is the infinite-horizon equivalent of the finite-horizon condition discussed in chapter 2, according to which it is suboptimal to hold positive wealth at the end of one's life.

By combining equations (7.5) and (7.7), we obtain:

$$\lim_{n \to \infty} \frac{A_{t+n}}{\Pi_{m=0}^{n-1} (1 + r_{t+n})} = 0,$$

which means that the limit term disappears from the IBC. This confirms that our extension of the finite-horizon consumption function in equation (2.10) to the *infinite-horizon* consumption function in equation (7.4) is valid.

7.1.3.2 THE NEUTRALITY OF THE TIMING OF TAXES

Now that we are on sound bases regarding household consumption, let us return to the Ricardian equivalence theorem. In equation (7.4) we see clearly how (lump-sum) taxes show up in the aggregate consumption function—an increase in their present value reduces C_t. However, as the government's IBC (equation (7.2)) shows, *the present value of lump-sum taxes is unchanged (whatever the actual path of lump-sum taxes) as long as the present value of government spending is itself unchanged.* To restate this formally, a modification of the path of lump-sum taxes $\{T_{t+k}\}_{k=0}^{\infty}$ has no effect on the present value of lump-sum taxes $\sum_{k=0}^{\infty}[T_{t+k}/\Pi_{m=0}^{k-1}(1+r_{t+k})]$ as long as the present value of government spending ($\sum_{k=0}^{\infty}[G_{t+k}/\Pi_{m=0}^{k-1}(1+r_{t+k})]$) is not modified. This implies that a transitory cut in the lump-sum tax that leaves the path of government spending $\{G_{t+k}\}_{k=0}^{\infty}$ unchanged must lead to a rise in future lump-sum taxes (possibly far into the future), whose present value exactly offsets the cut in the current tax.[4] To see this clearly, let us in the expression for C_t (equation (7.4)) replace the present value of lump-sum taxes by the value that is implied by the government IBC (equation (7.2)):

$$C_t = \frac{\rho}{1+\rho}\left[(A_{t-1}-B_{t-1})(1+r_{t-1})+\sum_{k=0}^{\infty}\frac{(W_{t+k}/P_{t+k})L_{t+k}^s}{\Pi_{m=0}^{k-1}(1+r_{t+m})}-\sum_{k=0}^{\infty}\frac{G_{t+k}}{\Pi_{m=0}^{k-1}(1+r_{t+m})}\right].$$

The latter expression does not feature the path of taxes, which confirms that $dC_t = 0$ after a tax cut $dT_t < 0$. Put differently, the rise in disposable income generated by the tax cut is entirely saved, so that households' assets rise exactly by the same amount as the quantity of newly issued public debt ($dA_t = -dT_t$). This implies that the rise in the demand for loanable funds by the government is matched by the rise in supply, leaving the market-clearing real interest rate unchanged. Since neither consumption nor the real interest have changed, aggregate demand does not change, and hence neither do output and inflation. The macroeconomic equilibrium is exactly the same as before the tax cut, except for the rise in the quantity of government bonds held by the households. However, these additional government bonds in households' portfolios are *not* additional net wealth, *for the taxes that the government will need to levy to pay them back exactly offset their value.*

---

4. For concreteness let us take the example of a tax cut in period t of amount dT_t financed by public debt, which will be reimbursed in period $t+1$ by a tax increase of amount $dT_{t+1}>0$. With this operation, the debt burden in the following period will be $(1+r_t)dT_t$, so that the present value of lump-sum taxes is modified by $-dT_t+\frac{1}{1+r_t}(1+r_t)dT_t=0$. This argument can be generalized to any modification of the path of lump-sum taxes that does not modify the present value of government spending.

7.1.4 Departures from Ricardian Equivalence

Is the Ricardian equivalence theorem verified empirically? Posed in this way, the question does not make much sense. Like any theorem, that of Ricardian equivalence is valid only under very specific assumptions; it turns out that these assumptions are quite restrictive, and it is unlikely they hold in practice. The interest of the theorem is not empirical but *theoretical*. By uncovering the set of assumptions leading to the neutrality of tax cuts, we are better able to understand, by contrast, the mechanisms that underlie the actual effects of concrete fiscal policies. We now discuss briefly the main reasons why the Ricardian equivalence theorem may not hold, so that a change in the timing of taxes (holding the path of government spending unchanged) *does* modify the current equilibrium.

7.1.4.1 Tax Distortions

First and foremost, in practice almost all taxes are not lump-sum but either proportional or progressive. The key feature of lump-sum taxes is that they only affect household behavior through so-called *wealth effects*. More specifically, a household who would see the present value of such taxes rising would be poorer in the sense that the present value of its disposable income would fall; accordingly, this household would adjust its consumption path downward, as is implied by equation (7.4). But since a pure change in the timing of lump-sum taxes that leaves the present value of government spending unchanged does not shift the present value of lump-sum taxes, it induces, precisely, no wealth effect, and is therefore neutral. What proportional or progressive taxes add to this picture is that they affect household behavior not only through wealth effects but also through *substitution effects*. For example, an increase in the VAT—a proportional tax on consumption goods—raises the cost of consumption goods relative to the cost of leisure and may thereby induce households to consume more leisure (that is, to work less) and fewer consumption goods. Similarly, a progressive income tax typically lowers the return on hours worked and may discourage labor supply. Taxes that generate such substitution effects are said to be *distortionary* because they affect household behavior—and thus modify the entire macroeconomic equilibrium—even in the absence of wealth effects. This implies that, even in the case where the path of government spending is not modified, a change in the timing of distortionary taxes will in general not be neutral. Farther down, we will analyze the macroeconomic effects of changes in the VAT and income tax rates and formally confirm this nonneutrality.

7.1.4.2 Financial Constraints

When deriving the Ricardian equivalence theorem, it has been assumed that all households were Ricardian: their consumption was not constrained by a binding debt limit, which led them to (optimally) consume a fraction of their total wealth.

As discussed in chapter 2, many households face a binding debt limit that constrains their consumption choices relative to that of a Ricardian household. A household facing a binding debt limit consumes any additional unit of income as soon as it is available (recall equation (2.11)). Hence, a tax cut—even lump-sum—directly boosts the consumption demand of a Keynesian household and is therefore not neutral. Computing the exact value of the induced variation in *aggregate* consumption—and ultimately on the full equilibrium—is not straightforward due to the heterogeneity of consumers (Ricardian and non-Ricardian) and the general-equilibrium effects at work—namely, the consumption response of Keynesian households modifies prices and wages and therefore *also changes the behavior of Ricardian households*. It is precisely to capture these subtle interactions that we perform a full general-equilibrium analysis of tax cuts, where Ricardian and Keynesian households interact, later in this chapter.

7.1.4.3   THE DILUTION OF THE FISCAL BURDEN

One of the underlying assumptions of the Ricardian equivalence theorem is that the life-span of the representative household be the same as that of the government (we focused on the infinite-horizon case above, but the same is true with a finite horizon). This household therefore must necessarily bear at some point the cost of any fiscal gift that it receives from the government, and this is precisely the reason why the present value of lump-sum taxes is not modified by their timing. However, the situation is different if new households enter the economy *after* the tax cut has taken place and bear some of its burden. In this case, the beneficiaries of a tax cut do not pay the full cost of it, and thus they see the present value of their disposable income increase. One part of this income gain will be consumed (by equation (7.4)), which will raise aggregate demand and thus shifts the equilibrium.

These three departures from the assumptions underlying the Ricardian equivalence theorem (tax distortions, financial constraints, and dilution of the fiscal burden due to new entrants) are present and important in the world we live in. Therefore the conditions of validity of the Ricardian equivalence theorem are far from being verified, which means that it would make little sense to try to test it empirically. Put differently, the so-called empirical rejections of the theorem are in fact rejecting a joint hypothesis, namely the theorem *and* its conditions of validity—which we already know are unlikely to hold in practice. Once again, the interest of the Ricardian equivalence theorem is not to produce testable predictions for econometricians, but rather to illuminate how and why concrete fiscal policies—which *do* involve departures from the conditions of Ricardian equivalence—alter the macroeconomic equilibrium. This is the question to which we now turn, starting, as is required for this enterprise, by spelling out the general-equilibrium foundations of the AS-AD model.

7.2 FISCAL POLICY IN GENERAL EQUILIBRIUM

In chapter 2 we were somewhat allusive about the impact of fiscal variables on aggregate demand. Government spending and taxes influenced aggregate demand via their effect on the generic demand parameter θ_t of the IS curve, but nothing specific was said about the scope of the expected effects. We were also careful to mention in chapter 4 that a fiscal shock was not a pure aggregate demand shock, since in general it shifted not only the AD curve (due to its effect on public and private demand) but also the AS curve (via its effect on the labor market and thus the marginal cost of production). We now study these mechanisms in a systematic way by explicitly introducing fiscal variables into individual choices and market equilibria.

In doing so, we will incorporate two important departures from the conditions of Ricardian equivalence: *distortionary taxation* and *debt constraints*. These are the most important ones in practice, so we focus on them here, leaving aside generational turnover and the future entry of new households. Debt constraints are introduced by assuming that a fixed proportion υ, $0 \leq \upsilon < 1$, of the households are *Keynesian* in the sense of chapter 2.[5] Distortionary taxation is introduced by means of *proportional* taxes on consumption (τ_t^c) and labor income (τ_t^l), in addition to the lump-sum tax (T_t). In reality, the income tax is usually not a pure labor income tax, since it also includes some asset income taxation; we will ignore this here for simplicity. Moreover, the income tax is usually progressive rather than proportional, but we will also abstract from this here in order to keep the problem as simple as possible. In what follows, we will simply call τ_t^c the value-added tax (VAT) and τ_t^l the income tax. The lump-sum tax T_t does not really have an empirical counterpart, but we still keep it for now, as it will allow us to better understand the impact of alternative fiscal policies in sections 7.3 and 7.4 below.

Finally, we are going to impose the following additional restrictions to preserve the clarity of the analysis:

- Just like in chapter 3, the economy is closed $(X_t - M_t = 0)$ and the stock of capital is constant so that investment is always zero $(I_t = 0)$. Thus, the only components of aggregate demand are private consumption C_t and government spending G_t (recall from chapter 1 that these two components represent more than three quarters of GDP in the United States and the euro area).

- Labor productivity is constant and normalized to $z_t = \xi \mu^*$ (in log). As discussed in the previous chapter, this amounts to normalizing log natural output without a public sector (i.e., $y_t^n = z_t - \xi \mu^*$) to zero.[6]

---

5. General-equilibrium models with nominal rigidities and both Ricardian and Keynesian consumers were initially formulated by Galí, Lopez-Salido, and Valles. (2007) and Bibiie (2008). They have come to be known as TANK models, for Two-Agent New Keynesian models.

6. Exercise 7.5.2 studies the effect of government-spending shocks that affect labor productivity.

7.2.1 THE GOVERNMENT AND THE CENTRAL BANK

The budget constraint of the government was described in section 7.1 above and there is nothing to add on this front; in sections 7.3 and 7.4 below we will further specify the alternative fiscal policies that the government can run. One crucial dimension of the policy mix to keep in mind from now on is that in a monetary economy with nominal rigidities *it is not possible to study fiscal policy independently of monetary policy*. This is a matter of a logical impossibility. In the presence of nominal rigidities, in the short run the value of the real interest rate is not determined by supply-side factors (unlike in the natural equilibrium) but is given by the behavior of the central bank (see Parts I and II). It follows that the effects of any fiscal policy is conditional on the presumed response of the central bank to the policy. For example, if the central bank wishes at all costs to fight the inflationary pressures generated by a fiscal stimulus, then it will tighten monetary policy so as to raise the real interest rate and reduce private spending; this will mechanically mitigate the direct effect of the stimulus. Conversely, a monetary policy that is expansionary at the same time as fiscal policy will magnify the impact of any fiscal stimulus. In what follows, we will make the most neutral possible assumption about the way the central bank responds alternative fiscal policies—we will assume that it always keeps the real interest unchanged at

$$r_t = \rho, \tag{7.8}$$

where ρ is households' rate of time preference (as defined in chapter 2). This may be interpreted as a minor form of policy coordination between monetary and fiscal authorities, in the sense that under this monetary policy the potential inflationary or deflationary pressures generated by the government's fiscal policy are not systematically countered by the central bank (through a rise or a fall in the real interest rate). Put differently, the central bank is not hawkish in the way it responds to fiscal policy—without being particularly dovish either.[7]

7.2.2 RICARDIAN HOUSEHOLDS

7.2.2.1 OBJECTIVE AND CONSTRAINTS OF THE REPRESENTATIVE RICARDIAN HOUSEHOLD

Let us assume that all Ricardian households are identical, so we can focus on a *representative* Ricardian household. This household chooses in every period its consumption demand C_t^R and labor supply L_t^R in such a way as to maximize its intertemporal utility. This intertemporal utility takes the form:[8]

---

7. Exercise 7.5.1 examines the impact of fiscal policy shocks under an alternative (hawkish) monetary policy according to which which the central bank never lets inflation depart from target after a fiscal shock.

8. This is the same utility function as the one we considered in the appendix to chapter 3, except that we are assuming here that the horizon n goes to infinity.

$$u_t^R = \sum_{k=0}^{\infty} \left(\frac{1}{1+\rho}\right)^k \left(\ln C_{t+k}^R - \xi \left(L_{t+k}^R\right)^{1/\xi}\right), \quad k = 0, 1, \ldots,$$

where ξ is a parameter determining the elasticity of labor supply, assumed to satisfy the following condition:

$$\upsilon < \xi < 1.$$

The budget constraint of the representative household in any period $t + k$ now takes into account the *proportional* consumption (τ_t^c) and labor (τ_t^l) taxes to which it is subject. It is written as follows, for $k = 0, 1, \ldots$:

$$\underbrace{C_{t+k}^R \left(1 + \tau_{t+k}^c\right)}_{\text{consumption, VAT included}} + \underbrace{A_{t+k}^R - A_{t+k-1}^R}_{\text{net financial savings}}$$

$$= \underbrace{A_{t+k-1}^R r_{t+k-1} + \frac{W_{t+k}}{P_{t+k}} \left(1 - \tau_{t+k}^l\right) L_{t+k}^R - T_{t+k}}_{\text{disposable income}}, \tag{7.9}$$

which generalizes equation (2.4) in chapter 2 .

In period t, $A_{t-1}^R \left(1 + r_{t-1}\right)$ is inherited from the past and hence taken as given. By using the budget constraints of periods $t + k$, $k = 0, 1, \ldots$ to eliminate all the A_{t+k}^R (see chapter 2 again for a similar computation), we obtain the *intertemporal budget constraint* (IBC) of the representative Ricardian household:

$$\textbf{IBC}: \quad \underbrace{\sum_{k=0}^{\infty} \frac{C_{t+k}^R \left(1 + \tau_{t+k}^c\right)}{\Pi_{m=0}^{k-1} \left(1 + r_{t+m}\right)}}_{\text{present value of consumption, VAT included}} \tag{7.10}$$

$$= \underbrace{A_{t-1}^R \left(1 + r_{t-1}\right)}_{\text{asset wealth and interest}} + \underbrace{\sum_{k=0}^{\infty} \frac{\frac{W_{t+k}}{P_{t+k}} \left(1 - \tau_{t+k}^l\right) L_{t+k}^R - T_{t+k}}{\Pi_{m=0}^{k-1} \left(1 + r_{t+m}\right)}}_{\text{present value of disposable labor income}}.$$

Note that, by virtue of the no-Ponzi and transversality conditions (see our discussion in section 7.1 above), the limit term $\lim_{n \to \infty} A_{t+n}^R / [\Pi_{m=0}^{n-1} \left(1 + r_{t+n}\right)]$ that appears on the left-hand side of equation (7.10) in this process of successive substitutions has been set to zero.

Equation (7.10) generalizes the IBC of the Ricardian household in the absence of a public sector (see equation (2.5)). On the right-hand side we again find total wealth, which is the sum of the asset wealth (with interest) and the present value of disposable labor income. And on the right-hand side, we see the present value of consumption spending, which now includes the VAT.

7.2.2.2 CONSUMPTION DEMAND

The representative Ricardian household maximizes its intertemporal utility under the IBC. The Lagrangian function is written:

$$
\mathcal{L}_t^R = \mathcal{U}_t^R + \Lambda_t \left\{ A_{t-1}^R \left(1 + r_{t-1}\right) + \sum_{k=0}^{\infty} \frac{\frac{W_{t+k}}{P_{t+k}} \left(1 - \tau_{t+k}^l\right) L_{t+k}^R - T_{t+k}}{\Pi_{m=0}^{k-1} \left(1 + r_{t+m}\right)} \right.
$$
$$
\left. - \sum_{k=0}^{\infty} \frac{C_{t+k}^R \left(1 + \tau_{t+k}^c\right)}{\Pi_{m=0}^{k-1} \left(1 + r_{t+m}\right)} \right\},
$$

where Λ_t is the Lagrange multiplier associated with the IBC.

The first-order conditions associated with consumption demand C_{t+k}^R and labor supply L_{t+k}^R are, for all t:

Consumption:
$$
\frac{\partial \mathcal{L}_t^R}{\partial C_{t+k}^R} = \frac{1}{C_{t+k}^R} - \frac{\Lambda_t \left(1 + \tau_{t+k}^c\right)}{\Pi_{m=0}^{k-1} \left(1 + r_{t+m}\right)} = 0, \tag{7.11}
$$

Labor:
$$
\frac{\partial \mathcal{L}_t^R}{\partial L_{t+k}^R} = -\left(L_t^R\right)^{\frac{1}{\xi}-1} + \Lambda_t \frac{\left(W_t/P_t\right) \left(1 - \tau_t^l\right)}{\Pi_{m=0}^{k-1} \left(1 + r_{t+m}\right)} = 0. \tag{7.12}
$$

By using the first-order conditions for consumption in two consecutive periods t and $t + 1$ to eliminate Λ_t and using the fact that the central bank sets $r_t = \rho$ for all t (see equation (7.8)), we obtain a new version of the Keynes-Ramsey rule (see equation (2.8)):

$$
\frac{C_{t+1}^R}{C_t^R} = \frac{1 + \tau_t^c}{1 + \tau_{t+1}^c}.
$$

This expression generalizes equation (2.8) to account for the effect of variations in VAT from one period to another on the slope of the consumption profile (while abstracting from changes in the real interest rate). When VAT increases between period t and period $t + 1$ (so that consumption goods become relatively more expensive in period $t + 1$), it becomes more advantageous to buy goods in period t rather than to wait until period $t+1$, and the slope of the consumption profile (C_{t+1}^R/C_t^R) is reduced. Conversely, an anticipated drop in VAT leads the representative household to defer its consumption, which increases the slope of the consumption profile. Therefore, anticipated variations in VAT have exactly the same impact on the slope of the consumption profile as do variations in the real interest rate.[9]

By turning the Keynes-Ramsey rule into log and by using the usual approximation (equation (1.3)) we can express log current consumption c_t^R as as follows:

$$c_t^R = c_{t+1}^R - \tau_t^c + \tau_{t+1}^c.$$

Replacing c_{t+1}^R by its value $(= c_{t+2}^R - \tau_{t+1}^c + \tau_{t+2}^c)$, then c_{t+2}^R by its value, and repeating these substitutions until time $t = \infty$, we find the current log consumption of a Ricardian households to be:

$$c_t^R = c_\infty^R - \tau_t^c + \tau_\infty^c, \tag{7.13}$$

where c_∞^R is the log-consumption of a Ricardian household in long-run equilibrium (to be determined later).

7.2.2.3 LABOR SUPPLY

By using the first-order conditions associated with the choice of C_t^R and L_t^R to eliminate Λ_t, we obtain the following optimality condition for labor supply:

$$\left(L_t^R\right)^{\frac{1}{\xi}-1} = \left(\frac{1-\tau_t^l}{1+\tau_t^c}\right) \frac{W_t}{P_t} \frac{1}{C_t^R}. \tag{7.14}$$

This condition states that the representative household increases its working hours L_t^R just to the point where one additional unit of labor supplied yields as much in terms of utility from consumption (the right-hand side of the equation) as it costs in terms of disutility of labor (left-hand side of the equation). In effect, an additional unit of labor reduces the utility of the household by $(L_t^R)^{\frac{1}{\xi}-1}$. This unit of labor yields $(1 - \tau_t^l)W_t$ monetary units (e.g., US dollars) after tax, with each monetary unit permitting the purchase $1/\left(1+\tau_t^c\right)P_t$ of units of goods (once VAT

---

9. In practice, VAT does not vary much. Note, though, that according to equation (7.13) it is theoretically possible to use fiscal policy (and not just conventional monetary policy) to manipulate the slope of the consumption path and thus influence aggregate demand. We will study this possibility in chapter 10, since it has actually been suggested as one of the unconventional fiscal policies capable of boosting aggregate demand in a liquidity trap.

has been added to the raw nominal price of goods), and an additional unit of good being consumed increases the utility of the household by $1/C_t^R$. We see immediately that, at a given value of C_t^R, the direct effect of a rise of either one of the tax rates (τ_t^c or τ_t^l) is a *reduction in labor supply*. Indeed, both taxes reduce the quantity of goods that an additional unit of labor permits purchasing, and thus they reduce the incentive to work. By contrast, the lump-sum tax T_t does not intervene in the optimality condition, precisely because it does not modify the price of goods in terms of labor units.[10]

Another way of presenting the optimality condition in equation (7.14) is in terms of the *marginal rate of substitution* (MRS) between consumption and hours worked. This marginal rate of substitution is the ratio of the marginal disutility of labor $(L_t^R)^{\frac{1}{\xi}-1}$ to the marginal utility of consumption $1/C_t^R$. Optimality requires that this MRS be equal to the price of labor in terms of goods, meaning the real wage times a correction due to distortionary taxation:

$$\underbrace{\frac{\left(L_t^R\right)^{\frac{1}{\xi}-1}}{1/C_t^R}}_{\text{MRS}} = (1 - \underset{\uparrow}{\tau_t}) \quad \times \quad \underset{\uparrow}{\frac{W_t}{P_t}} \quad , \quad \text{with } \tau_t = \frac{\tau_t^c + \tau_t^l}{1 + \tau_t^c}. \tag{7.15}$$

$$\text{tax wedge} \quad \text{real wage}$$

The gap between the MRS and the real wage due to the presence of proportional taxes is called the *tax wedge*. The tax wedge is a synthetic measure of the economic distortions caused by proportional taxation. In the absence of proportional taxes, we recover the classic optimality condition of equalization of the MRS and the real wage (which remains valid in the presence of lump-sum taxes). As soon as proportional taxes are positive, then the tax wedge is too, and thus the MRS is lower than the real wage. A low value of the MRS relative to the real wage generally materializes as both fewer hours worked (hence a lower marginal disutility of labor $(L_t^R)^{\frac{1}{\xi}-1}$) and lower consumption (hence a higher marginal utility of consumption $1/C_t^R$). In this way the burden of the tax is optimally spread between the consumption of goods and the consumption of leisure.[11]

---

10. Since it does not appear in the first-order condition, the lump-sum tax induces no substitution effect between consumption and leisure. On the other hand, the lump-sum tax has an income effect to the extent that it impoverishes households. This income effect in general causes the lump-sum tax to modify labor supply and consumption demand in general equilibrium, but these effects are not apparent by merely looking at equation (7.14).

11. The exact division between the two variables depends on the elasticity of labor supply ξ. The higher this elasticity, the more the household increases its hours worked after a tax increase in order to limit the drop in consumption that it would otherwise incur.

By taking the log of equation (7.14) and by using our usual approximation (equation (1.3)) for small τ_t^l and τ_t^c, we obtain the following expression for (log) labor supply, which generalizes equation (3.23):

$$l_t^R \simeq \frac{\xi}{1-\xi} \quad \underbrace{(w_t - p_t - \tau_t^c - \tau_t^l}_{\text{log disposable labor income}} - \underbrace{c_t^R)}_{\substack{\uparrow \\ \text{log consumption}}}. \tag{7.16}$$

7.2.3 KEYNESIAN HOUSEHOLDS

As discussed in chapter 2, the Keynesian households are those who face a binding debt limit in every period and therefore cannot choose the consumption level that would be granted on the basis of their intertemporal budget constraint only. For simplicity it is assumed here that Keynesian households are identical and face a binding debt limit of zero (i.e., they cannot borrow). Moreover, for expositional clarity (but without loss of generality), it is also assumed that they are not taxed lump-sum (only the Ricardian households are taxed thusly in situations where there are lump-sum taxes). Under these assumptions, and taking into account the proportional taxes, equation (2.11) gives the following consumption demand for the representative Keynesian household:

$$C_t^K = \frac{W_t}{P_t} \left(\frac{1 - \tau_t^l}{1 + \tau_t^c} \right) L_t^K.$$

It is important to keep in mind that the debt limit constrains the *intertemporal* choice of the household (between consuming and saving) but not its *intratemporal* labor supply choice—a Keynesian household who is forced to consume less than he would like by a binding debt limit will still choose its hours worked optimally. Formally, the Lagrangian function that summarizes the problem of the Keynesian household is the same as that of the Ricardian household, except for an additional term reflecting the bindingness of the debt limit; but since labor supply does not show up in this additional term, the optimality condition for the labor supply of the representative Keynesian consumer is exactly the same as that of the Ricardian consumer:

$$\left(L_t^K \right)^{\frac{1}{\xi} - 1} = \left(\frac{1 - \tau_t^l}{1 + \tau_t^c} \right) \frac{W_t}{P_t} \frac{1}{C_t^K}.$$

The latter two expressions imply that the labor supply of the representative Keynesian consumer is constant at $L_t^K = 1$.[12] Turning these expressions into log and

---

12. This is an implication of some of our simplifying assumptions and needs not be true in a more general specification (e.g., if the debt limit is not zero or if Keynesian households are taxed lump sum).

using the approximation (1.3) again, we get:

$$l_t^K = 0 \quad \text{and} \quad c_t^K = w_t - p_t - \tau_t^l - \tau_t^c.$$

7.2.4   FIRMS

The behavior of firms is identical in every way to what was described in chapter 3. This leads to two decisions: one about the price at which firms wish to sell their goods, and the other (which follows from the first) about the labor demand they express on the labor market. With our normalization $z_t = \xi \mu^*$, the expression of the optimal nominal price (3.4) becomes

$$p_t^* = w_t + (1 - \xi) \mu^*. \tag{7.17}$$

The total demand for labor in period t is given by the aggregation of individual labor demands. With $z_t = \xi \mu^*$ the equation for total labor demand (equation (3.6)) becomes:

$$l_t^d = y_t - \xi \mu^*. \tag{7.18}$$

7.2.5   MARKET CLEARING

The economy considered here includes three markets: a goods market, a labor market, and an asset market (where the securities that compose household wealth are traded). Walras's law implies that if two markets clear, then the third one clears also. Thus it suffices to consider the clearing of two markets out of the three, and so we will only look at the markets for goods and labor.

7.2.5.1   THE GOODS MARKET

In the market for goods, households and the government demand the goods that are produced by the firms. On the *supply* side, the production function of firms is identical to that in chapter 3: firm i, $0 \leq i \leq 1$, produces by means of the production function $Q_{i,t} = Z_t L_{i,t}$, where $Z_t (= e^{\xi \mu^*}$ under our normalization) is labor productivity and $L_{i,t}$ employment in the firm. Since each firm produces a quantity $Q_{i,t}$ equal to the demand $Y_{i,t}$ it faces, the supply of goods at the level of the economy as a whole is given by $Y_t = Q_t = Z_t L_t^d$, where L_t^d is the aggregate demand for labor. Switching to logs, the latter expression becomes

$$y_t = \xi \mu^* + l_t^d.$$

On the *demand* side, the aggregate demand for goods in period t comes from the private consumption of both Ricardian and Keynesian households, as well as from government spending:

$$Y_t = (1 - v)\, C_t^R + v C_t^K + G_t.$$

To simplify the analysis (but without loss of generality), we will study fiscal adjustments in the vicinity of a long-run equilibrium (indexed by ∞) where government spending is zero (i.e., $G_\infty = 0$) and where the long-run consumption levels of Ricardian and Keynesian households are the same (i.e., $C_\infty^R = C_\infty^K$).[13] It can then be shown, still using our usual approximation (equation (1.3)), that log aggregate demand is then given by

$$y_t \simeq (1 - v)\, c_t^R + v c_t^K + g_t,$$

where g_t is government spending expressed as a share of long-run output:

$$g_t = \frac{G_t}{Y_\infty}. \tag{7.19}$$

To summarize, the market-clearing condition for the goods market, in log form, is given by

$$\underbrace{\xi \mu^* + l_t^d}_{\text{supply of goods}} = \underbrace{(1 - v)\, c_t^R + v c_t^K + g_t}_{\text{demand for goods}}. \tag{7.20}$$

7.2.5.2 THE LABOR MARKET

The labor market clears when the aggregate demand for labor equals the aggregate supply of labor, and it is the real wage $w_t - p_t$ that adjusts to ensure market clearing at any given output level y_t. The aggregate demand for labor is $l_t^d = y_t - \xi \mu^*$. The aggregate supply of labor is $(1 - v)\, l_t^R$ (since $l_t^K = 0$). Hence, clearing of the labor market requires

$$\underbrace{y_t - \xi \mu^*}_{\text{labor demand}} = \underbrace{(1 - v)\, l_t^R}_{\text{labor supply}}. \tag{7.21}$$

7.2.6 SOLVING THE GENERAL-EQUILIBRIUM AS-AD MODEL

Solving the general-equilibrium AS-AD model is no easy task, due to the heterogeneity in household behavior (Ricardian versus Keynesian) and the presence of distortionary taxes. We will therefore proceed gradually, starting with a summary

---

13. Under the assumptions made so far the condition $C_\infty^R = C_\infty^K$ holds only if $\mu^* = \tau_\infty^c = \tau_\infty^l = 0$, but the analysis remains valid provided that those markup and long-run tax rates are sufficiently close to zero.

of the key equations of the model and from there deriving the *natural equilibrium* and the *long-run equilibrium* of the economy. Once this is done, we will be able to infer what the AS and AD curves are, before turning to the analysis of fiscal shocks in sections 7.3 and 7.4.

7.2.6.1 SUMMARY OF THE MODEL'S EQUATIONS

From the analysis above, the behavior of the economy can be summarized by the following four equations:

Consumption of Keynesian households : $c_t^K = w_t - p_t - \tau_t^l - \tau_t^c$, (CK)

Consumption of Ricardian households : $c_t^R = c_\infty^R + \tau_\infty^c - \tau_t^c$, (CR)

Labor supply of Ricardian households : $l_t^R = \dfrac{\xi}{1-\xi}(w_t - p_t - \tau_t^c - \tau_t^l - c_t^R)$, (LR)

Market clearing (goods and labor) : $\xi \mu^* + (1-v)\, l_t^R = v c_t^K + (1-v)\, c_t^R + g_t$. (MC)

The *endogenous* variables in this system of equations are the consumption levels c_t^R and c_t^K, Ricardian households' labor supply l_t^R, and the real wage $w_t - p_t$ (so that we have four endogenous variables for four equations). The exogenous variables are the fiscal variables—namely the tax rates τ_t^l and τ_t^c and government spending g_t. It may seem that c_∞^R is a fifth endogenous variable, but we will see later that c_∞^R is pinned down by the long-run values of the tax rates τ_∞^l and τ_∞^c, so it is actually an exogenous variable in this system. What we are going to do in the remainder of this section is to move from those four equations to a reduced-form AS-AD model that will look exactly like the AS-AD model of chapter 4.

The first thing to note here is that equations (CK), (LR), and (MC) allow rewriting l_t^R as a function of the real wage $w_t - p_t$ and the exogenous variables. Indeed, replacing c_t^K in (MC) by its value in (CK), solving (MC) for c_t^R, substituting the resulting expression into (LR), and rearranging the variables, gives the following expression for the labor supply of Ricardian households:

$$l_t^R = \frac{\xi}{1-v}(w_t - p_t - \xi\mu^* - \tau_t^c - \tau_t^l + g_t).$$ (LRb)

This labor supply is, unsurprisingly, increasing in the real wage. It is decreasing in the tax rates because, as explained above, both taxes raise the tax wedge and thus discourage labor supply. Finally, l_t^R is increasing in government spending *even if the latter is fully debt-financed* (so that current taxes do not change). This is an outcome of the so-called *wealth effects of government spending on labor supply*. Intuitively, an increase in government spending must be financed at some point in time and thus it lowers households' present value of disposable income. Ricardian households respond to this by working more in order to raise their pre-tax wage income, and thereby mitigate the fall in this present value.

7.2.6.2   NATURAL EQUILIBRIUM

In the natural equilibrium all firms set their selling price optimally; therefore, the price level p_t is equal to the optimal price p_t^*. Equation (7.17) then implies that the real wage in the natural equilibrium is equal to $-(1-\xi)\mu^*$. Equation (CK) gives c_t^{Kn}. Equation (LRb) gives l_t^{Rn}. Once l_t^{Rn} is known, equation (LR) can be solved for c_t^{Rn}. We get:

$$c_t^{Kn} = -(1-\xi)\mu^* - \tau_t^l - \tau_t^c, \tag{CKn}$$

$$c_t^{Rn} = \frac{(1-\xi)\left(\upsilon\mu^* - g_t\right) - (\xi - \upsilon)(\tau_t^c + \tau_t^l)}{1-\upsilon}, \tag{CRn}$$

$$l_t^{Rn} = \frac{\xi}{1-\upsilon}(-\mu^* - \tau_t^c - \tau_t^l + g_t). \tag{LRn}$$

Finally, since $y_t = \xi\mu^* + (1-\upsilon)l_t^R$, natural output y_t^n is given by:

$$y_t^n = \xi(g_t - \tau_t^c - \tau_t^l). \tag{7.22}$$

All else equal, an increase in proportional taxes (τ_t^c or τ_t^l) reduces natural output, because it reduces households' incentive to work. Government spending, on the contrary, increases natural output. It makes households poorer (since they must ultimately finance this spending, at one time or another, in the form of taxes), which leads them to increase their labor supply in order to partially offset the implied loss of disposable income (this is just the wealth effect of government spending on labor supply).

Importantly, equation (CRn) gives the long-run consumption level of Ricardian households c_∞^R that roots its current level c_t^R according to equation (CR) above. Since $g_\infty = 0$ (by assumption), we have:

$$c_\infty^R = c_\infty^{Rn} = \frac{(1-\xi)\upsilon\mu^* - (\xi - \upsilon)\left(\tau_\infty^c + \tau_\infty^l\right)}{1-\upsilon}. \tag{CR∞}$$

We are now in a position to derive the AS and AD curves implied by our general-equilibrium model with a public sector.

7.2.6.3   THE AS CURVE

The AS curve summarizes how firms respond to changes in the demand they face and their costs of production by adjusting their selling price and quantity produced. The building block of the AS curve is the labor-market equilibrium, which determines the real wage that firms pay to their workers and hence their unit cost of production. From equations (7.21) and (LRb) above, the labor market equilibrium can be rewritten as:

$$\underbrace{y_t - \xi\mu^*}_{\text{labor demand}} = \underbrace{\xi(w_t - p_t - \xi\mu^* - \tau_t^c - \tau_t^l + g_t),}_{\text{labor supply}}$$

which can be solved for the equilibrium real wage $w_t - p_t$ as a function of y_t and the fiscal variables:

$$w_t - p_t = \xi^{-1}y_t - (1 - \xi)\,\mu^* - g_t + \tau_t^c + \tau_t^l. \tag{7.23}$$

This equation generalizes the equilibrium real-wage equation (3.8) in the presence of public spending, taxes, and heterogeneous households. All else being equal, the real wage is increasing in output, since a high level of output translates into a high demand for labor, which tightens the labor market and ultimately raises the equilibrium real wage. An increase in proportional taxes reduces labor supply (since the tax increase discourages labor supply), which (at a given demand for labor) tends to raise the equilibrium real wage. An increase in government spending impoverishes households and thus leads them to work more in order to offset the income loss they will incur as a result of higher taxes. At a given demand for labor, this increase in labor supply leads to a drop in the equilibrium real wage.

We know that in the presence of nominal rigidities, and under the assumptions stated in chapter 3 about the evolution of nominal prices, the price level is a weighted average of indexed prices (in proportion ω) and optimized prices (in proportion $1 - \omega$). Thus we have:

$$p_t = \omega\left(p_{t-1} + \pi_{t-1}\right) + (1 - \omega)\,p_t^*.$$

We now show how, following the same steps as in chapter 3, we get to the exact same AS curve, the only difference being that natural output is now given by equation (7.22) above and thus incorporates fiscal variables. First of all, by adding $-(1 - \omega)$ to each side of the equation above and factorizing, we obtain the dynamics of inflation as a function of the optimal *real* price ($p_t^* - p_t$ in log):

$$\pi_t = \pi_{t-1} + \left(\frac{1 - \omega}{\omega}\right)(p_t^* - p_t).$$

Further, by using the expression of the optimal nominal price (7.17) and that of the equilibrium real wage (7.23), we see that the optimal real price is increasing in the output gap:

$$p_t^* - p_t = \xi^{-1} y_t - g_t + \tau_t^c + \tau_t^l$$
$$= \xi^{-1} \left(y_t - y_t^n \right).$$

Substituting this expression into the previous one gives our AS curve:

$$\textbf{AS}: \pi_t = \pi_{t-1} + \kappa \left(y_t - y_t^n \right). \tag{7.24}$$

Therefore, the only difference with the aggregate supply block of chapter 3 is indeed the presence of fiscal variables (g_t, τ_t^c, and τ_t^l) in the expression of natural output y_t^n (equation (7.22)).

7.2.6.4   THE AD CURVE

We may now turn to the AD curve. We already know that aggregate demand is given by:

$$y_t = \upsilon c_t^K + (1 - \upsilon) c_t^R + g_t.$$

In this equation, c_t^K is given by equation (CK) above, with $w_t - p_t$ given by (7.23). On the other hand, c_t^R is given by equation (CR), with c_∞^R given by (CR∞). Using those expressions we get the following AD curve:

$$\textbf{AD}: y_t = \xi \underbrace{\left[\frac{(1 - \upsilon) \left(g_t - \tau_t^c \right) + (1 - \xi) \tau_\infty^c}{\xi - \upsilon} \right]}_{\theta_t} - \xi \tau_\infty^l, \tag{7.25}$$

where we recall that $\xi - \upsilon > 0$ by assumption.

Equation (7.25) is just a special case of the general AD curve derived in chapter 2 and used in Part II to study the business cycle. This general AD curve was given by $y_t = \theta_t - \sigma \gamma (\pi_t - \bar{\pi})$, where θ_t was a generic aggregate demand shock and $\pi_t - \bar{\pi}$ the deviation of inflation from target. In the present chapter we are assuming that the central bank does not change the real interest rate following fiscal shocks, even when these shocks create inflationary or deflationary pressures; this amount setting $\gamma = 0$ in the AD curve of chapter 2. The AD curve is thus only made of the aggregate demand shock θ_t, as given by the right-hand side of equation (7.25). It is precisely the advantage of a full general-equilibrium analysis of fiscal shocks to allow *exactly mapping the fiscal variables* (g_t, τ_t^c, τ_∞^c, *and* τ_∞^l) *into aggregate demand* (θ_t) *and supply* (y_t^n) *shocks.* We now use this mapping to analyze the macroeconomic effects of alternative fiscal policies—what has come to be known as the *fiscal multipliers*.

7.3   THE GOVERNMENT-SPENDING MULTIPLIER

7.3.1   EMPIRICAL MULTIPLIER

Formally, the *government-spending multiplier* is defined as the rise in GDP generated by an exogenous increase of government spending, with the latter being expressed relative to the size of GDP. Empirically, the government-spending multiplier $\hat{M}_g$ is calculated as follows:

$$\hat{M}_g = \frac{\frac{Y_t - Y_{t-1}}{Y_{t-1}}}{\frac{G_t - G_{t-1}}{Y_{t-1}}}. \quad \begin{array}{l} \leftarrow \text{growth rate of output} \\ \leftarrow \text{variation in the gov't spending share of GDP} \end{array} \tag{7.26}$$

The empirical literature about this multiplier is considerable. The challenge it faces is to measure the causal chain running from government spending to output, while many mechanisms other than changes in government spending influence the empirical correlation between these two variables. To understand the difficulty, let us suppose (for argument's sake) that variations in government spending have no causal effect on output whatsoever. However, public spending would still covary systematically with output, since it is much higher in recession than in expansion by virtue of the automatic stabilizers. The endogenous response of government spending to output induces a negative correlation between these variables that could be attributed (wrongly) to a causal effect running from more spending to less output. In practice, the causality runs in both directions, and there are potentially other variables (called confounding factors) that correlate government spending and output independently of any direct causal link between these two variables.[14] In this context, how can one isolate the variations in government spending that are truly exogenous—that is, that are not themselves caused by fluctuations in output or by a confounding factor that correlates with output?

Until now, the empirical literature on the measurement of the multiplier has relied on two main identification strategies. The first strategy consists of focusing on particular types of government-spending shocks—namely those we have good reason to think they are not themselves generated by variations in GDP. From this perspective, the most popular way of proceeding is to take as exogenous government-spending shocks the *increases in military spending due to a sudden and unanticipated deterioration in the geopolitical context*. Such events generate variations in government spending that in principle should not depend on the business cycle (although the business cycle depends on them), and thus they constitute

---

14. For example, an earthquake may trigger both a recession and increased infrastructure spending but one would be wrong to compute the government-spending multiplier by using such an event. One might infer from this calculation that infrastructure spending *reduces* GDP, just as one could deduce from the presence of sick people in hospitals that these places are dangerous for one's health.

a valid basis for measuring the government-spending multiplier.[15] The government-spending multipliers obtained with this method range between 0.7 and 1.2 for the United States (Hall 2009).

The second approach relies on geographic variations in government spending to identify the component that is exogenous to nationwide GDP. The study by Suarez Serrato and Wingender (2016) offers a telling example of this approach. Every ten years, a census is taken in the United States that involves counting the population of every single county in the nation's states. After that, the federal government adjusts its financial contribution according to these demographic evolutions. The counties whose population is revised upward see their endowment increase, and those whose population is revised downward see a decrease. Unsurprisingly, this reallocation of federal funds among the counties leads each county to vary its local government spending. What is important about these variations is that *by construction their geographic dispersion is not linked to the GDP of the United States as a whole or to other factors that are systematically linked to the GDP in the United States* (such as the monetary policy of the US Federal Reserve, for example). Thus they may be used to calculate the local multipliers—that is, the increase in local output in a county that follows from a variation in federal spending induced by a revision in the population census. Suarez Serrato and Wingender (2016) find local multipliers between 1.7 and 2 using this method, which are much higher than the national multipliers obtained with macroeconomic data.[16] Likewise, Nakamura and Steinsson (2014) estimate the multipliers associated with regional military spending in the United States and find a multiplier of about 1.5. They stress, however, that cross-sectional variations in regional spending do not generate the general-equilibrium effects and monetary-policy response that are likely set in motion after an economy wide fiscal stimulus. It thus takes a general-equilibrium model to infer the value of the aggregate multiplier (what we care about) from those of the regional multipliers (what we measure).

7.3.2 THEORETICAL MULTIPLIERS

The AS-AD model developed in the last section enables us to understand the size of the government-spending multiplier as well as its underlying economic determinants. In order to isolate the pure effects of government spending on the equilibrium without mixing them with the fiscal distortions due to proportional taxation, we will assume in the present section that government spending is entirely financed

15. This method has been applied mostly in the United States. The government-spending shocks, then, are the Korean war (1950), the Vietnam war (1965), the rearmament policy of Ronald Reagan (1980), and the 9/11 attack (2001).

16. See also Acconcia, Corsetti, and Simonelli (2014), who studied the impact of an anti-Mafia law in Italy on regional budgets and thereby on local spending. They find that the local multiplier associated with a contraction in government spending in one region is about 1.5.

by lump-sum taxes (so that $\tau_t^c = \tau_t^l = 0$ for all t). Hence, from equation (7.25) the AD curve simplifies to:

$$\mathbf{AD}: y_t = \frac{\xi\,(1-\upsilon)}{\xi - \upsilon}\,g_t. \tag{7.27}$$

Note that Ricardian equivalence may not hold here, even without distortionary taxation, because some households (the Keynesian households) face debt constraints. Hence, in principle the timing of the lump-sum taxes that finance the rise in government spending could matter. However, our maintained assumption that only Ricardian households can be taxed lump-sum restores Ricardian equivalence here, so we need not worry about the timing of lump-sum taxes.[17] Of course, nothing prevents us later on from considering a government-spending shock financed by, say, a rise in the income tax; the overall impact of this policy on the equilibrium will just be the sum of a government-spending shock financed by lump-sum taxes (which we study now) and a hike in the income tax associated with a lower path of lump-sum taxes (a policy that we examine in section 7.4 below).

Finally, for expositional clarity we will proceed just like in chapter 4 by assuming that the economy was in long-run equilibrium in period $t-1$ before the government spending shock occurs, and we normalize the inflation target $\bar{\pi}$ to zero. Since long-run government spending g_∞ is zero and we are ruling out proportional taxes, we have

$$g_{t-1} = g_\infty = 0, \quad y_{t-1} = y_\infty = y_\infty^n = 0 \ \text{ and } \ \pi_{t-1} = 0.$$

In period t an increase in government spending of size $dg_t > 0$ occurs, and we wish to compute its impact on output (dy_t) and inflation ($d\pi_t$). This shock is potentially persistent, but necessarily transitory by virtue of our assumption of long-run government spending being nil. Note that the ratio dy_t/dg_t is here the direct theoretical counterpart of the empirical multiplier (equation (7.26)). In fact, dy_t is in first approximation equal to GDP growth following the government-spending shock while dg_t is the variation in the share of government spending in GDP. Indeed, from the definition of g_t in equation (7.19) and our approximation (1.3), we have

$$\frac{dy_t}{dg_t} = \frac{y_t - y_{t-1}}{g_t - g_{t-1}} = \frac{\ln Y_t - \ln Y_t}{\frac{G_t - G_{t-1}}{Y_{t-1}}} \simeq \frac{\frac{Y_t - Y_{t-1}}{Y_{t-1}}}{\frac{G_t - G_{t-1}}{Y_{t-1}}}.$$

17. This shows up in the fact that nowhere do lump-sum taxes explicitly appear in the system of equations describing the equilibrium. The path of lump-sum taxes that ensures the solvency of the government is implicit, and changes in the path of these taxes do not matter as long as the solvency of the government is maintained (i.e., as long as the intertemporal budget constraint of the government is satisfied).

7.3.2.1 THE MULTIPLIER IN THE NATURAL EQUILIBRIUM

Let us begin by calculating the multiplier that would prevail in the *natural* equilibrium, if all prices were optimally adjusted at all times after any aggregate shock. In this equilibrium, equation (7.22) gives

$$\frac{dy_t^n}{dg_t} = \xi < 1.$$

Thus, the government-spending multiplier is equal to the labor-supply elasticity parameter ξ and is thus *positive but necessarily lower than one*. The reason for this is as follows. One direct effect of the government-spending shock is to impoverish households, since the government will have to finance this expenditure by levying taxes, either now or in the future. Because Ricardian equivalence holds here, deferring in time the fiscal incidence of government spending has no effect on the size of this incidence. The response of households is to consume less but also to work more in order to buffer the effect of the shock on their labor income (that is, in order to limit the fall in consumption that higher taxes force). The increase in hours worked makes possible an increase in output, but the drop in consumption implies that output increases less than the amount of government spending—and therefore we say that government spending *crowds out* private consumption. The higher the elasticity of labor supply (ξ), the more the hours worked will increase after the government-spending shock, and hence the less labor income will diminish and the less consumption will fall.

7.3.2.2 THE MULTIPLIER UNDER NOMINAL RIGIDITIES

In the presence of nominal rigidities, the equilibrium (y_t, π_t) is given by the AS and AD curves (i.e., equations (7.25) and (7.27)). Hence, the government-spending multiplier is given by

$$\frac{dy_t}{dg_t} = \frac{\xi(1-\upsilon)}{\xi - \upsilon} \geq 1,$$

with an equality if $\upsilon = 0$ and a strict inequality whenever $0 < \upsilon < \xi$. Moreover, from the AS curve and the multiplier in the natural equilibrium, the variation of *inflation* following the shock is given by

$$\frac{d\pi_t}{dg_t} = \kappa \frac{dy_t - dy_t^n}{dg_t} = \frac{\kappa\xi(1-\xi)}{\xi - \upsilon} > 0.$$

To understand the size and workings of the government-spending multiplier, it is useful to start by considering an economy *without* Keynesian consumers (i.e.,

$v = 0$). In this case the multiplier dy_t/dg_t is equal to 1, while inflation rises by the amount $\kappa (1 - \xi)dg_t$. The reason why the multiplier is 1 in that scenario is that Ricardian consumers do not alter their consumption after a government-spending shock (see equation (CR) in the preceding section); hence output rises by exactly the same amount as government spending. Of course, this increase in output requires more labor input, and labor supply can rise only if the real wage does. Hence, the government-spending shock increases the unit production cost of the firms, which the firms that set their price optimally pass through to selling prices, and inflation rises. The adjustment to the shock is represented graphically in figure 7.1(a). The AS curve is given by $\pi_t = \kappa \left(y_t - y_t^n\right)$ (since $\pi_{t-1} = 0$ by assumption); the spending shock raises natural output y_t^n by the amount ξdg_t (see equation (7.22)) and thus it shifts the AS curve downward by a distance of $\kappa \xi dg_t$. In the absence of Keynesian consumers the AD curve is given by $y_t = g_t$; it is thus vertical in the (y, π) plane and is shifted to the right by a distance $dy_t = dg_t$ after the government-spending shock. The conjunction of the movements of the AS and AD curves shifts the equilibrium from point A to point B, which is associated with levels of output and inflation that are higher than before the shock.[18]

Let us now turn to the case where there *are* Keynesian consumers in the economy (i.e. $0 < v < \xi$). We have just seen that, in the absence of such consumers, the rise in government spending triggers a rise in the real wage; what this higher real wage does is to *boost the consumption demand of Keynesian households* (see equation (CK) above). The story does not stop here, because the greater consumption demand of Keynesian households itself reinforces the rise in the real wage, which further boosts consumption, and so on. This feedback loop explains why the government-spending multiplier is *necessarily* greater than one in the presence of Keynesian consumers; we say that government spending *crowds in* private consumption (which is the opposite as what happened in the natural equilibrium). For that matter, the multiplier can be *much* greater than 1 (think of what happens if v is close to ξ), a reflection of the feedback loop between the consumption of Keynesian consumers and the equilibrium real wage.[19] The impact of a government-spending shock on the equilibrium when $v > 0$ is represented on figure 7.1(b). The AS curve and its shift are the same as in the case where $v = 0$. The AD curve, however, is now given by equation (7.27), and therefore its rightward shift becomes larger as v rises. As a consequence, both y_t and π_t rise more than when $v = 0$.

18. We have just seen that $d\pi_t > 0$, which means that the AS curve can never be shifted to the point of generating a *drop* in inflation after a government-spending shock.

19. It is because of this feedback loop that the share of Keynesian consumers cannot be too large for an equilibrium to exist. As $v \to \xi$ the loop is so powerful that it causes output and inflation to shoot up to infinity following a government-spending shock of any size.

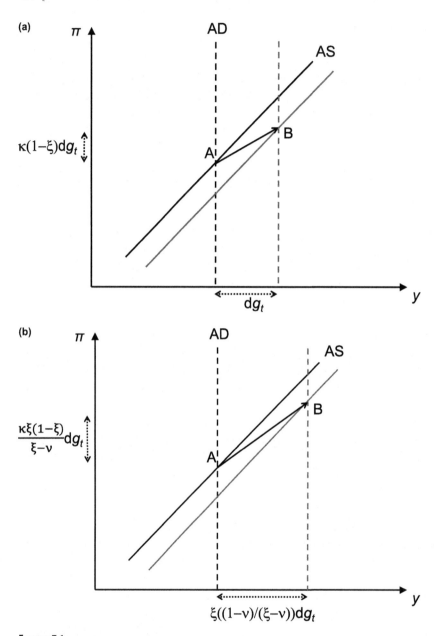

FIGURE 7.1
Impact of an increase in government spending (a) without Keynesian households and (b) with Keynesian households. An increase in government spending raises both aggregate demand and supply and, hence, shifts both the AS and AD curves. The shift of the AD curve and the implied impact on output and inflation are larger in the presence of Keynesian households.

7.4 THE TAX MULTIPLIERS

7.4.1 EMPIRICAL MULTIPLIERS

The empirical measurement of the tax multipliers poses exactly the same difficulties as does the government-spending multiplier. It is hard to isolate exogenous variations in taxes that would not be somehow a consequence of the business cycle. Therefore it is hard to precisely measure the causality running from changes in taxes to changes in output.

There are several reasons why taxes endogenously respond to the business cycle. For one thing, holding the tax code unchanged, tax revenues systematically rise with total income since most taxes are proportional or progressive; that is, taxes play the role of *automatic stabilizers*. Hence, the first thing to do when trying to measure the effect of taxes on output is to use a *cyclically adjusted* measure of tax revenues, in place of the raw measure (Blanchard and Perotti 2002). But the feedback from output to taxes does not stop here, because economic developments may elicit changes in the tax code itself— for example, when a tax cut is passed during a recession. Inasmuch as tax cuts are more likely to be passed during recessions, this again induces a positive correlation between tax revenues and output that adds up to that induced by the automatic stabilizers.

To get around this difficulty, Romer and Romer (2010) plunged into the details of the political and legislative history of the United States in order to isolate variations in the tax code that were *not* responses to economic developments. That is, they ignored changes in taxes that were motivated by the business cycle (or the willingness to offset variations in government spending), only to consider the tax changes that were politically or ideologically motivated (e.g., exogenous to economic developments). By correlating these exogenous tax shocks with the induced variations in output at various horizons, Romer and Romer (2010) showed that a drop in fiscal revenue by an amount equal to 1 percent of GDP generates a gradual increase in GDP that reaches its maximum (3 percent) after two-and-a-half years. Thus, the expansionary impact of tax cuts is large.

7.4.2 THEORETICAL MULTIPLIERS

When studying the government-spending multiplier we abstracted from simultaneous changes in proportional taxes. The symmetric assumption is made here by setting government spending to zero at all times ($g_t = g_\infty = 0$ for all t); again, this is without loss of generality since the impact of joint variations in government spending and proportional taxes is just the sum of their individual impacts. On the other hand, the government is assumed to be servicing a positive debt burden, which is financed by a combination of lump-sum taxes (T_t) and proportional taxes (τ_t^c, τ_t^l). Starting from this situation, we can examine the macroeconomic effect of a *cut* in either proportional tax, which will result in an increase in the present value of lump-sum taxes in such a way as to satisfy the government's intertemporal budget constraint. Finally, we will not confine ourselves to examining merely transitory fiscal shocks, but will also consider the effects of permanent fiscal shocks (fiscal reforms). More specifically, for the two proportional taxes τ_t^c and τ_t^l, we define a transitory tax cut as a reduction in τ_t that leaves τ_∞ unchanged, and a permanent tax cut as a reduction in τ_t and τ_∞ such that $\tau_t = \tau_\infty$.

7.4.2.1 THE TAX MULTIPLIERS IN THE NATURAL EQUILIBRIUM

We begin, as we did before, by calculating the tax multipliers in the natural equilibrium. In this equilibrium, and in the absence of government spending, the expression of natural output (equation (7.22)) implies

$$-\frac{\mathrm{d}y_t^n}{\mathrm{d}\tau_t^l} = -\frac{\mathrm{d}y_t^n}{\mathrm{d}\tau_t^c} = \xi.$$

In other words, a drop in either tax rate raises natural output, and does it by the same amount $(= \xi \mathrm{d}\tau_t)$ for both taxes whether the tax cut is transitory $(\mathrm{d}\tau_\infty^l = \mathrm{d}\tau_\infty^c = 0)$ or permanent $(\mathrm{d}\tau_\infty^l = \mathrm{d}\tau_t^l,\ \mathrm{d}\tau_\infty^c = \mathrm{d}\tau_t^c)$. This effect comes from the optimal labor supply of the households, which implies that lowering either tax incentivizes the households to work more.

7.4.2.2 THE TAX MULTIPLIERS UNDER NOMINAL RIGIDITIES

Under nominal rigidities the relevant AS-AD model is again given by equations (7.25) and (7.27). In particular, we infer from the AD curve above (equation (7.25)) that:

- a transitory cut in income tax $(\mathrm{d}\tau_t^l < 0)$ has a multiplier effect of zero (output does not change);

- a permanent cut in income tax $(\mathrm{d}\tau_t^l = \mathrm{d}\tau_\infty^l < 0)$ has a multiplier effect of ξ (output rises by $-\xi \mathrm{d}\tau_\infty^l > 0$);

- a transitory cut in VAT $(\mathrm{d}\tau_t^c < 0)$ has a multiplier effect of $\frac{\xi(1-\upsilon)}{\xi - \upsilon}$ (output rises by $-\frac{\xi(1-\upsilon)}{\xi - \upsilon}\mathrm{d}\tau_t^c > 0$);

- a permanent cut in VAT $(\mathrm{d}\tau_t^c = \mathrm{d}\tau_\infty^c < 0)$ has a multiplier effect of ξ (output rises by $-\xi \mathrm{d}\tau_t^c > 0$).

Let us explain those multipliers one by one, starting with the effect of a *transitory cut in income tax*. As we did for the government-spending multiplier, we first examine the effect of this policy in an economy *without* Keynesian consumers. In such an economy, the tax cut has no effect on output for the following reasons. First of all, this cut does not directly shift aggregate demand (as is apparent from equation (7.25)), because Ricardian households only respond to changes in VAT (see equation

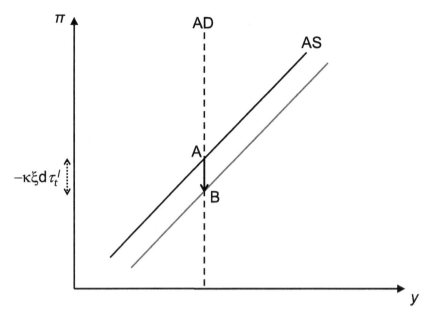

FIGURE 7.2
Impact of a transitory cut in income tax. A transitory income tax cut boosts labor supply, which shifts the AS curve downwards.

(CR)). What the income tax cut does, however, is to spur Ricardian households' labor supply (see (LRb)), which causes the equilibrium real wage to fall (see (7.23)). The firms that adjust their prices optimally respond to this drop in production costs by lowering their selling price, which leads to a drop in inflation. However, recall that, under the monetary policy assumed throughout, the central bank does not respond to changes in the inflation rate; hence aggregate demand is not moved indirectly either by a change in the real interest rate.[20] So the only impact of the tax cut here is a fall in both the real wage and inflation.

How does the presence of Keynesian households alter this picture? The direct effect of the cut is to raise their disposable income, which we could think from equation (CK) that it should boost consumption demand. However, under our assumptions this direct effect is *exactly* canceled by an indirect, general-equilibrium effect—namely, the downward adjustment of the real wage. Thus, the presence of Keynesian households does change the response of aggregate demand to the tax cut.

The shift of the equilibrium (y_t, π_t) after a transitory cut in income tax is represented in figure 7.2. The AD curve is still vertical and given by (7.25) and it is thus

---

20. As can be shown formally by solving Exercise 7.5.1, the tax cut would be expansionary if the central bank responded to the implied deflationary pressures by lowering the real interest rate. However, in that case the stimulus effect would be just as much the outcome of monetary policy as of fiscal policy.

not displaced at all by the tax cut. The AS curve, on the other hand, does move—the income tax cut raises natural output (here by an amount $\xi d\tau_t^l$; see equation (7.22)), which shifts the AS curve downward (by the amount $\kappa\xi d\tau_t$). So the equilibrium goes from point A to point B on figure 7.2.

Now let us consider the case of a *permanent cut in the income tax*. The essential difference between a transitory and a permanent cut in income tax is that the latter lifts aggregate demand, in addition to lifting aggregate supply. This channel works through the consumption demand of Ricardian households. From equation (CR∞), their long-run consumption level c_∞^R is raised, which is a reflection of the rise in their permanent income brought about by the permanence of the tax cut; and since they smooth consumption over time, this also raises their current consumption demand.

The economy's response to a permanent cut in income tax is represented graphically on figure 7.3. The shift of the AS curve is exactly the same as under a transitory tax cut. But the AD curve now shifts rightward by the distance $-\xi d\tau_\infty^l > 0$ (see equation (7.25) again). It is easily checked (using the the values of dy_t and dy_t^n) that the impact on inflation of the joint shift in the AS and AD curve exactly offset each other, so that $d\pi_t = 0$. Hence the equilibrium moves horizontally from point A to point B.

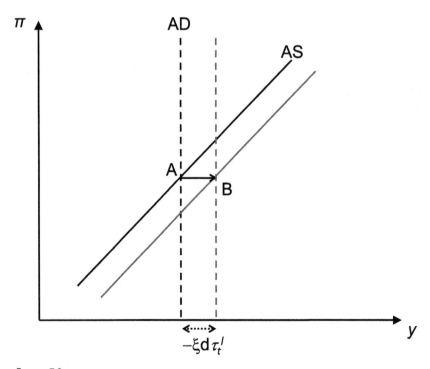

FIGURE 7.3
Impact of a permanent cut in income tax. The aggregate demand and supply effects of a permanent cut in income tax on inflation exactly offset each other.

A *transitory cut in VAT* also generates both aggregate supply and demand effects, and here again it is useful to examine a situation without Keynesian consumers before analyzing their additional impact on the equilibrium. On the *supply* side, the cut in VAT generates the same increase in natural output as a cut in income tax (see equation (7.22)), and hence the same downward shift of the AS curve. On the *demand* side, the cut has the effect of lowering the price of goods consumed in the current period relative to the price of goods consumed in the future. This invites Ricardian households to consume more in the current period (see equation (CR)). The AD curve is shifted to the right, by a distance $dy_t = -d\tau_t^C > 0$ (see equation (7.25)). The equilibrium moves from point A to point B in figure 7.4(a).

What does the presence of Keynesian consumers do to this adjustment? The boost in aggregate demand triggered by the consumption demand of Ricardian households pushes up the real wage (see equation (7.23)), which leads Keynesian households to consume more (see equation (CK)). This in turn raises aggregate demand further, which keeps on pushing up the real wage, and so on. In other words, in the presence of Keynesian consumers a transitory cut in VAT *sets in motion the very same expansionary feedback loop between the real wage and the consumption demand of Keynesian household as did a government-spending shock.* This is why the corresponding multiplier may be (very) large. Graphically, in the presence of Keynesian households the AD curve shifts out more (namely by a distance $-\xi \frac{(1-\upsilon)}{\xi-\upsilon} d\tau_t^C > 0$), leading to a larger increase in output and inflation. See figure 7.4(b).

The impact of a *permanent cut in VAT* does not generate the intertemporal substitution in consumption that was generated by a transitory cut, but it still shifts the AD curve since it changes the long-run level of output y_∞. According to equation (7.25), the shift of the AD curve when the VAT shock is permanent $(\tau_\infty^C = \tau_t^C)$ is of size $dy_t = -\xi d\tau_t^C$, meaning that the AD curve shifts significantly less than after a transitory tax shock. The shift in the AS curve is the same as with a transitory shock. The equilibrium moves exactly in the same way as in the case of a permanent cut in income tax. This is represented in figure 7.5.

Table 7.1 gathers the values of the various multipliers that we have computed. The last column (Liquidity trap) anticipates the results of chapter 10, where we will recompute all fiscal multipliers when the economy is in a situation of liquidity trap.

Reading Table 7.1, we see that two fiscal policies stand out in terms of multiplier effects: the transitory hike in government spending and the transitory cut in VAT. These two policies effectively stimulate aggregate demand (the former by the government, the latter by the private sector), and all the more so when the share of Keynesian consumers in the economy is large, so that the feedback loop between their consumption demand and the equilibrium real wage is powerful. In both cases, the multipliers are substantially larger in the economy with nominal rigidities than in the hypothetical flexible price (i.e., natural) equilibrium. The reason for this is that

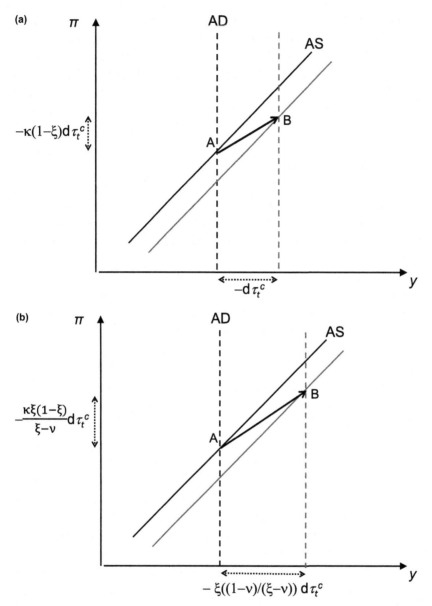

FIGURE 7.4
Impact of a transitory cut in VAT (a) without Keynesian households and (b) with Keynesian households. A transitory cut in VAT boosts current consumption (which shifts the AD curve to the right) as well as current labor supply (which shifts the AS curve downward). The shift of the AD curve and the implied impact on output and inflation are larger in the presence of Keynesian households.

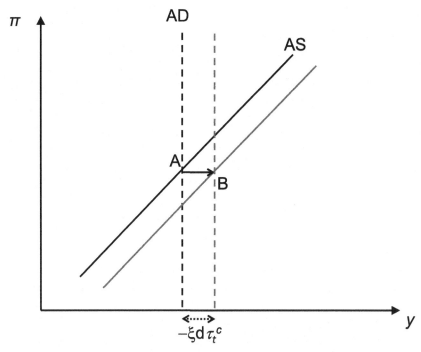

FIGURE 7.5
Impact of a permanent cut in VAT. A permanent cut in VAT has the same effect on output and inflation as does a permanent cut in income tax.

in the natural equilibrium expansionary fiscal policies only have aggregate *supply* effects (that is, they raise households' labor supply), whereas in the equilibrium with nominal rigidities these supply effects are complemented and reinforced by aggregate *demand* effects. In this respect, perhaps the most striking result is the reversal from *crowding out* to *crowding in* of private consumption by government spending when moving from the flexible price, natural equilibrium to the equilibrium with nominal rigidities (and Keynesian households).

There are two other factors that may further push up the size of the government-spending multiplier relative to that computed in section 7.3. First, one might realistically suppose that a significant portion of government spending represents *investments* that increase the stock of public capital, and thus raise the marginal product of complementary inputs—the foremost of which is labor (Baxter and King 1993). As an example, the American Jobs Act enacted by former President Barack Obama in November 2011 called for a modernization of infrastructure and an expansion of the high-speed internet network. When government spending raises the stock of public capital, then aggregate supply is directly

TABLE 7.1
Multiplier effects of fiscal shocks.

Fiscal multipliers	Natural equilibrium	Nominal rigidities	Liquidity trap (ch. 10)
Government spending (transitory rise)	ξ (<1)	$\frac{\xi(1-\upsilon)}{\xi-\upsilon}$ (≥ 1)	$\frac{\xi(1-\upsilon)(1-\kappa\xi)}{\xi(1-\kappa)-\upsilon(1-\xi\kappa)}$ $\left(> \frac{\xi(1-\upsilon)}{\xi-\upsilon}\right)$
Income tax (transitory cut)	ξ	0	$-\frac{\xi^2\kappa(1-\upsilon)}{\xi(1-\kappa)-\upsilon(1-\xi\kappa)}$ (<0)
Income tax (permanent cut)	ξ	ξ	ξ
VAT (transitory cut)	ξ	$\frac{\xi(1-\upsilon)}{\xi-\upsilon}$	$\frac{\xi(1-\upsilon)(1-\kappa\xi)}{\xi(1-\kappa)-\upsilon(1-\xi\kappa)}$
VAT (permanent cut)	ξ	ξ	ξ

Note: ξ is the elasticity of labor supply, κ the slope the AD curve, and υ the share of Keynesian consumers.

boosted (beyond the rise in labor supply) and the spending multiplier may be large *even in the natural equilibrium with flexible prices.* In this spirit, Exercise 7.5.2 below asks to compute the government-spending multiplier when government spending raises labor productivity. A second factor that may further raise the government-spending multiplier relates to monetary policy. As is apparent from the last column of Table 7.1, this multiplier (and also the transitory VAT cut multiplier) may be quite large when the economy is stuck in a *liquidity trap.* We will study in detail the mechanism underlying such large multiplier effects in chapter 10.

7.5   EXERCISES

7.5.1   FISCAL MULTIPLIERS WITH A HAWKISH CENTRAL BANK

Consider a variant of the general-equilibrium AS-AD model of section 7.2 in which (1) there are no Keynesian households and (2) the central bank is hawkish in the sense that it adjusts the real interest rate so that inflation never departs from its zero target after a fiscal shock:

$$\pi_t = 0 \text{ for all } t.$$

All other aspects of the model are the same as in section 7.2. Derive the government-spending multiplier and the tax multipliers under this assumption, and explain how and why they differ from those obtained under a constant real interest rate.

7.5.2 THE GOVERNMENT-SPENDING MULTIPLIER IN THE PRESENCE OF PUBLIC INVESTMENT

Consider a variant of the AS-AD model of section 7.2 in which (1) there are no Keynesian households and (2) labor productivity is given by

$$Z_t = e^{\xi \mu^*} \left(1 + g_t \right)^\alpha, \quad \alpha \geq 0,$$

or, in first approximation and in the vicinity of $g_t = 0$:

$$z_t \simeq \xi \mu^* + \alpha g_t.$$

The behavior of all agents (Ricardian households and firms) is identical to that described in section 7.2. The central bank implements a monetary policy of constant real interest rate ($r_t = \rho$), and the fiscal policy of the government is a one-shot increase in government spending occurring in period t:

$$g_{t-1} = g_{t+1} = g_{t+2} = \ldots = 0, \quad g_t > 0.$$

Finally, assume that government spending is entirely financed by lump-sum taxes.

1. Compute the natural levels of output and employment.

2. Derive the AS and AD curves and then compute the multiplier effects of government spending on output and inflation.

3. Represent graphically the effect of this fiscal shock in the (y, π) plane, and discuss the various relevant cases according to the value of the parameter α.

7.5.3 THE GOVERNMENT-SPENDING MULTIPLIER WHEN MONETARY POLICY IS OPTIMIZED

Consider a variant of the general-equilibrium AS-AD model of section 7.2 in which (1) there are no Keynesian households and (2) the central bank sets the real interest rate r_t to minimize in every period the following loss function:

$$\min_{\pi_t} \lambda c_t^2 + \pi_t^2, \quad \lambda \geq 0,$$

where $c_t = \ln C_t$ is log aggregate consumption (in other words, it is output *net of government spending* that the central bank is trying to stabilize jointly with inflation).

All the other aspects of the model are the same as in Section 7.2. In particular, a transitory rise in government spending occurs in period t (in the neighborhood of $g_t = 0$) and is entirely financed by lump-sum taxes.

When choosing the real interest rate, the central bank takes as given past inflation π_{t-1} as well as the behavior of private agents, as summarized by the AD and AS curves. Under the assumptions of this exercise, these curves are given by:

$$\text{AD}: y_t = c_t + g_t,$$

$$\text{AS}: \pi_t = \pi_{t-1} + \kappa \left(y_t - y_t^n \right), \ y_t^n = \xi g_t,$$

$$\pi_{t-1} \text{ and } g_t \text{ given.}$$

1. Write down the Keynes-Ramsey rule that describes the optimal slope of the consumption profile of the households.

2. Solve the central bank's problem and infer from it that the optimal path of inflation is given by:

$$\pi_t = \left(\frac{\lambda}{\lambda + \kappa^2} \right) \pi_{t-1} + \left(\frac{\kappa \lambda (1 - \xi)}{\lambda + \kappa^2} \right) g_t.$$

Provide an interpretation of this expression, relying on the discussion of optimal monetary policy in chapter 6.

3. Show that the government-spending multiplier is given by

$$\frac{dy_t}{dg_t} = \frac{\lambda + \xi \kappa^2}{\lambda + \kappa^2}.$$

Provide an interpretation of this result, notably by comparing this multiplier with those obtained under the monetary policies of constant real interest rate ($r_t = \rho$, the chapter's baseline specification) and of constant inflation rate ($\pi_t = 0$, as studied in Exercise 7.5.1).

7.5.4 Monetary Policy with Heterogeneous Households

The analysis of this chapter shows that household heterogeneity, and notably the presence of Keynesian consumers, matters greatly for the transmission of fiscal policy. However, as stressed by Bilbiie (2008), Galí and Debortoli (2017), and Kaplan, Moll, and Violante (2018), household heterogeneity also matters for the transmission of monetary policy. To see this, consider again the general-equilibrium framework of section 7.2, assuming away government spending and taxes (i.e., $g_t = \tau_t^c = \tau_t^l = 0$ for all t). However, assume that the real interest rate is equal to ρ at all times except in the current period t.

1. Show that the consumption Ricardian households is equal to $c^R_\infty = \frac{(1-\xi)v\mu^*}{1-v}$ at all times except in period t, where it is given by

$$c^R_t = c^R_\infty + \rho - r_t.$$

2. Infer that the AD curve is given by

$$y_t = \text{constant} - \left[\frac{\xi(1-v)}{\xi - v}\right] r_t.$$

3. Explain intuitively how the change in the fraction of Keynesian consumers v affects the response of output y_t to the real interest rate r_t (Hint: There is an *direct* and an *indirect* effect of r_t, both of which are affected by v).

THE LIQUIDITY TRAP AND UNCONVENTIONAL POLICIES

THE LIQUIDITY TRAP

There is the possibility … that, after the rate of interest has fallen to a certain level, liquidity-preference may become virtually absolute in the sense that almost everyone prefers cash to holding a debt which yields so low a rate of interest. In this event the monetary authority would have lost effective control over the rate of interest. But whilst this limiting case might become practically important in the future, I know of no example of it hitherto.

—John Maynard Keynes (1936)

Because it determines the level of aggregate demand at any given period, the real interest rate is the most important variable in the macroeconomic equilibrium. When the real interest rate is too high, aggregate demand is too weak and pulls down output and inflation. Conversely, a real interest rate that is too low leads to excessive levels of aggregate demand and output relative to the natural level of output, which generates inflationary pressures. The departures of output from its natural level are transitory but costly. A level of output lower than the natural level generates underemployment, while an output above its natural level leads to an excessive level of inflation which will have, at some point, to be resorbed.

In normal times, the central bank has control over the stance of monetary policy, in the sense that it is in principle capable of manipulating the real interest rate to reach the desired level of aggregate demand. Of course, this control is not direct since the central bank instrument is the short-term nominal interest rate and not the real interest rate (see chapter 6). Nevertheless, we have seen that, in normal times, the manipulation of the short-term nominal interest rate, coupled with an effective communication about the future path of this rate, allowed the control of longer-term nominal interest rates (by exploiting the term structure of interest rates), and thereby the real interest rate (by exploiting the Fisher equation).

Unfortunately, this macroeconomic configuration of effective monetary control does not always prevail, and it could prevail less and less in the future. Since the mid-1990s, Japan has been locked in a liquidity trap—that is, a situation in which extremely low (close to zero) short-term nominal interest rates are no longer sufficient to revive a chronically deficient level of aggregate demand. From late 2008 onward, most developed countries, including the United States and the euro area, have one after the other joined Japan in the liquidity trap, due to the macroeconomic repercussions of the financial crisis. This period took the name of Great Recession, a sad tribute to the Great Depression of the 1930s. As the time of this writing, neither the euro area nor Japan have emerged from the liquidity trap. The United States exited the liquidity trap in December 2015, but concerns remain that it could return to it as soon as aggregate demand weakens again.[1] This means that the scenario contemplated by John Maynard Keynes some eighty years ago, and summarized in the epigraph of this chapter, is nowadays a major concern for central bankers. Figure 8.1 illustrates the fact that, while short-term nominal interest rates were reduced dramatically in many Western countries at the onset of the Great Recession, they stopped falling below a value close to zero—just like what happened in Japan in the 1990s.

The purpose of this chapter and the next two is to understand the circumstances that may drive an economy into the liquidity trap and to examine whether there are unconventional macroeconomic policies capable of restoring aggregate demand in this situation. The present chapter formally introduces the liquidity trap into the analysis of the macroeconomic equilibrium. In particular, we show why and how an economy can become stuck in a liquidity trap, and how the real interest rate, aggregate demand, output, and employment are determined there. The liquidity trap is frequently presented as a situation in which the usual rules of macroeconomics no longer hold;[2] we illustrate this point by means of the three liquidity trap paradoxes—namely, the paradoxes of *flexibility*, of *toil*, and of *thrift*.

8.1   THE FINANCIAL CRISIS AND AGGREGATE DEMAND

We will see below that, under the current monetary institutions, the liquidity trap is the *necessary* outcome of a sufficiently large negative shock to aggregate demand. But before analyzing the liquidity trap problem at that level of generality, let us

---

1. According to Kiley and Roberts (2017), the US economy may in the future find itself in a liquidity trap as often as two-fifths of the time. The persistence of the liquidity trap has led Lawrence Summers to stir up the specter of a secular stagnation—understood as the chronic inability of the central bank to raise aggregate demand at the level that would be necessary to ensure full employment (Summers 2014).

2. Eggertsson and Krugman (2012) refer to the liquidity trap as "a world of topsy-turvy, in which many of the usual rules of macroeconomics are stood on their head."

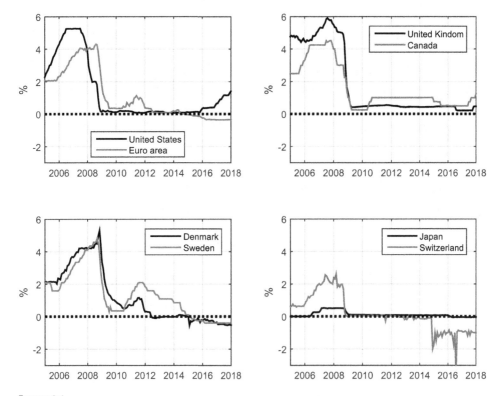

FIGURE 8.1
Interbank market rates. Since 2008, many central banks have adopted highly accommodative monetary poli-
cies, but short-term nominal interest rates have approached or hit a lower bound.
Source: OECD.

provide some contextual elements about the actual aggregate shocks that drove many
economies into the trap in the wake of the last financial crisis.[3]

8.1.1 THE FINANCIAL CRISIS OF 2007–2008

The financial crisis began in 2007 with a temporary freeze of the interbank market,
and then turned into a global financial crisis in 2008–2009. This crisis originated
in the financial imbalances accumulated in the US economy during the 2000s and
most prominently in the accumulation of toxic mortgages originated by commercial banks and diluted in the financial system worldwide through securitization.
The first manifestation of the crisis (i.e., the freezing of the interbank market in
August 2007) was the inevitable manifestation of growing and widespread doubts

---

3. Let us recall again that Japan did not wait until 2008 to enter the liquidity trap. It entered as early as
1995, shortly after the financial crisis that the country experienced in 1993. The historical experience of
the Japanese liquidity trap helps understand the situation of Western economies after 2008.

about the creditworthiness of banks following the increase in the delinquency rate on US mortgage borrowers. The interbank market is the one on which banks carry out short-term loans, with banks that are in surplus at the end of the day covering the temporary liquidity needs of those that are temporarily in deficit (see chapter 6 for details). This market operates smoothly when lending banks are certain that their counterpart will not go bankrupt overnight. As the information on this market is very asymmetric (each borrowing bank knows the quality of its own assets and loans, but the banks it is borrowing from do not), a diffuse doubt about the quality of assets leads surplus banks to retain their excess liquidity (technically, on their account with the central bank) rather than lending it to the other banks. This is precisely what happened in August 2007.

In the absence of a central bank, the freezing of the interbank market would immediately lead to the bankruptcy of all the banks experiencing a temporary liquidity shortage. But the central bank can substitute for a failing interbank market by lending the required liquidity directly to illiquid banks (this is called a loan of last resort). This is precisely what the major central banks did in August 2007, and it did effectively stem the liquidity crisis.[4] If we had stayed there, there would have been no global financial crisis and, in all likelihood, no Great Recession.

Unfortunately, the initial doubts about the quality of assets held by the banking system were partly justified, which meant that the system was not just experiencing a temporary liquidity crisis but a far more serious *solvency* crisis. Moreover, even the institutions that did not hold bad loans or assets but only suffered transitory illiquidity also saw their solvency deteriorating. Indeed, a key feature of the financial system is to hold assets of long maturity, together with liabilities of short maturity that must be constantly refinanced. A liquidity crisis may then contaminate a financial institution's creditworthiness because of *rollover risk*—that is, the risk of having to roll over past short-term debt with new debt at less favorable terms. During the period 2007–2009, the initial insolvency of certain financial institutions particularly exposed to the real estate market and the spreading of this insolvency to the rest of the financial system through roll over risk led to the collapse of several major financial institutions and to a generalized distrust in the financial markets. This in turn led to a phase of contraction in household debt accompanied by a sharp increase in credit spreads for all risky borrowers. These two channels—*rising credit spreads* and *household deleveraging*—are those by which the *financial* crisis muted into a collapse of aggregate demand and thereby a *real* recession. According to the US National Bureau of Economic Research, the US economy entered in a recession in the fourth quarter of 2007. It was shortly followed by the euro area, in the first quarter of 2008 (according to the European-based Center for Economic Policy Research). In September 2008, the major investment bank Lehman Brothers went bankrupt,

---

4. Bernanke (2013, Lecture 3) provides and extensive discussion of the emergency measures taken by the US Federal Reserve over the years 2007–2009.

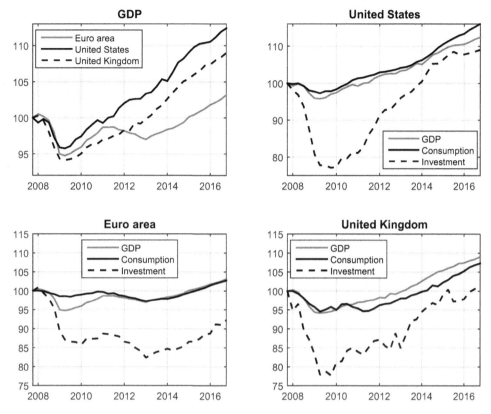

FIGURE 8.2
The Great Recession. All variables are in volume, normalized to 100 in the third quarter of 2007.
Sources: AWM database, BEA (NIPA tables), ONS.

plunging global financial markets into panic and sealing the worldwide spreading of the crisis. Figure 8.2 shows the economic contraction in the United States, the euro area, and the United Kingdom during the Great Recession.

8.1.2 THE INCREASE IN CREDIT SPREADS

The rise in the amount of credit risk perceived by lenders led to an explosion of *credit spreads* i.e., the difference between the risk-free interest rate and the effective interest rates faced by risky private borrowers (interest rate on bank loans or corporate bonds for firms, and interest rates on mortgages or consumer credit for households).

It is important to distinguish the credit spread from the *term premium* introduced in chapter 6, so let us first recall what the latter is. As we have seen in chapter 6, there is always a gap between the average of short-term nominal interest rates and the longer-term nominal interest rates—namely the term premium, which we had denoted by φ. The term premium compensates investors for the *interest-rate risk* that they are bearing—namely, the risk of changes in the resale value of long bonds following changes in interest rates on shorter-maturity bonds—and is therefore present even on securities that bear no income risk (such as the sovereign bonds issued by creditworthy governments). What we have deliberately ignored so far, for the sake of simplicity, is that there is also a gap between the nominal risk-free interest rate (the interest rate i_t, as it results from the average of short nominal rates $\tilde{i}_t$ and the term premium φ—see equation (6.2)) and the nominal interest rate on loans to risky private borrowers. The credit spread is thus an additional premium that compensates investors for the income risk that they are bearing—whether on a bank loan or a bond.[5] If ζ_t denotes the credit spread then the nominal interest rate faced by risky borrowers is no longer $i_t = \tilde{i}_t + \varphi$ but $i_t = \tilde{i}_t + \varphi + \zeta_t$. We have ignored the credit spread so far on the ground that in normal times its average level is low and its variations are of limited magnitude. But as figure 8.3 illustrates, the credit spreads (on mortgage loans and on bonds to non-financial corporations) underwent large fluctuations in the United States and the euro area in the wake of the financial crisis of 2008.[6] In both regions credit spreads shot up in 2008–2009; they shot up again in 2011 in the euro area as the region entered into recession again, and several southern European countries experienced sovereign debt crises.

An increase in the credit spread acts as a *negative aggregate demand shock*. Indeed, the interest rate faced by risky private borrowers includes the credit spread; thus, it is that interest rate—and not the risk-free rate—that determines their spending behavior, and for this reason it is the appropriate interest rate to consider in the IS curve. In chapter 2 we used r_t to denote *the* real interest rate, implicitly taken to be risk-free. If we keep the same notation, the real interest rate on risky loans is $r_t + \zeta_t$. The real interest rate on risky loans can then be decomposed as follows:

$$r_t + \zeta_t = \underbrace{\underset{\substack{\uparrow \\ \text{average of short-term nominal rates}}}{\tilde{i}_t} + \underset{\substack{\uparrow \\ \text{term premium}}}{\varphi} - \underset{\substack{\uparrow \\ \text{expected inflation}}}{\pi_{t+1}}}_{\text{real risk-free rate } r_t} + \underset{\substack{\uparrow \\ \text{credit spread}}}{\zeta_t}.$$

$$(8.1)$$

Denoting $\bar{\zeta}$ as the average value of the credit spread, one may write the IS curve in the presence of credit risk as follows:

---

5. A notion closely related to the credit spread is the *risk premium*, which compensates shareholders for the *dividend risk* that they are bearing (rather than the credit risk on a loan).

6. In the US, credit spreads are the difference between firms' and households' borrowing rate and the interest rate on US Treasuries with similar maturity. In the euro area these spreads are calculated against the interest rate on Bunds (i.e., the German sovereign bonds), which are considered to be free of credit risk.

FIGURE 8.3
Credit spreads in the United States and the euro area.
Sources: Gilchrist and Zakrajsek (2012), Gilchrist and Mojon (2018), European Central Bank, Freddie Mac (Primary Mortgage Market Survey), Board of Governors of the Federal Reserve System, and the author's calculations.

$$y_t = \theta_t - \sigma(r_t + \zeta_t - (\bar{r} + \bar{\zeta}))$$
$$= \underbrace{\theta_t - \sigma\left(\zeta_t - \bar{\zeta}\right)}_{=\hat{\theta}_t} - \sigma\left(r_t - \bar{r}\right). \tag{8.2}$$

The latter expression shows that a shock to the credit spread is formally identical to any aggregate demand shock θ_t, in the sense that it is a shock that shifts the IS curve at any given value of r_t. In this part of the book we will denote by $\hat{\theta}_t$ the aggregate demand shock in this augmented IS curve, to distinguish it from the variable θ_t that we used in earlier chapters and that did not incorporate the credit spread. Aside from this notational change, the IS curve has exactly the same form as before.

8.1.3 HOUSEHOLD DELEVERAGING

According to the Japanese economist Richard Koo (2008, 2011), the one thing that the Great Recession of the Western economies from 2008 onward and the Japanese recession of the 1990s have in common is that they have been preceded by an *over-accumulation of private debts* and, in particular, by an *overindebtedness of households following their home purchases*. Such a phase of overindebtedness leads mechanically to a recession that continues as long as the rise in mortgage debt has not reverted to more normal levels, whether this resorption is voluntary or else forced upon the households by tighter financing constraints. This phenomenon is referred to as a "balance-sheet recession" (Koo 2008, 2011) or "debt supercycle" (Rogoff 2015b). The characteristic of such recessions is that they end only when the deleveraging phase is sufficiently advanced.

The process of household leveraging and deleveraging has not had the same temporality and intensity in Anglo-Saxon countries and in the euro area. In the United States and the United Kingdom, the sharp reversal in the growth of mortgage debt was the main contributor to the decline in aggregate demand during the Great Recession. Figure 8.4 illustrates the sharp reversal in the dynamics of household debt in both countries. In the euro area, the situation is more heterogeneous. Private and public debts have increased significantly in some countries which subsequently experienced serious adjustment problems—most notably, Ireland, Portugal, and Spain. In other countries such as France and Italy, the growth in household debt before 2008 was limited in magnitude and did not lead to sharp deleveraging.

The household deleveraging process is naturally captured within the AS-AD model by a tightening of the debt limit (see, e.g., Eggertsson and Krugman 2012). We saw in chapter 2 that "Keynesian" households were constrained in their choice of consumption and asset accumulation by a (potentially time-varying) debt limit $\bar{D}_t$. The consumption of a Keynesian household was given by (see equation (2.11)):

$$C_t^{K,j} = \frac{-\bar{D}_t}{1+r_t} + (1 + r_{t-1}) A_{t-1}^j + \frac{W_t}{P_t} L_t^j - T_t^j.$$

The latter expression implies that a tightening of the debt limit, if it applies to a sufficient number of households, mechanically contracts aggregate demand—and thereby output and inflation. In chapter 2 this effect showed up in the composite parameter Θ_t (see equation (2.23)), wherein the debt limit appeared explicitly. In the rest of this chapter we assume that the IS curve has exactly the same form as that described in equation (8.2), bearing in mind that an increase in credit spreads or a tightening of the debt limit both have the effect of reducing the composite demand parameter $\hat{\theta}_t$.

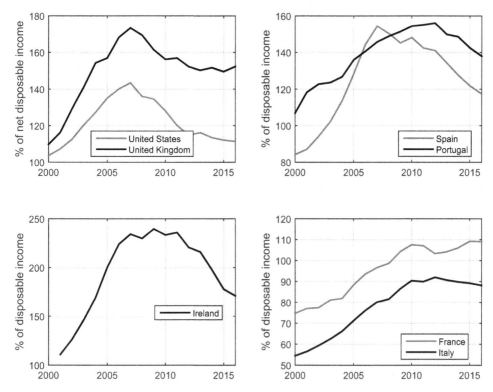

FIGURE 8.4
Household leveraging and deleveraging, 2000–2016.
Source: OCDE.

8.2   THE ZERO LOWER BOUND ON THE SHORT-TERM NOMINAL INTEREST RATE

Household deleveraging and rising credit spreads are *financial* shocks—the implication of which is a fall in the demand for consumption and investment. The question that naturally arises is why, in 2008, these shocks have not been effectively neutralized by appropriate actions on the part of central banks, in accordance with the conventional monetary policy described in chapters 2 and 6. Indeed, a sufficiently large decline in the real interest rate should in principle effectively stimulate the part of aggregate demand that depends on it (see the IS curve) and thereby counter any negative aggregate demand shock, whatever its size. From our analysis in chapter 6, such an expansionary monetary policy in the face of negative aggregate demand shocks is in principle not only possible but also desirable, since it is without cost in terms of inflation (by virtue of the "divine coincidence"). Why has this policy of low interest rates not been sufficient to sustain aggregate demand during the Great Recession? The answer is that central banks have used conventional monetary policy as much as they could; however, in many countries—including the United States, the United Kingdom, and the euro area—this conventional policy started losing effectiveness by the end of 2008, as short-term nominal interest rates approached or hit their *zero lower bound* (ZLB, for short).

8.2.1 BANKNOTES, RESERVE ACCOUNTS, AND INTERBANK LOANS

To understand why monetary policy can become ineffective when the economy is hit by a large negative shock to aggregate demand, let us go back to an implicit but central assumption we have made in all the previous chapters: we have considered that the central bank *was always able to implement the monetary policy that it wished.* Whether this monetary policy was represented by a reaction function (the MP curve introduced in chapter 2) or was outcome of an optimal choice (through the loss function of chapter 6), the central bank could always, by an appropriate choice of the path of short-term nominal interest rates, implement any targeted value of the (risk-free) real interest rate r_t.

Closer examination of how short-term nominal interest rates are determined on the interbank market in the current institutional setting shows that this assumption of effective monetary control is not always verified. Let us recall from chapter 6 that, at a given—and, in the very short run, constant—level of output y, the short-term nominal interest rate in the interbank market i^M is determined by the interest rate on reserves i^R and the supply of reserves R^s. More specifically, we had (see equation (6.4)):

$$i^M = i^M(\underset{+}{i^R}, \underset{+}{y}, \underset{-}{R^s}) \geq i^R. \tag{8.3}$$

The trade-off between, on the one hand, holding reserves or lending them to other banks in the interbank market and, on the other hand, holding reserves or paper currency (i.e., banknotes), implies that *there is a minimum possible value, close to zero, of the short-term interest rate on the interbank market i^M:*

- On the one hand, *the nominal interest rate on the interbank market i^M is bounded below by the nominal interest rate on reserves i^R.* If we had $i^M < i^R$, then banks holding excess reserves would always prefer to keep them on their account with the central bank, rather than lending them to the other banks; hence, the supply of reserve money on the interbank market would be zero. However, there would still be a demand for reserve money on this market by banks experiencing temporary liquidity shortages. It follows that if $i^M < i^R$ then market forces would push i^M up until the condition $i^M \geq i^R$ is restored (see chapter 6 for details).

- On the other hand—and this is a constraint that we had previously ignored—*the nominal interest rate on reserves i^R can not fall (much) below the nominal interest rate on banknotes, which is zero.* Banknotes and reserves are the two components of the monetary base (i.e., the liabilities of the central bank). These two components are only imperfectly substitutable from the point of view of the banks. Bank customers express a demand for banknotes for transaction purposes and thus force banks into holding zero-interest banknotes even when $i^R > 0$. But conversely, and more importantly, the costs of holding large amounts of banknotes (storage, transfer, security, and so on), as opposed to holding reserve money (which are electronic, and hence costless), imply that banks will not be discouraged from holding reserve money even when the latter pay a (slightly) negative interest rate. Let us call $\underline{i}^B$ (≤ 0) the nominal return on banknotes once the costs associated with holding them are counted (without such holding costs we would simply have $\underline{i}^B = 0$). At $i^R = \underline{i}^B$ the banks are indifferent between holding banknotes or reserve money, but at $i^R < \underline{i}^B$ the demand for reserve collapses and a run toward banknotes would take place. The central bank must thus always respect the constraint $i^R \geq \underline{i}^B$ if it is to avoid a monetary crisis.

Taken together, the two constraints imply that:

$$i^M \geq i^R \geq \underline{i}^B, \text{ with } \underline{i}^B \leq 0.$$

One of the difficulties facing central banks nowadays is their ignorance of the precise value of the floor $\underline{i}^B$ for the interest rate on reserves i^R, below which there would be a run toward banknotes. As of April 2018, six central banks, starting with the European Central Bank and the Bank of Japan, have set i^R to moderately negative values—while holding R^s at a sufficiently high level so that i^M stay close to i^R—without triggering such a run.[7] For example, in April 2018 we have $i^R = -0.40$ percent and $i^M \simeq -0.36$ percent in the euro zone and $i^R = -0.10$ percent and $i^M \simeq -0.02$ percent in Japan. However, central banks move cautiously into these negative territories, for fear of violating the condition $i^R \geq \underline{i}^B$ and causing a monetary crisis.

We present in the next chapter an unorthodox institutional arrangement that would in principle enable the central bank to escape the constraint $i^R \geq \underline{i}^B$. Leaving this aside for now, and for the sake of expositional clarity (but without loss of generality), we will assume in the rest of the book that $\underline{i}^B = 0$, i.e., i^M is bounded below by zero. This is what is meant by the expression of *zero lower bound* on the short-term nominal interest rate, even though in practice the bound may not be exactly zero.[8]

---

7. Those central banks are the European Central Bank and the central banks of Japan, Denmark, Switzerland, Sweden, and Hungary.

8. For this reason some economists refer to the *effective* (rather than *zero*) lower bound on the nominal interest rate.

8.2.2 The Zero Lower Bound and the Liquidity Trap

By virtue of the term structure of interest rates and the Fisher equation, the zero lower bound on the short-term nominal interest rate also constrains all other interest rates, including the longer-term real interest rate that affects aggregate demand. Hence, the zero lower bound may prevent the central bank from influencing aggregate demand the way it is able to in normal times. Sticking to our framework of analysis, if the short-term nominal interest rate i^M cannot be negative, then its average $\tilde{\imath}_t$ in equation (6.1) in chapter 6 cannot be negative either. It follows that the nominal interest rate between time t and time $t+1$ cannot lie below the term premium φ:

$$i_t = \tilde{\imath}_t + \varphi \geq \varphi.$$

By implication, the *real interest rate* between t and $t+1$ is also bounded below by the term premium *minus* future inflation:

$$r_t = i_t - \pi_{t+1} \geq r_t^{\min} = \varphi - \pi_{t+1}. \tag{8.4}$$

This constraint on the real interest rate in turn implies that the central bank is not always able to support aggregate demand as much as it wishes after a negative aggregate demand shock. From the IS curve and equation (8.4), one sees that the level of aggregate demand that the central bank can hope to reach by its monetary policy is bounded above:

$$y_t = \hat{\theta}_t - \sigma \, (r_t - \bar{r}) \leq y_t^{\max} = \hat{\theta}_t - \sigma \, (\varphi - \pi_{t+1} - \bar{r}) \,.$$

The central bank can respond to a negative aggregate demand shock $d\hat{\theta}_t < 0$ by adjusting r_t downward. However, once $\tilde{\imath}_t = 0$ has been reached, we have $r_t = r_t^{\min}$ and hence $y_t = y_t^{\max}$; but $y_t^{\max}$ *may be too low to ensure full employment.*

To summarize, the *liquidity trap* can equivalently be defined as follows:

- a situation in which the short-term nominal interest rate is equal to zero and cannot be lowered further by the central bank;

- a situation in which the real interest rate is too high relative to the value that would stabilize aggregate demand after it has been perturbed by a negative shock;

- a situation in which output, inflation, and employment are excessively low (in a sense that will be made more precise below).

We may now formally analyze the liquidity trap by generalizing our AS-AD model to the case where the zero lower bound on the nominal interest rate may be binding. To simplify the analysis, we study a situation in which the liquidity trap lasts at most one period.[9] One must thus interpret this single period as relatively long, possibly extending over several years. To simplify the expressions, but without loss of generality, we also assume that the inflation target is zero ($\bar{\pi} = 0$) and that labor productivity (in log) is constant at $z_t = z_\infty = \xi \mu^*$. Just as in chapters 6 and 7, this normalization implies that natural output y_t^n (see equation (3.10) in chapter 3) is zero, so that y_t denotes both actual output and the output gap.

At time $t - 1$ the economy is assumed to have been in long-run equilibrium, so that:

$$y_{t-1} = \pi_{t-1} = \hat{\theta}_{t-1} = 0.$$

At time t an aggregate demand shock $\hat{\theta}_t = \hat{\theta} < 0$ occurs, which may cause the economy to enter into the liquidity trap (it will do if $|\hat{\theta}|$ is sufficiently large, as we will show below). This shock was not anticipated at time $t - 1$ and lasts only one period. At time $t + 1$ we again have $\hat{\theta}_{t+1} = 0$, and the economy exits the liquidity trap it was there at time t.

We solve the intertemporal equilibrium *backward*—that is, by first computing the equilibrium at time $t + 1$ to then infer the equilibrium at time t. Since the economy no longer is in a liquidity trap at time $t + 1$, the behavior of the central bank at that time is described by the usual MP curve:

MP(t+1): $r_{t+1} = \bar{r} + \gamma \pi_{t+1}$.

By substituting the MP(t+1) curve into the IS(t+1) curve, which under our assumptions is simply $y_{t+1} = -\sigma (r_{t+1} - \bar{r})$, one obtains the AD(t+1) curve. The AS(t+1)-AD(t+1) system that results is a special case of the macroeconomic equilibrium "in normal times" studied in chapter 4:

AD(t+1): $y_{t+1} = -\sigma \gamma \pi_{t+1}$, \hfill (8.5)

AS(t+1): $\pi_{t+1} = \pi_t + \kappa y_{t+1}$. \hfill (8.6)

The solution to this system gives (y_{t+1}, π_{t+1}) as a function of π_t:

$$\pi_{t+1} = \left(\frac{1}{1 + \kappa \sigma \gamma} \right) \pi_t, \hfill (8.7)$$

$$y_{t+1} = -\left(\frac{\sigma \gamma}{1 + \kappa \sigma \gamma} \right) \pi_t. \hfill (8.8)$$

---

9. Exercise 8.4.2 studies a liquidity trap lasting several periods.

We may now study the time t equilibrium (y_t, π_t), depending on whether the zero lower bound is binding or not.

8.2.3   CASE 1: THE ZERO LOWER BOUND IS NOT BINDING

If the aggregate demand shock at time t is sufficiently mild, so that the economy remains outside the liquidity trap, then the central bank applies its conventional monetary policy, as given by the MP curve:

$$\mathbf{MP}: r_t = \bar{r} + \gamma \pi_t.$$

Since the demand parameter at time t is $\hat{\theta}$ (< 0), the IS curve is given by

$$\mathbf{IS}: y_t = \hat{\theta} - \sigma\,(r_t - \bar{r}).$$

As usual, we infer the AD curve from the MP and IS curves:

$$\mathbf{AD}: y_t = \hat{\theta} - \sigma \gamma \pi_t. \tag{8.9}$$

Finally, since $\pi_{t-1} = y^n_{t-1} = 0$ (by assumption), the AS curve is given by

$$\mathbf{AS}: \pi_t = \kappa y_t. \tag{8.10}$$

From the AD and AS curves, we get that the equilibrium at time t is given by

$$\pi_t = \left(\frac{\kappa}{1 + \sigma \gamma \kappa}\right) \hat{\theta} < 0, \tag{8.11}$$

$$y_t = \left(\frac{1}{1 + \sigma \gamma \kappa}\right) \hat{\theta} < 0. \tag{8.12}$$

In other words—and rather unsurprisingly—the negative aggregate demand shock takes down output and inflation. Down to what limit can the demand parameter $\hat{\theta}$ fall, or equivalently (from equation (8.11)) inflation π_t fall, without making the zero lower bound binding? Precisely down to the point where the real interest rate r_t implied by the MP curve meets its floor value of $r^{\min}_t$:

$$\underbrace{\bar{r} + \gamma \pi_t}_{r_t \text{ according to MP}} = \underbrace{\varphi - \pi_{t+1}}_{r^{\min}_t}.$$

Replacing π_{t+1} by its value (equation (8.7)) in the latter equation and factorizing, we can infer the minimal inflation rate $\pi^{\min}$ consistent with a nonbinding zero lower bound:[10]

$$\pi^{\min} = \frac{(\varphi - \bar{r})\,(1 + \kappa\sigma\gamma)}{1 + \gamma\,(1 + \kappa\sigma\gamma)}. \tag{8.13}$$

Then, using equations (8.11) and (8.13), one can infer the minimum value $\hat{\theta}^{\min}$ of the aggregate demand shock $\hat{\theta}$ such that the economy stays away from the liquidity trap if and only if $\hat{\theta} \geq \hat{\theta}^{\min}$. It is given by

$$\hat{\theta}^{\min} = \frac{(\varphi - \bar{r})\,(1 + \kappa\sigma\gamma)^2}{\kappa\,[1 + \gamma\,(1 + \kappa\sigma\gamma)]}. \tag{8.14}$$

To summarize, as long as $\hat{\theta} \geq \hat{\theta}^{\min}$, the negative aggregate demand shock is effectively stabilized by the central bank's conventional monetary policy (as summarized by the MP curve) and the economy stays away from the liquidity trap at time t. We now turn to the case where $\hat{\theta} < \hat{\theta}^{\min}$—that is, where the zero lower bound on the short-term nominal interest rate becomes binding.

8.2.4   CASE 2: THE ZERO LOWER BOUND IS BINDING

When $\hat{\theta} < \hat{\theta}^{\min}$, the real interest rate r_t reaches its floor value $r_t^{\min}\ (= \varphi - \pi_{t+1})$ and cannot fall further. The IS curve thus gives (see equation (8.4)):

$$\textbf{IS}: y_t = \hat{\theta} - \sigma\left(r_t^{\min} - \bar{r}\right)$$

$$= \hat{\theta} + \sigma\,(\bar{r} - \varphi) + \sigma\pi_{t+1}.$$

This expression reveals a fundamental property of the liquidity trap. Since conventional monetary policy becomes passive—in the sense that the average $\tilde{\imath}_t$ of the short-term nominal interest rates is stuck at zero—the real interest r_t depends directly (and negatively) on *future inflation* π_{t+1}. In other words, *any expected decline in inflation directly raises the current real interest rate and thus contracts current aggregate demand* (and the other way around).

We have assumed that the economy exits the liquidity trap at time $t+1$, and we have solved the equilibrium value of π_{t+1} accordingly (see equation (8.7)). Using equation (8.7) to eliminate π_{t+1} from the IS curve, we find the relationship between y_t and π_t (that is, the AD curve) in a liquidity trap to be:

---

10. We note that in the long run we have $\bar{r} = i_\infty + \varphi$ (since $\pi_\infty = 0$) and hence $\varphi - \bar{r} = -i_\infty < 0$. Thus, in our example $\pi_t^{\min}$ is negative, so that the liquidity trap can only be associated with a state of outright *deflation*. This property, however, is not general but related to the specific parameter restrictions that we have imposed, as Exercise 8.4.1 demonstrates.

$$\mathbf{AD}: y_t = \hat{\theta} + \sigma\,(\bar{r} - \varphi) + \left(\frac{\sigma}{1 + \kappa\sigma\gamma}\right)\pi_t. \tag{8.15}$$

Thus, when the zero lower bound is binding, the AD curve induces *an increasing, rather than decreasing, relation between output y_t and inflation π_t*. The reason for the inversion of the slope of the AD curve, relative the standard case where the zero lower bound is not binding, is as follows. First, the automatic component of monetary policy—in which the negative slope of the AD curve in normal times originates (see chapter 2)—becomes inoperative in a liquidity trap. In this configuration, the real interest rate is simply determined by the term premium and future inflation. Second, inflation is persistent, as shown by the curve AS(t+1) above (equation (8.6)). Thus, *low inflation in period t generates low inflation in period $t+1$, thereby raising the real interest rate in period t and decreasing aggregate demand at that time*.[11]

The AS curve, on the other hand, is still given by equation (8.10). This curve also establishes an increasing relation between output and inflation in period t. The fact that y_t and π_t are linked through *two* increasing relations instead of one sets the stage for the vicious circle that is set in motion when the zero lower bound becomes binding: the lower current inflation π_t, the lower *future* inflation π_{t+1} ($= \pi_t/(1 + \kappa\sigma\gamma)$), the greater the current real interest rate r_t ($= r_t^{\min} = \varphi - \pi_{t+1}$), the lower current output y_t ($= \hat{\theta} - \sigma(r_t^{\min} - \bar{r})$), the lower current inflation π_t ($= \kappa y_t$), and so on. This deflationary spiral is summarized in figure 8.5.

Does this spiral eventually stabilize? To answer this question, let us calculate the cumulative effects of an exogenous fall in the inflation rate at time t, of size $d\pi$. This fall leads to a decrease in output of size $dy_t = \frac{\sigma}{1+\kappa\sigma\gamma}d\pi$ (see equation (8.15)). The fall in output induces an additional fall in inflation of size $\kappa dy_t = \frac{\kappa\sigma}{1+\kappa\sigma\gamma}d\pi$ (see equation (8.10)). The latter in turn causes an additional fall in output of size $\frac{\sigma}{1+\kappa\sigma\gamma} \times \frac{\kappa\sigma}{1+\kappa\sigma\gamma}d\pi$, hence a fall in inflation of size $\kappa \times \frac{\sigma}{1+\kappa\sigma\gamma} \times \frac{\kappa\sigma}{1+\kappa\sigma\gamma}d\pi = \left(\frac{\sigma\kappa}{1+\kappa\sigma\gamma}\right)^2 d\pi$, and so on. Repeating the same reasoning over and over again, one finds that the total impact $D\pi$ of the initial deflationary shock $d\pi$ is given by:

$$D\pi = d\pi + \left(\frac{\sigma\kappa}{1+\kappa\sigma\gamma}\right)d\pi + \left(\frac{\sigma\kappa}{1+\kappa\sigma\gamma}\right)^2 d\pi + \left(\frac{\sigma\kappa}{1+\kappa\sigma\gamma}\right)^3 d\pi \ldots$$

The latter sum is positive and finite provided that:

$$\frac{\sigma\kappa}{1+\kappa\sigma\gamma} < 1, \tag{8.16}$$

---

11. We have already encountered a situation in which the slope of the AD curve was positive and not negative, namely when the Taylor principle is violated (see chapter 6). The similarity is more than apparent; violation of the Taylor principle corresponds to a situation in which the nominal interest rate responds too little to macroeconomic developments and the liquidity trap to a situation where this rate does not respond at all. In both cases monetary policy is passive, which explains the inversion of the slope of the AD curve.

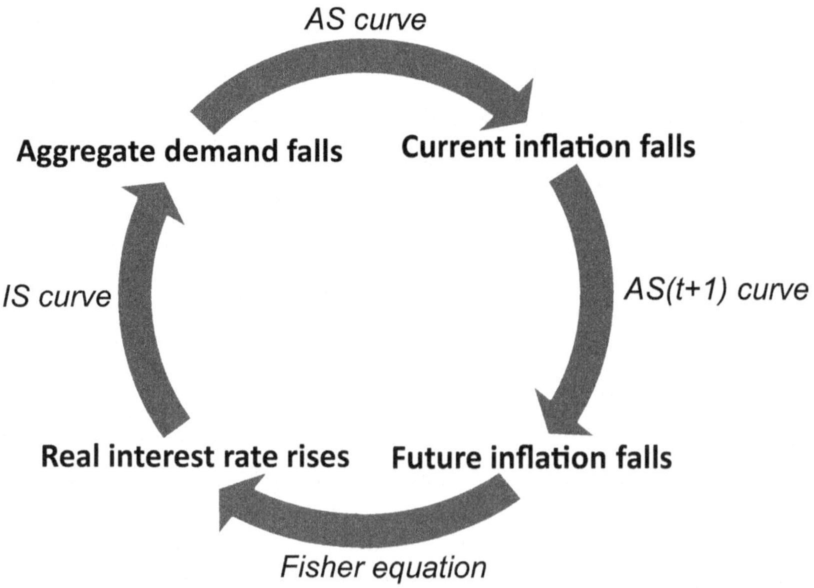

AS curve

Aggregate demand falls   Current inflation falls

IS curve   AS(t+1) curve

Real interest rate rises   Future inflation falls

Fisher equation

FIGURE 8.5
The deflationary spiral.

and we will assume throughout that this condition holds.[12] This condition has a simple interpretation in terms of the relative slopes of the AS and AD curves in a liquidity trap. Indeed, one may rewrite (8.16) as follows:

$$(0 <) \qquad \kappa \qquad < \qquad \frac{1}{\sigma} + \kappa \gamma .$$

$\underset{\text{slope of AS curve in the } (y, \pi)\text{-plane}}{\uparrow} \qquad \underset{\text{slope of AD curve in the } (y, \pi)\text{-plane}}{\underbrace{}}$

In other words, as long as the slope of the AD curve remains greater than that of the AS curve, the deflationary spiral induces cumulative effects that eventually settle down. The cumulated impact on inflation is given by:

$$D\pi = \frac{1}{1 - \frac{\sigma \kappa}{1 + \kappa \sigma \gamma}} d\pi = \frac{1 + \kappa \sigma \gamma}{1 - \kappa \sigma (1 - \gamma)} d\pi ,$$

12. Taylor rule estimates for the post-Volcker period in the United States (see chapter 6, section 6.1) give a nominal interest rate response to inflation of about 1.5; that is, a real interest rate response of $\gamma = 1/2$. Estimates of the slope (κ) of the AS curve suggest that it is no greater than one-third, while those of the interest-rate elasticity of output (σ) give it a value no greater than 1. This implies that condition (8.16) holds for plausible values of the parameters.

and is greater when $\kappa\sigma\,(1-\gamma)$ is closer to 1 (that is, when the slope of the AD curve gets closer to that of the AS curve).

In a liquidity trap the equilibrium (y_t, π_t) is determined by equations (8.10) and (8.15). The solution to those equations is given by

$$y_t = \frac{\sigma\,(1+\kappa\sigma\gamma)\,(\hat{\theta}+\bar{r}-\varphi)}{1-\kappa\sigma\,(1-\gamma)},$$

$$\pi_t = \frac{\kappa\sigma\,(1+\kappa\sigma\gamma)\,(\hat{\theta}+\bar{r}-\varphi)}{1-\kappa\sigma\,(1-\gamma)}.$$

By comparing this value of y_t with that in equation (8.12), it can be verified that the impact of a given decrease in the demand parameter $\hat{\theta}$ has a larger effect on y_t (and possibly *much* larger) in the liquidity trap than outside the trap. The reasons for this impact is first, that the aggregate demand shock is effectively buffered by the central bank in the latter case (through a decrease in the policy rate) but not in the former. And second, absent this buffering, any negative aggregate demand shocks sets in motion the deflationary feedback loop between current and future inflation that is depicted in figure 8.5.

8.2.5 THE FALL INTO THE LIQUIDITY TRAP

So far we have characterized the equilibrium (y_t, π_t) depending on whether or not the economy was in a liquidity trap. We are now in a position to study the complete AS-AD system and examine how a negative aggregate demand shock at time t can cause the economy to fall into the trap, starting from a situation where the economy was not yet in the trap.

The AS curve (equation (8.10)) is the same whether the economy is in a liquidity trap or not (the trap is an aggregate demand phenomenon that leaves the mechanisms of aggregate supply unchanged, at least under our assumptions).[13] The AD curve is given by equation (8.9) outside the liquidity trap—that is, as long as $\pi_t \geq \pi^{\min}$—and by equation (8.15) in the liquidity trap (i.e., whenever $\pi_t < \pi^{\min}$). Thus, the complete AS-AD system is given by

$$\mathbf{AS}: \pi_t = \kappa y_t,$$

$$\mathbf{AD}: y_t = \begin{cases} y_t = \hat{\theta} - \sigma\gamma\pi_t & \text{for } \pi_t \geq \pi^{\min} \\ y_t = \hat{\theta} + \sigma\,(\bar{r}-\varphi) + \left(\frac{\sigma}{1+\kappa\sigma\gamma}\right)\pi_t & \text{for } \pi_t < \pi^{\min} \end{cases}.$$

This system is depicted in figure 8.6. The AS curve has the usual shape. The AD curve, however, is kinked; it is decreasing outside the liquidity trap region (this

---

13. Benigno and Fornaro (2018) show that in a liquidity trap, weak aggregate demand can deter firms from innovating, thereby slowing down productivity growth, impoverishing households, and ultimately perpetuating the liquidity trap. Our analysis abstracts from this aggregate supply effect.

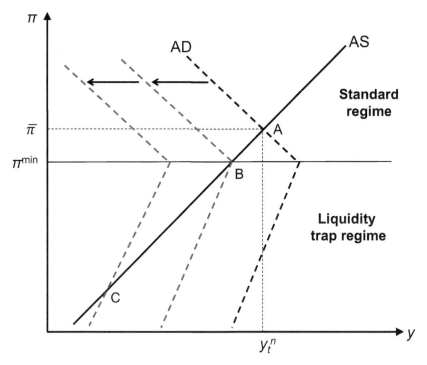

FIGURE 8.6
The fall into the liquidity trap. A sufficiently powerful negative aggregate demand shock necessarily pushes the economy into the liquidity trap.

is the case studied in chapter 4) but increasing inside the liquidity trap region (as showed in the present chapter). It is easily verified that the AD curve is continuous.[14] Under condition (8.16), which we have assumed to hold, the slope of the AD curve below $\pi^{\min}$ is greater than that of the AS curve.

Point A in figure 8.6 corresponds to the equilibrium before the negative aggregate demand shock (at time $t-1$), when output was equal to its natural level ($=0$) and inflation was on target ($\bar{\pi}=0$). This equilibrium lies in the standard monetary regime where the zero lower bound is not binding. The negative aggregate demand shock occurring at time t results in a horizontal, leftward shift of the AD curve. As long as the shock remains of moderate size, the equilibrium (y_t, π_t) stays in the standard regime and therefore the fall in these two variables remains itself moderate. This is what occurs as long as the aggregate demand shock is such that the new

14. We have:

$$\hat{\theta} - \sigma\gamma\pi^{\min} = \hat{\theta} + \sigma\,(\bar{r} - \varphi) + \left(\frac{\sigma}{1+\kappa\sigma\gamma}\right)\pi^{\min},$$

with $\pi^{\min}$ given by equation (8.13).

equilibrium does not move beyond point B, at which $\hat{\theta} = \hat{\theta}^{\min}$ and thus $\pi_t = \pi^{\min}$. Beyond this point the economy enters the liquidity trap regime and any further shift of the AD curve has a much larger effect on y_t and π_t. One can observe from figure 8.6 that the very same change in $\hat{\theta}$ (i.e., the same translation of the AD curve) shifts the equilibrium from point A to point B, where the variations of y_t and π_t are of limited magnitude, and from point B to point C, where both are large. Again, the change from normal times to the liquidity trap is due to two factors: (1) in the liquidity trap (beyond point B) the central bank is no longer able to stabilize inflation because of the zero lower bound; (2) the feedback loop between current and future inflation (see figure 8.5) amplifies the effect of any aggregate demand shock.

8.3   THE LIQUIDITY TRAP PARADOXES

8.3.1   THE PARADOX OF FLEXIBILITY

The liquidity trap is sometimes described as a situation in which traditional macroeconomic adjustments are turned upside down. Let us review the first manifestation of this—which Eggertsson and Krugman (2012) refer to as the *paradox of flexibility*. In the AS-AD model, the degree of nominal price rigidities determines the parameter κ; that is, the slope of the AS curve. Figure 8.7 shows how the equilibrium shifts as a result of a negative aggregate demand shock for two different values of κ, corresponding to more or less price rigidities. As long as $\pi_t \geq \pi^{\min}$, we get the same property as in chapter 4—that greater price flexibility tends to reduce the impact of a demand shock on output. The shift from point A to point B is associated with a smaller fall of y_t (and a greater fall of π_t) when compared with a shift of the equilibrium from point A to point B'. The reason for this stabilizing effect of price flexibility in normal times is as follows (see, for example, chapter 3): when a negative aggregate demand shock occurs, it pushes firms to (1) reduce their selling price (since the price that was set before the shock turns out to be excessively high) and (2) discourage consumers from purchasing the goods. The higher the proportion of firms that effectively adjust their selling price downward (to their new optimal level) following the shock, the less the demand for goods (and hence output) shrink as a result of the shock. Price movements thus serve to buffer the impact of aggregate shocks on output.

Things, however, work differently in a liquidity trap. In that situation, the firms that optimally adjust their prices downward following the fall in aggregate demand tend to *aggravate the vicious circle* described in figure 8.5 above. Thus, when the aggregate demand shock is large enough to push the economy into the liquidity trap, greater price flexibility turns out to amplify—rather than dampen—the fall in output. One goes from point A to point C when prices are relatively flexible, but from point A to point C' when they are relatively rigid. It can also be seen that greater nominal rigidities tend to keep the economy away from the liquidity trap region (at point B, the economy enters the liquidity trap region, whereas at point B' it is still away from

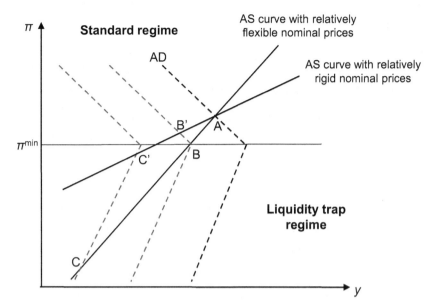

FIGURE 8.7
The paradox of flexibility. In normal times, the flexibility of nominal prices buffers output fluctuations, but the opposite is true in a liquidity trap.

it). The impact of price flexibility on macroeconomic stability is thus ambiguous as soon as there is a risk that the economy may enter into a liquidity trap regime after a negative aggregate demand shock.

8.3.2   The Paradox of Toil

The *paradox of toil*, so named by Gauti Eggertsson (2010a), states that in a liquidity trap *households' desire to work more may lead to a decrease, rather than an increase, in total employment*. The explanation for this paradox is that when everybody tries to work more, this creates an excess supply of labor in the labor market which causes a reduction in the equilibrium real wage. Following this fall in production costs, the firms that can adjust their selling price optimally lower it in order to gain market share (see chapter 3). This brings down current inflation and, in the liquidity trap, sets in motion the deflationary feedback loop depicted on figure 8.5. And since labor productivity has not changed, the fall in output triggered by the deflationary spiral necessarily translates into lower employment.

One can formally analyze the paradox of toil by generalizing the analysis of chapter 3 to incorporate exogenous variations in labor supply. To be more specific, assume that household labor supply (equation (3.7)) now takes the form:

$$l_t^s = \xi \left(w_t - p_t - \xi \mu^* + \varsigma_t \right), \tag{8.17}$$

where ς_t is a *labor supply shock*, and where labor productivity z_t has been normalized to $\xi\mu^*$. An increase in ς_t corresponds to a common desire to work more at the prevailing real wage, and we want to understand how this affects equilibrium employment.

Exercise 8.4.3 asks to formally prove that a positive labor-supply shock $\varsigma_t > 0$ (1) raises natural output and employment, (2) raises output and employment when the economy is *not* in a liquidity trap, but (3) *contracts employment when the economy is in the trap*. The key to these results is that, while the AS curve is the same as usual, namely

$$\mathbf{AS}: \pi_t = \pi_{t-1} + \kappa \left(y_t - y_t^n \right),$$

now natural output is directly affected by labor-supply shocks:

$$y_t^n = \xi \varsigma_t.$$

The latter equation shows that an exogenous increase in labor supply is a positive aggregate supply shock which shifts the AS curve downward. In normal times (i.e., outside the liquidity trap), such a shock has the beneficial effects described in chapter 4. It increases output and reduces inflation, and since this shock does not affect labor productivity, total employment ($l_t = y_t - z_t$) must also rise. However, the opposite occurs in the liquidity trap, as shown in figure 8.8. The AS curve and its shift are exactly the same as those in chapter 4. But the slope of the AD curve is *positive* in the liquidity trap, and therefore this shift of the AS curve *brings both inflation and output down* (and also employment, since labor productivity is unchanged). Again, this is because the exogenous rise in labor supply brings down labor costs and inflation and thus triggers the deflationary feedback loop at work in the liquidity trap. Moreover, the loop is stronger when price are more flexible—yet another implication of the paradox of flexibility discussed above (graphically, the slope of the AS curve gets closer to that of the AD curve as κ rises).

While the term "toil" in the paradox refers to a labor supply phenomenon, the expression has now come to refer to the impact of any positive aggregate supply shock—that is, any shock that boosts natural output (including shocks to productivity, markups, costs, and so on).[15] The AS-AD model implies that such shocks necessarily take down inflation, output, and employment if the economy is in the liquidity trap. This is a strong prediction of the model that can in principle be tested in the data. In this spirit, Wieland (2017) examines whether or not *negative* aggregate

---

15. Our derivation of the natural level of output in chapter 3 only made room for shocks to labor productivity (z_t). However, it is apparent from that analysis that any change in the degree of competition that would affect the optimal mark-up rate (μ^*) would equivalently affect natural output. Finally, we saw in exercise 2 of chapter 4 that, once one incorporates *energy* (e.g., oil) as a production input, then exogenous changes in the price of energy change firms' real marginal cost and, thereby, natural ouput.

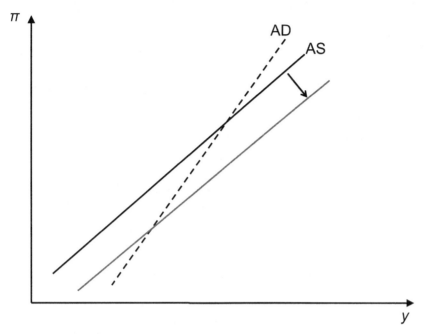

FIGURE 8.8
The paradox of toil. If, in a liquidity trap, all households wish to work more at the existing wage, then they reinforce the deflationary pressures on wages, prices, and output, and total employment actually falls. The same is true of any positive aggregate supply shocks.

supply shocks in Japan—a country that has been in a liquidity trap since the mid-1990s—have led to output *expansions*. Looking at the Great East Japan Earthquake of 2011, as well as at numerous oil price hikes, Wieland (2017) finds no expansionary impact on output, casting doubt on the empirical validity of the paradox of toil. Datta et al. (2017) adopt a different empirical strategy, based on the joint behavior of oil and equity returns. They observe that, when oil prices rise in a liquidity trap, then we should observe an expansion in aggregate demand and output (according to the paradox of toil) and therefore a rise in the demand for, and price of, capital inputs. This implies that the *ex post* returns on oil and equity should be positively correlated in a liquidity trap *and only there*.[16] This prediction is borne out in US data, where this correlation is clearly positive throughout the Great Recession but close to zero before 2008. In other words, there is no consensus on the empirical validity of paradox of toil—the jury is still out.

---

16. Out of the liquidity trap, the central bank would stabilize the inflationary pressures generated by the rise in oil prices by adopting a contractionary monetary policy, causing aggregate demand to *fall*, not rise.

8.3.3 THE PARADOX OF THRIFT

According to the *paradox of thrift*, aggregate savings *may decline when all households seek to save more.* The underlying idea is that an increase in households' desire to save leads to a fall in aggregate demand—driven by lower aggregate consumption—and thereby in aggregate output and income. If the fall in income is sufficiently pronounced, it can lead to a reduction in the total quantity of savings even if the savings *rate* has increased.

Graphically, the decline in aggregate demand that follows households' willingness to cut consumption results in a leftward shift of the AD curve. When the economy is in a liquidity trap (so that the AD curve has positive slope), then output, and therefore the aggregate income distributed to the households, can fall sharply as a result (see figure 8.9). If the fall in income is sufficiently strong, it can dominate the direct effect on aggregate savings of the of increased desire to save at the individual level and ultimately lead to a contraction in total savings.

It should be noted that the effect of the increase in desired savings can only bring about the paradox of thrift in a situation of liquidity trap and *not* in normal times. Indeed, when the central bank is able to freely adjust the short-term nominal interest rate, and thereby influence the real interest rate (see chapter 6), then it is

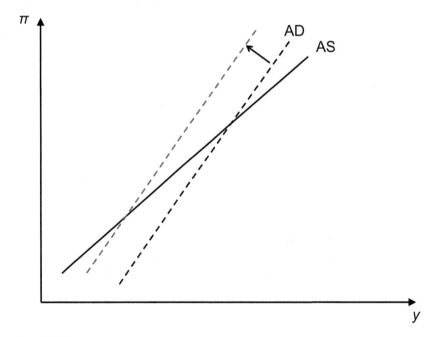

FIGURE 8.9
The paradox of thrift. If, in a liquidity trap, all households wish to save more at the existing real interest rate, then aggregate demand, and thereby output and household income, may contract so much that total savings actually fall.

always able to stabilize, even marginally, the fall in aggregate demand resulting from households consumption-saving choices. It follows that in equilibrium aggregate demand necessarily falls *less* than what would be implied by the initial savings shock and an unresponsive central bank. In other words, in normal time the general equilibrium effect coming from the reduction in household income is never so strong as to revert the direct effect coming from households' increased desire to save. So it is the lack of responsiveness to the shock by the central bank, and the associated deflationary feedback loop, that is responsible for the paradox of thrift.

In essence, the paradox of thrift states that if the output contraction induced by the increase in the desire to save is sufficiently large, then it may frustrate this desire (through the induced fall in aggregate income). It can be shown analytically that in a liquidity trap, a given rise in households' desire to save can cause a contraction in output of arbitrarily large magnitude. A rigorous proof of this point requires a full general-equilibrium analysis of the AS-AD model in the liquidity trap—an analysis which is introduced in chapter 10. Exercise 10.4.3 in that chapter asks to prove (under certain simplifying assumptions) that the AD curve has the form:

$$\mathbf{AD} : y_t = \text{constant} + \rho_t + \pi_t,$$

where $\rho_t > 0$ is households' common rate of time preference, which may vary over time. This rate determines how the future utility flows of a Ricardian household are valued relative to the current utility flow (see chapter 2)—the higher ρ_t, the lower the utility of future consumption and the lower the desire to save. An exogenous increase in households' desire to save (at any given value of the real interest rate r_t) thus corresponds to a decrease in ρ_t below its long-run value ρ_∞.

The AS curve, on the other hand, is the same as in section 8.2:

$$\mathbf{AS} : \pi_t = \kappa y_t.$$

The two curves are depicted in figure 8.9. Condition (8.16) in section 8.2, which requires that the slope of the AD curve be greater than that of the AS curve, boils down to $\kappa < 1$ here. An exogenous increase in households' desire to save is a decrease in ρ_t that moves the AD curve leftward in the (y, π) plane and thereby causes y_t and π_t to fall. This fall is greater when the slope of the AS curve ($= \kappa < 1$) is close to that of the AD curve ($= 1$). Formally, the AD curve gives $dy_t = d\rho_t + d\pi_t$ and the curve AS curve gives $d\pi_t = \kappa dy_t$. Thus, in the liquidity trap, a given fall in ρ_t generates a fall in y_t of size

$$\frac{dy_t}{d\rho_t} = \frac{1}{1 - \kappa} > 0,$$

which gets arbitrarily large as κ approaches 1.

8.4 EXERCISES

8.4.1 THE LIQUIDITY TRAP WITH POSITIVE INFLATION

Let us consider the same liquidity trap model as in section 8.2, with one modification: the inflation target $\bar{\pi}$ is not zero but is strictly positive. The economy is in long-run equilibrium at time $t-1$ (so that $\pi_{t-1}=\bar{\pi}$ and $y_{t-1}=\hat{\theta}_{t-1}=0$), but a shock $d\hat{\theta}_t<0$ at time t occurs, which may push the economy into the trap. The demand parameter returns to its long-term level at time $t+1$ ($\hat{\theta}_{t+1}=0$), so that the economy exits the liquidity trap at time $t+1$ if it were there at time t. The term premium φ is set to zero for simplicity.

1. Compute the equilibrium at time $t+1$, (y_{t+1},π_{t+1}), as a function of π_t.

2. Compute the value of $\pi^{\min}$—that is, the inflation floor below which the economy falls into the liquidity trap.

3. Show that $\pi^{\min}>0$ if and only if

$$(1-\gamma)(1+\kappa\sigma\gamma)<1 \quad \text{and} \quad \bar{\pi}>\frac{\bar{r}(1+\kappa\sigma\gamma)}{1-(1-\gamma)(1+\kappa\sigma\gamma)}.$$

8.4.2 A MULTIPERIOD LIQUIDITY TRAP

Let us consider the following model economy. The IS and AS curves are as follows:

$$\textbf{IS}: y_t=\hat{\theta}_t-\sigma\,(r_t-\bar{r}),\quad \sigma,\bar{r}>0,$$

$$\textbf{AS}: \pi_t=\pi_{t-1}+\kappa y_t,\quad \kappa>0,$$

where the following condition holds:

$$\sigma\kappa<1.$$

When it is able to, the central bank implements a monetary policy that fully stabilizes inflation at its target $\bar{\pi}=0$. We assume that at time $t-1$ the economy is in long-run equilibrium, so that:

$$\hat{\theta}_{t-1}=y_{t-1}=\pi_{t-1}=0.$$

The economy is subject to aggregate demand shocks—that is, negative values of $\hat{\theta}_t$. When such shocks occur, they are sufficiently large to push (or keep) the economy in the liquidity trap. However, the economy exits the trap whenever $\hat{\theta}_t$ returns to zero. The term premium φ is set to 0 for simplicity.

1. Compute the equilibrium (y_t, π_t) when $\hat{\theta}_t = \hat{\theta} < 0$ and $\hat{\theta}_{t+k} = 0$ for all $k \geq 1$.

2. Compute the equilibrium values of (y_t, π_t) and (y_{t+1}, π_{t+1}) when $\hat{\theta}_t = \hat{\theta}_{t+1} = \hat{\theta} < 0$ and $\hat{\theta}_{t+k} = 0$ for all $k \geq 2$.

3. Explain intuitively how and why the values of (y_t, π_t) obtained in questions 1 and 2 differ.

8.4.3   PROOF OF THE PARADOX OF TOIL

Consider the very same aggregate supply block as in chapter 3 (sections 3.1 to 3.4), assuming that household labor supply is now given by equation (8.17) and that $z_t = \xi \mu^*$ at all times.

1. Show that the equilibrium real wage is given by

$$w_t - p_t = \xi^{-1} y_t - (1 - \xi) \mu^* - \varsigma_t,$$

and explain intuitively this expression.

2. Compute the natural levels of output (y_t^n) and employment (l_t^n).

3. Derive the AS curve in the presence of nominal price rigidities.

4. Compute the value of $dl_t / d\varsigma_t$:

(a) in normal times, so that the AD curve is given by (2.28);

(b) in a liquidity trap, so that the AD curve is given by (8.15).

UNCONVENTIONAL MONETARY POLICIES

> The residential housing sector has now shrunk so much that the only real assurance that it will ever stabilize seems to be the fact that construction spending cannot go negative. This is just about the only zero lower bound that is working on our side.
> —J. Yellen, then-president of the San Francisco Federal Reserve (2009)

The liquidity trap, as we have seen in the previous chapter, is a situation in which conventional monetary policy (that is, the unconstrained adjustment of the short-term nominal interest rate in order to reach the desired value of the real interest rate) becomes inoperative (due to the zero lower bound on the short-term nominal interest rate). The objective of this chapter is to present the *unconventional* monetary policies that can take over from conventional monetary policy during episodes of liquidity trap. In this perspective, we will first analyze the transmission channels of the main two unconventional monetary policies discussed (and implemented) since 2008—notably in the United States and the United Kingdom: Forward Guidance (section 9.1) and Large-Scale Asset Purchases (section 9.2), of which the much debated *Quantitative Easing* policy is part. Section 9.3 will then turn to a menu of entirely original unconventional monetary policies, which may even be called iconoclastic— either because they have never been implemented in the past or because they challenge the most firmly established monetary policy dogmas. These monetary policies are *(very) negative interest rates* (which would require the phasing out, or at least devaluation, of banknotes), the *adoption of a high inflation target* (twice the historical target of the typical inflation targeting regime) or even the simple *abandonment of inflation targeting* (in favor of price-level targeting).

9.1 FORWARD GUIDANCE

9.1.1 FUTURE MONETARY POLICY AS AN UNCONVENTIONAL POLICY TOOL

We have seen in the preceding chapter that the liquidity trap equilibrium has two key features:

- the central bank is unable to freely control the short-term nominal interest rate and thus to implement the desired value of the real interest rate;

- the current real interest rate depends on future (anticipated) inflation.

The policy of forward guidance follows naturally from these two properties. The central bank does not have direct control over interest rates as long as the economy is in a liquidity trap, hence it has limited influence on the macroeconomic equilibrium at that time, but it will regain control once the economy has emerged from the trap and thus is, in principle, able to influence output and inflation then. Consequently, if the central bank can credibly communicate about the monetary policy it will implement *once it has emerged from the trap*, then it can influence inflation expectations at that horizon in a way that affects outcomes *while the economy is still in the trap*. More specifically, if the central bank promises during the liquidity trap (in period t) to adopt an expansionary monetary policy stance once out of the trap (in period $t+1$) so as to raise inflation at that time (i.e., π_{t+1}), then it will lower the real interest rate during the trap (since $r_t = \varphi - \pi_{t+1}$), which will lift output and inflation in period t.

To illustrate this point formally, let us consider, within the framework developed in chapter 8 (section 8.2), the effect of choosing an interest rate that would be exceptionally low (relative to that implied by the MP curve) for some time still after the economy has left the trap. To take a somewhat extreme example of this, let us assume here that the central bank is committed to maintaining the nominal interest rate at zero in period $t+1$—even though the economy has left the trap by that time. From period $t+2$ onward the central bank follows again its conventional monetary policy, as summarized in the usual MP curve. To simplify the expressions, but without loss of generality, we assume here that the term premium φ is zero.

As usual, we solve the equilibrium backward, starting here with the equilibrium at time $t+2$. Since the economy is not in a liquidity trap at that time, so that monetary policy is described by the MP curve, the macroeconomic equilibrium is the standard equilibrium of chapter 4. Under the parameter restrictions of section 8.2 in chapter 8 ($y_t^n = \bar{\pi} = 0$ for all t), the AS(t+2)-AD(t+2) equilibrium is given by

$$\textbf{AD(t+2)}: y_{t+2} = -\sigma\gamma\pi_{t+2},$$

$$\textbf{AS(t+2)}: \pi_{t+2} = \pi_{t+1} + \kappa y_{t+2},$$

which gives the equilibrium values of (y_{t+2}, π_{t+2}) as a function of π_{t+1}:

$$y_{t+2} = -\left(\frac{\sigma\gamma}{1+\sigma\gamma\kappa}\right)\pi_{t+1}, \quad \pi_{t+2} = \left(\frac{1}{1+\sigma\gamma\kappa}\right)\pi_{t+1}.$$

We have assumed that at time $t+1$ the economy has left the liquidity trap but, nevertheless, the central bank maintains its zero interest rate policy. It follows that the real interest rate at that time is given by $r_{t+1} = -\pi_{t+2}$, and we have just computed the value of π_{t+2} $(=\pi_{t+1}/(1+\sigma\gamma\kappa))$. It follows that the AD(t+1) curve is given by

$$\textbf{AD(t+1)}: y_{t+1} = -\sigma\,(r_{t+1} - \bar{r}) = \sigma\bar{r} + \left(\frac{\sigma}{1+\sigma\gamma\kappa}\right)\pi_{t+1}.$$

Finally, the AS(t+1) curve is simply

$$\textbf{AS(t+1)}: \pi_{t+1} = \pi_t + \kappa y_{t+1}.$$

The latter two expressions give the equilibrium values of output and inflation at time $t+1$ (we shall call them y_{t+1}^{FG} and π_{t+1}^{FG}, for "forward guidance") as a function of π_t. It is easily verified (but left to the reader) that, under our maintained assumption that inequality (8.16) in the previous chapter holds, π_{t+1}^{FG} is strictly greater than the inflation rate that prevailed when the central bank implemented the conventional monetary policy (given by the MP curve) from period $t+1$ onward (equation (8.7) in the previous chapter). In other words, under the *unconventional* forward guidance policy of setting $i_{t+1} = 0$, even though the economy has left the trap at time $t+1$, the real interest rate *in the trap is lower than under the conventional monetary policy*. It follows that aggregate demand, output, and inflation at time t are greater under the forward guidance policy. By implementing a policy that is more accommodative than the conventional monetary policy *after* the liquidity trap period, the central bank manages to effectively stimulate the economy *during* the liquidity trap.

Following this insight, several central banks have more or less explicitly adopted the policy of forward guidance to circumvent the zero lower bound. In practice, forward guidance consist in making explicit statements about future monetary policy, insisting notably on the fact that short-term nominal interest rates will be kept lower for longer, relative to what would be warranted on the basis of the mere inflation targeting regime. As an example of this monetary policy strategy, here is a sequence of forward guidance statements on the part of the US Federal Open Market Committee (FOMC) over the years 2008–2016 (emphasis added):

- December 2008: "[T]he Committee anticipates that weak economic conditions are likely to warrant **exceptionally low levels** of the federal funds rate **for some time**" (Board of Governors of the Federal Reserve System 2008).

- January 2009: "[T]he Committee continues to anticipate that economic conditions are likely to warrant **exceptionally low levels** of the federal funds rate **for some time**" (Board of Governors of the Federal Reserve System 2009).

- From 2009 to 2011 (repeated statements): "[T]he Committee ... continues to anticipate that economic conditions ... are likely to warrant **exceptionally low levels** for the federal funds rate **for an extended period**" (Board of Governors of the Federal Reserve System 2010).

- August to December 2011: "[T]he Committee ... currently anticipates that economic conditions ... are likely to warrant **exceptionally low levels** for the federal funds rate **at least through mid-2013**" (Board of Governors of the Federal Reserve System 2011).

- January to August 2012: "the Committee ... currently anticipates that economic conditions ... are likely to warrant **exceptionally low levels** for the federal funds rate **at least through late 2014**" (Board of Governors of the Federal Reserve System 2012a).

- September-October 2012: "[T]he Committee expects that a highly accommodative stance of monetary policy will remain appropriate **for a considerable time after the economic recovery strengthens**. In particular, the Committee ... currently anticipates that **exceptionally low levels** for the federal funds rate are likely to be warranted **at least through mid-2015**" (Board of Governors of the Federal Reserve System 2012b).

- December 2012 to June 2013: "[T]he Committee expects that a **highly accommodative stance** of monetary policy will remain appropriate **for a considerable time after the asset purchase program ends and the economic recovery strengthens**" (Board of Governors of the Federal Reserve System 2012c).

- March-April 2014: "The Committee currently anticipates that, **even after employment and inflation are near mandate-consistent levels**, economic conditions may, for some time, **warrant keeping the target federal funds rate below levels the Committee views as normal** in the longer run" (Board of Governors of the Federal Reserve System 2014).

Note that the last statements explicitly mentions that monetary policy accommodation will last *after* the recovery, which literally corresponds to the forward-guidance policy as we have defined it. Earlier statements point toward the same policy, though in a less explicit way. From 2013 onward the Governing-Council meeting of the European Central Bank started issuing similar-sounding statements (interest rates will remain "at present or lower level," and this "for an extended period of time"), and so have the Bank of England and the Bank of Canada. Swanson (2017) examined the effect of forward guidance statements on the yield curve in the

US economy. He found that such statements transitorily lowered the short end of the yield curve.

9.1.2 THE DEFLATION BIAS

While forward guidance seems to offer a natural solution to the zero lower bound problem, it nevertheless raises a more fundamental question. Conventional monetary policy as implemented outside the liquidity trap has reasons for being what it is. It corresponds to the policy that the central bank wishes to implement when macroeconomic conditions are considered normal. This policy must somehow correspond to what is indeed optimal to do in these circumstances, at least from the central bank's point of view. However, forward guidance requires the central bank to deviate from this policy after the economy has exited the trap, when macroeconomic conditions have returned to normal. There is a contradiction here. To put it another way, forward guidance faces a credibility problem: if it is indeed desirable for the central bank to announce in a liquidity trap that it will pursue an exceptionally accommodative policy once the economy has emerged from the trap, there is every reason to believe that, at that time, it will let bygones be bygones and return to the conventional monetary policy which it has always considered optimal under normal conditions. Private agents, anticipating this, have no reason to believe in the central bank's promise of an extraordinarily accommodative policy after the trap.

This lack of credibility of forward guidance is a manifestation of the *time-inconsistency of optimal plans* of the type diagnosed by Kydland and Prescott (1977)—the monetary policy that it will be optimal to implement in the future from the point of view of the current period (an inflationary policy aimed at reducing the real interest rate in the trap) will no longer be optimal once the time of implementing the policy has come. Hence, it will ultimately *not* be implemented. We have already encountered a time inconsistency problem earlier in the book, when we examined the inflation bias in chapter 6. We showed then that the time inconsistency of optimal policy could lead to excess inflation without benefits in terms of output. Here the time inconsistency has the opposite manifestation: committing to future *inflationary* policies is beneficial but time inconsistent; hence the current real interest rate is too high and current demand, output, and inflation are too *low*—there is a *deflation* bias, rather than an inflation bias. The time inconsistency of future inflationary policies was identified by Paul Krugman (1998) in the context of the Japanese liquidity trap.

Let us now analyze the deflation bias formally. First of all, we need to make monetary policy decisions the outcome of an optimal choice on the part of the central bank, rather than that of an ad hoc reaction function. Without a welfare criterion to maximize, it would be impossible to compare the relative efficiency of the various policy options and hence even to diagnose situations of policy inefficiency. We shall focus on the case that is analytically simplest to handle—namely, the case where the sole objective of the central bank is to stabilize inflation at its target $\bar{\pi} = 0$ in every period (but the argument holds much more generally). The intertemporal loss function of the central bank thus takes the form:[1]

$$L_t^I = \pi_t^2 + \beta \pi_{t+1}^2 + \beta^2 \pi_{t+2}^2 + \dots, \quad 0 \le \beta < 1.$$

Aside from this modification—the replacement of the MP curve by an explicit objective function—we work under exactly the same set of assumptions and parameter restrictions as in chapter 8. In particular, we assume that the demand parameter $\hat{\theta}_t$ is zero at all times except in the current period, during which $\hat{\theta}_t = \hat{\theta} < 0$ falls to the point of pushing the economy into the liquidity trap. This will indeed happen provided that the aggregate demand shock is sufficiently bad, namely whenever

$$\hat{\theta} < \hat{\theta}^{\min} = \sigma \, (\varphi - \bar{r}) \;\; (< 0), \tag{9.1}$$

a condition that is assumed to hold here.[2] In period $t + 1$ the demand parameter $\hat{\theta}_{t+1}$ reverts to 0 and the economy leaves the liquidity trap.

In what follows we compare the monetary policy that is (optimally) chosen by the central bank under two alternative assumptions about its ability to commit to future policy. In the first case, the central bank freely sets its monetary policy instrument in every period and is not tied to past policy announcements. Monetary policy is thus at the central bank's *discretion*, which corresponds pretty much to how the world actually works. In the second case, the central bank chooses *at time t* the monetary policy that it will implement *in all future periods* $t + k$, $k \ge 0$; once this optimal policy path has been announced, the central bank is tied to it and just unfolds it over time. This situation of policy *commitment* is not realistic from an empirical point of view. However, it is a useful benchmark in that it delivers the best

---

1. The normative approach to monetary policy analysis is discussed extensively in chapter 6. Assuming that the central bank only cares about stabilizing inflation means that the weight on output stabilization in its loss function is zero.

2. Condition (9.1) is exactly the same as condition (8.14) in the previous chapter, applied to the case where $\gamma = \infty$ (which corresponds to a situation where the central bank responds so strongly to deviations of inflation from its target that it effectively eliminates any discrepancy between the two). Indeed, applying l'Hospital rule (see chapter 6, footnote 16), it can be seen that:

$$\hat{\theta}^{\min} = \frac{(\varphi - \bar{r}) \, (1 + \kappa \sigma \gamma)^2}{\kappa \, [1 + \gamma \, (1 + \kappa \sigma \gamma)]} \xrightarrow[\gamma \to +\infty]{} \sigma \, (\varphi - \bar{r}).$$

If the negative aggregate demand shock were too weak to cause the economy to enter the liquidity trap, then the question whether forward guidance is optimal or even feasible would not arise. The optimal policy would be of the conventional type analyzed in chapter 6 and, given the central bank's objective, it would be to set $\pi_t = 0 \; \forall \, t \ge 0$.

feasible macroeconomic outcome. This will allow us, by comparison, to diagnose the inefficiencies associated with the discretionary regime.

9.1.2.1 DISCRETION

Given the objective of the central bank, the discretionary outcome is particularly simple to analyze. The central bank minimizes its intertemporal loss *in each period*, regardless of the policies that have been announced or implemented in the past. At time t the central bank minimizes $L_t^I = \pi_t^2 + \beta\pi_{t+1}^2 + \beta^2\pi_{t+2}^2 + \ldots$, but has no control over π_t (since the economy is in a liquidity trap). The central bank can in principle compute the optimal values of $\pi_{t+1}, \pi_{t+2}, \ldots$, but in any case those inflation rates will be chosen again and implemented at the relevant times, due to the discretionary nature of the central bank's decisions.

At time $t+1$, and given its loss function at that time ($L_{t+1}^I = \pi_{t+1}^2 + \beta\pi_{t+2}^2 + \beta^2\pi_{t+3}^2 + \ldots$), the central plans to implement $\pi_{t+1} = \pi_{t+2} = \ldots = 0$. At time $t+2$ it will similarly plan to implement $\pi_{t+2} = \pi_{t+3} = \ldots = 0$, and so on. The path of inflation that results from these successive choices is simply

$$\pi_{t+1} = \pi_{t+2} = \pi_{t+3} = \ldots = 0.$$

Private agents, on the other hand, understand the choices of the central bank and are thus fully able to predict the inflation rates that will be implemented in every period. Hence, at time t they anticipate $\pi_{t+1} = 0$, and thus face the real interest rate $r_t = i_t + \varphi - \pi_{t+1} = \varphi$ (recall that the zero lower bound is binding at time t; hence $i_t = 0$). The IS curve ($y_t = \hat{\theta} - \sigma(r_t - \bar{r})$) and the AS curve ($\pi_t = \kappa y_t$) then give output and inflation at time t:

$$y_t = \hat{\theta} - \sigma(\varphi - \bar{r}) < 0, \tag{9.2}$$

$$\pi_t = \kappa\hat{\theta} - \kappa\sigma(\varphi - \bar{r}) < 0. \tag{9.3}$$

One can see (from condition (9.1)) that inflation π_t (<0) is below target ($=0$)—the monetary policy that will be optimally chosen by the central bank at time $t+1$ causes inflation to undershoot its target at time t.

The evolution of the main macroeconomic variables under discretion is shown in figure 9.1 for the (somewhat arbitrary) parameters $\varphi = 0$, $\sigma = 1$, $\kappa =$, $\bar{r} = 4$ percent, $\hat{\theta} = -6$ percent, and $\beta = 0.9$.[3] At the time of the liquidity trap the nominal interest rate falls to zero, and then gradually returns to its long-run value ($\bar{i} = \bar{r} + \bar{\pi} = 4$).

---

3. The AS(t+k) curves ($y_{t+k} = \kappa^{-1}(\pi_{t+k} - \pi_{t+k-1})$) allow us to compute the levels of output at all future dates $t+k$, $k \geq 1$:

AS(t+1) : $y_{t+1} = -\hat{\theta} + \sigma(\varphi - \bar{r})$,

AS(t+k) : $y_{t+k} = 0$ for $k \geq 2$.

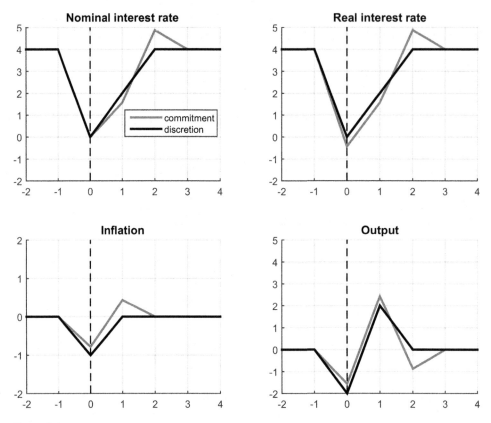

FIGURE 9.1
Discretion versus commitment in a liquidity trap. If the central bank could credibly commit to adopt an inflationary policy once out of the liquidity trap, then this policy would lift output and inflation during the trap.

Inflation and output fall at the time of the aggregate demand shock. Inflation returns to target ($= 0$) at time $t + 1$ and stays there thereafter. To implement $\pi_{t+1} = 0$, which is greater than π_t, the central bank must keep an expansionary stance in period $t + 1$, which consists in setting the nominal rate i_{t+1} at a relatively low value in order to boosts output y_{t+1}.

With the values of y_{t+k} and π_{t+k} for all $k \geq 0$, we can infer the values of the real interest rate r_{t+k} by inverting the IS(t+k) curves, and then the values of the nominal interest rate i_{t+k} by inverting the Fisher equation.

9.1.2.2 COMMITMENT

We now work out the optimal policy plan chosen by the central bank under the alternative assumption that it *is* able to commit to future monetary policy. Under this assumption, private agents anticipate that the central bank will honor its past commitments, so the central bank is able use future policy to affect the current equilibrium. Formally, under policy commitment the central bank chooses its policy plan once and for all at time t. After time t the central bank does not reoptimize but merely implements the originally chosen plan.

A time t the central bank solves

$$\min_{\pi_{t+1}, \pi_{t+2} \ldots} L_t^I = \pi_t^2 + \beta \pi_{t+1}^2 + \beta^2 \pi_{t+2}^2 + \ldots,$$

subject to

$$\mathbf{IS}: y_t = \hat{\theta} - \sigma \left(\varphi - \pi_{t+1} - \bar{r} \right),$$

$$\mathbf{AS(t+k)}: \pi_{t+k} = \pi_{t+k-1} + \kappa y_{t+k}, \quad k = 0, 1, \ldots,$$

$$\text{and } \pi_{t-1} = 0 \text{ given.}$$

As before, the central bank has no control over π_t (since the economy is in a liquidity trap at time t) but knows it will be able to control π_{t+1} π_{t+2} ... (since the economy will have left the trap by then). The key difference with the discretionary outcome analyzed above is that the π_{t+k}s, $k = 1, 2, \ldots$, will not be freely chosen in the future; they will just be implemented according to the plan that solves the above time t problem.

Using the IS and AS curve, one may rewrite the problem of the central bank at time t as follows:

$$\min_{\pi_{t+1}, \pi_{t+2} \ldots} L_t^I = (\kappa [\hat{\theta} - \sigma \left(\varphi - \pi_{t+1} - \bar{r} \right)])^2 + \beta \pi_{t+1}^2 + \beta^2 \pi_{t+2}^2 + \ldots.$$

One immediately sees that the choice of π_{t+1} affects L_t^I in two ways:

- it directly affects the future loss $\beta \pi_{t+1}^2$, to the extent that π_{t+1} deviates from its target value of zero;

- it indirectly affects the current loss $\pi_t^2 = (\kappa [\hat{\theta} - \sigma \left(\varphi + \pi_{t+1} - \bar{r} \right)])^2$ through the effect of π_{t+1} on π_t (see the IS and AS curves).

These two effects reflect the intertemporal trade-off that the central bank faces: increasing π_{t+1} above target induces a direct loss, but at the same time this policy raises y_t and π_t (through its expansionary effect in the current period) *and thereby takes π_t closer to its target of zero*. The optimal solution to this trade-off is given by the first-order condition with respect to π_{t+1}, which is given by

$$\frac{\partial L_t^I}{\partial \pi_{t+1}} = 2\sigma\kappa^2[\hat{\theta} - \sigma\,(\varphi - \pi_{t+1} - \bar{r})] + 2\beta\pi_{t+1} = 0.$$

Solving the latter for π_{t+1} gives:

$$\pi_{t+1}^* = \left(\frac{\kappa^2\sigma}{\kappa^2\sigma^2 + \beta}\right)[\sigma\,(\varphi - \bar{r}) - \hat{\theta}] > 0.$$

Hence, *the optimal policy under commitment implements at time $t+1$ an inflation rate that is strictly greater than the inflation rate under discretion.* Given the value of π_{t+1}^* and the IS and AS curves above, one may compute the time t equilibrium under policy commitment (y_t^*, π_t^*). It is given by

$$y_t^* = \left(\frac{\beta}{\sigma^2\kappa^2 + \beta}\right)\left[\hat{\theta} - \sigma\,(\varphi - \bar{r})\right] < 0,$$

$$\pi_t^* = \left(\frac{\beta}{\sigma^2\kappa^2 + \beta}\right)\left[\kappa\hat{\theta} - \kappa\sigma\,(\varphi - \bar{r})\right] < 0.$$

Thus, output and inflation still fall at time t, but since $\beta/\left(\sigma^2\kappa^2 + \beta\right) < 1$ *they fall less under commitment than under discretion* (see equations (9.2) and (9.3)). The fact that the central bank is committed to choose for time $t+1$ a higher rate of inflation than under discretion implies that the time t real interest rate is lower than under discretion; this in turn raises time t output and inflation. Overall, inflation at time t is closer to the target (= 0), which offsets the fact that inflation at time $t+1$ is farther away from the target. To put it another way, the optimal policy under commitment delays part of the welfare cost of the negative shock to aggregate demand occurring at time t to period $t+1$. In contrast, under discretion the full welfare cost of the shock fell onto period t. Smoothing intertemporally the impact of the aggregate demand shock is optimal, given the quadratic shape of the loss function.[4]

From date $t+2$ onward the central bank implements the same inflation rates as under discretion. Indeed, the first-order conditions with respect to the π_{t+k}s, $k \geq 2$, give

$$\frac{\partial L_t^I}{\partial \pi_{t+k}} = 2\beta^k\pi_{t+k} = 0 \Rightarrow \pi_{t+k} = 0.$$

---

4. See chapter 6 for a general discussion of how the shape of the central bank's loss function affects its intratemporal and intertemporal choices.

Since all the π_{t+k}s are equal to zero from $k = 2$ on, all the y_{t+k}s also are from $k = 3$ on (as can be inferred from the AS(t+k) curves for $k \geq 3$). The values of y_{t+1} and y_{t+2} can be recovered using the AS (t+1) and AS(t+2) curves:

$$\textbf{AS(t+1)}: y_{t+1} = \kappa^{-1}\,(\pi_{t+1} - \pi_t) = \left(\frac{\kappa\sigma + \beta}{\kappa^2\sigma^2 + \beta}\right) [\sigma\,(\varphi - \bar{r}) - \hat{\theta}] > 0,$$

$$\textbf{AS(t+2)}: y_{t+2} = \kappa^{-1}\,(\pi_{t+2} - \pi_{t+1}) = -\left(\frac{\kappa\sigma}{\kappa^2\sigma^2 + \beta}\right) [\sigma\,(\varphi - \bar{r}) - \hat{\theta}] < 0.$$

Figure 9.1 shows the adjustment of the economy to the negative aggregate demand shock under policy commitment (the grey lines). The main characteristic of this equilibrium is that the central bank implements for period $t + 1$ an inflation rate that is higher than its target. It does so by setting the nominal interest rate at a lower level than under discretion. The implied higher level of inflation in period $t + 1$ limits the impact of the negative aggregate demand shock on output and inflation at time t. Subsequently, the central bank takes back inflation to its target by raising interest rates.

9.1.3   EFFICIENCY AND CREDIBILITY OF FORWARD GUIDANCE

The optimal policy under commitment corresponds to the forward guidance policy discussed above. It consists of a commitment on the part of the central bank regarding its future policy, with the purpose of limiting the current economic contraction. It is easily verified that the equilibrium under commitment dominates that under discretion in terms of welfare. Since all inflation levels are all zero from period $t + 2$ onward (whether the central bank operates under discretion or commitment), the intertemporal loss is $L_t^I = \pi_t^2 + \beta\pi_{t+1}^2$ in both cases. Using the values of π_t and π_{t+1} in each equilibrium we obtain:

$$\textbf{discretion}: L_t^I = \pi_t^2 + \beta\pi_{t+1}^2 = \kappa^2[\hat{\theta}_t - \sigma\,(\varphi - \bar{r})]^2,$$

$$\textbf{commitment}: L_t^I = \pi_t^2 + \beta\pi_{t+1}^2 = \left(\frac{\beta}{\beta + \kappa^2\sigma^2}\right)\kappa^2[\hat{\theta}_t - \sigma\,(\varphi - \bar{r})]^2.$$

Since $\beta/(\beta + \kappa^2\sigma^2) < 1$, the equilibrium under commitment dominates the equilibrium under discretion (the loss is lower). The issue with forward guidance is not with its effectiveness but with its *credibility*. As noted earlier, there is no formal mechanism tying the central bank to its past commitments, and in practice central banks operate in a largely discretionary manner. Now, under discretion the central bank implements conventional inflation targeting as soon as the economy has emerged from the liquidity trap, simply because this is precisely what has become optimal by that time! To put it another way, forward guidance is not time consistent, since what was optimal to plan ahead when the economy was in the liquidity trap is no longer optimal once the economy has left the liquidity trap—and will, therefore, not be implemented. Private agents, who know the loss function of the central bank and therefore understand its incentives and future choices, have no reason to believe in policy promises that they know will not be kept. In the words of Paul Krugman (1998), a central bank cannot "commit to being irresponsible"—the irresponsibility here being to engineer excess inflation while the liquidity trap is past.

9.2 LARGE-SCALE ASSET PURCHASES

9.2.1 QUALITATIVE VS. QUANTITATIVE EASING

Since 2008, the major central banks, starting with the US Federal Reserve, the Bank of England, the Bank of Japan, and the European Central Bank, have embarked on so-called *Large-Scale Asset Purchase* (LSAP) programs. These operations, as their name implies, involve massive purchases of assets (notably public debt) by the central bank in order to support their price and, at the same time, increase the amount of liquidity (i.e., reserve money) held by the banking system as a whole.

There are two types of LSAPs: *qualitative* and *quantitative* easing operations. Qualitative easing operations are interventions on the interbank market that do not change the size of the central bank's balance sheet because they are *sterilized*. The central bank buys some assets from private banks (usually with the purpose of influencing the equilibrium price of those assets), and at the same time it resells other assets to the banking system for the same dollar amount. In consequence, the total amount of reserves held by banks on their accounts with the central bank is left unchanged.[5] The effect of these transactions on the central bank's balance sheet is (typically) a change in the structure of its portfolio toward riskier assets or assets with longer maturity. Symmetrically, the financial sector as a whole holds less risky, long assets and more of the safer, shorter assets sold by the central bank. Examples of qualitative-easing operations are the *Securities Markets Program* (2010–2012) and *Outright Monetary Transactions* (2012–), by which the European Central Bank supported the sovereign bond markets of the troubled southern European economies, as well as the *Maturity Extension Program* (2011–2012) by which the US Federal Reserve simultaneously sold short-term treasuries and bought long-term treasuries. Inasmuch as the qualitative-easing policies generally target certain asset classes explicitly, they are occasionally referred to as "targeted easing."

In contrast, *quantitative easing* operations are *not* sterilized. The central bank purchases assets from private banks, pays for these assets by raising the amount

---

5. The working of the interbank market and the open market operations by which the central banks buys or sells assets from private banks is described in chapter 6.

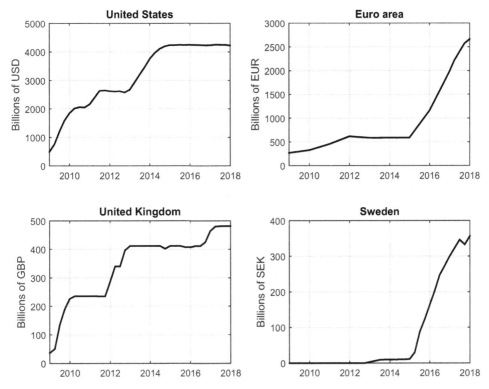

FIGURE 9.2
Large-Scale Asset Purchases (LSAP) by central banks.
Sources: U.S. Federal Reserve, European Central Bank, Bank of England, Sveriges Riksbank, and the author's calculations.

of reserve money on the account of the selling banks, and just lets the size of its balance sheet increase by the amount of the purchase. The Bank of Japan inaugurated this policy in 2001 and continued it until 2006 (with limited success, as we discuss below); they started it again at the end of 2012 in the context of the set of expansionary policies known as "Abenomics" (from the name of the prime minister Shinzo Abe). During the Great Recession the US Federal Reserve implemented three successive rounds of quantitative easing, dubbed "QE1" (2009–2010), "QE2" (2010–2011), and "QE3" (2012–2014); these cumulative transactions led to a five-fold increase in the size of its balance sheet between 2007 and 2014. The Bank of England also adopted quantitative easing from 2009 onward. Finally, the European Central Bank followed suit beginning in March 2015, as part of a program which, at the time of writing, is expected to last at least until the end of 2018. Figure 9.2 illustrates the sharp rise in asset holdings on the part of several central banks over the period 2008–2017.

9.2.2 THE IMPLEMENTATION OF QUANTITATIVE EASING

Concretely, a QE operation consists in the purchase of assets by the central bank from a private bank. This transaction results in the following:

- For the private bank, a portfolio substitution on the asset side of the balance sheet that keeps the size of the balance sheet unchanged (the sold security disappears from the assets, but the reserve account with the central bank is credited by the same dollar amount).

- For the central bank, an equal increase in its assets and liabilities by the exact amount of the purchase (the purchased security enters the asset side of the balance sheet, while the corresponding credit on the account of the private bank appears on the liability side).

In other words, from as strict operational point of view there is no substantial difference between a QE operation and a standard open-market operation (OMO), whereby the central banks intervene on the interbank market to influence the short-term nominal interest rate (see chapter 6). There are, however, several important differences from an economic point of view:

- QE operations differ from standard OMOs by their long-term impact on the balance sheet of the central bank. In practice, an OMO generally takes the form of a purchase of a security against a *repurchase agreement*, or repo—that is, a reverse operation that is scheduled to take place in the near future.[6] A repo is formally equivalent to a collateralized loan; the central bank lends reserve money to a private bank against a security, and the loan is repaid to the central bank against the return of the security to the bank, when the repo reaches maturity. This means that standard OMOs phase out mechanically and therefore do not persistently and significantly increase the size of the central bank's balance sheet. In contrast, QE operations do not include any automatic buyback mechanism and therefore have the (intended) effect of raising, if not permanently, at least persistently the size of the central bank's balance sheet.[7]

- OMOs vary the amount of total reserves R^s so as to implement the desired value of the equilibrium interest rate on the interbank market i^M (see equation (6.4)). The exact size of these transactions is therefore endogenous to the target value

---

6. For example, the Main Refinancing Operations (MRO) of the European Central Bank have a maturity of one week.

7. Of course a repo can be renewed from one period to the next (as is the case in practice), while a QE operation can be reverted by reselling the assets initially purchased by the central bank. But neither the renewal of a repo nor the reversion of a QE operation are planned in the contract; hence they remain at the discretion of the central bank.

of i^M and the market equilibrium; the central bank increases R^s as long as i^M is above target, and vice versa. In contrast, a QE operation involves a nominal amount of purchased assets scheduled in advance, so that the explicit target is the rate of change of reserves ΔR^s. For example, the QE of the European Central Bank from the beginning of 2015 onward specified that 60 billion euros worth of assets would be bought every month. This amount became 80 billion every month between March 2016 and March 2017, and then back to 60 billion every month from April 2017 onward. In Japan, the QE that was initiated at the end of 2012 targets an expansion of the monetary base of 80 trillion yen a year until the monetary base is doubled. In all these cases the policy is explicitly about the *quantity* of reserves to be injected in the banking system.

- Finally, QE operations differ from open market operations in terms of the interest rates they seek to influence. Whereas open market transactions aim to control the short-term nominal interest rate on the interbank market i^M, QE operations are typically aimed at increasing the price of assets with a longer maturity, with the goal of lowering their required rate of return and ultimately easing the financing conditions of all borrowers. We shortly describe why and how QE operations affect those longer-term interest rates and thereby aggregate demand.

9.2.3 CHANNELS, IMPACT, AND LIMITS OF QE

The ultimate goal of QE operations is to lower the real interest rate faced by private agents—that is, the interest rate that ultimately determines consumption and investment expenditures. In order to decompose the channels by which quantitative easing affects the real interest rate, let us use again equation (8.1) of the previous chapter:

$$r_t + \zeta_t = \underbrace{\underset{\substack{\uparrow \\ \text{average of short-term nominal rates}}}{\tilde{\imath}_t} \quad + \quad \underset{\substack{\uparrow \\ \text{term premium}}}{\varphi} \quad - \quad \underset{\substack{\uparrow \\ \text{expected inflation}}}{\pi_{t+1}}}_{\text{real risk-free rate } r_t} \quad + \quad \underset{\substack{\uparrow \\ \text{credit spread}}}{\zeta_t} \quad ,$$

where $r_t + \zeta_t$ is the real interest rate faced by risky borrowers (which includes the credit spread ζ_t).

When the zero lower bound is binding (so that $\tilde{\imath}_t = 0$), a decrease in $r_t + \zeta_t$ can only come from a decrease in the term premium or the credit spread ($\varphi + \zeta_t$) or an increase in (expected) future inflation (π_{t+1}). QE operations can reduce the term premium and the credit spread through the so-called "portfolio balance channel." Moreover, these operations can *signal* the accommodative nature of future monetary policy and thus potentially influence inflation expectations (upward). Before going into the details, let us succinctly summarize how these two channels affect the relevant interest rate $r_t + \zeta_t$ at the zero lower bound (where $\tilde{\imath}_t = 0$):

$$r_t + \zeta_t = \underbrace{\varphi + \zeta_t}_{\downarrow \text{ (portfolio-balance channel)}} - \underbrace{\pi_{t+1}}_{\uparrow \text{ (signaling channel)}} .$$

9.2.3.1 THE PORTFOLIO-BALANCE CHANNEL

According to the portfolio-balance channel, when the central bank massively acquires a specific type of assets, it raises their equilibrium price and thus reduces their yield.[8] For example, when the European Central Bank acquires some government bonds of the euro area countries, it reduces the interest rate at which these securities are issued and hence the cost of public debt for the concerned governments. These lower financing cost are then transmitted to other asset classes that are close in terms of maturity and risk (e.g., low-risk corporate bonds), as investors seek elsewhere the profitability they no longer find on government bonds. The initial effect of the purchase thus gradually contaminates other assets, lowering their own term premia and credit spreads, which ultimately relaxes financing conditions throughout the entire economy.

What does it take for the portfolio channel to be operative? Recall from section 6.1 of chapter 6 that, according to the strict term structure of interest rates applied to bonds without credit risk, the nominal interest rate on a long bond is just the average of the expected interest rates on shorter-maturity bonds. In the example used there, the interest rate on a two-year maturity bond could be expressed as the mean of current and future interest rates on three-month maturity bonds. However, we argued that risk-averse investors facing interest-rate risk required a *term premium* in excess of the mere average of short-term yields to hold long assets. Hence, the yield on a two-year maturity bond without income risk could be written as:

$$i_s^{2y} \simeq \frac{1}{8} \left(i_s^{3m} + \sum_{j=1}^{7} i_{s+j \times 3m}^{3m} \right) + \varphi^{3m,2y}.$$

The presence of the term premium $\varphi^{3m,2y} \geq 0$ is the manifestation of the fact that purchasing a long bond is *not a perfect substitute to a series of purchases of shorter-maturity bonds*. Holding a long bond is a riskier investment strategy, because a long bond may have to be liquidated before maturity at unfavorable terms. The longer the bond, the most likely this event becomes, and the greater the required term premium.

---

8. The portfolio-balance channel is not related to the amount of reserve money in the economy but only to the buying pressure that the central bank exerts on certain securities. This channel is therefore at work whether the easing is quantitative (i.e., unsterilized) or qualitative/targeted (i.e., sterilized). See Woodford (2012) for an informal but systematic discussion of the transmission channels of QE.

To understand the conditions under which the portfolio-balance channel of QE works, suppose instead that investors do not care about the interest rate risk associated with holding long bonds; for example, they may be all risk-neutral, or the risk could be perfectly diversified away. In this scenario bonds of short and long maturities all become perfect substitutes from the point of view of investors, and the strict term structure of interest rates holds (without any term premium). But at the zero lower bound, interbank loans as well as short-maturity bills *are also almost perfect substitutes with reserve money*, since all have close maturities and pay almost the same interest rates (i^M and i^R). Hence, if bonds of various maturities were perfect substitutes while the economy is in a liquidity trap, then *reserve money and loans and bonds of all maturities would all become perfect substitutes*, and they would all pay a nominal interest rate of zero. In this situation, the purchase by the central bank of a bond of any maturity from a private bank (against the creation of reserve money) would amount to a substitution of two equivalent assets in the bank's portfolio. Therefore, this should have no effect on the behavior of the private bank, leaving the macroeconomic equilibrium entirely unchanged.

It follows that the effectiveness of the portfolio-balance channel *entirely rests on the imperfect substitutability of bonds of various maturities*. One way of generating this imperfect substitutability is by assuming that there is an interest-rate risk commanding a term premium, but there are other ways. For example, some investors may have a preference for some specific bonds (e.g., bonds denominated in the local currency) or may be constrained by regulation to hold bonds of particular maturities (e.g., pensions funds constrained to hold long-maturity bonds). When bonds are imperfect substitutes and command a positive term premium, the latter becomes sensitive to the buying pressure exerted by the various investors—the premium falls when the bond is in high demand, so its yield gets closer to the yield on short-run maturity bonds, and the other way around. The portfolio-balance channel of QE denotes the reduction in the term premium of the bonds directly purchased by the central bank, as well as the spillover of this purchase to other asset markets. As the price of the purchased bonds rises, and consequently their yield-to-maturity falls, investors rebalance their portfolio toward other assets to find the return they no longer get on the assets directly affected by the central bank intervention somewhere else. These other assets include bonds free of credit risk, but of different maturities, whose term premium falls, as well as corporate bonds that involve some credit risk, whose credit spreads then also falls.

There is both indirect and direct evidence about the portfolio-balance channel of QE. Event studies that look at the market impact of QE announcements find that they significantly reduce term premia and credit spreads, which is consistent with the portfolio-balance channel.[9] Joyce, Liu, and Tonks (2017) have studied how

---

9. See Swansson (2017), and the references therein, for the impact of QE in the United States, and Andrade et al. (2016) for similar evidence in the euro area.

insurance companies and pension funds have rebalanced their portfolios following QE by the Bank of England over the period 2009–2013. They showed that these operations lowered the yield on sovereign bonds and pushed these investors to rebalance their portfolio toward riskier corporate bonds. This provides direct evidence on the workings of the portfolio-balance channel.

Let us examine the impact of the portfolio-balance channel on the macroeconomic equilibrium using our AS-AD model. The AD curve in a liquidity trap is given by equation (8.15) in chapter 8, where the demand parameter $\hat{\theta}_t$ includes the term premium φ and the credit spread ζ_t (see equation (8.2)). Making this dependence explicit in the AD curve, we can rewrite it as follows:

$$\textbf{AD}: y_t = \underbrace{-\sigma\,(\varphi + \zeta_t)}_{\uparrow \text{ (portfolio channel)}} + \underbrace{\theta_t + \sigma\left(\bar{r} - \bar{\zeta}\right)}_{\text{constant (by assumption)}} + \left(\frac{\sigma}{1 + \kappa\sigma\gamma}\right)\pi_t.$$

The latter formulation of the AD curve makes it clear that a quantitative-easing operation that successfully reduces term premia and/or credit spreads shifts the AD curve rightward in the (y, π) plane, thereby raising output and inflation (see figure 9.3).

Note that, while the portfolio-balance channel can effectively lead to a reduction in term premia and in credit spreads, its scope is necessarily limited. Indeed, these premia and spreads can be reduced only to the extent that they are significantly positive in the first place. The issue is of the same nature as the zero lower bound problem. Term premia and credit spreads cannot fall below zero because they both compensate investors for some risk: *interest-rate risk* for the term premium and *credit risk* for the credit spread. No investor would agree to hold a long maturity bond with a yield to maturity lower than the yield on a short bond that bears no interest-rate risk. Similarly, no investor would agree to hold a risky bond yielding less than a risk-free bond. Therefore, it must be that, inasmuch as QE is successfully implemented, the extra room for further successful QE naturally shrinks over time as term premia and credit spreads are themselves shrinking. As an illustration of this, Swanson and Williams (2014) show that in the United States ten-year sovereign bond futures cease to decline by the end of 2011, stabilizing at around 1.8 percent, despite the continuation of quantitative-easing operations thereafter.

9.2.3.2 THE SIGNALING CHANNEL

QE operations, as we have seen, aim to raise the amount of reserves held by banks on their account with the central bank. This goal may seem somewhat surprising. Indeed, at the zero lower bound, the short-term term nominal interest rate on the interbank market (i^M in equation (6.4) of chapter 6) is very close to the interest rate on reserves (i^R); hence the opportunity cost of reserves (the difference $i^M - i^R$) is very low. Banks therefore get little benefit from lending their additional holdings of

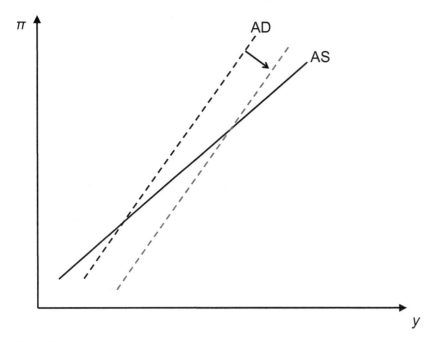

FIGURE 9.3
The portfolio-balance effect. Quantitative easing lowers term premia and credit spreads, which eases financing conditions and raises aggregate demand.

reserves (ΔR^s in the aggregate), which therefore remain on their account with the central bank. This is the very meaning of the liquidity trap: a situation where liquidity injections by the central bank fail to circulate, as if they were falling in a trap. But if this is indeed the case, what can be the impact of ΔR^s on the macroeconomic equilibrium?

Bernanke and Reinhart (2004) have argued that the significant increase in the quantity of bank reserves following QE operations can serve as a *signal* about future monetary policy, if private agents anticipate that the amount of reserves injected into the banking system will remain high *after the economy has come out of the trap*. To understand the logic of this argument, let us examine again how the short-term nominal interest rate i^M is determined, as is summarized in equation (6.4). During the liquidity trap (let us index this period by 0) the economy is at the zero lower bound and hence

$$i_0^M = i^M(i_0^R, y_0, R_0^s) \simeq i_0^R = 0.$$

Once R_0^s has increased so much that i_0^M is already very close to 0, increasing R_0^s to the value $R_1^s = R_0^s + \Delta R^s > R_0^s$ has no further effect on i_0^M. Nevertheless, if those extra reserves are maintained over time, this extra ΔR^s *will* affect the equilibrium once the economy has left the liquidity trap (let us index this period by 1), at a time when output will be greater (at $y_1 > y_0$) and when reserves will have become a scarce resource again. Indeed, in period 1 we necessarily have:

$$i^M(i_1^R, \ y_1, \ R_0^s) > i^M(i_1^R, \ y_1, \ R_0^s + \Delta R^s) > 0,$$

since the zero lower bound is no longer binding in period 1 and i^M falls with R^s. In other words, if private agents anticipate that the central bank will maintain its reserves at the high level $R_0^s + \Delta R^s$ in period 1, then they anticipate that the short-term interest rate i_1^M will be low at that time—lower than if the quantity of reserves were reverted to R_0^s. This policy is thus expansionary, and as such raises inflation in period 1. It follows that this policy reduces the real interest rate in period 0 (r_0), which has an expansionary effect on inflation and output in period 0. Put differently, according to this logic QE (i.e., $\Delta R^o > 0$) successfully implements what forward guidance was unable to do—namely, *raising inflation expectations so as to bring down the real interest rate and stimulate aggregate demand during the liquidity trap.*

As convincing as it may look, however, there are two immediate objections to this logic:

- First, the signaling channel merely shifts (toward the quantity of reserves) the problem of credibility of forward guidance emphasized in the previous section. Indeed, the economic stimulus effect at date 0 of maintaining high reserves ($= R_0^s + \Delta R^s$) until period 1 comes from the fact that this policy raises future inflation, precisely at a time when the economy has left the liquidity trap. Consequently, if the central bank targets a certain rate of inflation in normal times (for example, because its intertemporal loss function is of the type described in Section 9.1), then it will revert its QE operations once the economy has left the trap in order to meet the inflation target. Since private agents rationally anticipate this, raising the quantity of reserves during the liquidity trap is unlikely to successfully signal high future inflation.

- Second, even if the central bank *could* credibly commit to maintain a large balance sheet (for example, because reselling the assets on the market would take time or would be associated with a capital loss), it remains true that the interest rate on the interbank market i_1^M cannot be lower than the interest rate on reserves i_1^R, which is freely set by the central bank in every period. Hence, even with a large balance sheet the central bank could in principle reach its inflation target in period 1 by raising i_1^R, which would mechanically push i_1^M upward. To put it differently, the central bank has not one but two ways of keeping inflation low at time 1: reverting QE (by massively reselling assets)

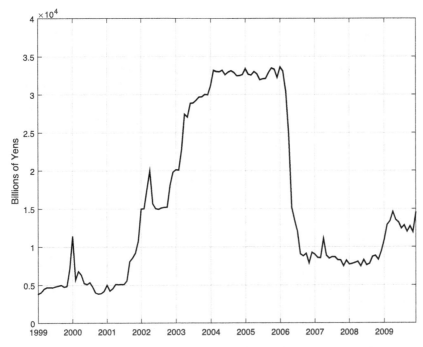

FIGURE 9.4
The first QE in Japan.
Source: Bank of Japan.

or raising the interest rate on reserves. The signaling channel thus requires a double commitment—on the future quantity of reserves *and* on the interest rate that they will be paying.

The QE experiment undertaken in Japan between 2001 and 2006 perfectly illustrates the limits of the signaling channel. This QE led the Bank of Japan to sharply increase the quantity of bank reserves in 2001, with the explicit goal of raising inflation expectations. This policy, however, was largely unsuccessful. It did not significantly change inflation expectations, nor did it raise actual inflation or output. A possible explanation for this ineffectiveness is that private agents understood that QE could be readily reverted at the first sign of inflation pick-up. As shown in figure 9.4, they were right to be skeptical. In 2006 the Bank of Japan contracted the quantity of reserves sharply until it returned to its pre-2001 trend. A natural interpretation of this episode is that the Bank of Japan lacked the ability to commit to maintaining high levels of reserve money, and that the private sector perfectly understood the consequences of this.

9.3   ICONOCLASTIC MONETARY POLICIES

9.3.1   (VERY) NEGATIVE INTEREST RATES

We have seen in section 8.2.1 that the zero lower bound on the short-term nominal interest rate in the interbank market (i^M) is not exactly equal to zero. This interest rate is limited by the nominal interest rate on reserves held by banks on their account with the central bank (i^R), while the latter rate cannot be set at a level below the nominal interest rate on banknotes *adjusted for their holding cost* (we denoted this nominal return $\underline{i}^B \leq 0$). We summarized these arbitrage constraints by the following double inequality:

$$i^M \geq i^R \geq \underline{i}^B.$$

The central bank controls the aggregate supply of reserves R^s, and thus the equilibrium value of $i^M - i^R$, as well as the interest rate on reserves i^R (see section 8.2.1 in chapter 8). In the wake of the Great Recession, R^s grew rapidly in most developed countries due to direct liquidity support to illiquid banks by the central bank and to QE operations. As a consequence, i^M became very close to i^R; for example, the difference between these two rates at the time of this writing is less than 10 basis points (0.1 percent) in the United States, the euro area, and Japan. A number of central banks today fix i^R at a level slightly below zero. For example, in April 2018 these rates were −0.4 percent in the Euro area and −0.1 percent in Japan. However, the existence of the lower bound $\underline{i}^B$ prevents central banks from going much further. The exact value of $\underline{i}^B$ is unknown, but risking to cross this floor is potentially disastrous due to the run toward banknotes that this would cause. In the absence of the constraint $i^R \geq \underline{i}^B$, the central bank could lower i^R as much as it wishes and then keep i^M arbitrarily close to i^R through its control of R^s.

Rogoff (2015a) recently put forward a radical proposal to solve the $i^R \geq \underline{i}^B$ problem—to gradually phase out banknotes and ultimately use electronic money exclusively. The lower bound $\underline{i}^B$ would mechanically disappear. The banks would no longer have an asset alternative to their reserves with the central bank; hence they would be stuck with their reserves even if i^R were to become very negative. The banks' only option to maintain their intermediation margin would then be to pass through the fall of i^R to the interest rate that they pay on deposits (i.e., they would effectively *charge* deposits). And in the face of a negative deposit rate the customers would no longer have an alternative asset to run toward, either.[10] Other, less radical institutional proposals aim at keeping banknotes while raising their holding

---

10. Phasing out paper currency would have other benefits. One of them is that it would harm the most important private user of banknotes—namely, the underground economy. The main drawback of living in a world of pure electronic money is the lack of transactional anonymity that paper currency allows and to which many citizens are wedded.

costs so as to allow the central bank to lower $\underline{i}^B$ to more negative values than under the current system. For example, Rogoff (2017) stresses that removing large denominations from circulation but maintaining small ones would already significantly raise the cost of storing banknotes. The nominal return on cash $\underline{i}^B$, and by way of consequence the interest rate on reserves i^R, could both be substantially lowered as a result. Relatedly, Mankiw (2009) has proposed to regularly invalidate certain banknotes, randomly drawn based on their issue number; this would reduce the expected return on all banknotes $\underline{i}^B$.[11] Last but not least, Agarwal and Kimball (2015) have proposed to temporarily introduce a crawling peg between electronic reserve money and paper currency. In this way, paper currency could be gradually depreciated relative to reserve money, to the point where the returns on these two forms of money are equalized even in situations where reserve money pays a negative nominal return.

Let us illustrate this point by means of an example (assuming for simplicity that there is no cost of holding banknotes other than their nominal depreciation against reserve money). The current system is one in which banknotes and electronic reserve money trade at par. When a bank purchases a $500 banknote from the US Federal Reserve, its reserve account is debited by the amount of $500 (and vice versa when the bank sells a banknote to the central bank). Suppose that such a parity prevailed until day $s - 1$, when the nominal interest rate was zero ($i^R = \underline{i}^B = 0$), but the central bank now wishes to implement a negative interest rate $i^R < 0$ between day s and day $s + 1$. The Fed can fix i^R at any value it wants, provided that it ensures that banknotes depreciate sufficiently between day s and day $s + 1$ (relative to electronic reserve money), in such a way that their return $\underline{i}^B$ remains no greater than i^R (otherwise there would be a run toward the banknotes). Since the two forms of money are traded at par until day s, at the time the negative interest rate policy is implemented the price of a $1 banknote is … $1 of electronic reserve money. The central bank can align the return on banknotes with that on reserves between day s and day $s + 1$ by announcing that the price of the banknote on day $s + 1$ in terms of electronic reserve money will not be $1 but $ $(1 + i^R) < \$1$. For example, a bank that is willing to sell a $500 note to the central bank to credit its reserve account will only be credited with $500 \times (1 + i^R) < \$500$. This operation can be pursued over several periods so as to ensure a continuous devaluation of the banknotes (for example, a negative interest rate on reserves $i^R < 0$ can be maintained for two days if the price of the $500 banknote in terms of electronic money is set at $500 \times (1 + i^R)$ at time $s + 1$, then $500 \times (1 + i^R)^2 < \$500 \times (1 + i^R)$ at time $s + 2$, and so on).

This crawling peg between paper and electronic reserve money can in principle be maintained over any duration and be used to implement any value of i^R. Of course, when negative interest rates cease to be necessary and the policy comes

---

11. See also Buiter and Panigirtzoglou (2003) for a related proposal.

to an end, paper currency can be strongly depreciated relative to electronic money. Agarwal and Kimball (2015) propose then to gradually restore parity between the two forms of money. In our example, if i^R goes back to the value of zero in $s+2$, then a crawling peg ensuring a gradual reappreciation of paper currency from day $s+2$ onward will ultimately restore parity. During this adjustment period the return on banknotes is bound to be greater than that on electronic money, but the difference between the two returns can be made small if the reappreciation of paper currency is sufficiently slow.

One important limitation of the theoretical analysis of negative interest rates policies is that it is based on the presumption that the traditional transmission channels of monetary policy (from a lower policy rate to lower bank deposit and lending rates) are left unchanged by the crossing of the zero lower bound. In this view, there is nothing special about the way the banking sector passes through changes in the policy rate to other interest rates, once the former has turned negative. Recent empirical work casts serious doubts on this view (Heider, Saidi, and Schepens 2017; Eggertsson, Juelsrud, and Getz Wold 2017). First, the evidence shows that the *deposit rate* remains nonnegative despite negative policy rates; that is, banks are reluctant to charge households deposits, even though their own deposits with the central bank are charged (via negative interest rates on reserves). Second, inasmuch as deposits are the main sources of funding for commercial banks, the *lending rate* at which households and firms borrow from the banks also remains nonnegative—or else banks would lose money by lending. Third, the downward pressure on the lending rate in the face of a nonnegative deposit rate implies that the intermediation margin contracts, which undermines banks' incentives to lend. These results suggest that the transmission channels of monetary policy work differently at the zero lower bound and that negative policy rates may actually be counter-productive.

9.3.2 A HIGHER INFLATION TARGET

We have examined in detail the reasons why it was difficult for the central bank to commit to an inflationary monetary policy for periods in which the economy is no longer in the liquidity trap (see section 9.1). In practice, an *excessive* level of inflation is nothing else than a level greater than the inflation target that the central bank has set for itself (possibly under the guidance of the government). And the reason why private agents may rightly doubt that the central bank will let inflation deviate from the target is that they have observed the central bank tracking the target untiringly and, often, actively communicating on its immutability.

Most central banks in developed countries, including the US Federal Reserve and the European Central Bank, have more or less explicitly adopted a 2 percent inflation target. This target has been internalized by households and firms. Since the nominal interest rate cannot fall below zero, it follows that the *real* interest rate r_t, which depends on expected inflation, cannot fall below $r_t^{\min} = \varphi - \pi_{t+1} > -2\%$

($r_t^{\min}$ is equal to -2 percent in the best scenario where the term premium is zero, but greater if $\varphi > 0$). Ball (2014) and others have argued that this lower bound on the real interest rate is too high to effectively stabilize negative aggregate demand shocks that may push the economy into the liquidity trap. Ball proposes to reset the inflation target at the level of 4 percent, thereby allowing $r_t^{\min}$ to potentially go down to -4 percent (or a bit higher due to the term premium). This policy would mechanically relax the zero lower bound constraint, which would become binding less often. For example, if the term premium is zero and the economy is periodically hit by negative aggregate demand shocks requiring a -3 percent real interest rate to be neutralized, then the economy hits the zero lower bound every time a shock occurs if the inflation target is 2 percent, but it never does if the inflation target is above 3 percent.

The impact of the choice of the inflation target on the economy's exposure to the risk of liquidity trap can be analyzed formally by generalizing our analysis to allow the inflation target $\bar{\pi}$ to take any value (and not only $\bar{\pi} = 0$). Apart from this generalization all the assumptions of section 8.2 are maintained, so we do not discuss them here. As usual, we first solve the equilibrium of period $t+1$ (when, by assumption, aggregate demand resumes and the economy leaves the liquidity trap), and then infer the equilibrium of period t.

With a generic inflation target $\bar{\pi}$, the AS(t+1)–AD(t+1) equilibrium is given by:

AD(t+1) : $y_{t+1} = -\sigma\gamma\,(\pi_{t+1} - \bar{\pi})$,

AS(t+1) : $\pi_{t+1} = \pi_t + \kappa y_{t+1}$.

Substituting y_{t+1} in the AD(t+1) curve into the AS(t+1) curve and rearranging, we obtain:

$$\pi_{t+1} = \bar{\pi} + \frac{\pi_t - \bar{\pi}}{1 + \kappa\sigma\gamma},$$

which generalizes equation (8.7) of chapter 8.

The economy stays away from the liquidity trap region as long as the zero lower bound on the short-term nominal interest rate is not binding, or equivalently (from equation (8.4)) as long as

$$\underbrace{\bar{r} + \gamma\,(\pi_t - \bar{\pi})}_{=\ r_t \text{ according to the MP curve}} \geq \underbrace{\varphi - \pi_{t+1}}_{=\ r_t^{\min}}.$$

Replacing π_{t+1} by its value and solving this inequality, we see that the economy stays away from the liquidity trap as long as the equilibrium inflation rate stays above the threshold $\pi^{\min}$:

$$\pi_t \geq \pi^{\min} = \bar{\pi} + \frac{(\varphi - \bar{\pi} - \bar{r})(1 + \kappa\sigma\gamma)}{1 + \gamma(1 + \kappa\sigma\gamma)},$$

which generalizes equation (8.13) of chapter 8.

What is the size of the aggregate demand shocks that the economy can take without π_t falling below $\pi^{\min}$? To answer this question, we must compute the equilibrium value of π_t, and thus determine the equilibrium of period t. As long as the economy avoids the liquidity trap, the AS-AD equilibrium is given by the following equations (see chapter 4):

AD : $y_t = \hat{\theta}_t - \sigma\gamma(\pi_t - \bar{\pi})$,

AS : $\pi_t = \bar{\pi} + \kappa y_t$,

where we have assumed that inflation was equal to target before the aggregate demand shock occurred (i.e., $\pi_{t-1} = \bar{\pi}$). Solving the time t macroeconomic equilibrium gives:

$$\pi_t = \bar{\pi} + \frac{\kappa\hat{\theta}_t}{1 + \kappa\sigma\gamma}.$$

Using the value of $\pi^{\min}$ above, we find that the minimal value of the demand parameter $\hat{\theta}_t$, below which the economy enters the liquidity trap, is now given by

$$\hat{\theta}^{\min} = \frac{(\varphi - \bar{r} - \bar{\pi})(1 + \kappa\sigma\gamma)^2}{\kappa[1 + \gamma(1 + \kappa\sigma\gamma)]}.$$

To summarize, the economy enters into liquidity trap whenever $\hat{\theta}_t$ falls below $\hat{\theta}^{\min}$, while $\hat{\theta}^{\min}$ is a (linearly) decreasing function of $\bar{\pi}$. In this sense, *a high inflation target effectively protects the economy against the risk of liquidity trap.*

If raising the inflation target allows us, in principle, to steer away the spectrum of the liquidity trap, this policy should nevertheless be interpreted with caution. Indeed, the above analysis is not a welfare analysis that would explicitly balance the macroeconomic gains associated with avoiding the liquidity trap and the costs associated with a higher inflation trend. When inflation is high and firms reoptimize their prices infrequently, inflation raises the dispersion of nominal prices and hence distorts the relative prices of goods. This is a source of economic inefficiency that generate some welfare costs in the aggregate. Coibion, Gorodnichenko, and Wieland (2012) sought to evaluate these gains and costs in a full dynamic general-equilibrium model with nominal price rigidities. They concluded that as long as liquidity trap episodes are relatively infrequent, then the optimal inflation rate (i.e., the one that exactly balances the costs of high inflation and the gains associated with avoiding the liquidity trap) is unlikely to be greater than 2 percent. Of course, this result depends on the assumed frequency and duration of liquidity trap episodes. The reference scenario used by Coibion, Gorodnichenko, and Wieland (2012) was that of a liquidity trap that lasts for two years and occurs once every twenty years on average. The experience of Japan, the United States, the euro area, and many other countries shows that liquidity trap episodes can last much longer. In a more recent assessment of the optimal inflation rate under more plausible frequencies and durations of liquidity trap episodes, Carreras et al. (2016) find this optimal rate to be about twice as large as originally thought—namely around 4 percent and hence close the value advocated by Ball (2014).

9.3.3 PRICE-LEVEL TARGETING

Another way to generate high inflation expectations in a liquidity trap, so as to lower the real interest rate, would be to adopt a *price-level targeting* regime instead of the inflation targeting regime (Eggertsson and Woodford 2003; Evans 2012). In the inflation targeting regime, the central bank seeks to bring inflation back to target whenever it temporarily deviates from it. In the price-level targeting regime, it is a *price trend*, not the inflation rate, that is being targeted. Hence, any unanticipated shock to the level of inflation must necessarily be followed by a *change in inflation of opposite sign* in order take the price level back to its trend. For example, if inflation rises temporarily from 2 percent (a rate consistent with the targeted price trend) to 3 percent, then the central bank must implement an inflation rate of 1 percent over the same length of time in order to bring down the price level back to target.

The price-level targeting regime is beneficial in a liquidity trap because it mechanically commits the central bank to implement an *inflationary* monetary policy whenever the macroeconomic outcome has become *deflationary*—which is precisely what occurs in a liquidity trap. Even though high inflation cannot be implemented during the trap (due to a binding zero lower bound), it will be after the economy has left the trap and will be maintained until the price level is back to trend. Hence anticipations of high, future inflation lower the real interest rate during the liquidity trap and lift up current output and inflation. To put it differently, an explicit (institutional) price-level targeting regime makes future inflation credible—that is, it solves the credibility problem faced by forward guidance policies under the inflation targeting regime.

The main limitation of price-level targeting is that, while it would certainly be helpful during liquidity traps, it is very constraining for the central bank *in normal times*. To understand this, observe that, in the inflation targeting regime, a temporary surge in inflation, eventually tamed by the central bank, leaves a permanently higher price *level* about which the central bank does not need to care.

In contrast, after the same temporary increase in inflation, the price-level targeting regime requires the central bank to engineer a contraction in inflation (which may even lead to an outright deflation) as long as the price level has not returned to target. Overall, it seems doubtful that the benefits of this regime in terms of commitment capacity (during liquidity trap episodes) are sufficient to offset the costs of this regime in terms of flexibility (in normal times). The price-level targeting regime does not therefore seem to constitute a serious alternative to the inflation targeting regime.

9.4   EXERCISES

9.4.1   PREDETERMINED PRICES AND OPTIMAL POLICY AT THE ZERO LOWER BOUND

This problem revisits the issue of the credibility of forward guidance using the form of nominal price rigidities introduced in section 6.3.1 of chapter 6. The natural level of output is normalized to zero, so output y_t and the output gap are the same. The AS curve relates y_t to the difference between *actual* inflation and *rationally expected* inflation:

$$\pi_t = \pi_{t-1,t}^e + \kappa y_t, \text{ with } \kappa > 0 \text{ and } \pi_{t-1,t}^e = \mathbb{E}_{t-1}(\pi_t). \tag{9.4}$$

Moreover, the IS curve relates output and the real interest rate r_t as follows:

$$y_t = \theta_t - r_t, \tag{9.5}$$

where r_t is given by

$$r_t = i_t - \pi_{t,t+1}^e. \tag{9.6}$$

Finally, we assume that the instantaneous loss function of the central bank is given by

$$L_t = y_t^2 + \pi_t^2, \tag{9.7}$$

and its intertemporal loss by

$$L = L_1 + L_2.$$

The central bank is assumed to perfectly control inflation (via its action on the real interest rate, and thereby on the AS-AD equilibrium) except in situations of liquidity trap; in such situations, the nominal interest rate is equal to zero (its lower bound) and the central bank loses control of current inflation.

Let us assume that private agents were anticipating an inflation rate of $\pi_{0,1}^e = 0$ for period 1. However, in period 1 a negative aggregate demand shock $\theta_1 < 0$ occurs, which is sufficiently strong to push the economy into the liquidity trap. This shock is transitory; the economy exits the liquidity trap in period 2, and this is perfectly anticipated by private agents and the central bank as of period 1.

1. Explain intuitively equations (9.4) to (9.7).

2. Under discretion the central bank minimizes its instantaneous loss L_t in every period, taking inflation expectations as given. Assuming that private agents anticipate this behavior on the part of the central bank,

- Compute the levels of output and inflation $(\hat{y}_t, \hat{\pi}_t)$ at times $t = 1, 2$ under discretion and provide an interpretation of your results. (Hint: Start with period 2.)

- Infer the realized value of the intertemporal loss under discretion $(\hat{L})$.

3. Now assume that the central bank announces at time $t = 1$ the inflation rate that it will set at time $t = 2$. Assuming that private agents trust the central bank and the central bank keeps its promise,

- Compute the corresponding levels of output and inflation (y_t^*, π_t^*), $t = 1, 2$ and explain intuitively why these values differ from $(\hat{y}_t, \hat{\pi}_t)$, $t = 1, 2$. (Hint: L_1 and L_2 are no longer independent.)

- Infer the realized value of the intertemporal loss under commitment (L^*).

4. Prove formally that the equilibrium (y_t^*, π_t^*), $t = 1, 2$, is more efficient than $(\hat{y}_t, \hat{\pi}_t)$, $t = 1, 2$, but not time consistent.

9.4.2 FORWARD GUIDANCE IN A MULTIPERIOD LIQUIDITY TRAP

Consider the following economy. Natural output is normalized to zero, so the output gap y_t and actual output are the same. The IS curve is given by

$$\mathbf{IS} : y_t = \hat{\theta}_t - r_t,$$

where r_t is the real interest rate and $\hat{\theta}_t$ and exogenous demand parameter. Following Ball (2008), assume that the AS curve has the following form:

$$\mathbf{AS} : \pi_t = \pi_t^* + \kappa y_t, \ \kappa < 1,$$

with

$$\pi_t^* = \max\{\pi_{t-1}, 0\}.$$

The AS curve implies that when the economy is in deflation at time t ($\pi_t < 0$), then the output gap at time $t+1$ (y_{t+1}) determines the inflation rate at that time (π_{t+1}) and not the *variation* in the inflation rate ($\pi_{t+1} - \pi_t$). We assume that the demand parameter $\hat{\theta}$ is zero until period $t = T_1 - 1$, takes the constant value $\hat{\theta} < 0$ from period $t = T_1$ to period $t = T_2$ (inclusive), and then reverts to $\hat{\theta}_t = 0$ for all $t > T_2$. This aggregate demand shock is strong enough to push the economy into the liquidity trap during the time interval $[T_1, T_2]$, but the economy gets out of the trap at time $T_2 + 1$. The central bank announces at time T_1 that it will adopt a highly accommodative monetary policy at time $T_2 + 1$, consisting of implementing the inflation rate $\check{\pi} > 0$. This policy is assumed to be credible; hence it is the inflation rate that private agents expect will prevail then. Show that output at the time the economy enters the liquidity trap is given by

$$y_{T_1} = \left(\frac{1 - \kappa^{T_2 - T_1 + 1}}{1 - \kappa} \right) \hat{\theta} + \kappa^{T_2 - T_1} \check{\pi},$$

and provide a discussion of this result.

FISCAL POLICY AND STRUCTURAL REFORMS IN A LIQUIDITY TRAP

> I pledge you, I pledge myself, to a new deal for the American people. Let us all here assembled constitute ourselves prophets of a new order of competence and courage
> —Franklin D. Roosevelt (1932)

In this chapter, we examine the effects in a liquidity trap of economic policies other than monetary policy: *fiscal policy,* on the one hand, and *structural reforms* on the other. Both types of policies have been the subject of much discussion in the recent years. In the United States the paralysis of conventional monetary policy during the Great Recession and the uncertainty surrounding the effectiveness of unconventional monetary policy have immediately led policy makers to shift their attention toward fiscal policy.[1] It was even argued that, somewhat paradoxically, the liquidity trap could in fact make the impact of some forms of fiscal stimulus *stronger* than in normal times.[2] The first objective of this chapter is to understand why this can be the case and to evaluate which type of fiscal stimulus is likely to be most effective in this situation.

Fiscal policy was less of an option in the euro area, due to the important size of public debts in many countries prior to the Great Recession and the tight constraints

---

1. Christina Romer recalls her first encounter with (then) President Obama, just before her appointment as president of the Council of Economic Advisers, in these terms: "The very first meeting I ever had with the President-Elect was on exactly this topic ... . The President-Elect began the discussion by saying that the economy was very sick and there was not much more the Fed could do—so we needed to use fiscal policy" (Romer 2011).

2. This point was notably made by Eggertsson (2010b), Christiano, Eichenbaum, and Rebelo (2011), and Woodford (2011). It found some empirical support recently in the work of Ramey and Zubairy (2018).

on fiscal deficits imposed by the Stability and Growth Pact.[3] In that region the debate instead revolved around the desirability of implementing *structural reforms* aimed at intensifying competition in the goods and labor markets and thereby raising potential output and growth. The second objective of this chapter is to analyze how such structural reforms affect aggregate demand and supply in a liquidity trap, and ultimately whether or not we should expect them to be effective at mitigating its contractionary impact.

We explained in chapter 7 why the effects of fiscal policies could not be properly studied without a fully specified general-equilibrium framework—that is, a framework that specifies all the flows of resources and expenditures between the agents (including the government) as well as the optimal responses of private agents to fiscal policy. This remains equally valid here, so we shall use the same general-equilibrium framework, extended to allow for a situation where the zero lower bound on the short-term nominal interest rate is binding (section 10.1). We then use this framework to recompute the value of the various fiscal multipliers (government spending, income tax, and VAT multipliers) in the liquidity trap (section 10.2). Finally, we use it to study the effects of structural reforms in a liquidity trap (section 10.3). As we shall see, the impact of alternative fiscal policies and structural reforms usually depends on two key factors: the *persistence* of the policy under consideration and the *pervasiveness of financing constraints*—as measured by the share of Keynesian consumers in the economy.

10.1 THE GENERAL-EQUILIBRIUM AS-AD MODEL AT THE ZERO LOWER BOUND

The present chapter builds on the analysis of chapter 7 (section 7.2) and extends it to a situation where the zero lower bound is binding. It also extends it to make room for two additional macroeconomic shocks:

- A (negative) shock to households' rate of time preference ρ, now indexed by time: ρ_t. This shock will act as a transitory, negative shock to aggregate demand since it makes all households more patient and thus causes a decline in the consumption demand of Ricardian households (see chapter 2).[4] Moreover, we

---

3. According to this pact, countries belonging to the European Union should not let their fiscal deficit be larger than 3 percent of GDP.

4. Equivalently, one could assume that it is a rise in the credit spread (see chapter 8) that triggers the negative demand shock causing the economy to enter the liquidity trap. The two shocks are formally equivalent here, while assuming a discount-rate shock saves on notations.

assume for simplicity that ρ_t is equal to its long-run value $\rho > 0$ in every period except in period t, where ρ_t falls below ρ sufficiently to push the economy into the liquidity trap. In period $t+1$ this aggregate demand shock completely reverts, and the economy leaves the liquidity trap.

- A (negative) shock to the optimal markup rate of firms (now also time indexed: μ_t^*), which we will interpret in the broad sense as a deregulation of the goods market. Because we allow this markup to vary we must abandon the normalization of chapter 7 (i.e., $z_t = \xi \mu^*$). Labor productivity, for its part, is assumed to be constant at z.

The following presentation is succinct, because the general-equilibrium AS-AD model used in the present chapter is just a generalization of the framework introduced in chapter 7. It is thus advisable to have the material of chapter 7 well in mind before reading what comes next.

10.1.1 THE GOVERNMENT AND THE CENTRAL BANK

The government has the same menu of fiscal policies as in chapter 7: it can raise government spending g_t (above its long-run value $g_\infty = 0$) or cut the income tax rate τ_t^l or the VAT rate τ_t^c, either temporarily or permanently. In doing so the government must satisfy its intertemporal budget constraint, which may require some adjustments in the lump-sum taxes paid by Ricardian households. For simplicity we will also assume in this chapter that an increase in government spending or a temporary tax cut have no persistence at all. This implies that $g_{t+1} = g_\infty = 0$ and also that $\tau_{t+1}^l = \tau_\infty^l$ and $\tau_{t+1}^c = \tau_\infty^c$, whether the corresponding tax cut be permanent or temporary.

Since the economy is in a liquidity trap in period t, the central bank has no influence on the real interest rate at that time and the latter is simply given by equation (8.4) in chapter 8. To simplify the exposition, we assume here (without loss of generality) that the term premium φ is zero. Thus, the real interest rate of period t is given by

$$r_t = -\pi_{t+1}.$$

On the other hand, since the economy leaves the liquidity trap in period $t+1$, the central bank is able to implement the interest rate it wishes from that period onward. We will assume, just like in chapter 7, that the central bank then adopts the monetary policy of equalizing the real interest rate r_t to the rate of time preference:

$$r_{t+k} = \rho, \quad \text{for all } k \geq 1. \tag{10.1}$$

10.1.2 HOUSEHOLDS AND FIRMS

Just as in the general-equilibrium AS-AD model of chapter 7, there is a share $1 - v$ of identical Ricardian households (where $0 \leq v < \xi$ and $\xi < 1$ is the labor supply elasticity parameter) and a complementary share v of identical Keynesian households. The key difference with the system (CK)–(MC) in chapter 7 is that the real interest rate may not be equal to ρ in period t—hence we cannot readily eliminate r_t in the intertemporal optimality condition of Ricardian households. Rather, using the first-order condition (7.11) of chapter 7 in periods t and $t+1$ to eliminate the Lagrange multiplier Λ_t, turning the resulting expression into log and rearranging, we get the following version of the Keynes-Ramsey rule for these households:

$$c_t^R = c_{t+1}^R + \rho_t - r_t + \tau_{t+1}^C - \tau_t^C. \tag{10.2}$$

The dependence of the slope of the consumption profile $(c_{t+1}^R - c_t^R)$ on the real interest rate (r_t) was explained in chapter 2, and its dependence on changes in VAT rates $(\tau_{t+1}^C - \tau_t^C)$ was explained in chapter 7. The new element here is the rate of time preference. When ρ_t falls, so that households become more patient in period t, Ricardian households consume less and save more, which raises the slope of their consumption profile. The other choices of the households (i.e., the consumption demand of Keynesian households and the labor supplies of Keynesian and Ricardian households) are described by the same equations as in chapter 7.

10.1.3 AS-AD EQUILIBRIUM

The AS-AD model, under the assumptions discussed above, is derived in the appendix of this chapter. The AS curve takes the usual form:

$$\textbf{AS} : \pi_t = \pi_{t-1} + \kappa \left(y_t - y_t^n \right), \tag{10.3}$$

where natural output y_t^n is here given by

$$y_t^n = z - \xi(\mu_t^* + \tau_t^C + \tau_t^l - g_t). \tag{10.4}$$

Equation (10.4) is similar to equation (7.22) in chapter 7, except for the fact that z_t is no longer tied to $\xi \mu_t^*$.

On the other hand, the AD curve is given by

$$\textbf{AD} : y_t = \underbrace{y_\infty + \xi \left(\frac{1-v}{\xi - v} \right) (\rho_t + \tau_\infty^C - \tau_t^C + g_t)}_{=\hat{\theta}_t} + \xi \left(\frac{1-v}{\xi - v} \right) \pi_t, \tag{10.5}$$

where y_∞ is *long-run output* and is given by

$$y_\infty = z - \xi(\mu_\infty^* + \tau_\infty^l + \tau_\infty^c). \tag{10.6}$$

The AD curve in equation (10.5) is a special case of the more general AD curve of chapter 8, with the demand parameter $\hat{\theta}_t$ now being endogenous to the fiscal variables as well as to ρ_t.

The effects of the various variables appearing on the right side of equation (10.5) are intuitive. The term ρ_t reflects the degree of impatience of the households. When ρ_t falls, Ricardian households value future consumption more, so they save more and consume less in the current period; this causes aggregate demand to fall. The term y_∞ reflects Ricardian households' willingness to smooth consumption over time and their implied permanent-income behavior (see chapter 2)—the higher the long-term level of output y_∞, the more Ricardian households want to increase their consumption already at time t, and this tends to raise aggregate demand. The terms $\tau_\infty^c - \tau_t^c$ and g_t reflect the effects of fiscal policy. A reduction in current VAT τ_t^c relative to future VAT τ_∞^c stimulates current consumption (since it increases the relative price of goods consumed in the future) and hence current aggregate demand and output. An increase in public expenditure g_t directly stimulates aggregate demand. Finally, we maintain our assumption that in the (y, π) plane the slope of the AD curve $(= (\xi - \upsilon)/\xi(1 - \upsilon))$ is strictly greater than that of the AS curve (κ) (see condition (8.16) in chapter 8 and the discussion therein). In the present case this boils down to the following parameter restriction, which we will assume to hold henceforth:

$$\frac{\kappa\xi(1 - \upsilon)}{\xi - \upsilon} < 1. \tag{10.7}$$

This condition is satisfied, provided that neither κ nor υ are too large while ξ is not too small.

10.2 FISCAL POLICY IN A LIQUIDITY TRAP

In this section, we formally study the effects of alternatives fiscal policies in a liquidity trap. We therefore ignore macroeconomic shocks except for the discount-rate shock that sends the economy into the trap. In particular, the optimal markup rate is held constant, so we can adopt same normalization as in chapter 7 to simplify the expressions:

$$z = \xi\mu^*.$$

Let us recall again the thought experiment that is performed here to compute the values of the various fiscal multipliers. We assume that the economy was in its long-run equilibrium at time $t - 1$ (where $\pi_{t-1} = g_{t-1} = 0$ and $y_{t-1} = y_\infty$), and that an aggregate demand shock $\rho_t < \rho$ brings the economy into a liquidity trap at time t (but only for that period). We then examine how changing government spending or taxes affects the equilibrium at time t.

10.2.1 THE GOVERNMENT-SPENDING MULTIPLIER

To isolate the effect of government spending, we abstract from fiscal distortions and thus assume that all proportional taxes (τ_t^c and τ_t^l) are zero at all times (government spending is therefore financed entirely through lump-sum taxes).

Under our assumptions, the AS-AD system (equations (10.3)–(10.5) above) becomes

$$\mathbf{AD}: y_t = \frac{\xi (1 - \upsilon)}{\xi - \upsilon} \left(\rho_t + g_t + \pi_t \right),$$

$$\mathbf{AS}: \pi_t = \kappa \left(y_t - \xi g_t \right).$$

From these expressions, the impact of a government-spending shock of size dg_t on inflation and output is such that:

$$dy_t = \frac{\xi (1 - \upsilon)}{\xi - \upsilon} \left(dg_t + d\pi_t \right) \quad \text{and} \quad d\pi_t = \kappa \left(dy_t - \xi dg_t \right),$$

from which we can compute the government-spending multiplier:

$$\frac{dy_t}{dg_t} = \frac{\xi (1 - \upsilon) (1 - \kappa \xi)}{\xi (1 - \kappa) - \upsilon (1 - \kappa \xi)} \quad (> 1),$$

where the denominator is positive under our maintained assumption that condition (10.7) holds.

This multiplier is large in the sense that it is strictly greater than the corresponding multiplier outside the liquidity trap, which was itself no less than 1 (see the second row of Table 7.1 in chapter 7). The multiplier can even be considerably higher than 1; this notably occurs when the denominator $\xi (1 - \kappa) - \upsilon (1 - \kappa \xi)$ gets closer to zero, or, put differently, when the slope of the AD curve ($= (\xi - \upsilon) / \xi (1 - \upsilon)$ in the (y, π) plane) gets close to that of the AS curve ($= \kappa$). Importantly, the multiplier increases with the share of Keynesian consumers υ (which was also the case out of the liquidity trap).

We have already discussed at some length in chapter 7, for an economy *outside* the liquidity trap, how the government-spending shock was propagated through the endogenous adjustment of the consumption demands of Ricardian and Keynesian consumers. In particular, in the presence of Keynesian consumers, a feedback loop between rising real wages and rising consumption arises that magnifies the impact of the fiscal stimulus. The reason why the multiplier is still greater in a liquidity trap comes from the impact of government spending on inflation. By creating inflationary pressures at time t, government spending raises inflation at time $t + 1$ (since inflation is persistent), which reduces the real interest rate at time t and thus *further boosts the consumption of Ricardian households*. This effect operates in addition to the direct effect of government spending on aggregate demand as well as the indirect effect due to the feedback loop between the real wage and *Keynesian* households' consumption. To summarize, the size of the government-spending multiplier in a liquidity trap ultimately results from three effects:

- the direct effect of the rise in government spending;

- a feedback loop ("feedback loop #1") between the real wage and the consumption demand of Keynesian households, already studied in chapter 7;

- a feedback loop ("feedback loop #2") between inflation, the real interest rate, and the consumption demand of Ricardian households, which is specific to the liquidity trap.

To disentangle these effects and their potential interactions, it is useful to decompose the government-spending multiplier in a liquidity trap as follows:

$$\frac{\mathrm{d}y_t}{\mathrm{d}g_t} = \underbrace{\underbrace{1}_{\text{direct effect}} + \underbrace{\upsilon\left(\frac{1-\xi}{\xi-\upsilon}\right)}_{\text{feedback loop \#1 (>0)}}}_{\text{normal-time multiplier (see Chap. 7)}} + \underbrace{\frac{\kappa\,(1-\xi)}{1-\kappa}}_{\text{feedback loop \#2 (>0)}}$$

$$+ \underbrace{\upsilon\left\{\frac{(1-\xi)^2\,\xi\kappa}{(1-\kappa)\,(\xi-\upsilon)\,[\xi\,(1-\kappa)-\upsilon\,(1-\kappa\xi)]}\right\}}_{\text{interaction between the two feedback loops (>0)}}.$$

Let us examine the various terms of this decomposition one by one. The first term is the direct effect of the government spending shock. The second term measures the effect of the first feedback loop (working through Keynesian households' consumption), abstracting from the second (due to the liquidity trap). The first two terms thus give the government-spending multiplier in normal times (i.e., out of the liquidity trap) computed in chapter 7, which is equal to 1 in the absence of Keynesian consumers but is strictly greater than 1 in their presence (see Table 7.1). The third term of the decomposition measures the effect of the second feedback loop (due to the liquidity trap), abstracting from the first feedback loop (due to the presence of Keynesian households). So if we add the first and third terms in the right-hand side of the equation we obtain the government-spending multiplier *in the liquidity trap without Keynesian households* $(= (1 - \xi\kappa) / (1 - \kappa))$. Note that even in this simple scenario the government-spending multiplier is strictly greater than 1 (since $\xi < 1$); in other words, either feedback loop (#1 or #2) is enough to push the government-spending multiplier above 1. In general we should expect the two feedback loops to be operative, and this even gives rise to a fourth term reflecting the interactions between the two feedback loops. Under condition (10.7) and with $v > 0$, this term is strictly positive, reflecting the fact that *the two feedback loops tend to reinforce each other*.

Figure 10.1 shows the impact of a government-spending shock in a liquidity trap in the (y, π) plane, distinguishing the case without (a) and with (b) Keynesian consumers. The government-spending shock moves the AD curve to the right (this is the *aggregate demand effect* of the shock) and the AS curve downward (this is the *aggregate supply effect*, due to the rise in households' labor supply). In both cases, the joint effect of these shifts is a northeast translation of the equilibrium toward higher output and inflation.[5] The presence of the Keynesian consumers lowers the slope of the AD curve in the (y, π) plane, hence taking it closer to the slope of the AS curve (the slope is 1 when $v = 0$ but somewhere between $\kappa < 1$ and 1 when $v > 0$). Consequently, the equilibrium shifts more in the presence of Keynesian consumers.

10.2.2 THE TAX MULTIPLIERS

We now examine the effects of a change in the proportional tax rates τ_t^l and τ_t^c on the equilibrium in a liquidity trap. Thus we shut down government spending (i.e., $g_t = 0$) and assume that the government inherits at time t some quantity of public debt—some of which is financed through proportional taxes (τ_t^c, τ_t^l)—so that we can actually operate a cut in these taxes (financed through a rise in lump-sum taxes). A *transitory tax cut* is a downward shift in τ_t^c or τ_t^l that leaves the values of τ_{t+k}^c, τ_{t+k}^l, $k \geq 1$, unchanged, while a *permanent tax cut* is downward shift in all the τ_{t+k}^cs or τ_{t+k}^ls by the same amount for all $k \geq 0$.

From equations (10.3)–(10.6), in the absence of government spending (and our normalization for z) the AS-AD equilibrium becomes:

$$\mathbf{AS} : \pi_t = \pi_{t-1} + \kappa \left(y_t - y_t^n \right),$$

$$\mathbf{AD} : y_t = \hat{\theta}_t + \xi \left(\frac{1 - v}{\xi - v} \right) \pi_t,$$

where the supply and demand shifters y_t^n and $\hat{\theta}_t$ are given by

---

5. By checking the intercepts of the two curves in the (y, π) plane, one can verify that the AS curve never moves so much as to cause a drop in inflation following the shock.

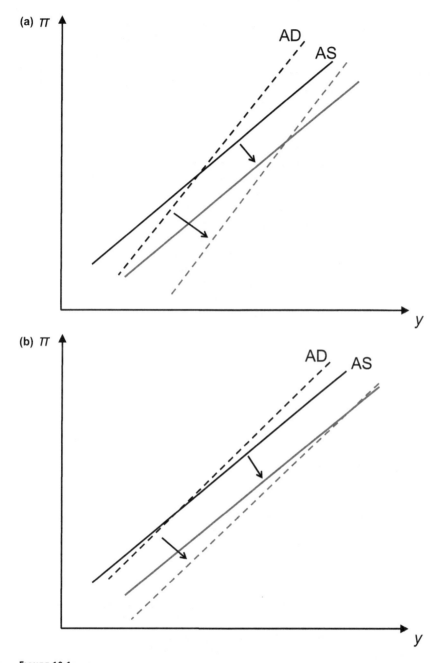

FIGURE 10.1
Impact of a rise in government spending in a liquidity trap (a) without Keynesian households and (b) with Keynesian households. Government spending raises aggregate demand directly, and also indirectly, via its impact on inflation; as a result, the government spending multiplier is greater than 1. This expansionary effect is even greater in the presence of Keynesian households.

$$y_t^n = -\xi(\tau_t^c + \tau_t^l) \text{ and } \hat{\theta}_t = -\xi\left(\tau_\infty^l + \tau_\infty^c\right) + \xi\left(\frac{1-\upsilon}{\xi-\upsilon}\right)(\rho_t + \tau_\infty^c - \tau_t^c).$$

Just as in chapter 7, a cut in proportional taxes has both aggregate demand and supply effects—it shifts both the AD curve (through $\hat{\theta}_t$) and the AS curve (through y_t^n). On the *demand* side, the consumption demand of Ricardian households is directly affected by the slope of the VAT profile $\tau_\infty^c - \tau_t^c$ (which alters the price of current consumption relative to future consumption) and also by the long-run level of taxes $(\tau_\infty^c + \tau_\infty^l)$, which affects permanent income $y_\infty = -\xi(\tau_\infty^c + \tau_\infty^l)$ and feeds back to current consumption demand. On the *supply* side, current taxation $(\tau_t^c + \tau_t^l)$ influences the incentive to work and thereby natural output y_t^n.

10.2.2.1   IMPACT OF A TEMPORARY INCOME TAX CUT

The first paradoxical effect of taxation in a liquidity trap is that *a transitory cut in income tax has a negative effect on output*.[6] Since long-run taxes do not change, the total differentiation of the AS and AD curves above gives us:

$$d\pi_t = \kappa\left(dy_t + \xi d\tau_t^l\right) \text{ and } dy_t = \xi\left(\frac{1-\upsilon}{\xi-\upsilon}\right)d\pi_t,$$

from which we get:

$$\frac{dy_t}{d\tau_t^l} = \frac{\xi^2\kappa(1-\upsilon)}{\xi(1-\kappa)-\upsilon(1-\xi\kappa)},$$

so that output and the tax rate move in the same direction.

This negative effect of a transitory tax cut is yet another manifestation of the *paradox of toil* discussed in chapter 8. Indeed, as the income tax rate falls, the incentive to work rises and so does the labor supply of Ricardian households. This exerts a downward pressure on the equilibrium real wage, lowers current and future inflation, and ultimately raises the real interest rate and lowers aggregate demand. While Keynesian households consume any additional unit of disposable income, the general-equilibrium fall in the real wage dominates the direct effect of the tax cut on that income, so their consumption demand also falls; this reinforces the downward pressure on the real wage, hence on their consumption demand, and so on. The presence of Keynesian households thus reinforces the deflationary spiral that is set in motion after the tax cut.[7]

---

6. This paradoxical effect was highlighted by Eggertsson and Woodford (2006) and Eggertsson (2010b).

7. It is easy to verify that the multiplier becomes larger in absolute value when υ rises.

Here again, it is useful to decompose this multiplier in order to track the overall effect of the policy to its fundamental determinants. We obtain:

$$\frac{dy_t}{d\tau_t^l} = \underset{\uparrow}{0} + \underbrace{\frac{\xi\kappa}{1-\kappa}}_{\text{feedback loop \#2 (>0)}} + \upsilon \underbrace{\left\{ \frac{\xi\kappa(1-\xi)}{[\xi(1-\kappa)-\upsilon(1-\xi\kappa)](1-\kappa)} \right\}}_{\substack{\text{interaction between the two feedback}\\ \text{loops (> 0)}}}.$$

$$\underset{\text{normal-time multiplier}}{}$$

We already know from the analysis of chapter 7 that the first feedback loop is inoperative in normal times after a transitory cut in income tax (the multiplier was zero, regardless of the number of Keynesian consumers; see Table 7.1). What is interesting here is that the first feedback loop *starts mattering when it interacts with the second one*, which is specific to the liquidity trap (since it works through the impact of inflation on the real interest rate). Absent the first feedback loop, we would still have a negative effect of the tax cut due to the second feedback loop, but just like in the case of government spending the interaction between the two feedback loops tends to magnify their individual effects (to be clear, in a liquidity trap, a temporary income tax cut depresses output *more* in the presence of Keynesian households that in their absence).

Figure 10.2(a) and 10.2(b) illustrate these adjustments in the (y, π) plane. The AS curve has a slope equal to κ. In the absence of Keynesian consumers, the AD curve has a slope equal to 1 $(> \kappa)$. The tax cut causes an increase in natural output (of size $\xi d\tau_t^l$) and thus a downward shift of the AS curve (of length $\kappa\xi d\tau_t^l$). Given the slopes of the AS and AD curves, the shift in the AS curve drags the equilibrium (y_t, π_t) along the AD curve in the southeast direction, with the effect of lowering both y_t and π_t (see figure 10.2(a)). The presence of Keynesian households takes the slope of the AD curve closer to that of the AS curve and thus magnifies the shift of the equilibrium (see figure 10.2(b)).

10.2.2.2 IMPACT OF A PERMANENT INCOME TAX CUT

Let us now turn to the macroeconomic effect of a *permanent* cut in income tax (i.e., such that $d\tau_\infty^l = d\tau_t^l$). Total differencing the AS and AD curves above (taking into account the effect of the tax cut on the supply and demand shifters) gives us:

$$d\pi_t = \kappa(dy_t + \xi d\tau_t^l) \quad \text{and} \quad dy_t = -\xi d\tau_t^l + \xi \left(\frac{1-\upsilon}{\xi-\upsilon} \right) d\pi_t,$$

so that

$$\frac{dy_t}{d\tau_t^l} = -\xi \quad \text{and} \quad \frac{d\pi_t}{d\tau_t^l} = 0.$$

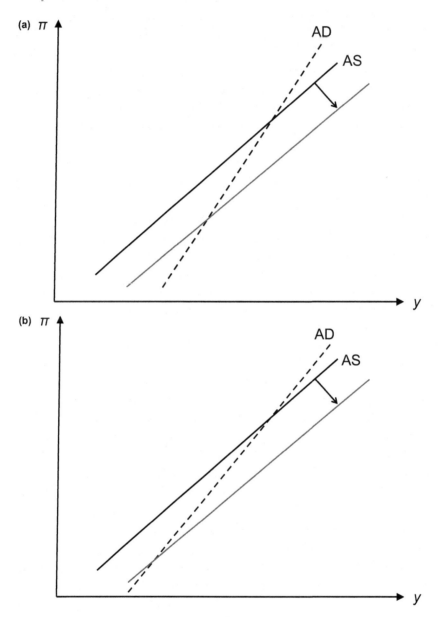

FIGURE 10.2
Impact of a transitory income tax cut in a liquidity trap (a) without Keynesian households and (b) with Keynesian households. The policy boosts labor supply, which lowers the real wage and aggravates the deflationary spiral. The situation is even worse in the presence of Keynesian households.

In other words, a permanent cut in income tax $(d\tau_t^l < 0)$ *successfully lifts up output* $(dy_t = -\xi d\tau_t^l)$ while leaving inflation unchanged. The key difference between a transitory and a permanent cut in income tax is that the latter raises long-run output y_∞ in addition to raising current natural output y_t^n. While the rise in natural output could generate a paradox-of-toil deflationary feedback loop, the rise in long-run output raises the consumption demand of Ricardian households sufficiently to neutralize this loop.

The impact of a permanent cut in income tax is exactly the same as in normal times (see chapter 7), and in both cases the impact is the same whether there are Keynesian households in the economy or not. This is essentially saying that the two feedback loops that were activated with government-spending shocks and transitory income tax cuts are inoperative here.

The expansionary effect of a permanent tax cut is illustrated on figure 10.3. The effect on the AS curve is the same as in the case of a transitory cut in income tax. On the other hand, the fact that the tax cut is permanent causes an expansion in

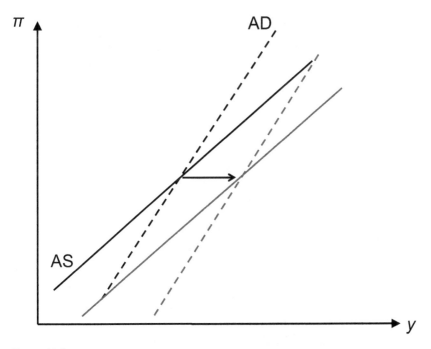

FIGURE 10.3

Impact of a permanent income tax cut in a liquidity trap. The policy boosts labor supply and lowers the real wage (which is deflationary) but also boosts aggregate demand (which is inflationary). In equilibrium, inflation is unchanged, but output rises.

aggregate demand so that the AD curve shifts rightward. The joint shifts of the AS and AD curves causes output to rise, with no effect on inflation.

While this result on the impact of permanent income tax cuts seems to pave the way for an effective expansionary fiscal policy in the liquidity trap, its scope should not be exaggerated. Indeed, in order to theoretically isolate the effects of a cut in income tax independently of any other consideration, we have implicitly assumed that it was entirely financed by an increase in lump-sum taxes. In practice, lump-sum taxes are virtually nonexistent, so a permanent cut in income tax would in practice have to be financed either by a permanent increase in VAT or by a permanent decrease in government spending. A permanent increase in VAT would offset at least some the effect of the lower income tax —since both taxes change long-run output in the same way—while a fall in government spending would depress current aggregate demand and output. Either way, the strong expansionary effect of the permanent cut in income tax would be dampened.

10.2.2.3   IMPACT OF A TEMPORARY CUT IN VAT

We turn now to the only tax policy that seems *both effective from a theoretical point of view and easily implementable in practice: a transitory cut in VAT* (i.e., such that $d\tau^c < 0$ but $d\tau^c_\infty = 0$).[8] The AS-AD curves tell us that such a policy has a powerful effect on output in a liquidity trap. Again, total differencing the AS and AD curves and taking into account the shifts in $\hat{\theta}_t$ and y^n_t, we find the corresponding multiplier to be

$$\frac{dy_t}{d\tau^c_t} = -\frac{\xi\,(1-\upsilon)\,(1-\kappa\xi)}{\xi\,(1-\kappa)-\upsilon\,(1-\xi\kappa)}.$$

Thus, no only does a fall in τ^c_t raise output, but the multiplier effect is potentially large—it is exactly same as that associated with an increase in government spending. The reason for this similarity is as follows. On the demand side, a transitory cut in VAT boosts the consumption demands of both Ricardian households (by lowering the cost of current consumption relative to future consumption) and Keynesian households (by raising their disposable income). This initial rise in *private* demand then sets in motion the two feedback loops discussed above. On the supply side, the temporary cut in VAT increases labor supply, which tends to lower inflation.

Looking at the normal-time multiplier effect in chapter 7 (Table 7.1), we can again decompose the overall multiplier into the contributions of the two feedback loops:

---

8. This policy was initially suggested by Feldstein (2002) in the context of the Japanese liquidity trap and subsequently formalized by Eggertsson (2010b) in the context of the Great Recession (but in an economy without Keynesian consumers).

$$\frac{\mathrm{d}y_t}{\mathrm{d}\tau_t^c} = \underset{\uparrow}{-1} \quad \underbrace{-\upsilon\left(\frac{1-\xi}{\xi-\upsilon}\right)}_{} \quad \underbrace{-\frac{1-\kappa\xi}{1-\kappa}}_{} \quad \text{— interaction between loops.}$$

$$\underbrace{\text{direct effect} \quad \text{feedback loop \#1} \quad \text{feedback loop \#2}}_{\text{normal-time multiplier}}$$

Graphically, a temporary cut in VAT shifts the AS and AD curves in exactly the same way as an increase in government spending (see figure 10.1). Here again, a greater share of Keynesian households tends to magnify the overall impact of the fiscal stimulus.

10.2.2.4 IMPACT OF A PERMANENT CUT IN VAT

It is easy to verify that a *permanent* cut in VAT has exactly the same effect on the equilibrium as a permanent cut in income tax (see figure 10.3 above). This is not surprising. First, the two policies move the long-run level of output $y_\infty = -\xi(\tau_\infty^l + \tau_\infty^c)$ in exactly the same way. Second, the permanent nature of the shock eliminates intertemporal substitution in consumption on the part of Ricardian households (since the relative price of goods at different points in time is left unchanged). And third, the impact on the disposable income, and thereby the consumption demand, of Keynesian households are the same as with an income tax cut.

10.2.3 UNCONVENTIONAL FISCAL POLICIES

10.2.3.1 TEMPORARY TAX SWAP

We have just studied the effects of changes in income tax and VAT separately. Can these changes in taxation be optimally combined to maximize their joint impact on output and employment during liquidity trap episodes? Correia et al. (2013) propose an original combination of tax policies that can effectively stimulate the economy in a liquidity trap, at zero cost for the fiscal authorities. They suggest to temporarily lower the VAT rate τ_t^c and to simultaneously raise the income tax rate τ_t^l to compensate the implied loss in government revenue. The transitory cut in VAT has the same expansionary effect as that illustrated in figure 10.4. At the same time, the transitory increase in income tax has the opposite effect to that described in figure 10.2. By discouraging labor supply and thus reducing the natural level of output, this policy generates inflationary pressures, which we know are beneficial in a liquidity trap. Thus, the *unconventional fiscal policy* of transitorily cutting the VAT rate and simultaneously raising the income tax rate optimally combines the aggregate demand and supply effects of taxation in a liquidity trap. This unconventional fiscal policy is depicted in figure 10.4.

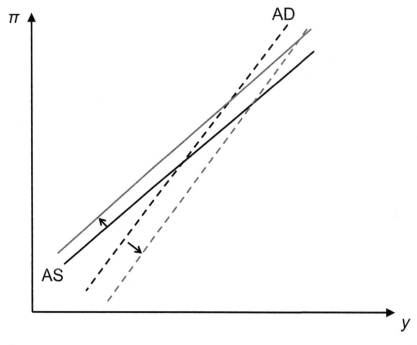

FIGURE 10.4
Impact of a temporary tax swap in a liquidity trap. A temporary cut in VAT financed by a transitory rise in income tax produces an expansion in aggregate demand and a contraction in aggregate supply, both of which contribute to boosting inflation and output.

10.2.3.2   HELICOPTER MONEY

In seeking to understand the short- and long-term effects of expansionary monetary policies, Milton Friedman (1969) proposed as a thought experiment a situation where a helicopter would throw banknotes to the population. If one wished to literally implement this experiment within the existing monetary institutions, one could imagine that the central bank would print banknotes and send them by mail to all households. But a simpler and formally equivalent mechanism exists provided that the treasury and the central bank are willing and able to coordinate their actions. The treasury reduces the taxes it collects from the households and finances the revenue shortfall by issuing an additional stock of public debt bought by the central bank and destined to be permanently rolled over, so that the treasury never actually pays it back. The term "helicopter money" is thus now referring to a monetization of the fiscal deficit to the benefits of the households. Although such a monetization was, before the crisis of 2008, considered taboo (at least in developed countries), this form of monetary-fiscal stimulus has made a comeback into the public debate due to the gradual exhaustion of the other unconventional policy options.

A helicopter drop is akin to a lump-sum transfer to households financed by public debt. If all the households were Ricardian, then the Ricardian equivalence would hold (see chapter 7, section 7.1), and this fiscal shock should be completely neutral (Krugman 1998). However, if there are Keynesian households in the economy, then the effect of the tax cut on their disposable income could in principle be expansionary (by raising their consumption demand). An important condition is that this tax cut be indeed lump-sum and not proportional to household income; otherwise it could worsen the recession by increasing the labor supply of Ricardian households (see our discussion above about the impact of a temporary income tax cut). But even in this case, it is unclear why a helicopter money drop would be preferable to a more standard cut in lump-sum taxes implemented by the government. In any case, the main issue with this policy is political and regulatory. The form of policy coordination between the treasury and the central bank that would be required to implement it likely goes well beyond what is allowed to most central banks, which are supposedly independent from the government.

10.3   STRUCTURAL REFORMS IN A LIQUIDITY TRAP

10.3.1   TEMPORARY AND PERMANENT STRUCTURAL REFORMS IN THE AS-AD MODEL

We conclude this chapter and the book by studying another manifestation of the paradox of toil—namely, the effect of structural reforms. In the most general sense, a structural reform is the elimination (be it temporary or permanent) of a source of economic inefficiency. The typical example of a structural reform in the goods market is the deregulation of a regulated profession (e.g., taxis, pharmacists, notaries, and so on), which tends to reduce the monopoly power and rents of incumbent firms. Such a reform can also increase labor productivity if new entrants use more efficient technologies, and even more so if they force existing firms to adopt those new technologies to survive. A basic microeconomic intuition tells us that such a reform, even temporary, is beneficial because it reduces the selling price of goods and increases the volume and quality of trades. This leads to an increase in consumer surplus, and possibly in the profits of new entrants, which more than offset the decline in profits incurred by incumbent firms.

Does this microeconomic intuition extend to the macroeconomic equilibrium? If we look at the natural equilibrium, it certainly does so—a fall in the optimal markup rate of size $\mathrm{d}\mu_t^*$ raises output by

$$\mathrm{d}y_t^n = -\xi\,\mathrm{d}\mu_t^* > 0.$$

However, in an economy with nominal rigidities that is stuck in a liquidity trap, this intuition extends only under certain conditions. To evaluate the macroeconomic effects of a structural reforms in a liquidity trap, let us use the AS-AD model again, abstracting from variations in fiscal variables. From equations (10.3) to (10.6) it is apparent that a *permanent* cut in μ_t^* shifts y_t^n and $\hat{\theta}_t$ in exactly the same way as a permanent cut in income tax or VAT. Therefore, it has the same macroeconomic effect on output and inflation. More specifically, a fall in the markup rate of size $d\mu_t^*$ has multiplier effects of

Permanent reform : $\dfrac{dy_t}{d\mu_t^*} = \dfrac{dy_t^n}{d\mu_t^*} = \xi > 0$ and $\dfrac{d\pi_t}{dy_t^n} = 0.$

This expansionary impact of a structural reform does not extend to the case of a *temporary* reform, just as the impact of a permanent cut in income tax does not extend to the case of a temporary cut. In fact, the temporary nature of the reform *reverts* its effect on output, with a multiplier effect equal to that of a temporary income tax cut. This is because a structural reform that temporarily lowers the markup rate by $d\mu_t^*$ shifts natural output upward (by the amount $-\xi d\mu_t^*$) but does not change long-run output. Hence it shifts aggregate supply but not aggregate demand and therefore sets in motion the usual deflationary spiral between inflation and output. To be more specific, a temporary cut in firms' markup of size $d\mu_t^*$ has the following multiplier effect:

Temporary reform : $\dfrac{dy_t}{d\mu_t^*} = \dfrac{\xi^2 \kappa (1 - \upsilon)}{\xi (1 - \kappa) - \upsilon (1 - \xi\kappa)}$ and $\dfrac{d\pi_t}{d\mu_t^*} = \dfrac{\xi\kappa (\xi - \upsilon)}{\xi (1 - \kappa) - \upsilon (1 - \xi\kappa)},$

so that both output and inflation fall with μ_t^*.

It follows from this discussion that *a structural reform in a liquidity trap has very different effects depending on whether it is perceived as permanent or temporary*. This is represented in figure 10.5. A temporary reform only shifts the AS curve (downward), and the resulting deflationary spiral takes down output and inflation. A permanent reform also shifts the AD curve (rightward), which breaks this feedback loop and causes an expansion in output (with no effect on inflation).

We have just seen that once a structural reform is perceived as transitory—either because it is announced as such or (for example) because it is anticipated that lobby groups or political pressures will get it repealed—then it may become counterproductive and aggravate the economic crisis. For this reason, Eggertsson, Ferrero, and Raffo (2014) criticized the notion that structural reforms provide the appropriate recipe to get the euro area out of its economic slump.[9] In several countries in the euro area, resistance to reforms are strong and trust in politicians is limited. As a

---

9. The perception of the need for structural reform in Europe is well reflected in Manuel Baroso's speech in 2012, when he chaired the European Commission: "The biggest problem we have for growth in Europe is the problem of lack of competitiveness that has been accumulated in some of our Member States, and we need to make the reforms for that competitiveness .... to get out of this situation requires structural

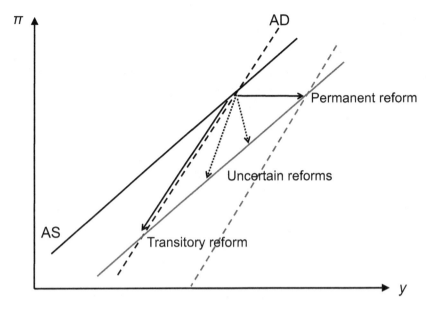

FIGURE 10.5
Impact of a structural reform in a liquidity trap. Structural reforms aimed at cutting markups always boost aggregate supply, but raise aggregate demand only to the extent that they are perceived as persistent.

result, although some reforms may be perceived as necessary and acceptable when the macroeconomic outlook is bleak, there is always a risk that they will be called into question once the outlook improves.

We can formally capture the risk of reversion of a structural reform by assigning a probability χ, $0 \leq \chi \leq 1$, to the fact that it will be maintained after time t. More specifically, suppose that the optimal markup rate was at its long-run value of μ_∞^* in period $t-1$ and is shifted by the amount $d\mu_t^*$ (<0) in period t, but is expected to return to μ_∞^* with probability $1-\chi$ in period $t+1$ (in which case it stays there forever). In this situation, natural output in period t is $y_t^n = z - \xi(\mu_\infty^* + d\mu_t^*)$ but *expected* long-run output $\mathbb{E}_t(y_\infty)$ shifts less than natural output:

$$\mathbb{E}_t(y_\infty) = z - \xi[\chi(\mu_\infty^* + d\mu_t^*) + (1-\chi)\mu_\infty^*]$$
$$= z - \xi(\mu_\infty^* + \chi d\mu_t^*).$$

Graphically, as the expected persistence of the reform falls, the AD curve moves less and less, and there is a critical value of χ below which the impact of the reform on output goes from positive to negative (see figure 10.5 again). Exercise 10.4.1 asks to compute the corresponding multipliers.

---

reforms, because there is an underlying problem of lack of competitiveness in some of our Member State" (cited by Eggertsson, Ferrero, and Raffo 2014).

10.3.2   THE NEW DEAL (1933–1937)

The negative effect of temporary structural reforms—or reforms that are perceived as such with high probability—illustrates the paradoxical nature of macroeconomic adjustments in a liquidity trap. This shows that economic policies that are *a priori* desirable in normal times can become harmful in times of major crisis. In the present case, the paradox of temporary structural reforms is perhaps even more striking when turned upside down. Since a temporary increase in the degree of competition turns out to be detrimental in a liquidity trap, is it not desirable, in this situation, to engineer a structural reform in the *opposite* direction—that is, to *temporarily reduce competition between firms and strengthen their market power?* In a fascinating study, Eggertsson (2012) argues that the expansionary effect of Franklin D. Roosevelt's (FDR's) New Deal in the United States between 1933 and 1937 was precisely due to the anticompetitive policies of the package. These policies were explicitly aimed at breaking the deflationary spiral of the Great Depression and as such were perceived as temporary. Although these anticompetitive policies were received with skepticism—if not outright hostility—by most economists at the time (starting with John Maynard Keynes), the implementation of the New Deal was followed by a cumulative growth of 40 percent of GDP between 1933 and 1937.

The AS-AD model offers a natural explanation for the expansionary effect of temporary anticompetitive policies in a liquidity trap. These policies increase the markup rate μ_t^* and thus lower the natural level of output y_t^n. The AS curve shifts upward, while the AD curve does not shift as long as the reform is seen as temporary. The equilibrium (y_t, π_t) is thus shifted northeast (see figure 10.6). This is just the mirror image of the paradox of toil: supply-side reforms that would be disastrous in normal times may become beneficial once the liquidity trap has turned the economy's mechanics upside down.

10.4   EXERCISES

10.4.1   IMPACT OF UNCERTAIN STRUCTURAL REFORMS

Compute analytically, under the assumptions of section 10.3, the effects on output $(dy_t/d\mu_t^*)$ and inflation $(d\pi_t/d\mu_t^*)$ of a structural reform that is expected to last beyond period t only with probability χ. Express the threshold value of χ below which structural reforms aggravate the recession as a function of the other parameters, and discuss the formula obtained.

10.4.2   IMPACT OF A DROP IN OIL PRICES IN A LIQUIDITY TRAP

1. Solve Exercise 4.5.2 in chapter 4 and infer the natural level of output in an economy that uses both labor and energy as productive inputs.

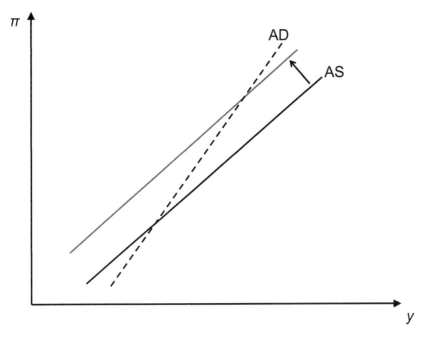

FIGURE 10.6
The New Deal, 1933-1937. By temporarily reducing competition and raising markups, the New Deal broke the deflationary spiral of the Great Depression and lifted inflation and output.

2. Oil prices have fallen dramatically between 2014 and 2016. Using the analytical framework of the present chapter, study graphically and analytically:

(a) the impact of a transitory drop in oil prices in a liquidity trap;

(b) the impact of a permanent drop in oil prices in a liquidity trap.

10.4.3   PROOF OF THE PARADOX OF THRIFT
Provide a formal proof of the paradox of thrift of chapter 8 by using the general-equilibrium model of the present chapter.

10.5 APPENDIX: DERIVATION OF THE GENERAL-EQUILIBRIUM AS-AD MODEL IN A LIQUIDITY TRAP

The derivation of the general-equilibrium AS-AD model used in this chapter follows the same steps as in section 7.2 of chapter 7, except for two additional complications. First, labor productivity z_t is not normalized to $\xi\mu_t^*$; second, and more importantly, the economy is in the liquidity trap in period t, so the real interest rate r_t in that period is $-\pi_{t+1}$. This means that we must first solve for the equilibrium in period $t+1$ (once the economy has left the liquidity trap) before computing the equilibrium in period t.

To solve the model, let us start with the same system of equation as in section 7.2 of chapter 7, except that equation (CR), which gives the consumption of a Ricardian household, is now given by equation (10.2):

$$c_t^K = w_t - p_t - \tau_t^l - \tau_t^c, \tag{CK}$$

$$c_t^R = c_{t+1}^R + \rho_t - r_t + \tau_{t+1}^c - \tau_t^c, \tag{CR}$$

$$l_t^R = \frac{\xi}{1-\upsilon}(w_t - p_t - z_t - \tau_t^c - \tau_t^l + g_t), \tag{LRb}$$

$$y_t = z + (1-\upsilon)l_t^R = \upsilon c_t^K + (1-\upsilon)c_t^R + g_t. \tag{MC}$$

Total labor demand by the firm sector is $l_t^d = y_t - z_t$ and equating it with the total supply $(1-\upsilon)l_t^R$ in (LRb) gives the real wage:

$$w_t - p_t = \xi^{-1}y_t + z\left(1 - \xi^{-1}\right) + \tau_t^c + \tau_t^l - g_t. \tag{RW}$$

The natural equilibrium is such that $p_t = w_t + \xi\mu_t^* - z_t$, so that $w_t - p_t = z_t - \mu_t^*$. Then, from equations (CK), (LRb), and (MC) we find the natural equilibrium to be

$$c_t^{Kn} = z - \mu_t^* - \tau_t^l - \tau_t^c, \tag{CKn}$$

$$c_t^{Rn} = z - \frac{(1-\xi)g_t + (\xi - \upsilon)\left(\mu_t^* + \tau_t^c + \tau_t^l\right)}{1-\upsilon}, \tag{CRn}$$

$$l_t^{Rn} = \frac{\xi}{1-\upsilon}(-\mu^* - \tau_t^c - \tau_t^l + g_t), \tag{LRn}$$

$$y_t^n = z - \xi\mu_t^* + \xi(g_t - \tau_t^c - \tau_t^l). \tag{MCn}$$

From the natural equilibrium we may compute the values of c_t^K and y_t in long-run equilibrium, which we are going to need later on:

$$c_\infty^R = z_\infty - \frac{(\xi - \upsilon)\left(\mu_\infty^* + \tau_\infty^C + \tau_\infty^l\right)}{1 - \upsilon} \quad \text{and} \quad y_\infty = z - \xi(\mu_\infty^* + \tau_\infty^C + \tau_\infty^l).$$

Aggregate demand is given by $y_t = (1 - \upsilon) c_t^R + \upsilon c_t^K + g_t$. From equations (CK) and (RW) above we can rewrite c_t^K as follows:

$$c_t^K = \xi^{-1} y_t + z\left(1 - \xi^{-1}\right) - g_t.$$

We compute c_t^R backward, by first computing c_{t+1}^R and then by substituting the resulting value into equation (CR). From period $t + 1$ onward we have $r = \rho$ in every period (the assumed monetary policy out of the liquidity trap). Iterating (CR) forward as of period $t + 1$ and then using (CR∞), we get:

$$c_{t+1}^R = c_{t+2}^R + \tau_{t+2}^C - \tau_{t+1}^C = c_{t+3}^R + \tau_{t+3}^C - \tau_{t+1}^C = \ldots = c_\infty^R + \underbrace{\tau_\infty^C - \tau_{t+1}^C}_{=0}$$

$$= z - \frac{(\xi - \upsilon)\left(\mu_\infty^* + \tau_\infty^C + \tau_\infty^l\right)}{1 - \upsilon}.$$

At the end of the first line we have $\tau_\infty^C - \tau_{t+1}^C = 0$, because we only consider tax shocks that are either permanent or purely temporary (in which case they occur in period t and are fully reverted in period $t + 1$); both cases imply $\tau_\infty^C = \tau_{t+1}^C$. Substituting the value of c_{t+1}^R in the latter equation into equation (CR), we get:

$$c_t^R = z - \frac{(\xi - \upsilon)\left(\mu_\infty^* + \tau_\infty^C + \tau_\infty^l\right)}{1 - \upsilon} + \rho_t - r_t + \tau_\infty^C - \tau_t^C,$$

where again we have used the fact that $\tau_\infty^C = \tau_{t+1}^C$.

In period t, when the economy is in the liquidity trap, we have $r_t = -\pi_{t+1}$, with π_{t+1} given by the AS($t+1$) curve:

$$\pi_{t+1} = \pi_t + \kappa\left(y_{t+1} - y_{t+1}^n\right).$$

Since all shocks are either purely transitory of permanent we have:

$$y_{t+1}^n = y_\infty = z_\infty - \xi \mu_\infty^* - \xi(\tau_\infty^C + \tau_\infty^l).$$

Moreover, from the AD curve of period $t+1$, which is given by equation (7.25) in chapter 7 with a one-period lead, we have:

$$
y_{t+1} = z - \xi\mu^*_{t+1} + \xi\left[\frac{(1-\upsilon)\left(g_{t+1} - \tau^C_{t+1}\right) + (1-\xi)\tau^C_\infty}{\xi - \upsilon}\right] - \xi\tau^I_\infty,
$$

$$
= z - \xi\mu^*_\infty - \xi\left(\tau^C_\infty + \tau^I_\infty\right),
$$

where we have used the fact that government-spending shocks are purely transitory (so that $g_{t+1} = 0$) while all the other shocks (on μ^*_t, τ^I_t, and τ^C_t) are either purely transitory or permanent (hence their value at $t+1$ is the same as that at infinity). From the last three equations we can infer that $\pi_{t+1} = \pi_t$, and hence we can replace r_t by $-\pi_t$ in the last expression for c^R_t. Aggregate demand is then given by:

$$
y_t = \upsilon\underbrace{\left[\xi^{-1}y_t + z_t\left(1 - \xi^{-1}\right) - g_t\right]}_{=c^K_t}
$$

$$
+ (1-\upsilon)\underbrace{\left[z - \frac{(\xi-\upsilon)\left(\mu^*_\infty + \tau^C_\infty + \tau^I_\infty\right)}{1-\upsilon} + \rho_t + \pi_t + \tau^C_\infty - \tau^C_t\right]}_{=c^R_t} + g_t
$$

$$
= \upsilon\xi^{-1}y_t + \left(1 - \upsilon\xi^{-1}\right)z - (\xi-\upsilon)\left(\mu^*_\infty + \tau^I_\infty\right) + (1-\xi)\tau^C_\infty + (1-\upsilon)\left(\rho_t - \tau^C_t + \pi_t + g_t\right)
$$

$$
= \underbrace{\left[z - \xi\left(\mu^*_\infty + \tau^I_\infty + \tau^C_\infty\right)\right]}_{= \, y_\infty \text{ in (MC}\infty)} + \frac{\xi(1-\upsilon)\tau^C_\infty + \xi(1-\upsilon)\left(\rho_t - \tau^C_t + \pi_t + g_t\right)}{\xi - \upsilon}
$$

$$
= y_\infty + \frac{\xi(1-\upsilon)}{\xi-\upsilon}\left(\rho_t + \tau^C_\infty - \tau^C_t + g_t + \pi_t\right).
$$

This is just the AD curve. The AS curve is easily derived following exactly the same steps as in chapters 3 and 7, with natural output now given by equation (CMn).

REFERENCES

Acconcia, A., G. Corsetti, and S. Simonelli. 2014. "Mafia and Public Spending: Evidence on the Fiscal Multiplier from a Quasi-Experiment."*American Economic Review* 104 (7): 2185–2209.

Agarwal, R., and M. Kimball. 2015. "Breaking through the Zero Lower Bound." IMF Working Paper No. 15/224, International Monetary Fund, Washington, DC, October 23.

Alesina A., and L. H. Summers. 1993. "Central Bank Independence and Macroeconomic Performance: Some Comparative Evidence." *Journal of Money, Credit and Banking* 25 (2): 151–162.

Alvarez, L. J., E. Dhyne, M. M. Hoeberichts, C. Kwapil, H. Le Bihan, et al. 2006. "Sticky Prices in the Euro Area: A Summary of New Micro-Evidence." *Journal of the European Economic Association* 4: 575–584.

Andrade, P., J. Breckenfelder, F. De Fiore, P. Karadi, and O. Tristani. 2016. "The ECB's Asset Purchase Programme: An Early Assessment." European Central Bank Discussion Paper No. 1956, European Central Bank, Frankfurt Am Main, Germany, September.

Backus, D., and J. Drifill. 1985. "Inflation and Reputation." *American Economic Review* 75: 530–538.

Ball, L. 1994. "What Determines the Sacrifice Ratio?" In *Monetary Policy*, edited by N. G. Mankiw, 155–193. Chicago, IL: University of Chicago Press.

Ball, L. M. 2014. "The Case for a Long-Run Inflation Target of Four Percent." IMF Working Paper No. 14/92, International Monetary Fund, Washington, DC, June 9.

Barattieri, A., S. Basu, and P. Gottschalk. 2014. "Some Evidence on the Importance of Sticky Wages." *American Economic Journal: Macroeconomics* 6 (1): 70–101.

Barnichon, R., and P. Garda. 2016. "Forecasting Unemployment across Countries: The ins and outs." *European Economic Review* 84: 165–183.

Barro, R. J. 1974. "Are government bonds net wealth?"*Journal of Political Economy* 82: 1095–1117.

Barro, R. J. 1989. "The Ricardian Approach to Budget Deficits." *Journal of Economic Perspectives* 3 (2): 37–54.

Barro, R. J., and D. B. Gordon. 1983a. "A Positive Theory of Monetary Policy in a Natural Rate Model." *Journal of Political Economy* 91: 589–610.

Barro, R. J., and D. B. Gordon. 1983b. "Rules, Discretion and Reputation in a Model of Monetary Policy." *Journal of Monetary Economics* 12: 101–121.

Basu, S., J. G. Fernald, and M. Kimball. 2006. "Are Technology Shocks Contractionary?" *American Economic Review* 96 (5): 1418–1448.

Baxter, M., and R. G. King. 1993. "Fiscal Policy in General Equilibrium." *American Economic Review* 83 (3): 315–334.

Benigno, G., and L. Fornaro. 2018. "Stagnation Traps." *The Review of Economic Studies* 85 (3): 1425–1470.

Bernanke, B. S. 2013. *The Federal Reserve and the Financial Crisis.* Princeton, NJ: Princeton University Press.

Bernanke, B. S., and V. Reinhart. 2004. "Conducting Monetary Policy at Very Low Short-Term Interest Rates." *American Economic Review* 94 (2): 85–90.

Bilbiie, F. O. 2008. "Limited Asset Market participation, Monetary Policy and (Inverted) Aggregate Demand Logic." *Journal of Economic Theory* 140 (1): 162–196.

Bils, M., P. J. Klenow, and B. A. Malin. 2018. "Resurrecting the Role of the Product Market Wedge in Recessions." *American Economic Review* 108: 1118–1146.

Blanchard, O. J. 2016. "The Phillips Curve: Back to the '60s?" *American Economic Review* 106 (5): 31–34.

Blanchard, O. J. 2018. "Should We Reject the Natural Rate Hypothesis?" *Journal of Economic Perspective* 32 (1): 97–120.

Blanchard, O. J., and J. Galí. 2007. "Real Wage Rigidities and the New Keynesian Model." *Journal of Money, Credit and Banking* 39 (1): 35–65.

Blanchard, O. J., and N. Kiyotaki. 1987. "Monopolistic Competition and the Effects of Aggregate Demand." *American Economic Review* 77: 647–666.

Blanchard, O., and R. Perotti. 2002. "An Empirical Characterization of the Dynamic Effects of Changes in Government Spending and Taxes on Output." *Quarterly Journal of Economics* 126 (February): 51–102.

Board of Governors of the Federal Reserve System. 2008. "FOMC Statement." Press release, December 16, https://www.federalreserve.gov/newsevents/pressreleases/monetary20081216b.htm.

Board of Governors of the Federal Reserve System. 2009. "Text of the Federal Reserve's Statement on Rates." *The New York Times*, January 28.

Board of Governors of the Federal Reserve System. 2010. "FOMC Statement." Press release, December 14, https://www.federalreserve.gov/newsevents/pressreleases/monetary20101214a.htm.

Board of Governors of the Federal Reserve System. 2011. "FOMC Statement." Press release, August 9, https://www.federalreserve.gov/newsevents/pressreleases/monetary20110809a.htm.

Board of Governors of the Federal Reserve System. 2012a. "FOMC Statement." Press release, March 13, https://www.federalreserve.gov/newsevents/pressreleases/monetary20120313a.htm.

Board of Governors of the Federal Reserve System. 2012b. "FOMC Statement." Press release, October 24, https://www.federalreserve.gov/newsevents/pressreleases/monetary20121024a.htm.

Board of Governors of the Federal Reserve System. 2012c. "FOMC Statement." Press release, December 12, https://www.federalreserve.gov/newsevents/pressreleases/monetary20121212a.htm.

Board of Governors of the Federal Reserve System. 2014. "Federal Reserve Issues FOMC Statement." Press release, March 19, https://www.federalreserve.gov/newsevents/pressreleases/monetary20140319a.htm.

Buiter, W., and N. Panigirtzoglou. 2003. "Overcoming the Zero Bound on Nominal Interest Rates with Negative Interest on Currency: Gesell's Solution." *Economic Journal* 113 (490): 723–746.

Campbell, J., C. Evans, J. Fisher, and A. Justiniano. 2012. "Macroeconomic Effects of Federal Reserve Forward Guidance." Brookings Papers on Economic Activity 1, Brookings Institution, Washington, DC, March.

Campbell, J. Y., and N. G. Mankiw. 1989. "Consumption, Income, and Interest Rates: Reinterpreting the Time Series Evidence." *NBER Macroeconomics Annual* 4: 185–246.

Carreras, M. D., O. Coibion, Y. Gorodnichenko, and J. Wieland. Infrequent but Long-Lived Zero Lower Bound Episodes and the Optimal Rate of Inflation." *Annual Review of Economics* 8: 497–520.

Christiano, L., M. Eichenbaum, and S. Rebelo. 2011. "When Is the Government Spending Multiplier Large?" *Journal of Political Economy* 119 (6): 1227–1228.

Christiano, L. J., M. Eichenbaum, and C. L. Evans. 2005. "Nominal Rigidities and the Dynamic Effects of a Shock to Monetary Policy." *Journal of Political Economy* 113: 1–45.

Christopoulou, R., and P. Vermeulen. 2012. "Markups in the Euro Area and the U.S. over the Period 1981–2004: A Comparison of 50 Sectors." *Empirical Economics* 42: 53–77.

Clarida, R., J. Galí, and M. Gertler. 2000. "Monetary Policy Rules and Macroeconomic Stability: Evidence and Some Theory." *Quarterly Journal of Economics* 115 (1): 147–180.

Coibion, O., Y. Gorodnichenko, and J. Wieland. 2012. The Optimal Inflation Rate in New Keynesian Models: Should Central Banks Raise Their Inflation Targets in Light of the Zero Lower Bound?" *Review of Economic Studies* 79 (4): 1371–1406.

Correia, I., E. Farhi, J. P. Nicolini, and P. Teles. 2013. "Unconventional Fiscal Policy at the Zero Bound." *American Economic Review* 103 (4): 1172–1211.

Datta, D., B. K. Johannsen, H. Kwon, and R. J. Vigfusson. 2017. "Oil, Equities, and the Zero Lower Bound." BIS Working Paper No. 617, Basel, Switzerland, March.

Davis, S. J., and T. Von Wachter. 2011. "Recessions and the Cost of Lost Jobs." Brookings Papers on Economic Activity No. 2, The Brookings Institution, Washington, DC.

Debortoli, D., and J. Galí. 2017. "Monetary Policy with Heterogeneous Agents: Insights from TANK Models." Unpublished paper, UPF, CREI, and Barcelona GSE, September.

Eggertsson, G. B. 2006. "The Deflation Bias and Committing to Being Irresponsible." *Journal of Money, Credit and Banking* 38 (2): 284–320.

Eggertsson, G. B. 2010a. "The Paradox of Toil." Federal Reserve Bank of New York Staff Report No. 433, FRB of New York, New York.

Eggertsson, G. B. 2010b. "What Fiscal Policy Is Effective at Zero Interest Rates?" *NBER Macroeconomics Annuals* 25: 59–112.

Eggertsson, G. B. 2012. "Was the New Deal Contractionary?" *American Economic Review* 102 (1): 524–555.

Eggertsson, G. B., A. Ferrero, and A. Raffo. 2014. "Can Structural Reforms Help Europe?" *Journal of Monetary Economics* 61: 2–22.

Eggertsson, G. B., R. E. Juelsrud, and E. Getz Wold. 2017. "Are Negative Nominal Interest Rates Expansionary?" NBER Working Paper No. 24039, The National Bureau of Economic Research, Cambridge, MA, November.

Eggertsson, G. B., and P. Krugman. 2012. "Debt, Deleveraging, and the Liquidity Trap: A Fisher-Minsky-Koo Approach." *Quarterly Journal of Economics* 127 (3): 1469–1513.

Eggertsson, G. B., and M. Woodford. 2003. "The Zero Bound on Interest Rates and Optimal Monetary Policy." Brookings Papers on Economic Activity No. 1, Brookings Institution, Washington, DC, 212–219.

Eggertsson, G. B., and M. Woodford. 2006. "Optimal Monetary and Fiscal Policy in a Liquidity Trap." In *NBER International Seminar on Macroeconomics 2004*, edited by R. H. Clarida, J. A. Frankel, F. Giavazzi, and K. D. West, 75–144. Cambridge, MA: The MIT Press.

Elsby, M. W. L., B. Hobijn, and A. Sahin. 2013. "Unemployment Dynamics in the OECD." *The Review of Economics and Statistics* 95 (2): 530–548.

Elsby, M. W. L., R. Michaels, and D. Ratner. 2015. "The Beveridge Curve: A Survey." *Journal of Economic Literature* 53 (3): 571–630.

Evans, C. L. 2012. "Monetary Policy in a Low-Inflation Environment: Developing a State-Contingent Price-Level Target." *Journal of Money, Credit and Banking* 41 (S1): 147–155.

Feldstein, M. 2002. "Commentary: Is There a Role for Discretionary Fiscal Policy?" Paper presented at The Changing Policy Landscape: Economic Policy Symposium Proceedings, Jackson Hole, WY, August 30–September 1.

Friedman, M. 1957. *A Theory of the Consumption Function.* Princeton, NJ: Princeton University Press.

Friedman, M. 1968. "The Role of Monetary Policy." *American Economic Review* 58 (1): 1–17.

Friedman, M. 1969. "The Optimum Quantity of Money." In *The Optimum Quantity of Money, and Other Essays.* Chicago, IL: Adline Publishing.

Frish, R. 1933. "Propagation Problems and Impulse Problems in Dynamic Economics." In *Economic Essays in Honour of Gustav Cassel*, 171–205. London: G. Allen & Unwin.

Galí, J. 2008. *Monetary Policy, Inflation, and the Business Cycle.* Princeton, NJ: Princeton University Press.

Galí, J., and M. Gertler. 1999. "Inflation Dynamics: A Structural Econometric Analysis." *Journal of Monetary Economics* 44: 195–222.

Gali, J., M. Gertler, and D. López-Salido. 2001. "European Inflation Dynamics." *European Economic Review* 45 (7): 1237–1270.

Galí, J., J. D. Lopez-Salido, and J. Valles. 2007. "Understanding the Effects of Government Spending on Consumption." *Journal of the European Economic Association* 5(1): 227–270.

Galí, J., and P. Rabanal. 2005. "Technology Shocks and Aggregate Fluctuations: How Well Does the RBC Model Fit Postwar U.S. Data?" In *NBER Macroeconomics Annual 2004*, edited by M. Gertler and K. Rogoff, 225–288. Cambridge, MA: The MIT Press.

Gilchrist, S., and B. Mojon. 2018. "Credit Risk in the Euro Area." *Economic Journal* 128 (February): 118–158.

Gilchrist, S., and E. Zakrajsek. 2012. "Credit Spreads and Business Cycle Fluctuations." *American Economic Review* 102 (4): 1692–1720.

Grilli, V., D. Masciandaro, and G. Tabellini. 1991. "Political and Monetary Institutions and Public Financial Policies in the Industrial Countries." *Economic Policy* 6 (13): 341–392.

Gu, G. W., and E. Prasad. 2018. "New Evidence on Cyclical Variations in Labor Costs in the U.S." IZA Discussion Paper No. 11311, IZA Institute of Labor Economics, Bonn, Germany.

Hall, R. E. 2005. "Employment Fluctuations with Equilibrium Wage Stickiness." *American Economic Review* 95 (1): 50–65.

Hall, R. E. 2009. "By How Much Does GDP Rise If the Government Buys More Output?" *Brookings Papers on Economic Activity* 2 (Autumn): 183–231.

Heider, F., F. Saidi, and G. Schepens. 2017. "Life below Zero: Bank Lending under Negative Policy Rates." Unpublished paper, European Central Bank, Center for Economic Policy Research, and Stockholm School of Economics, October 27, https://www.ecb.europa.eu/pub/conferences/shared/pdf/20161027_monetary_policy_pass_through/Life_Below_Zero_Bank_Lending_Under_Negative_Policy_Rates.pdf.

Hodrick, R. J., and E. C. Prescott. (1981) 1997. "Postwar U.S. Business Cycles: An Empirical Investigation." *Journal of Money, Credit and Banking* 29(1): 1–16.

Joyce, M. A. S., Z. Liu, and I. Tonks. 2017. "Institutional Investors and the QE Portfolio Balance Channel." *Journal of Money, Credit and Banking* 49 (6): 1225–1246.

Kaplan, G., B. Moll, and G. L. Violante. 2018. "Monetary Policy According to HANK." *American Economic Review* 108 (3): 697–743.

Kaplan, G., G. L. Violante, and J. Weidner. 2014. "The Wealthy Hand-to-Mouth." Brookings Papers on Economic Activity, Brookings Institution, Washington, DC (Spring): 77–138.

Keynes, J. M. 1933. "An Open Letter to Franklin D. Roosevelt. *New York Times*, December 31.

Keynes, J. M. 1936. *The General Theory of Employment, Interest, and Money*. London, UK: MacMillan and Co.

Keynes, J. M. (1936) 2017. *The General Theory of Employment, Interest, and Money*. N.p.: CreateSpace Independent Publishing Platform.

Kiley, M. T., and J. M. Roberts. 2017. "Monetary Policy in a Low Interest Rate World." Brookings Papers on Economic Activity, Brookings Institution, Washington, DC, Spring, 317–372.

Koo, R. 2008. *The Holy Grail of Macroeconomics: Lessons from Japan's Great Recession*. New York: Wiley.

Koo, R. 2011. "The World in Balance Sheet Recession: Causes, Cure, and Politics." *Real-World Economics Review* 58: 19–37.

Krugman, P. 1998. "It's Baaack: Japan's Slump and the Return of the Liquidity Trap." Brookings Papers on Economic Activity No. 2, Brookings Institution, Washington, DC, 137–205.

Kydland, F. E., and E. C. Prescott. 1977. "Rules Rather than Discretion: The Inconsistency of Optimal Plans." *Journal of Political Economy* 85: 473–492.

Le Bihan, H., J. Mortornes, and T. Heckel. 2012. "Sticky Wages: Evidence from Quarterly Microeconomic Data." *American Economic Journal: Macroeconomics* 4 (3): 1–32.

Lucas, R. E. 1972. "Expectations and the Neutrality of Money." *Journal of Economic Theory* 4: 103–124.

Lucas, R. E. 1976. "Econometric Policy Evaluation: A Critique." *Carnegie-Rochester Conference Series on Public Policy*: 19–46.

Lunnemann, P., and L. Wintr. 2009. "Wages Are Flexible, Aren't They? Evidence from Monthly Micro Wage Data." European Central Bank Working Paper No. 1074, Frankfurt, Germany, July.

Mankiw, G. 1985. "Small Menu Costs and Large Business Cycle: A macroeconomic Model of Monopoly." *Quarterly Journal of Economics* 100: 529–539.

Mankiw, N. G. 2009. "It May Be Time for the Fed to Go Negative. *The New York Times*, April 18.

Mortensen, D. T., and C. A. Pissarides. 1994. "Job Creation and Job Destruction in the Theory of Unemployment." *Review of Economic Studies* 61 (3): 397–415.

Mortensen, D. T., and C. A. Pissarides. 1999. "Job Reallocation, Employment Fluctuations and Unemployment." In *Handbook of Macroeconomics*, edited by J. B. Taylor and M. Woodford, 1171–1228. New York: Elsevier.

Nakamura, E., and J. Steinsson. 2008. "Five Facts about Prices: A Reevaluation of Menu Cost Models." *Quarterly Journal of Economics* 123: 1415–1664.

Nakamura, E., and J. Steinsson. 2014. "Fiscal Stimulus in a Monetary Union: Evidence from US Regions." *American Economic Review* 104 (3): 753–792.

Nekarda, C. J., and V. A. Ramey. 2013. "The Cyclical Behavior of the Price-Cost Markup." NBER Working Paper No. 19099, National Bureau of Economic Research, Cambridge, MA.

Orphanides, A., and J. C. Williams. 2013. "Monetary Policy Mistakes and the Evolution of Inflation Expectations." In *The Great Inflation: The Rebirth of Modern Central Banking*, edited by M. D. Bordo and A. Orphanides. Chicago, IL: University of Chicago Press.

Petrongolo, B., and C. A. Pissarides. 2001. "Looking into the Black Box: A Survey of the Matching Function." *Journal of Economic Literature* 39: 390–431.

Phelps, E. S. 1970. "Introduction: The New Microeconomics in Employment and Inflation Theory." In *Microeconomic Foundations of Employment and Inflation Theory*, by E. S. Phelps et al. New York: Norton.

Ramey, V., and N. Francis. 2009. "A Century of Work and Leisure." *American Economic Journal: Macroeconomics* 1 (2): 189–224.

Ramey, V. A., and S. Zubairy. 2018. "Government Spending Multipliers in Good Times and in Bad: Evidence from US Historical Data." *Journal of Political Economy* 126 (2): 850–901.

Ricardo, D. (1820) 1888. "Essay on the Funding System." In *The Works of David Ricardo,* edited by J. R. McCulloch. London, UK: John Murray.

Rogoff, K. 1985. "The Optimal Degree of Commitment to an Intermediate Monetary Target." *Quarterly Journal of Economics* 100: 1169–1189.

Rogoff, K. 2015a. "Costs and Benefits to Phasing out Paper Currency." *NBER Macroeconomics Annuals* 29 (1): 445–456.

Rogoff, K. 2015b. "Is a Debt Supercycle to Blame for Slow Growth?" World Economic Forum, April 23. https://www.weforum.org/agenda/2015/04/is-a-debt-supercycle-to-blame-for-slow-growth/.

Rogoff, K. 2017. "Dealing with Monetary Paralysis at the Zero Bound." *Journal of Economic Perspectives* 31 (3): 47–66.

Romer, C. D. 2011. "What Do We Know about the Effects of Fiscal Policy? Separating Evidence from Ideology." Speech given at Hamilton College, Clinton, NY, November 7.

Romer, C. D., and D. H. Romer. 2010. "The Macroeconomic Effects of Tax Changes: Estimates Based on a New Measure of Fiscal Shocks." *American Economic Review* 100: 763–801.

Romer, D. 2000. "Keynesian Macroeconomics without the LM Curve." *Journal of Economic Perspectives* 14 (2): 149–169.

Roosevelt, F. D. 1932. "Acceptance Speech." The Democratic National Convention in, Chicago, IL, July 2.

Sigurdsson, J., and R. Sigurdardottir. 2011. "Evidence from Nominal Wage Rigidity and Wage Setting from Icelandic Microdata." Economics Working Paper 55, Department of Economics, Central Bank of Iceland.

Slutzky, E. 1937. "The Summation of Random Causes as the Source of Cyclic Processes." *Econometrica* 5(2): 105–146.

Smith, A. (1776) 1975. An Inquiry into the Nature and Causes of the Wealth of Nations. Oxford: Oxford University Press.

Suarez Serrato, J. C., and P. Wingender, 2016. "Estimating Local Fiscal Multipliers." NBER Working Paper No. 22425, National Bureau of Economic Research, Cambridge, MA, July.

Summers, L. H. 2014. "U.S. Economic Prospects: Secular Stagnation, Hysteresis, and the Zero Lower Bound." *Business Economics* 49 (2): 65–73.

Swanson, E. T. 2017. "Measuring the Effects of Federal Reserve Forward Guidance and Asset Purchases on Financial Markets." NBER Working Paper No. 23311, The National Bureau of Economic Research, Cambridge, MA, April.

Swanson, E. T., and J. C. Williams. 2014. "Measuring the Effect of the Zero Lower Bound on Medium- and Longer-Term Interest Rates." *American Economic Review* 104 (10): 3154–3185.

Taylor, J. B. 1999. "A Historical Analysis of Monetary Policy Rules." In *Monetary Policy Rules*, edited by J. B. Taylor. Chicago, IL: University of Chicago Press.

Thornton, D. L. 2012. "How Did We Get to Inflation Targeting and Where Do We Need to Go to Now? A Perspective from the U.S. Experience." *Federal Reserve Bank of St. Louis Review* (January/February): 65–81.

Wicksell, K. (1898) 1936. *Interest and Prices*, trans. R.F. Kahn. London: Macmillan.

Wieland, J. F. Forthcoming. "Are Negative Supply Shocks Expansionary at the Zero Lower Bound?" *Journal of Political Economy*.

Woodford, M. 2003. *Interest and Prices: Foundations of a Theory of Monetary Policy*. Princeton, NJ: Princeton University Press.

Woodford, M. 2011. "Simple Analytics of the Government Spending Multiplier." *American Economic Journal: Macroeconomics* 3 (January): 1–35.

Woodford, M. 2012. "Methods of Policy Accommodation at the Interest-Rate Lower Bound. Paper presented at The Changing Policy Landscape: Economic Policy Symposium Proceedings, Jackson Hole, WY, August 30–September 1.

Yellen, J. 2009. "Comments." Joint Meeting of the Federal Open Market Committee and Board of Governors of the Federal Reserve System, Federal Reserve System, Washington, DC, January 27–28, 124. https://www.federalreserve.gov/monetarypolicy/files/FOMC20090128meeting.pdf.

Index

Printed in the United States
by Baker & Taylor Publisher Services